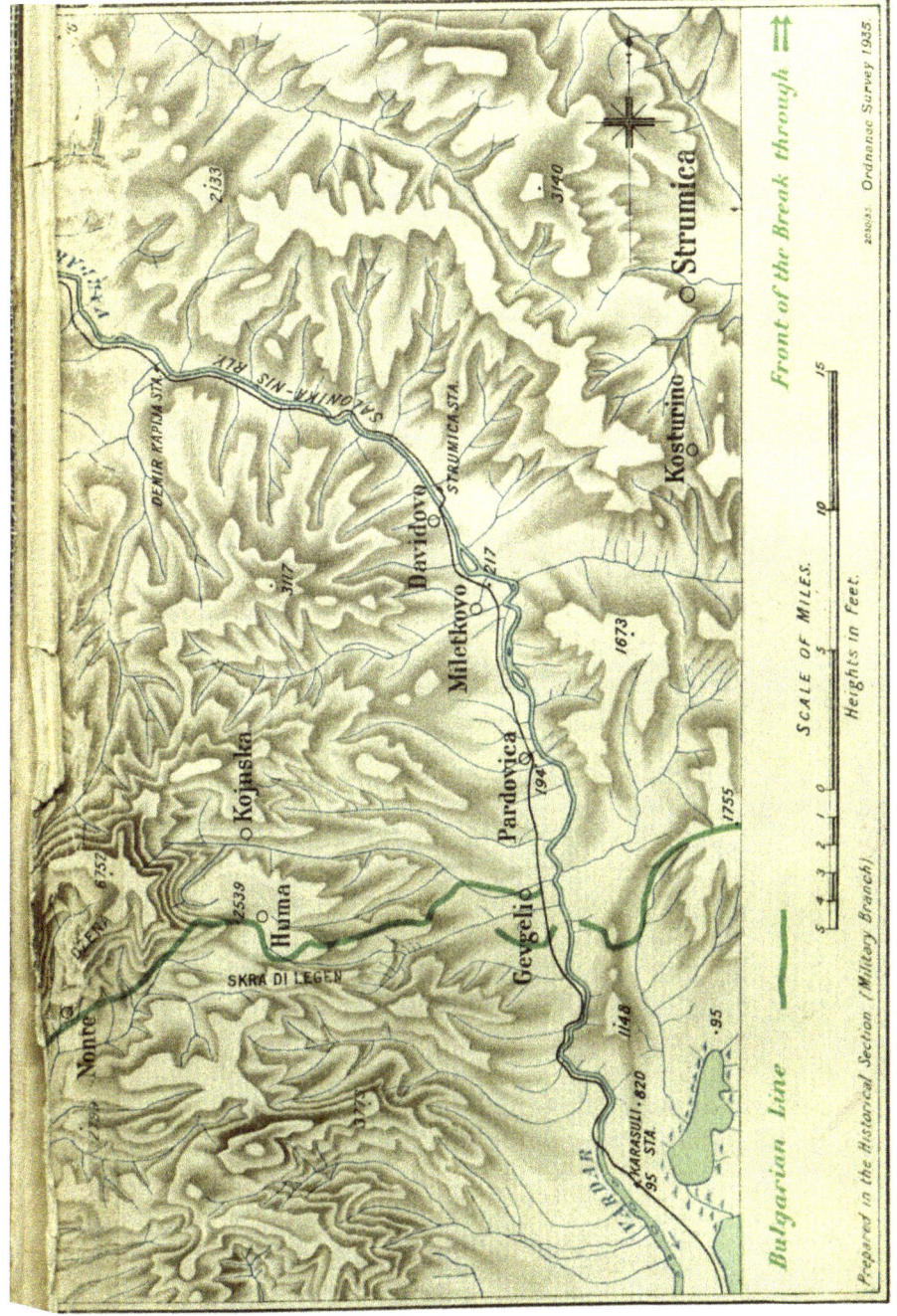

History of the Great War.

MILITARY OPERATIONS.

HISTORY OF THE GREAT WAR
BASED ON OFFICIAL DOCUMENTS
BY DIRECTION OF THE HISTORICAL SECTION OF THE
COMMITTEE OF IMPERIAL DEFENCE

MILITARY OPERATIONS MACEDONIA

FROM THE SPRING OF 1917 TO
THE END OF THE WAR

COMPILED BY
Captain CYRIL FALLS
LATE R. INNIS. FUS. AND GENERAL STAFF

MAPS COMPILED BY
Major A. F. BECKE
R.A. (RETIRED), HON. M.A. (OXON.)

The Naval & Military Press Ltd

Published by

The Naval & Military Press Ltd
Unit 5 Riverside, Brambleside
Bellbrook Industrial Estate
Uckfield, East Sussex
TN22 1QQ England

Tel: +44 (0)1825 749494

www.naval-military-press.com
www.nmarchive.com

Cover image: The Salonika 1916 displaying soldiers of all Allied nations taking part in the campaign. From left to right standing: Montenegrin, British, Serbian, Italian, French Colonial Zouave, Indian, Greek. Kneeling: French Colonial Cochin Chinese, Russian, French, French Colonial.

In reprinting in facsimile from the original, any imperfections are inevitably reproduced and the quality may fall short of modern type and cartographic standards.

PREFACE.

This volume completes the narrative of British military operations in Macedonia. The first volume, published in 1933, brought the military record up to the Allied offensive of May 1917. On the political side, in order that it should not be broken off in the midst of the Greek crisis, the story was carried a little further, up to the dethronement of King Constantine of Greece and the accession to the throne of his second son Alexander in June. The second volume begins, therefore, with a new phase, with Eleutherios Venizelos President of the Council of Ministers, and with the Kingdom of Greece a belligerent on the side of the Entente. Political events in Greece, which were so important a factor in the earlier period of the campaign, play but a small part in the present volume.

From the military point of view, too, another phase is opening. As recorded in the previous volume, the British Government had announced at a conference held in Paris on the 4th and 5th May that it was their intention to withdraw from Macedonia one infantry division and two cavalry brigades. They had, it is true, stated that if the offensive then preparing were remarkably successful they might reconsider this decision. The offensive having failed, the decision remained in force. But the Government had gone further than this. The destination of the troops was Egypt; they were, as will appear, shortly to be followed by another infantry division and by some heavy artillery. Dissatisfied with results in Macedonia, hopeful of better fortune in Palestine, and anxious to lessen the losses to shipping from submarine attacks in the Mediterranean, the Government were contemplating a great effort in Palestine largely at the expense of the British force in Macedonia. At the same conference they had stated that in their view the essential needs of the civil populations of the Allies could be met only by reducing the force at Salonika to what was necessary to hold an entrenched camp surrounding the harbour. For the moment this was only an expression of opinion, but as such it should be borne in mind in reading the record of the next twelve months.

At the end of May the general situation of the Allies was as follows. The Commander-in-Chief of the Allied

Armies of the East [1] was General Sarrail. The British Army, under the command of General G. F. Milne, held the front from the Gulf of Orfano to the Vardar, its line following the Struma and the northern slopes of the Krusha Ridge, and running from the southern shore of Lake Dojran to the Vardar at Machukovo. On the right was the XVI Corps, consisting of the 10th, 27th, and 28th Divisions, to the last-named of which was attached the 228th Brigade, formed from Garrison battalions; on the left was the XII Corps, consisting of the 22nd, 26th, and 60th Divisions. The 60th Division was under orders for Egypt, as were the two brigades of Yeomanry, the 7th and 8th Mounted Brigades. From the Vardar to south of Lake Malik, beyond the Albanian border, the Allied forces consisted of 18 divisions: eight French, six Serbian, two Greek, one Italian, and one Russian. A proportion of these troops were, however, either in Thessaly or about to proceed to Athens, Piræus, and the Isthmus of Corinth on account of the Greek crisis. On their left the Allied Armies of the East were in touch with an independent Italian force, the XVI Corps, which was based on Valona and held southern Albania to the Adriatic.

The Greek troops mentioned were the Seres and Archipelago Divisions, part of the Greek " Corps of National Defence," a Venizelist formation which had its birth at Salonika and developed in the Greek islands before the dethronement of King Constantine. The Seres Division was already in the line, while the Archipelago was under instruction behind the front. The third division of this Corps, the Crete, reached Salonika in June. The Regular Army, often described as the Royal Hellenic Army—though all Greek troops were, strictly speaking, " Royal " from the 27th June—had been demobilized. M. Venizelos intended to bring it into the field, but gradually. Not only had he to keep his finger on the pulse of public opinion; he had also to await from France and Britain arms, equipment, and supplies.

In the previous volume it was found necessary, in

---

[1] This title does not appear in Vol. I. The French first of all designated their force " Armée d'Orient." As it grew, they gave this title to the whole force and entitled their contingent " Armée Française d'Orient." Finally, they dropped " Armée d'Orient " and substituted " Armées Alliées en Orient," which is translated throughout this volume as " Allied Armies of the East." The term " Armée d'Orient " still, however, occasionally appears in French documents.

PREFACE   vii

compiling the history of this campaign, to depart from precedent; instead of making only incidental allusion to politics, it seemed desirable, in the words of the preface, to " set the military history in a political framework and to trace all events from their political sources." This, as has been stated, applies much less to the second volume because one major political issue, the Greek question, has been disposed of. There is, however, another respect in which precedent has here not been strictly followed. That is the space which has been given to the operations of Allied contingents other than the British and the Greek troops acting with them.

The great, the only great event of this volume is the final victorious offensive. Few operations of the war have a higher interest for military students than the fortnight's campaign which ended when Bulgaria laid down her arms. The whole period of fifteen months preceding it is dreary, except for the discussions and preparations leading up to the attack. It has seemed right not only to devote the greater part of the volume to the offensive, but, since the Anglo-Greek attacks were subsidiary ones, to devote a considerable proportion of this space to the main attack, of which the Serbian Armies formed the spearhead. A mere sketch of these operations would not have sufficed to make clear their nature, or have afforded material for any estimate of their influence upon modern mountain warfare and their relation to the great mountain campaigns of the past. They have therefore been treated, not, indeed, in as much detail as the Anglo-Greek, but as far as possible from a tactical as well as a strategical point of view.

Somewhat rashly, it was announced in the preface to the first volume that the second would probably contain a sketch of post-war events. Examination of the material soon showed that a narrative up to the evacuation of Turkey in October 1923 was undesirable because it would involve discussion of happenings and problems rightly belonging to another era, when the whole political and military situation had changed. The Græco-Turkish War alone is a very big subject, which, although it may be said to be an offshoot of the Great War, has a comparatively slight link with it. Any detailed description, however much abridged, of British policy and problems must have involved constant reference not only to the growth of the Turkish Nationalist movement in Anatolia but also to the campaigns of Denikin and Wrangel, and even to the expeditionary forces at Murmansk and Archangel; the attitude of new states such as Poland, Finland, Esthonia, and Latvia; and the campaigns in Siberia, including the parts played by Czecho-Slovak and Japanese forces in that vast area. In any case there is a possibility that, to wind up the history of British military operations in the Great War, a post-war volume devoted to the various occupations and expeditions will some day be written.

It has therefore been decided to limit the projected narrative to a bare record of the chief British movements up to May 1919, the month of the Greek occupation of Smyrna, which may be taken as the turning-point in the Near East. This record will be found in Appendix 1.

As before, two sets of maps are included: " sketches " bound in the volume, and larger " maps " in a separate case. A map covering the whole British front has, again as before, been placed in a pocket of the text volume for the convenience of the general reader. It will be observed that Map 8, of the Exploitation and Pursuit, covers that phase only, without taking account of the Anglo-Greek attacks east of the Vardar, which were launched subsequently to the Franco-Serbian assault known as the Battle of the Dobropolje. It would not have been possible to show all these attacks on the same map. Map 8 should therefore be read in conjunction with Maps 5 and 7, of the Battle of Dojran. All the maps and sketches, with the exception of two maps which are parts of existing publications, have been prepared with his usual skill and care by Major A. F. Becke, and drawn by Mr. H. Burge. The difficulties, always great when rapid movement over very large areas has to be recorded, have been increased by the wide divergence between the printed maps drawn on different scales and from different surveys. The passage in Chapter I describing the British Survey will make this clear.

The two panoramic photographs of the Dojran front are the copyright of the Imperial War Museum. Lieut.-Colonel W. C. Holden, R.A., who commanded the 8-inch howitzer battery on the Dojran front, lent copies on which he had marked at the time the position of every point of importance. The photographs of the Dobropolje and the Sokol, where the main attack took place, are reproduced by arrangement with the Geneva firm of Boissonnas. The originals of those entitled " The Trail of the Retreat " and " The Pass into the Valley of the Strumica " were lent by Lieut.-Colonel J. E. Cairnes, R.A.

The compiler desires to express his gratitude to the Historical Service of the French Army, and its Chief, General Halbwachs, for invaluable assistance. Three separate tracings of dispositions during the final offensive were furnished from this source. It will readily be understood that, as the supreme command in Macedonia was in French hands, orders were addressed to and reports received from all the Armies by French G.H.Q., with the consequence that French information regarding the campaign as a whole is more complete than that of any other nationality. In these circumstances it would have been convenient had the French account appeared first, but, in fact, the British history is ahead of the French. The second volume of the latter reached the compiler's hands only when he was engaged in correcting the galley proofs of his own second volume. In any case, the French second volume does not complete the record of the campaign, but covers the period from August 1916 to April 1918. It thus overlaps the British second volume only between June 1917 and April 1918, a relatively unimportant period. The account of this overlapping period has been checked by the French narrative, and two or three minor corrections have been made in proof; but no reference to the French volume will be found in this.

The compiler has also to thank the Bulgarian General Staff for a complete Order of Battle of the Bulgarian Armies on the 14th September 1918.

Acknowledgment is due to a great number of officers who took part in the campaign for valuable comments on the chapters submitted to them in draft, and in some cases for the loan of maps or papers.

As in the case of the first volume, the compiler is indebted to Mr. W. B. Wood, M.A., for his careful commentary on the final text.

November 1934.   C. B. F.

CONTENTS.

CHAPTER I.
IN THE DOLDRUMS: LATE MAY TO EARLY SEPTEMBER 1917.

	PAGE
The Gloomy Prospect of the Campaign	1
Minor Operations of the Summer	14
The British Survey in Macedonia	17
The Salonika Fire	21

CHAPTER II.
THE AUTUMN OF 1917.

Operations in the Struma Valley	24
Autumn Conditions	31
The Influence of other Fronts	36

CHAPTER III.
THE THIRD WINTER.

The Recall of General Sarrail	43
A New Broom	48
Events of January and February 1918	54

CHAPTER IV.
THE SHADOW OF THE GERMAN OFFENSIVE IN FRANCE: MARCH AND APRIL 1918.

Greek Mobilization and Serbian Reinforcements	61
The Defence Scheme	70
Projects of General Guillaumat	76
Operations of March and April	79

CHAPTER V.
GENERAL GUILLAUMAT'S REHEARSAL.

The Greek and French Operations in May and June	88
A Greek Corps in the Struma Valley	92

CHAPTER VI.
THE GENESIS OF THE OFFENSIVE.

Salonika—Paris—Versailles—London—Rome	103
General Milne's Problem	112
Events in July and August	117
Note: Ammunition Supply and Expenditure	122

xii   CONTENTS

Chapter VII.

Plans and Preliminaries.

The Strategical Scheme	124
The Opposing Forces	131
The British Plans and Preparations	135
The Capture of the Roche Noire Salient	141
Note : The Bulgarian Effectives	145

Chapter VIII.

The Final Offensive : the Battle of the Dobropolje.

The Capture of the Vetrenik, Dobropolje, and Sokol	147
The Capture of the Second and Third Systems of Defence	154
Note : The Battle from the Enemy's Side	157

Chapter IX.

The Final Offensive : the Battle of Dojran.

The Dojran Defences and Defenders	159
The Attack of the XII Corps—18th September	163
The Attack of the XVI Corps—18th September	172
The Attack of the XII Corps—19th September	178
Notes : I. XII Corps Artillery Dispositions and Chain of Command in Attack of 18th September	191
II. The Dispositions of the Enemy	192

Chapter X.

The Final Offensive : the Exploitation.

The Exploitation West of the Vardar, 18th–21st September	193
The Pursuit on the British Front, 21st–24th September	202
The Passage of the Vardar	212
The Widening Breach, 22nd–24th September	216

Chapter XI.

The Final Offensive : the Pursuit.

The Pursuit on the British Front, 25th–30th September	223
The General Pursuit on the Franco-Serbian Front, 25th–28th September	237
The Capture of Skoplje	243
The Armistice with Bulgaria	246
Note : Terms of the Armistice with Bulgaria	252

CONTENTS xiii

CHAPTER XII.
THE LAST ACT.

The Danube or Constantinople? 254
The British Move against Turkey 262
The Opening of the Dardanelles 267
The Advance to the Danube 271
The Austrian, German, and Hungarian Armistices .. 279

CHAPTER XIII.
CONCLUSION.

Some Open Questions 285
Some Deductions 297

TABLE OF APPENDICES.

1. Summary of Events concerning the British Army of the Black Sea, December 1918 to May 1919 306
2. Order of Battle of the Allied Armies of the East, 14th September 1918 309
3. Order of Battle of the British Salonika Army, 14th September 1918 311
4. Order of Battle of the Bulgarian and German Forces in Macedonia, 14th September 1918 316
5. Instructions for the General Commanding-in-Chief the Allied Armies of the East, 16th December 1917 318
6. Directive to the General Commanding-in-Chief the Allied Armies of the East, 23rd June 1918 321
7. Instructions of General Franchet d'Espérey to General Milne, 24th July 1918 323
8. Telegram from General Milne to War Office, 25th July 1918 325
9. Telegram from War Office to General Milne, 27th July 1918 325
10. Rôle of the 1st Group of Divisions (General Franchet d'Espérey to General Milne), 4th August 1918.. .. 326
11. Instructions for the Exploitation by General Franchet d'Espérey, 31st August 1918 327
12. XII Corps Instructions, 7th September 1918 333
13. 22nd Division Order No. 120, 15th September 1918 .. 339
14. XVI Corps Plan of Operations of the Cretan Division, 7th September 1918.. 344
15. XII Corps Order No. 33, 18th September 1918 347
16. Telegram from German O.H.L. to Bulgarian G.H.Q., (probably) 19th September 1918 348
17. Telegram from French G.H.Q., 22nd September 1918 .. 348
18. Telegraphic Order by British G.H.Q., 22nd September 1918 349
19. Telegraphic Order by British G.H.Q., 28th September 1918 349
20. Instructions for the Armies by General Franchet d'Espérey, 25th September 1918 349
21. A Note on Casualties 351

SKETCHES, MAPS AND ILLUSTRATIONS.

SKETCHES.
(Bound in Volume.)

Sketch A.	Theatre of the Main Allied Attack, September 1918	*At beginning*	
,,	1.	Sea to Vardar, 1st September 1917	*Facing p.* 13
,,	2.	Sea to Vardar, 10th April 1918	,, 63
,,	3.	Combat of the Skra di Legen, 30th May 1918	,, 89
,,	4.	Sea to Vardar, 15th July 1918	,, 95
,,	5.	Plan of Break-through	,, 125
,,	6.	Capture of the Roche Noire Salient, 1st September 1918	,, 141
,,	7.	Front of the Break-through: Bulgarian Positions, 15th–25th September 1918	,, 155
,,	8.	Battle of Dojran, 18th September 1918	,, 161
,,	9.	Battle of Dojran, 18th September 1918, Attack of XVI Corps	,, 173
,,	10.	Allied Offensive of September 1918, Situation on 30th	,, 239

ILLUSTRATIONS.

The Dobropolje	*Facing p.* 146
The Sokol	,, 150
Dojran to " P " Ridge (panorama)	,, 166
Looking up " P " Ridge (panorama)	,, 178
The Trail of the Retreat..	,, 226
The Pass into the Valley of the Strumica	,, 230

LIST OF BOOKS CONSULTED

(In addition to the British Official Histories.)

"ARMÉES FRANÇAISES DANS LA GRANDE GUERRE, Les," Tome VIII, 2ᵐᵉ Volume. (Paris: Imprimerie Nationale.)·
It is explained in the Preface (p. ix) why no reference is made to this volume of the French Official History.

BUJAC: "Les Campagnes de l'Armée Hellénique, 1918–1922." (Paris: Charles-Lavauzelle.)
An excellent work by a well-known veteran military historian.

CALLWELL: "Field-Marshal Sir Henry Wilson, His Life and Diaries." (Cassell.)
An occasional light on the attitude of the Chief of the Imperial General Staff to the campaign in Macedonia is thrown by entries in his diary.

COLLINSON OWEN: "Salonica and After." (Hodder & Stoughton.)
A well-written and entertaining book which gives a good notion of life behind the lines and especially in Salonika.

"ÉTUDE SUR LA GUERRE DE MONTAGNE, D'APRÈS LES ENSEIGNEMENTS DE LA CAMPAGNE D'ORIENT." (Paris: Imprimerie Nationale.)
An official work, which exactly lives up to its title and is of the highest value.

FEYLER: (iii) "La Campagne de Macédoine, 1917–1918." (Geneva: Editions d'Art Boissonnas.)
Only the third of Colonel Feyler's volumes applies where this period is concerned.

"HISTORIQUE DES TROUPES COLONIALES, pendant la Grande Guerre, 1914–1918 (Fronts Extérieurs)." (Paris: Charles-Lavauzelle.)
This official work has been found indispensable here, as it was in the compilation of the first volume.

HOFFMANN: "Der Krieg der Versäumten Gelegenheiten." (Munich: Verlag für Kulturpolitik.)
There is an English translation of this book (Secker), but references are to the German edition.

LARCHER: "La Grande Guerre dans les Balkans." (Paris: Payot.)
A strategical and political study.

LEPETIT: "La Genèse de l'Offensive de Macédoine." (Paris: Revue Militaire Française, July 1922.)
A valuable article based on official sources.

LUDENDORFF: "My War Memories." (English Edition, Hutchinson.)
Gives the official German view of the final Allied offensive in Macedonia.

NÉDEFF: "Les Opérations en Macédoine, l'Epopée de Doïran." (Sofia: Imprimerie Armeyski Voeno-Isdatelski Fond.)
This French translation of a Bulgarian work is of particular value for the operations on the British front.

PHOTIADÈS: "La Victoire des Alliés en Orient." (Paris: Plon-Nourrit.)
This book is not quoted but has been useful as a general guide, as it is known to embody the views of Marshal Franchet d'Espérey and to have been corrected by him. The author is a French airman of Greek descent.

REVOL: " La Victoire de Macédoine." (Paris : Charles-Lavauzelle.)
A useful work, based on official sources, by one of the most celebrated of French military historians. It does not go beyond the Bulgarian Armistice.

SARRAIL: " Mon Commandement en Orient (1916–1918)." (Paris : Flammarion.)
Useful up to the date of the writer's departure.

VILLARI: " The Macedonian Campaign." (English Edition, Fisher Unwin.)
A general study, but particularly useful as regards the Italian troops.

" WELTKRIEGSENDE AN DER MAZEDONISCHEN FRONT." (Berlin : Stalling.)
One of the well-known German monographs, and one of the best of them. To no other published source is the compiler so deeply indebted.

NOTE.—Reference to other works occasionally consulted is made in footnotes in the text.

CHAPTER I.

IN THE DOLDRUMS:
LATE MAY TO EARLY SEPTEMBER 1917.

(Maps A, 1, 2; Sketch 1.)

THE GLOOMY PROSPECT OF THE CAMPAIGN.

SPRING had once more carpeted the Macedonian plain with flowers, but had brought small promise to the British Salonika Army. Behind it was a failure; in front of it was no visible prospect of success. All the omens pointed to a summer of military inactivity, but of no welcome sort. There would be never-ending work on roads, on railways, and on defences. There would be intense heat, dust, and swarms of flies. The unequal battle with the mosquito would be renewed. Previous sufferers from malaria who had struggled somehow through the colder weather without going sick would be smitten again, would be sent to hospital, would return to their units, and would go back once more to hospital after their first serious exertion. There would, it seemed likely, be no more leave than formerly—and there were men in plenty who had now been on service for two years and more without sight of their families or their homes.   Maps A, 2. Sketch 1.

All this would have been more easily endurable had the objects of the campaign or its chances of ultimate success been clearer. As it was, men could not avoid wondering what cause they were serving. The last attacks on the shore of Lake Dojran could hardly fail to have made those who had taken part in them pessimistic as to the possibility of a successful offensive. On the other hand, some disappointment had been caused among the troops in the Struma valley—the more ardent spirits, at least—by the breaking-off of the operations there. " If victory cannot " be won here, are we doing any good by rotting here with " fever ? " was a question which must naturally have occurred to any critical mind.

If the man in the ranks reasoned thus, his uninstructed view was not very different from that of the General Staff at the War Office, which had all the factors set out before it. Macedonia was becoming more and more an isolated theatre of war. By early May, six months before the Bolshevik *coup d'état* in Petrograd, it was already possible that Russia might collapse and drop out of the war. If she did, it was certain that Rumania could not hold out for long. The strain upon British shipping, on which all the Allied forces in Macedonia mainly depended, was becoming more intense. The losses from submarine attack were in themselves very serious, but the delays caused by waiting for favourable opportunities to sail resulted in a heavy additional waste of tonnage. The General Staff had never believed in the possibility of a successful offensive from Salonika and was even more pessimistic after the events of May, which not only emphasized the difficulties in the path of the Allied Armies but aroused doubts as to the quality of their leadership.

Since the capture of Monastir in November 1916 the question of the command had been more or less in abeyance. After the failure of the May offensive it was raised again by Great Britain. At a meeting of the War Cabinet held on the 6th June, it was decided that the Prime Minister should make, in a personal letter to M. Ribot, a definite demand that General Sarrail should be replaced immediately. To this letter the President of the Council replied that he could scarcely remove the Commander-in-Chief at the moment of the dethronement of King Constantine, when the affairs of Greece were in a critical state, but that he would do so later. However, he was not again seriously pressed on the subject. At first, the British Government seems to have shrunk from causing embarrassment or worry to the French after the failure of General Nivelle's offensive, which had had dangerous effects upon the French Army and upon the country in general. Afterwards, there was question of withdrawing a second British division from Salonika to Palestine, and the British Government thought it wiser not to couple the two demands. And, after all, if the Army were not going to fight, it did not so much matter who commanded it. Such, literally, was the argument. It may have had some truth, but it was something less than high-spirited from the point of view of a great nation and unpromising from that of the Army.

The entry of Greece into the war was at first regarded by the General Staff almost in the light of a new embarrassment. No longer could it contemplate largely reducing the forces in Macedonia and then falling back upon the

Entrenched Camp, because Greece would thus be left open to attack. In an appreciation which Sir William Robertson wrote for the War Cabinet on the 29th July, after the Russian summer offensive had failed disastrously, he urged the necessity of laying down definitely the policy to be followed in the Balkans.

"I am afraid [he went on] I cannot advise the War
" Cabinet what the policy should be, except by repeating
" that the Salonika forces will never materially contribute
" to the winning of the war, while we may well lose it if we
" fail to have sufficient shipping to meet all and sundry
" requirements. As I have always pointed out to the War
" Cabinet, the Salonika expedition has been from the first
" strategically unsound. . . . We cannot use the large
" Army we have there for any offensive, and when we desire
" to move some of the troops elsewhere for urgent and
" necessary purposes we are compelled to consider potential
" dangers arising from the false position in which they are
" placed. . . . If they were properly commanded and
" adequate measures for defence, for which ample time has
" been available, had been taken, the troops on the
" Macedonian front are more than is necessary for defence.
" But the force is not adequately commanded, and I have
" no assurance that adequate measures for defence have
" been taken. If it becomes necessary to withdraw any
" considerable number of troops from Salonika, as it will be
" if the Russian collapse continues and extends, the only
" way of doing so which appears to be possible now is to
" abandon that place, sacrificing a large quantity of stores
" and material which we shall be unable to move, and fall
" back upon Greece, which the Serbians and Greeks, with
" the stiffening of three or four French, British, or Italian
" divisions, should be able to defend."

These extremely pessimistic views were not those of General Milne, except that he believed the maintenance of the present position and the evacuation of Macedonia to be the only alternatives; nor did they reflect the spirit of his reports to the C.I.G.S. In a personal letter to Sir William Robertson after the failure of the May attack he declared once more that he still thought the Bulgars could be beaten, if the means were provided; if attacks prepared as they were in France could be launched, his opinion was that the enemy would collapse at the first blow.

However that might be, now that summer was at hand there could be no immediate question of a renewed attack. It was necessary to wait on events, adopting a defensive attitude and meanwhile doing what was possible for the health, comfort, and general efficiency of the troops.

General Milne's first duty was to send to Egypt the division and the two mounted brigades which were to reinforce General Sir Archibald Murray in southern Palestine.[1] The first formation to be despatched was the 8th Mounted Brigade, which began embarkation on the 31st May. The relief of the 60th Division on the front of the XII Corps was completed by the 6th June, but owing to lack of shipping the move was a slow one and the headquarters of the division did not sail until the 30th. The 7th Mounted Brigade began embarkation on the 22nd. In view of his shortage of cavalry—two corps cavalry regiments of two squadrons apiece being all that was left—the War Office permitted General Milne to keep the Derbyshire Yeomanry of this brigade, and it remained in Macedonia until the end. General Milne, in accordance with later instructions, also despatched the 209th Siege Battery and headquarters and one section of the 292nd to Egypt. He was also asked if he could spare No. 6 Armoured Motor Battery, required in Mesopotamia, and agreed to send it. It was suggested to General Sarrail that he should place some French troops east of the Vardar in order to compensate the British Salonika Army for the loss of a division and two mounted brigades, but he found it impossible to agree owing to the number of his troops then in Old Greece.[2]

Next, the troops were to be withdrawn from the valleys of the Struma and Butkovo, so that they should not have to live in the low malarial ground during the heat of the summer. This move had to be carried out carefully and deliberately, in order to keep the Bulgarians in the dark until the last moment and to deny to them the material and stores of all sorts accumulated in the valleys, especially in that of the Struma. The pace of the withdrawal was also governed by the rate at which fresh water supplies could be developed in the hills. The Struma itself was to be the main line of defence on the front of the XVI Corps, but that

---

[1] See Vol. I, p. 318. [2] See Vol. I, p. 357.

WITHDRAWAL FROM STRUMA VALLEY 5

did not mean that any considerable number of troops would have to be kept on its banks. The strongly-defended bridgeheads were to be held by permanent garrisons ; the remainder of the river line could be swiftly and easily reinforced from the hills. On the other hand, it was intended that a wide belt on the left bank should be patrolled daily by two cavalry regiments, the Derbyshire and the Surrey Yeomanry. The enemy was to be prevented from occupying permanently the villages of Yeni Mahale, Osman Kamila, Hristian Kamila, Yeniköi, Nevolyen, Cuculuk, Elishan, Ormanli, and Haznadar. Should he occupy any part of this line in force, he was to be driven off it, if necessary with the aid of infantry and artillery from behind the Struma. He would thus be given no opportunity to prepare a surprise attack upon the line of the river. The 80th Brigade at the mouth of the Struma was not to be affected by the withdrawal. Its position was vital ; moreover, its troops were for the most part on fairly high ground, and its area was healthier than that above Lake Tahinos.

1917.
June.

The removal of material across the Struma took some three weeks, one of the divisions bringing out no less than two thousand wagon-loads. The wire was in general left standing, but gaps were cut in it for the passage of the cavalry. A few telephone lines were left out for the use of patrols. Otherwise everything portable, down to the floor-boards of the trenches, was taken across the river. Observation posts were dismantled ; such works as might be of service to the enemy were filled in. On the night of the 12th June the bulk of the infantry and all the artillery still on the left bank were withdrawn, leaving only small posts, with rather stronger supports, on the outpost line. On the following night the remainder of the infantry crossed to the right bank, and at dawn on the 14th the cavalry began its patrolling. That morning it found no enemy in the evacuated villages. During the following fortnight there were numerous encounters of patrols in them, but the enemy showed no intention of occupying them permanently. Though malaria affected his men far less than the British, he had no incentive to concentrate troops on the fever-haunted floor of the valley, where, into the bargain, he ran the risk of being constantly raided. On the right of the XII Corps, the troops of the 78th Brigade, in what was known as the " Independent Brigade Area," east of Lake Dojran, were likewise withdrawn to a summer line on the slopes of the Krusha Ridge.

In order to train, rest, and recreate the troops, General Milne decided to alter his dispositions, holding his line as lightly as possible and forming an Army Reserve consisting of the 28th Division and 228th Brigade, which would hold the centre on the Krusha Ridge with two brigades, and keep a brigade on either flank in reserve. The XVI Corps (27th and 10th Divisions) would then be responsible for the front from the mouth of the Struma to Kran Mah, four miles south-west of Butkovo; the Army Reserve (28th Division and 228th Brigade, under the orders of Major-General H. L. Croker) from thence to Surlovo, east of Dojran Station; and the XII Corps (22nd and 26th Divisions) from thence to the Vardar. The two corps commanders were instructed to keep one brigade from each of their divisions in reserve; there would thus be in reserve always six out of the 16 brigades in the force. The general method of defence was to be that of holding lightly essential points, with reserves in readiness to eject the enemy if he broke into the line. Losses from artillery fire would thus be reduced to a minimum. General Milne did not, however, intend that the defence should become wholly passive. On the contrary, a policy of harassing the enemy was to be maintained all along the front. For this purpose he had the 228th Brigade withdrawn from the line for further training and in order that a more active brigade should replace it in the Butkovo valley sector. For the two cavalry regiments and the XVI Corps Cyclists in the Struma valley, at least, there was little repose. Daily they patrolled up to a distance of five miles beyond the river, despite heat, a country made blind by long grass and giant thistles, and the constant prospect of ambushes. As regards these, however, they gave as good as they got, and so played on the enemy's nerves that he never ventured to establish posts in front of his permanent lines.

General Milne also directed that advantage should be taken of the lull in operations to carry out as much training as possible of other formations, so as to prepare the force for whatsoever tasks the future had in store for it. Divisional commanders would now be freer to devote themselves to training, a responsibility peculiarly theirs, since the division was the formation in which the close co-operation of all arms

MEASURES TO FIGHT MALARIA

1917.
June.

was attained. Special attention was to be paid to the two distinct phases of individual and combined training. The instruction of junior officers was to be taken in hand, and was to include lectures by representatives of one arm to those of others. So that the artillery should not miss its share, batteries were to be taken out in turn for training in open warfare. The training of drafts at Summerhill Camp was to cease and was to be carried out in future under the eyes of divisional commanders in their own areas. Only a small staff was to be kept at Summerhill for such training as was necessary for men discharged from hospital.

Every measure to combat malaria which ingenuity could devise was employed. Regular dosage with quinine was carried out throughout the force. Streams were canalized and stagnant water was drained off. Long grass near camps or bivouacs was cut or burnt. In certain cases mosquito-proof huts were built by the engineers to accommodate men when out of the line. Sentries were provided with gloves and masks. Sleeping nets were issued, though in this case the evil of the previous summer recurred, and the supply was late in arriving from home. In early June the 28th Division, on a rather healthier but by no means safe front, had to hand over 2,500 nets to the 10th and 27th Divisions, because the latter were short of them. The consequence was that in the 84th Brigade, from which the nets were withdrawn, the sick rate increased to alarming proportions. The troops fully understood the significance of the precautions and carried them out faithfully. In General Milne's words, the mosquito-curtain was looked upon as being " as important as the rifle." The number of sick, however, rose steadily as the summer advanced. By the end of June there were about 11,000—chiefly malarial cases—in the hospitals, by the end of July about 12,500, by the end of August about 18,000. The peak of the casualty chart, 21,434, was not reached until the 16th October, after the beginning of cooler weather, but from that time forward the graph dipped sharply. A convalescent depot at Corfu, where the climate was superior to that of Macedonia, proved of service for patients who had been the severest sufferers.

Wherever else they have failed, British commanders have generally had a large measure of success in their efforts to preserve the morale of their troops. To keep officers and men from growing stale was perhaps the chief task of that summer, and here, certainly by comparison with other national contingents, good results were achieved in the British Salonika Army. The problem in Macedonia was unusually difficult on account of the stagnation of the campaign, the absence of all civilized surroundings, the lack of leave, and the sickness which afflicted thousands of men not in hospital, inducing melancholy and lethargy. For this reason particular care had to be taken to avoid boredom by making the training as interesting as possible and providing such amusement as could be devised. A balance had to be struck between minor offensive operations, training, and work, on the one hand, and rest and play on the other. All troops not compelled to be abroad were kept in their camps during the heat of the day, work, training, and sport alike being confined to the cooler hours. Football, cross-country running, and boxing were organized in the form of cup competitions or tournaments, which aroused great interest and strong rivalry.

The horse shows held by the corps and divisions were on an elaborate scale. That of the 27th Division, in particular, was a social event very impressive to the foreign guests who witnessed it. It took place at divisional headquarters at Jum'a Mahale, on the edge of the Struma valley some four miles off the Seres road, and lasted three days, from the 23rd to the 25th July. On the last day General Sarrail, whose personal charm always made him a welcome guest on these occasions, came with General Milne. Visitors from the whole force, and from the other contingents, nursing sisters from the hospitals, officers from the fleet watched the jumping and the competitions, and admired the gleaming horses and mules, while aeroplanes circled above the crowd to keep any curious German or Bulgarian aviators from spoiling the show.

In preparation for the cold weather, Lieut.-Colonel H. G. Pleydell-Railston, commanding the dismounted Scottish Horse in the 27th Division, determined to form a pack of hounds, with the backing of his divisional commander, Major-General Forestier-Walker. There were many difficulties and disappointments. English Hunts made gifts of a few couples of hounds, but always when the officers returning from leave brought them to the railway station they were stopped by the R.T.O. Efforts to obtain hounds from Gibraltar, India, Egypt, and Cyprus failed. Finally

Lieut.-Colonel Pleydell-Railston managed to buy or borrow some twelve couples of a rough but useful type of harrier, of which most well-to-do farmers possessed one, taught to run hares to a point where his master waited with a gun. Having been trained to nobler methods, the pack provided very good sport that winter with both fox and hare. Hounds met every Saturday afternoon, the meets being advertized "war permitting." Fields frequently numbered over one hundred, and generally included the divisional commander. Higher up the Struma valley on the 28th Division front a second pack was hunted by Major W. H. Brooke, 1/K.O.Y.L.I., who had a few beagles and harriers. More than once these hounds, hunting between the river and the line of redoubts beyond the west bank, ran full cry through the enemy's wire; but on each occasion they returned within 36 hours—proof, if would appear, that the Bulgarians had not absorbed the doctrine of unlimited ferocity in war. It would be hard to over-estimate the effect of these interludes of healthy and exciting sport in dispelling the boredom and depression induced by fever, lack of leave, and general monotony.

In proportion to the size of the force, theatrical entertainments and shows of the music-hall type were organized probably on a greater scale than on any other front. In the XII Corps area two brick theatres and one of wood were built. Some of the acting was of a high order. In the spring of 1918 the fame of a pantomime song, "Boris the Bulgar," spread to the Bulgar himself; he translated the verses and posted them outside the trenches of the 28th Division with a request that he should be supplied with the music. The enemy, in fact, had a kindly eye for other relaxations than hunting. He often allowed football to be played within range of his field artillery batteries, but tossed over a warning shell if any attempt were made to carry out drill. On one occasion he actually sent a message that, while sport was welcome in that particular field, training was barred.

Another very useful institution was the Expeditionary Force Canteen, the sales of which, only some £12,000 a week in the autumn of 1916, had by the spring of 1917 risen to £44,000, a figure representing a considerable proportion of the force's pay. The British Red Cross Society, whose services were at the disposal not only of the British Army but of all the Allies, and the Young Men's Christian Association, made an invaluable contribution to the cause of health, comfort, and morale. And, somehow or another, the force was well fed. At various times comparative luxuries such as cheese and bacon had to be cut out of the ration; occasionally, after a period unusually disastrous to shipping, even the bread or meat ration, the essential basis, had to be reduced. In general, however, though at one moment there was a margin of only one day's frozen and twelve days' preserved meat, it was contrived to provide amply sufficient food.

Doubtless these efforts from above were aided from below by the traditional British good nature and patience; nevertheless, the Army owed a debt of gratitude to its commander, who was constantly in the midst of his troops to ensure that his instructions regarding discipline, training, and the provision of all possible comforts and relaxations were being carried out. The success of the combination was proved by the testimony of an experienced observer from outside. At the beginning of August Lieut.-General Henry Lawson arrived to study the question of economy in man-power, a mission which he had already carried out to other fronts. He was deeply impressed by the appearance and discipline of the troops, which seemed to him to be superior to what he had seen either in France or in Egypt.

It was proved, too, by what happened in other contingents. The Russian brigades, which had now been formed into a division, were in a deplorable condition. At the end of June the Russian detachment at Athens, some 2,500 strong, was sent back to Salonika. Certain units refused to re-embark, and the French commander, General Regnault, had to use force. Affairs then seemed to improve, and a month later the Russian division entered the line in the region of Lakes Prespa and Ohrid without serious trouble. Unfortunately, General Dietrichs, formerly Quartermaster-General to General Brusilov and one of the ablest of the younger Russian soldiers, who would have been an excellent divisional commander, was recalled to Russia. The conduct of the division was never again satisfactory, and in the course of the following winter it mutinied and dissolved. A handful volunteered for service in the French Foreign Legion, and a far larger proportion

FATIGUE OF THE SERBIANS

for work in labour companies, some of which were employed on the British front.

The Serbians also had unrest in their ranks. Their difficulties were, as has been recorded, chiefly due to dynastic feuds.[1] Yet the Crown Prince confided to General Milne, who spent a night with him at his advanced headquarters in the latter part of August, that he had other anxieties. The withdrawal of British troops, for whom the Serbians had great admiration, had had a depressing effect. The strain of the Battle of Monastir had told upon the rank and file, who were far from being in the condition which had enabled them to accomplish such great feats of arms during the previous years. For the first time, the British Commander-in-Chief was able to study the ground over which they had fought. He was more than ever impressed by their achievement, impossible to any but troops fighting for their homes and experienced in all the arts of mountain warfare. Now, however, that the Bulgarians were strongly entrenched in their new positions in the mountains, the difficulties of a renewed offensive would be very great.

If in the cases of Russians and Serbians the trouble was mainly political, that among the French was caused by war-weariness. In July, a number of men at Salonika about to go on leave to France had to be sent back to the front owing to lack of shipping. Serious mutinies broke out in the 57th Division and in the 2nd *bis* Regiment of Zouaves. Generals Sarrail and Grossetti succeeded in restoring order without bloodshed, but 90 men, the last and most intransigent of the mutineers, had to be disarmed. The affair was largely due to the indiscretion of the French Press and the speeches of members of the Chamber of Deputies, who declared that every man had right to leave after 18 months' service in the field. As the French had 20,000 men in this situation, leave for them all had hitherto been considered impossible,[2] though after the mutiny they were sent in greater numbers.

General Milne was in agreement with the War Office that some of his best officers should be given a chance to prove their merits in theatres of war which offered greater scope. His two senior staff officers left him during the summer: Major-General Webb Gillman, the Major-General

---

[1] See Vol. I, p. 343. [2] Sarrail, p. 264.

General Staff, being sent to Mesopotamia, and Major-General Travers Clarke, the Deputy Quartermaster-General, to G.H.Q. in France. Br.-General G. N. Cory, from the staff of the XVI Corps, replaced Major-General Gillman. Major-General W. H. Rycroft, Deputy Adjutant-General at G.H.Q., was transferred to the Quartermaster-General's branch, his own former post being taken by Br.-General H. J. Everett, formerly chief administrative staff officer of the XVI Corps.[1] The Commander-in-Chief also sent to France a number of commanders from both artillery and infantry, and senior staff officers, for the most part holding the rank of lieutenant-colonel and in a few cases that of major.

The demands upon the British Salonika Army were by no means at an end. The British Government now saw in the arrival of three Venizelist divisions and the approaching mobilization of the Greek Regular Army an opportunity to withdraw troops from Salonika. At a conference in Paris held on the 25th and 26th July they announced their intention of removing at once to Palestine one division and a proportion of heavy artillery, and of withdrawing further troops as Greek divisions became available to replace them. This resolution was strongly opposed by the representatives of all the other Allies. It drew from Serbia a protest in the form of an *aide-mémoire* addressed to the Foreign Office. In this document, after the statement that a victory could be won in Macedonia more easily than on any other front and that a reinforcement of 100,000 men would make it certain, the Serbian Government declared that any weakening of the Macedonian front would be exceedingly dangerous and would cause the Serbian Army to " cease to have trust " in the Allies." The British Government, which had now completely adopted the views of their General Staff on Macedonia and were looking forward to a great victory in Palestine, stuck firmly to their decision. Their nearest approach to a concession was made at the next conference, held at 10 Downing Street on the 7th August, when they

---

[1] Br.-General H. L. Knight, who had recently succeeded Br.-General Roberts (died in England) in command of the 80th Brigade, was appointed to succeed Br.-General Cory as B.G.G.S. XVI Corps, the command of the brigade being taken over by Lieut.-Colonel W. J. N. Cooke-Collis. Lieut.-Colonel E. D. Young became D.A. and Q.M.G. of the XVI Corps in place of Br.-General Everett.

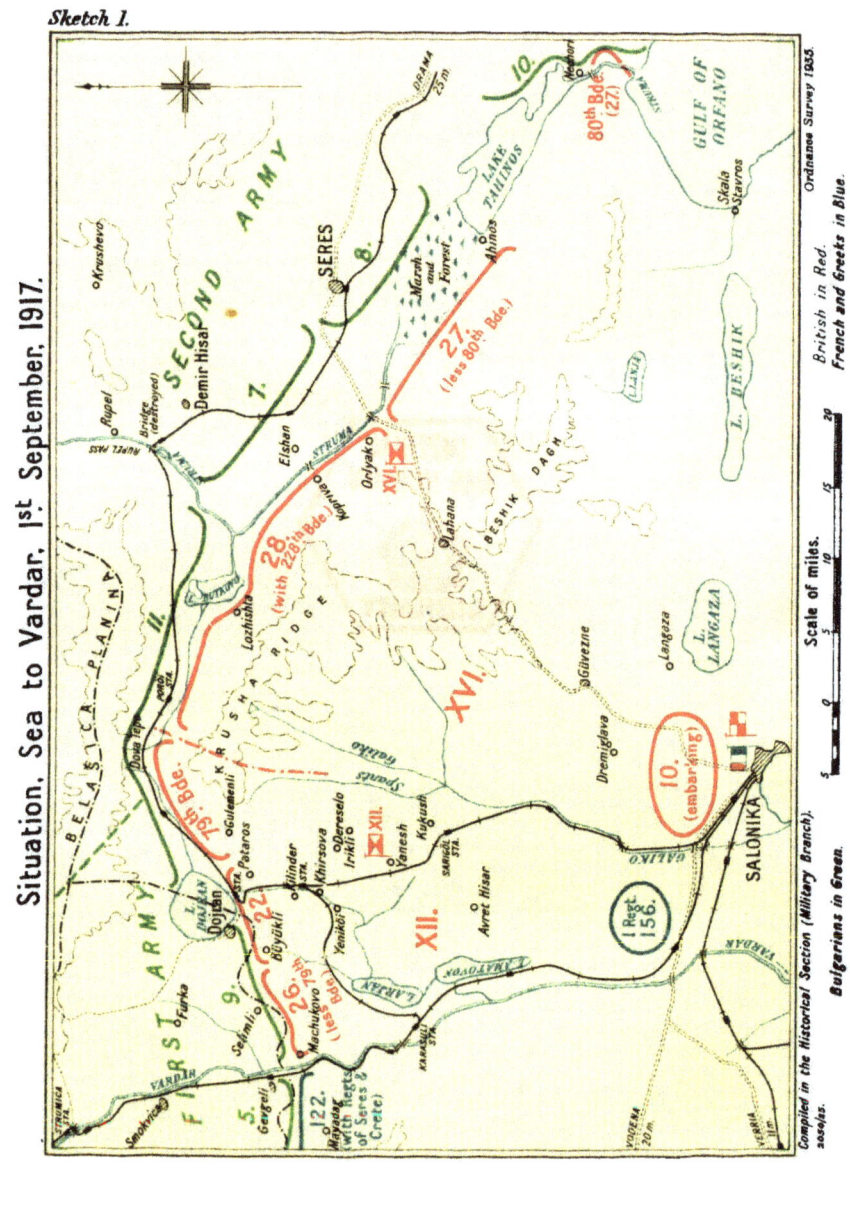

TROOPS DESPATCHED TO EGYPT 13

agreed not to withdraw any further troops "unless un- **1917.** "expected events occurred," in which case the question **Aug.** would be submitted to the Allies for discussion.

General Milne had already been ordered, on the 3rd August, to despatch two 6-inch guns, two 6-inch howitzer batteries, and one 60-pdr. battery, with a considerable quantity of ammunition, to Egypt. He selected one section of the 43rd Siege Battery (6-inch gun),[1] the 134th and 205th Siege Batteries, and the 181st Heavy Battery. On the 9th came orders to transfer an infantry division and to arrange with General Sarrail to relieve as much of his front as was necessary. General Milne issued orders for the withdrawal of the 10th Division from the XVI Corps front, but found it impossible to induce General Sarrail to take over any portion of his line. As recorded, a similar request had been made after the departure of the 60th Division, but at that time General Sarrail's statement that he could not find any French troops for the purpose had been admissible; besides, the British had then had five divisions, whereas now they would have but four for their 90-mile front. By August all the Allied troops which had been in Old Greece had returned to Macedonia and, though the French divisions were all below strength, there were sufficient forces at General Sarrail's disposal—18 French, Serbian, Greek, Italian, and Russian divisions— west of the Vardar. Even in face of pressure from the French General Staff General Sarrail absolutely refused any relief, and none was in fact carried out until the following November, though some French infantry and cavalry, without artillery, were temporarily moved to Salonika as a reserve.

Reduced to his own slender resources, an army of four divisions and one brigade, much weakened by sickness and once more grievously short of heavy artillery, General Milne again altered his dispositions. The Army Reserve

---

[1] This battery, which had consisted of three Mk. VII guns, had in the course of the spring been brought up to the strength of five, one being permanently detached in the Struma valley. (This was known as the "Detached Section," and had its own transport.) The departure of a section of two guns left the battery, therefore, at its earlier strength of three. In November a Mk. XI gun, taken from the 84th Siege Battery and placed on a wheeled mounting, was added. In August 1918 a second Mk. XI gun was added, bringing the battery again up to five, including the "Detached Section."

was broken up and the 228th Brigade was put back into the line. The two corps extended their inner flanks, taking over the front of the Army Reserve to Dova Tepe. The relief of the 10th Division began on the 19th, and its transshipment to Palestine was carried out during the month of September. The corps reserves now consisted, in addition to the cavalry and cyclists, of one brigade in the case of the XII Corps and only two battalions in that of the XVI Corps.

MINOR OPERATIONS OF THE SUMMER.

Maps A, 1, 2.
Only in the air was there any great activity during the summer months. The Royal Flying Corps and Royal Naval Air Service machines carried out bombing raids almost daily on railway stations, aerodromes, and depots. Drama, Angista, and Porna Stations, on the Constantinople Railway; Tushchuli, north-east of Lake Butkovo, where there was a large camp; Dedeli, the headquarters of the Bulgarian *First Army*; depots at Petrić, in the valley of the Strumica, and the Platanenwald on the left bank of the Vardar; and aerodromes at Drama, Livunovo, and Gereviz, near Xanthi, were the chief targets. Against the last-named two big raids were carried out on the 11th August from Thasos, twelve machines of the R.F.C. and three of the R.N.A.S. taking part and dropping over 3,000 lbs. of explosives. Considerable damage was done, and all the machines returned safely, though heavily engaged. This attack was in retaliation for one on the Thasos aerodrome a week earlier which resulted in the destruction of a hangar and some stores.

On the 9th August the enemy had scored a far more considerable success against the R.F.C., though not by means of aircraft. He brought up three field howitzers to Kalendra Wood and opened fire on the advanced aerodrome near Orlyak bridge at the big range of 8,500 yards with such accuracy that it was at first impossible for the pilots to reach their machines. Of the six on the aerodrome two were completely destroyed and one badly damaged; the workshop lorry was smashed, and a hangar burnt. The three remaining machines flew to the neighbouring Marian aerodrome, where they were out of range.

FIRST RAID ON HOMONDOS

On the ground the most important operation during June and July was a raid by the 1/Royal Scots of the 81st Brigade on the village of Homondos. The force at the disposal of Lieut.-Colonel R. R. Forbes, commanding the Royal Scots, consisted of his own battalion, two companies 13/Black Watch, a squadron of the Surrey Yeomanry, two sections of the 11th Battery R.F.A., the 153rd Heavy Battery,[1] and a Stokes mortar of the 81st Light Trench-Mortar Battery. An aeroplane was also allotted to him for contact patrol duty. The assaulting companies, which had to cover four miles from Komaryan bridge before reaching their objective, took the Bulgarian garrison by surprise when they advanced to the assault at 4.15 a.m. on the morning of the 22nd July. Small parties of the enemy fought doggedly among the houses, but were finally driven out or killed with bombs. An hour later the raiders began their withdrawal with their prisoners. As they fell back, they came upon a section of two mountain guns which had been overlooked in the darkness. The guns were completely wired in, but the wire was close enough to enable the Scottish bombers to destroy the detachment of 12 men. It was found impossible to bring in the guns, but they were damaged as much as possible and the sights were removed. By 8.45 a.m. the whole force had regained the right bank of the Struma with 35 prisoners, at a cost of 25 casualties, which included one man killed and eight missing.

One small but daring and successful action was carried out against P.4¼, the foremost Bulgarian work on the " P " Ridge. A party of one officer and 20 men of the 12/Lancashire Fusiliers (65th Brigade) moved out after dark on the 9th August, actually to examine the damage done to the work, which had been bombarded all day. Greeted with a volley of bombs, the patrol instantly closed with the enemy, killed 14 with the bayonet, captured a prisoner, and returned to its lines with a loss of one man missing.

On the 11th August orders were received from General Sarrail to simulate attacks by strong artillery preparations, followed by local raids, while he carried out an attack elsewhere. The demand came just after General Milne had been instructed to withdraw the 10th Division and had been

---

[1] The 60-pdrs. did not cross the river.

refused relief on any part of his front. He could not therefore effect very much. After the dispositions had been readjusted, the XII Corps began a heavy bombardment on the 27th August, chiefly on the front of the 22nd Division, behind which was the bulk of the corps heavy artillery.[1] On the fourth night, that of the 30th, small raids were carried out by the 22nd Division on three works between Lake Dojran and the "P" Ridge. They had no great success, a company of the 9/South Lancashire being repulsed at O.2 with loss, and one of the 12/Cheshire finding O.6 evacuated. At P.4¼, however, a party of the 12/Lancashire Fusiliers killed six of the enemy and brought in four prisoners, its own losses being only six. The total British casualties were two killed, 40 wounded, and two missing.

1917.
Sept.
On the Serbian and Italian fronts similar holding operations were carried out. Then, on the 7th September a composite division [2] under the orders of General Jacquemot began an advance on the extreme left flank. This was the only part of the Allied front where there was now room for manœuvre, if we except the valley of the Struma, where it was indeed possible to manœuvre, but only in front of a strong Bulgarian position. On the 10th Pogradec was captured, the advance being then pushed to the outskirts of Lin, on the western shore of Lake Ohrid. Upwards of 500 prisoners, chiefly Austrian, and four guns were captured, the French losses being 175. "Pogradec" was a very minor operation, yet it represented the one real success in the Balkans in the gloomy year of 1917. Its main object was to prevent the withdrawal of enemy troops to Rumania, where the front had again become lively and the Austro-German troops had been sharply checked in August by the reorganized Rumanian Army. It also strengthened the left flank of the Allies, which had hitherto run between Lakes Prespa and Ohrid. Later in the month there was a very successful raid mainly by the troops of the Albanian,

---

[1] Eight 6-inch howitzers, 22 60-pdrs., two 6-inch guns. The daily allowance was 100 rounds per 18-pdr., 150 rounds per 4·5-inch howitzer, 150 rounds per 6-inch howitzer, 100 rounds per 60-pdr., and 50 rounds per 6-inch gun. An extra 5,000 rounds of 18-pdr. ammunition was allotted for wire-cutting, and a small allowance of 18-pdr. and 60-pdr. ammunition for harassing fire by night.

[2] So many men of the 57th and 156th Divisions were on leave that these divisions had been temporarily amalgamated.

Essad Pasha, into the valley of the Shkumbi, west of Lake Ohrid, resulting in the capture of 442 more prisoners.[1]

1917. Sept.

One of the rare Bulgarian raids on the British front was carried out in the early hours of the 4th September against the works held by the 79th Brigade on the Dova Tepe spur. The enemy, between 200 and 300 strong, cut 70 yards of wire and entered the trenches of the 8/D.C.L.I. at two points, but was promptly driven out again without supports having been called upon. He left three prisoners in the hands of the garrison and 12 bodies were found in the trenches or outside the wire. The casualties of the D.C.L.I. were 10 killed and 11 wounded, no prisoners being taken by the raiders.

From time to time throughout the summer and autumn there were rumours that the enemy was contemplating an offensive. Their chief foundation would appear to have been that very doubtful guide, an appreciation made from his point of view. It seemed possible that he would decide to attack before the Greek Army was ready to reinforce the Allies in Macedonia. In fact, he had no great incentive to do so; nor had his means increased. Though he had brought down his *4th Division*, or part of it, from Rumania, he had already lost some German units and was to lose more as time went on. The Turkish *50th Division* left the lower Struma in July to follow the *46th* to Aleppo. If one side could seek a decision on a new front, so could the other. By a curious coincidence, the British 10th Division and the Turkish *46th Division*, both from the Struma valley, were to face one another in Palestine in the spring of 1918.

The British Survey in Macedonia.

British survey work in Macedonia began in January 1916, when a topographical section arrived; but as in the summer of 1917 the work had to a great extent to be done over again, it may be shortly described at this point.

The existing map was that of the Austro-Hungarian General Staff, on a scale of 1/200,000, which covered practically all south-eastern Europe. On this was based the

---

[1] Essad (see Vol. I, p. 35) had come to Salonika in August 1916 with a contingent of five to six hundred Albanians, but his little force had not been actively employed until the capture of Pogradec. He was regarded with extreme distrust by the Italian authorities, who feared that he would poach upon what they regarded as their Albanian preserves.

British War Office 1/250,000 map, and also the Admiralty War Staff 1/400,000 map. The Austrian map was indispensable; upon it and the adaptations mentioned above the Allies relied entirely in the event of any considerable advance. It was, however, at its worst in southern Macedonia, where it was so full of errors that its enlargement was almost useless. The innkeeper at Skala Stavros informed the first British officers quartered there that the Austrian surveyor often sent peasants to pace the distances between villages, while he sat over a bottle of wine. This was possibly a slander, but British officers, when they came to compare the ground with the map, found no difficulty in believing it. It was therefore decided, while the troops were holding the Entrenched Camp of Salonika, to begin a new survey.

The first triangulation was unsatisfactory. The base, on the Ortach plateau, was a short one of 1355·1 metres, measured with a steel tape which had not been checked since leaving Southampton and had been roughly handled on the Gallipoli Peninsula. No astronomical observations were made for latitude or azimuth. The base was extended by small triangles to Salonika and, after the advance from the Entrenched Camp, to the Langaza plain, where a junction was effected with the French system. The French triangulation, from a base in the flats near the Vardar, was very much more accurate than the British. It included the Dojran front and all the country in rear of it, the eastern boundary being roughly the line of the Galiko river. For this area maps on a scale of 1/50,000, and for the country close to the front line on a scale of 1/20,000, were produced by the French, and handed over to the British when the latter took over that sector. It is thus that we find on British maps up to the end of the war names such as Petit Couronné, Piton Rocheux, and Les Bagatelles, originated by French troops and map-makers. The British triangulation was next carried eastward to Stavros from the Ortach base to connect with a naval system. The British produced the 1/50,000 and such 1/20,000 sheets as were required for the area east of the French.

To cut a long story short, when Major H. Wood, R.E., arrived on the 29th December 1916, a complete reorganization was found necessary. First—as in France—the topographical, printing, and survey sections were amalgamated into one unit, which became No. 8 Field Survey Company R.E. Next, the production was commenced of a new series of British 1/50,000 maps, all of the same size and with edges corresponding with those of the French sheets, which was not the case with the preceding British series.

It was presently discovered, however, that a much more radical change was needed. When new triangulation was begun from any part of the old and attempts were made to " tie up " with the other work based on a different side, large differences in the co-ordinates were found, as much as 200 metres in the Struma valley. As there had been overlapping and differences had not been adjusted, most points had more than one value, and some had three or four. It was clear that from the old triangulation, with its short base and badly shaped triangles (of which only two angles had in some cases been observed), no agreement could be expected. There was nothing for it but to begin a new network of triangles depending on a new base and with as many stations as possible on the sites of the old. Thus the old triangulation could be recomputed.

In June 1917 a base of approximately $6\frac{1}{4}$ kilometres was measured in the Langaza plain with apparatus borrowed from the French, observations for latitude and azimuth being made. A new triangulation net was then extended over the whole British front, on a spherical instead of a rectangular basis. Finally, the old triangulation was recomputed, and all new subsidiary triangulation was based on the sides of the main network. The results were very satisfactory, and when the British triangulation was carried by the Serbians to the neighbourhood of Monastir and made a junction with the French and Serbian systems there, the agreement was found to be very close.

At the same period it became obvious that, in view of the decision to employ sound-ranging for the location of hostile battery positions,[1] there would be a demand for improved maps and for battery-boards, such as were provided for the artillery by the field survey companies on the Western Front. Major Wood reported that the staff of the topographical sections suffered from lack of experience in the use of the plane-table ; in three months the output had

---

[1] As recorded in Chapter III, two sound-ranging sections arrived in January 1918.

been 400 square miles on the 1/50,000 scale, whereas in his view a thoroughly efficient staff could have done nearly three times as much. Less than one third of the British area had then been surveyed on this scale; and the 1/50,000 sheets for the remainder had been produced partly by enlargement of the Austrian staff map and of a rough 1/100,000 map covering part of this area which had been made by the British, and partly from air photographs and cavalry reconnaissances. At this rate of progress it would have taken years to complete the survey. Major Wood therefore advised the General Staff that application should be made to India, which had available large numbers of highly qualified surveyors. The War Office agreed, but it was not until the 23rd October 1917 that a survey detachment from the Survey of India, consisting of a British officer and nine Indian surveyors, with orderlies and followers, arrived at Salonika. The Indian detachment then took over the survey completely, while the British sections, reduced to one containing only the best men, began the accurate fixation of batteries and observation posts and the preparation of battery-boards in the area of the XII Corps. Some maps of country behind the enemy's lines were also produced, based on skeleton surveys from observation posts into which air photographs were fitted, and also on data supplied by the Greek Government, which had begun a survey during the short period between the end of the Second Balkan War and the outbreak of the Great War. For the country beyond the crest of the Belašica Planina and the Bulgarian frontier east of the Struma, it was decided to rely upon the Austrian staff map and the British adaptations from it. These adaptations included not only the War Office and Admiralty maps mentioned above, but also, for the Strumica valley, rough 1/100,000 sheets, which were produced just before the final offensive.

The sound-ranging sections from England and an improvised flash-spotting section were subsequently incorporated in No. 8 Field Survey Company, which then carried out all the functions of a similar unit in France.

The British survey's history was thus like that of many British improvisations in time of war. Map-making began with the handicap of indifferent apparatus and lack of expert knowledge, so that it was for a long time far behind that of the French in efficiency. Finally, however, it may be said that it not only caught up but went ahead. The later British work was at least equal in accuracy to the French; in clarity it was distinctly superior, and some of the sheets were really handsome examples of the draughtsman's art.

The Salonika Fire.

Between three and four o'clock on the afternoon of the 18th August a fire broke out in the Turkish quarter at Salonika. It was not by any means the first among these flimsy old houses, but, as ill-luck would have it, on this occasion a strong "Vardar wind" was blowing out of the north-west and swept the flames before it. There was a poor water supply in the upper parts of the town, and the two fire-engines possessed by the civil authorities were small, antiquated, and, in a word, useless. Nevertheless, though the fire advanced swiftly and spread out to the east and south-west, it was not at first taken very seriously in the lower town. The Turkish quarter might be doomed, but it was not thought probable that the flames would cross the Rue Egnatia, the main east-to-west street, which divided the old town from the new. Actually, when they reached it they leapt across it with scarcely a check.

1917. Aug.

Following their custom of taking the evening meal late in summer, after the heat of the day was over, people were still sitting at dinner in hotels and restaurants at ten o'clock. A little later they were snatching up what belongings they could carry and running for safety, joining a great throng, wailing and terror-stricken, which had poured down from the upper town. The sight was a ghastly but magnificent one; the area of the fire was now one red glow, topped by enormous pillars of smoke, and the sound of the burning had become a continuous crackling roar, above which could be distinguished ever and anon the crash of roofs falling in.

Finally, the water-front caught fire, despite the efforts of the Navy, which played hoses on the buildings from lighters. Lighters were also used to take off refugees. For a time it looked as though this would be the only way of escape and that the exit by the Monastir road, the only one now remaining for lorries, would be closed. Fortunately this did not happen, and many thousands of refugees were rushed out in British lorries. The tragic splendour of the scene was heightened when some light inflammable matter was blown out over the sea and fell upon a lighter filled with petrol. The burning oil then spread over the surface of the sea, which seemed itself to be afire, and the flames illumined the whole harbour and the dense crowds massed upon the water-front. Little property was saved. Few had taken measures to do so in time, the majority of the civilians having fallen back from street to street as the fire advanced upon them, till they were finally driven down to the water-front. At one moment the port buildings were in serious danger, but they were saved, mainly by means of two British fire-engines, which by great good fortune had just been landed. The French Quartier-General was evacuated on the morning of the 19th, but was not actually destroyed. The British lost their Base headquarters, their post office, the Provost Marshal's office and the police barracks, and the Base Depot of Medical Stores. All documents and the greater part of the stores were, however, removed in time.

The fire, though somewhat abated, burnt fiercely throughout the 19th. On the 20th it was still burning, but had been got under control by the dynamiting of houses and because the wind had dropped, and it was no longer spreading. By the next morning it had almost burnt itself out, though it smouldered for several days longer.

Between one third and one half of the city was destroyed, the destruction involving the richest quarters and the finest houses—and some in the modern part really were fine. Many historical buildings, such as the fifth-century church of St. Demetrius, also perished. The Kalamaria road, on which were the biggest of the new houses, was, however, fortunately left intact. Altogether, over 9,000 buildings were burnt, with the great bulk of their contents, whether personal property or merchandize. Eighty thousand people, two-thirds of them Jews, were rendered homeless, but the loss of life, so far as could be ascertained, was small. The fire was said to be the most costly in the history of insurance, the damage being estimated at £8,000,000.[1]

In addition to bringing out thousands of refugees, the British did what they could for the sufferers afterwards. Camps, at first of tents, but later in some cases of wooden

---

[1] H. Collinson Owen, "Salonica and After," p. 103.

huts, were established for the most indigent and helpless. All the food stores in abandoned and partially destroyed warehouses were requisitioned for them, and a small proportion of them were fed entirely by the Allies until the Greek Government were in a position to undertake their rationing. Large numbers were later on evacuated into Old Greece. The British set to work so quickly on measures of relief that camps at Karaissi, Dudular, and Kalamaria were opened by the 20th, while the fire was still burning.

1917. Aug.

During the rest of the war and for a long period after its close Salonika remained a ruined shell. To the British Intelligence this was actually in one respect an advantage. A considerable proportion of the inhabitants of Salonika and an even larger one of those in the whole British area were potential enemies, there being in addition to the Turkish population of the city a number of Turkish and Bulgarian villages outside it. This situation made the work of contre-espionage and civilian censorship difficult, and necessitated the employment of Intelligence officers speaking French, Greek, Judæo-Spanish, and Italian, as well as of Turkish agents. Immigration from the Ægean islands had hitherto added to the difficulty, especially as, prior to the entry of Greece into the war, there had been communication between some of the islands and the coast of Asia Minor. After the fire, practically all applications to enter Salonika were refused at the request of the Greek civil authorities, on the grounds of scarcity of accommodation and the difficulties of feeding an increased population.

In general, however, such as the amenities of Salonika were, their loss was a serious one to the Allied Armies. The Cercle des Etrangers, a comfortable club used by officers as well as civilians, was gone ; so, too, was Floca's, the most popular and expensive of the cafés, and in fact every hotel and restaurant with the exception of the White Tower. It was a bare and desolate city that officers and men, on their rare leave from the front, were to visit henceforth.

CHAPTER II.

THE AUTUMN OF 1917.

(Maps A, 1, 2.)

OPERATIONS IN THE STRUMA VALLEY.

Maps A, 2. AFTER the Bulgarian raid at Dova Tepe on the night of the 3rd, the month of September was uneventful on the British Front. General Milne decided that as soon as the unhealthy season was past the troops withdrawn from the valleys of the Struma and Butkovo should return to the lower ground. His chief reason was that during the winter months supply would be almost impossible in the hills overlooking the valley; whereas, if a line were held on the left bank of the Struma, full use could be made of the light railway following the right. From Lake Tahinos to the Struma's junction with the Butkovo the former river was still to be the main line of defence, but there was to be a really strong outpost position on the left bank.

General Milne gave the corps commanders warning of over a month, so that they should have ample time for their preparations. It was not proposed to advance the outpost line as far beyond the Struma as during the previous winter because the force had been meanwhile considerably reduced. The line was now to run from Gudeli bridge through the villages of Agomah, Hristian Kamila, Yeniköi, Nevolyen, Cuculuk, Elishan, and Cavdarmah, to Artillery Bridge, or approximately 2¼ miles from the river, whereas that of the greater part of the previous winter had been twice as far distant.[1] The right flank was to be covered by constant patrolling by the Corps Mounted Troops, consisting of the Derbyshire and the Surrey Yeomanry, the XVI Corps Cyclists, and the Argyll Mountain Battery, all under the command of Lieut.-Colonel W. Neilson of the Derbyshire Yeomanry.

The occupation of the " winter line " was to take place on the night of the 14th October. On the front of the 28th Division it would consist mainly of old redoubts which had been visited by patrols and were known to be defensible. On that of the 27th Division on the right there would be far

---
[1] See Vol. I, Map 8.

more digging and wiring to be done. It was therefore 1917.
necessary to seize the villages of Osman Kamila and 13 Oct.
Homondos and hold them until the redoubts were in a state
advanced enough to provide for their own defence. As
Homondos was occupied in some strength, Major-General
Forestier-Walker was instructed by General Briggs to take
it by surprise and capture as big a proportion of its garrison
as possible, on the night of the 13th. Agomah and Osman
Kamila were to be occupied by the 82nd Brigade (Br.-
General C. C. M. Maynard) on the right; Hristian Kamila,
Karajaköi Bala and Karajaköi Zir by the 81st Brigade
(Br.-General B. F. Widdrington) on the left. This brigade
was also to carry out the attack on Homondos.

Rain began to fall in the evening and continued all
night, broken only by a snowstorm in the small hours of the
morning. This favoured the chances of a surprise, but
rendered the advance very difficult, especially as the scheme
was an ambitious one calling for absolute precision in a
complicated programme. The villages of Hristian Kamila
and the Karajaköis were first of all occupied without event
by the 1/Argyll and Sutherland Highlanders, which enabled
the batteries of the I Brigade R.F.A.[1] to cross the Struma
and take up positions in the open on the left bank. The
artillery was, however, only to be used in case of emergency
and for the defence of Homondos, and did not register until
the village had been taken.

The attack was carried out in two columns, the right
consisting of the 2/Cameron Highlanders and the left of the
13/Black Watch (Scottish Horse) with one company 1/Argyll
and Sutherland Highlanders. The right column left
Komaryan at 8.15 p.m. on the 13th. After crossing the
Meander Stream it deployed into five columns in fours at 14 Oct.
close intervals and advanced on a compass bearing to cross
the Belitsa about 1,500 yards east of Homondos. Having
driven in two Bulgarian listening posts, it crossed the stream,
which was found fordable despite recent rains, so that the
bridging material painfully carried up was not required.
The column then turned sharply left-handed, in order to get
behind Homondos, to reach which it had to recross the
stream. One company pushed on to attack some small
works 500 yards north-east of the centre of the village, while

---

[1] Consisting for the occasion of the 11th, 39th, and 98th Batteries
(18-pdr.) and D/I and D/CXXIX Batteries (4·5-inch howitzer).

the rest of the battalion deployed between them and the Belitsa. As it was thus turning its back on the outlying works and recrossing the Belitsa at the same moment as these works were being assaulted by the detached company, the extreme daring of the plan will be apparent.

Meanwhile the left column, which had crossed by Wessex bridge at midnight and moved to Hristian Kamila, left this village at 3.5 a.m. It likewise had to turn inwards to get behind Homondos, and just at the point where it was to do so and to assume attack formation, it ran into a flurry of snow. The scouts of the Scottish Horse, who knew the ground well, moved on ahead, aligned themselves at right angles to the former line of march, and held up their helmets on the points of their bayonets. The column then wheeled on to the new alignment, forming into line of half companies as it did so. For the remainder of the advance Lieut.-Colonel H. G. Pleydell-Railston appointed a pacer to each company, as it was impossible to see more than ten yards and progress was bound to be so slow as to preclude accurate estimation of the distance covered. The column was shot at by rifles, machine guns, and trench mortars as it passed enemy posts, but no man spoke a word or shifted in the ranks. On approaching the village, the attached company of the Argylls assaulted and captured a work at the northwest corner. One company of the Scottish Horse crossed the Belitsa and found touch with the right column.

At 6 a.m. on the 14th the whole line advanced southward into Homondos. Both here and in the works in rear of the village—where a Bulgarian battalion headquarters was established—the enemy was taken by surprise. His machine-gun fire inflicted a certain number of casualties, and at isolated points his defence was stout enough. He was, however, not given time to recover from his first disorganization, and when the attackers came to close quarters all was quickly over. The 1/Royal Scots from brigade reserve, which had advanced as far as the Meander south of Homondos, then took over the defence of the village, the attacking battalions withdrawing across the Struma.

"Homondos II," as it became known to the Army, to distinguish it from the successful raid of July, well deserved to be studied officially by the enemy—as it was afterwards discovered it had been—as a perfect example of night operations. It was perhaps the cleverest of many skilful ones carried out in the Struma valley, seeing that the starting-points of the two columns, Komaryan and Hristian Kamila, were three miles apart ; that the right column and a company of the left had to cross the Belitsa, a considerable stream, twice ; and that it rained or snowed the whole night. The captures amounted to 153, including 30 wounded, three machine guns, a great quantity of ammunition, and some valuable documents. Seventy-nine dead Bulgarians were buried. The casualties were one officer and 10 other ranks killed, one officer and 35 other ranks wounded.

1917. Oct.

Meanwhile the 82nd Brigade had occupied Osman Kamila and the old British works in its neighbourhood. Six platoons of the 10/Hampshire advanced from the village up the Agomah-Seres road at 5.50 a.m. on the 14th, to prevent any movement by the enemy against the rear of the 81st Brigade's right column. The scouts having observed that the enemy's works on the Belitsa had been evacuated, the detachment was halted 500 yards from the stream and soon afterwards withdrawn. Work was at once begun on the new line of redoubts, and on the evening of the 18th all troops except three companies of the 2/Gloucestershire—to hold six redoubts with two platoons apiece—were withdrawn across the Struma.

On the left of the 27th Division the 28th occupied the villages north of the Seres road without opposition. In front of the Krusha Ridge the troops advanced simultaneously to the lower slopes of the hills from Lozhishta to Lake Dojran. On the 17th, the front of the 28th Division was readjusted, the 228th Brigade now entering the Struma valley, and the division's line from Yeniköi to Akbusalik being held, from right to left, by the 85th, 228th, 83rd, and 84th Brigades. Between the 83rd and 84th, however, was a novel force holding a front of some three miles south of Lake Butkovo, a front where there was no possibility of even a small attack but every probability of the passage of spies. By day it was patrolled by the inner flank battalions of the two brigades, the patrols meeting half-way. At night it was entrusted entirely to the " 28th Divisional Agents," a picturesque little body of Macedonians whose early training as banditti proved useful and who carried out their duties fairly satisfactorily under two British officers. The Bulgarians occasionally opened fire upon their posts from boats on the lake.

On the 25th October the 27th Division followed up its success at Homondos by a raid on the enemy's outpost line, through the villages of Salmah, Kispeki, and Ada, which lay along the Meander stream below its junction with the Belitsa. On the right of this line Kakaraska was simultaneously attacked by the Corps Mounted Troops.

The mounted troops, who had to march six miles from Gudeli bridge to their objective, found it impossible to keep up to their time-table, and the enemy made off from Kakaraska when the attack of the 82nd Brigade developed. Only three prisoners were taken, the Corps Cyclists having five casualties.

The attack of the 82nd Brigade was carried out in two columns. The right, consisting of the 10/Cameron Highlanders (Lovat's Scouts), 2½ companies of the 10/Hampshire, and a sub-section of the 82nd Machine-Gun Company, under the orders of Lieut.-Colonel D. G. Baillie of the Lovat's Scouts, left Gudeli bridge at 10 p.m. on the 24th October. Having passed between Kakaraska and Salmah, it was to assault the latter village at 6.10 a.m. on the 25th, and after clearing the place to pass on to the capture of Kispeki. The left column, 2/Gloucestershire and 1½ companies 10/Hampshire, under the orders of Lieut.-Colonel J. D. M. Beckett of the Hampshire,[1] crossed the bridge at 11 p.m., when the right column was well clear of it. Moving up east of Osman Kamila, it was to cross the Meander and drop one company north of Ada, the remainder moving on to take up a position facing south from this point to the big bend of the Meander north of Salmah. It would thus be covering Kispeki, so as to prevent the escape of the garrison until the right column should be ready to attack that village. At 6.10 a.m. on the 25th Ada was to be captured from the north. Two sections of the 95th Battery R.F.A., two of the 133rd, and one of D/CXXIX were to be at Gudeli bridge by 5.30 a.m. on the 25th ready to cross the Struma and take up positions in and west of Yeni Mahale. It was not proposed to employ artillery in the assault; in fact, seeing that the attack was to be carried out mainly from the north, its use would have

---

[1] The officer commanding the Gloucestershire, Lieut.-Colonel K. M Davie, would naturally have been in command of the column, but he had left that morning to take over command of the 85th Brigade, 28th Division, owing to the illness, while on eave in England, of Br.-General B. C. M. Carter.

RAID ON SALMAH

1917.
25 Oct.

been very limited. The intention was, indeed, to carry out the whole operation with bayonet, bomb, and rifle grenade, without firing a shot.

Though the weather was better than on the night of the 14th, this undertaking was even more difficult than the attack on Homondos, because the country was fairly thickly wooded and covered with undergrowth where it was not, the going was heavier after ten days' generally wet weather, and the objective was a bigger one. The right column, admirably guided by officers who knew the ground well, struggled on doggedly, disregarding fire from some small posts, and reached a point mid-way between Kakaraska and Salmah well within its time-table. Two companies of the Lovat's Scouts were then despatched to take up a position north of Salmah, whence they were to assault the village at the hour agreed upon, Lieut.-Colonel Baillie co-operating by means of an attack with the rest of the force from the east. As these companies reached their position, they saw some reinforcements moving into the village from the direction of Seres. Maintaining complete silence, they halted, allowed the Bulgarians to pass in, and then got into position and attacked. A trench on the north side of Salmah was carried by a rush with the bayonet, but the Bulgarians fought hard amidst the houses and for a time held up the advance. A bombing attack from a flank coupled with a frontal rush carried their main trench, and they then threw down their arms. At 6.30 a.m. a company of the Lovat's Scouts and one of the 10/Hampshire advanced on Kispeki. Here the garrison had begun to withdraw, and the left column had not arrived in time to intercept it.

The left column had reached Osman Kamila, previously occupied by a company of the 2/D.C.L.I., at 12.45 a.m. on the 25th, and had crossed the Meander by 2.30. From now onwards the advance was a constant struggle through ditches and thick undergrowth. The head had frequently to halt in order to allow the tail to close up; sometimes it did not leave distance enough after passing an obstacle, and the rear files, trying to climb out of some boggy nullah, found themselves obstructed by those in front. Then at 5 a.m. the leading company was fired on by a line of Bulgarian posts running north from Ada. It was impossible to disregard these posts, which were dangerously near the spot where the company detailed for the assault on Ada was to form up; on the other hand, the broken and boggy nature of the ground prevented their quick capture. They were taken eventually, the enemy retreating in haste, but the various delays had made the column late in taking up its blocking position, and the greater part of the garrisons of both Ada and Kispeki escaped.

The scheme had been an ingenious one and had failed to attain complete success by not more than half an hour at most. Br.-General Maynard had, as we have seen, allowed the left column seven hours and ten minutes for the completion of its task, and could hardly have made more exact calculations. All reasonable precautions had been taken, even to remembering that the needles of compasses might be deflected by steel helmets and ordering the compass-bearers not to wear them. The programme had been worked out with the greatest care, and, if it was one which made high demands on troops and leaders, they were not excessive in view of previous achievements in the valley. But the raid did not need this justification; its actual measure of success sufficed, even though the balance of fortune had gone against it. It resulted in the capture, almost all of them in Salmah, of 106 prisoners and a machine gun, while between 60 or 70 of the enemy were killed. The casualties in the three battalions were 77, including 14 killed.

On the front of the XII Corps the only operation of any importance in the course of the autumn was a raid by 12/Argyll and Sutherland Highlanders of the 77th Brigade on Boyau Hill, three miles east of the Vardar, on the night of the 4th November. Though there had been a preliminary bombardment lasting three days, the enemy was found holding his trenches in strength. A barrage was therefore called for, and when it lifted the raiding-party forced its way in. Then followed a fierce fight with bomb and bayonet in intense darkness. All the Bulgarians in the front line, including three machine-gun detachments, were killed, and many bombs were dropped into crowded communication trenches as the enemy attempted to counter-attack. His casualties could not, however, be calculated, and no prisoners were taken. The British losses were fairly heavy, the total, including those of parties making demonstrations at other points, being 54.

Autumn Conditions.

Except on the front of the 27th Division in the Struma valley, autumn had brought no increase of activity, though that in the air was maintained. The Allies were now obviously not strong enough to gain any considerable success. In the course of the last few months their forces had been reduced by two infantry divisions, two cavalry brigades, and a large proportion of the heavy artillery from the British front. They had virtually lost the Russian division, which was unreliable and was soon to disappear. The ranks of both French and Serbians were greatly depleted, the former by the numbers now always absent on leave, the latter by casualties which could not be replaced. In September the official rifle strength with fighting formations of the Serbian Army was given as 34,000 out of a ration strength of 129,000, but there were actually not 20,000 rifles available for operations, the rest having of necessity been withdrawn to recover from their hardships. Similarly, both French and British contingents were carrying a dead weight of thousands of men afflicted by chronic malaria, subject to constant relapses, passing in and out of hospital, and never fit for a hard day's work in the field.

1917. Oct. Map 1.

The only hope of being able to undertake a major offensive, supposing that the Allied Governments ever agreed to allow another to be undertaken, lay in the Greek Army, and it would obviously be a long time before that was ready. The second and third divisions of the National (Venizelist) Army, the Crete and Archipelago Divisions, had now joined the Seres Division in Macedonia,[1] but the old Regular Army had not yet made its appearance. A general mobilization was not ordered until October. M. Venizelos had to move slowly, weeding out the majority of the senior officers, whose sympathies were with King Constantine; he also had to await the despatch of equipment and stores from Great Britain and France.

The French operations in Albania, which General Sarrail had intended to continue in October, came to nothing. On the 20th three columns began an advance west of Lake Ohrid. Next day a telegram was received from the Ministry of War forbidding any extension of the French

---

[1] See Vol. I, p. 257.

front in the region of Pogradec. Once again international rivalry had stepped in ; for there could be no doubt that the message was the result of pressure by the Italian authorities, who did not want French troops in what they regarded as their political zone.

The left flank of the Armée d'Orient, in magnificent country of mountains covered with forests of oak, beech, chestnut, and pine, of green valleys and limpid lakes, was, indeed, politically an open sore. General Sarrail is in this matter deserving of every sympathy, though it is possible that his handling of affairs was not always as tactful as it might have been. When he had, as far back as August 1916, occupied Koritza, he had found four parties eager to push in there—Venizelist Greeks, Italians, Albanians of Essad Pasha, and, less insistently, Serbians—not to speak of the Royalist Greeks, who had been long in possession, Greece having occupied the Kaza of Koritza since the Balkan Wars. The district was also, he alleges, a centre of Austro-Bulgarian espionage.[1] He had taken the natural course of refusing to allow in anyone but the French, under that old acquaintance of the British on the Struma front, Colonel Descoins, chosen because he had commanded the Greek cavalry before the war. In December 1916 the Kaza had proclaimed its autonomy, become a "republic" under the benevolent but watchful eye of the French colonel, and issued postage stamps now much sought after by collectors.[2] Light opera, perhaps, but without the combats, pillage, and burnings of the melodrama which had preceded it. Asked for an explanation by the Ministry of War at the request of Italy, General Sarrail had stuck to his guns.

Not only here but for some 70 miles further south and within the frontier of Greek Epirus bitterness continued. At Preveza and elsewhere the Italian troops, after their advance in June,[3] had removed the Greek authorities. From Yannina the British Vice-Consul reported in July to the Athens Legation his fear that, if the Protecting Powers did not intervene, the populace would attack the Italians. To the representations of M. Barrère, the French Ambassador

---

[1] Sarrail, p. 220.
[2] The first issue of stamps by Koritza had been, according to the catalogue of Yvert et Tellier, in 1914.
[3] See Vol. I, p. 357. Preveza is on the Gulf of Arta, and just off Map 1. Yannina (below) is spelt Ioannina on Map 1.

AFFAIRS IN ALBANIA

in Rome, Baron Sonnino replied that Italy must continue to hold the Santi Quaranta route, which was of great importance to her and had already proved of some small service to the other Allies in Macedonia.[1] As the result of friendly pressure by Great Britain and France, neither of whom had an axe to grind here, Italy by October permitted the reinstallation of the Greek authorities, withdrew her troops from Yannina and Preveza, and recalled all the detachments on Greek soil except those necessary to cover the Santi Quaranta route. *(1917. Oct.)*

Ill feeling did not disappear, but comparative quiet reigned thenceforward. The Albanians furnished contingents which rendered useful service to the French, though it was perhaps balanced by that rendered by their fellow-countrymen on the other side of the line to the Austrians. In addition to the followers of Essad Pasha, the French recruited a battalion which they placed under the command of a French officer, and raised a gendarmerie upwards of a thousand strong.

From the military point of view all this was not of the first importance. Neither side was ever likely to turn the other's flank from beyond the lake district, and the Italian corps at Valona was not likely to move at all. It was, however, a constant distraction and irritation, and it is only right to remember, if General Sarrail is reproached with having been too much preoccupied by political affairs, that here the preoccupation was inevitable and unwelcome.

Mention has been made of the difficulties under which the Serbians were labouring. The British Government decided to send out a senior officer, who would act as representative of the C.I.G.S. with their Army and be something more than a liaison officer. He was, in fact, not to be placed under General Milne's orders, though he was to furnish the British Commander-in-Chief with whatever interesting information he became possessed of. His duty was to report direct to the C.I.G.S., to keep the Serbians informed of the part which Great Britain was playing in the war, and to let them see that the dark clouds overhanging the cause of the Allies in 1917 had a lining of silver. There was no *arrière pensée* as regards his mission, which was designed for the common good; but as the Serbian

---

[1] See Vol. I, p. 259.

Army was under General Sarrail's command and had never been in touch with the British in Macedonia, it was perhaps excusable that the French Commander-in-Chief should have regarded his arrival with some suspicion.[1] Indeed, General Milne did not see the necessity for the appointment, though he afterwards found that its holder, Br.-General C. E. Corkran, carried out his duties with great skill and tact. The latter reached Salonika on the 7th October. He succeeded in gaining the confidence of the senior Serbian officers, from the Crown Prince downwards. That, at a moment when they were distressed by the British withdrawals, was more valuable than the detailed reports which he sent at intervals to Sir William Robertson, and which could also have been furnished through the British Salonika Army.

Though the British provided a large proportion of the shipping on which the campaign depended, it was lack of shipping which prevented as much leave being given to them as was given to the French. In six months, from May to October, only two leave parties sailed for home. The opening of the Taranto route [2] in October did not at once produce the improvement which had been expected, because it coincided with the naval reorganization necessitated by the introduction of the convoy system in the Mediterranean, which caused serious delay. A rest camp was established at Itea, and was badly needed, as leave parties were occasionally held up there for weeks at a time.

This question of shipping was eternal. After malaria it was the most insistent of all the problems which had to be faced. In General Milne's words, his weakest point was now, as it had always been, "the L. of C. with England." At one moment in the following winter the supply of petrol was so short that the tram service in Salonika had to be suspended. Even on the maritime route between Salonika and Stavros, round the peninsula of Khalkidike, which required as a rule only three small ships, there were serious delays. It was mainly because of the uncertainty of this service that General Milne obtained permission to lay a light railway from Sarakli along the southern shores of

---

[1] Sarrail, p. 279.
[2] See Vol. I, p. 276. The route was by rail from Salonika to Bralo, by lorry to Itea on the Gulf of Corinth, by ship to Taranto, and thence by rail to Cherbourg.

Lakes Langaza and Beshik to Stavros.[1] He would have been glad to lay a standard gauge line, which he thought might be required for operations on this flank, but the War Office was unable to provide him with the rails. Even for a light railway the question of labour was a difficulty, as he had lost a number of his Macedonian labourers owing to the Greek mobilization, and had other urgent railway work in hand at the same time. He could hardly have laid a fifty-mile line without the services of 4,000 Turkish prisoners of war, shipped in batches from Cyprus. Work on the Stavros light railway was begun on the 14th November, and lasted nearly six months. The other work consisted of the complete relaying of the Sarigöl-Snevche light railway, hastily constructed over a year earlier by the French, and the laying of a new branch from it at Gramatna, through Kürküt and Krushova, to Rajanovo. Turkish prisoners were also employed on this branch, progress on which was hindered by lack of material, so that it was not open for traffic until February 1918.

1917. Oct.

On the 19th October General Sarrail at last announced that he would give the British some relief by taking over their left brigade sector east of the Vardar. This was the most satisfactory assistance he could have afforded, as the troops of one nationality would now be holding both banks of the river, perhaps the most vital position on the whole front. The French, moreover, would be able to place more heavy artillery in this area than had been possible for the British. The infantry relief was completed on the night of the 9th November, when the 1st Regiment de Marche d'Afrique relieved the 78th Brigade. The British left flank was now upon the Selimli Deresi, a stream running parallel with the Vardar. On the following night the 26th Division took over a frontage of one battalion from the 22nd, so that each division should have its share in the relief. On the British left there was now a group of divisions—a large army corps, in effect, though it was not given this designation—commanded by General Gérôme and consisting of the French 122nd Division with one regiment of the 156th, and the three Greek divisions, the Seres, the Archipelago, and the Crete. As its frontage, from the Selimli Deresi to Nonte, was only 24 miles, it had ample reserves by the

Map A.

---

[1] See Vol. I, p. 279.

standards of Macedonia, even if the Greek divisions were still not fully trained. General Milne, for his part, was able to place two battalions in Army reserve.

Once more, then, the winter was at hand. It had been said, after the failure of the offensive in May, that an opportunity had then been lost but that it would probably recur in the autumn. If it had recurred, there had been no possibility of taking advantage of it. So much had been clear to all the Allied Governments and commanders, and no plan of action had even been seriously discussed. There was really nothing to be done but clench teeth, endure what might come, and hope for better times.

The Influence of other Fronts.

It is time to glance at what had been happening recently in the theatres of war nearest to Macedonia and most closely affecting the fortunes of the Allied Armies there. In the previous volume there was a brief sketch of the victorious campaign by General von Falkenhayn and Field-Marshal von Mackensen against Rumania, which resulted in the overrunning of the greater part of that country. After being checked upon the lower Siret in January 1917, however, the Germans abandoned the attempt to continue what had now become a purely frontal advance. The Rumanian Government, now established at Jassy, was thus given a respite, and a French Military Mission under General Berthelot undertook the reorganization of the Army. A really powerful German thrust from the north, through Tarnopol in the direction of Odessa, would have put the Russian forces in the Carpathians in an untenable position and finally driven Rumania out of the war. That the Germans were capable of making it with success is not to be doubted, considering the then state of the Russian Armies. But in January 1917, when this operation was suggested to General Ludendorff by General Hoffmann, the Supreme Command was preparing to meet a great Allied offensive in the west and could not spare the necessary troops. On the 12th March the Russian Revolution broke out, and it then became even more to the German interest to play a waiting game. It might well be that the fruit was ripe enough to be on the point of falling, without there being any necessity to shake the tree.

The Tsar of Russia abdicated on the 15th March, and

Great Britain, France, Italy, and Rumania hastened to give official recognition to the Provisional Government. Perhaps only those whose memories go back to the event are capable of realizing how extravagant and fallacious were the hopes which the democracies of the Allies built upon this revolution. They even believed, or cheated themselves into the belief, that it would bring fresh nerve to Russia's arm. They saw her in their imaginations, like France a century and a quarter earlier, inspired by a Kerenski in place of a Danton, hurling invaders forth from her frontiers.

1917. June–Dec.

The reality was very different. The new leaders of the nation professed loyalty to Russia's alliances and undertakings, but they were not Dantons. They were unable to control the monster which they had unchained. By their own ordinances, especially the notorious "Prikaz No. 1," they ruined irretrievably the discipline of the Armies. Some troops, notably the Caucasians, remained fairly sound, but as a whole the fighting machine lapsed immediately into chaos and anarchy.

Nevertheless, preparations went forward for the offensive planned before the outbreak of the Revolution, and though they consisted in large part of speech-making and it was doubtful until the last moment whether the troops would attack at all, the offensive actually began on the 29th June. The main attack was on the southern front, with Lemberg as the material objective and the destruction of the Austrian forces as the real goal. This front had been chosen in order to avoid German troops. Subsidiary attacks further north and on the Rumanian front would encounter German troops, but in Rumania the Russians appeared to be less affected by the Revolution, while the Rumanians themselves were well trained and confident.

Attacking in overwhelming superiority of numbers, the Russians broke completely through the Austrians astride the Dniester. But the offensive immediately petered out. Some formations did not advance at all; some marched back as soon as they met the slightest resistance; some which did not wish to fight actually fired on others which did. The net result may be said to have been the destruction of such few troops as remained loyal to their colours. Then came the counter-offensive.

Inevitably, seeing that there had been fraternization, encouraged by the enemy, and numerous Russian desertions, the Russian plan had long been known to the German command, though the date was not. Prince Leopold of Bavaria, the Commander-in-Chief in the East, and his staff officer General Hoffmann were prepared to parry it by an action of the same nature as the latter had suggested in January, a thrust in the direction of Tarnopol. This time General Ludendorff agreed, and was bold enough to despatch his " Central Reserve " of six divisions from France for the purpose. They were too late to anticipate the attack, and Hoffmann had to stiffen the Austrian *Third Army* south of the Dniester before he could strike. Yet the blow, if made with weakened forces, sufficed. Preceded by an artillery preparation planned by an obscure artillery commander of a *landwehr* division, whose name was shortly to be on every lip, Colonel Bruchmüller, it was made on the 19th July. Ten miles were gained on the first day and Tarnopol fell on the 25th of the month. By the beginning of August scarcely any Austrian territory remained in Russian hands. Then the lack of communications brought the advance to a halt. On the 1st September the Germans turned to the other end of the huge front, with the same Central Reserve. Another " Bruchmüller preparation," and, with hardly any opposition, they were across the Dwina and in possession of the great fortress of Riga. They could march on Petrograd now at any moment they chose.

Meanwhile in Rumania the Russian troops had been responsible for the failure of a promising Allied offensive, in which the Rumanians had gained important initial successes. Here also the Austro-Germans counter-attacked, but here they were rudely disillusioned. Their offensive between the Siret and the Oitoz Pass—known to the Rumanians as the Battle of Marasesci—lasted from the 6th August until the end of the month. Nowhere did they do more than regain the losses of July, and at many points they were completely repulsed. The Rumanians fought excellently and even the Russians fairly well here. " Thanks " to the influence of the French," writes General Ludendorff, " the Rumanian Army had become so much stronger that " strategic successes seemed out of the question for us so " long as the offensive in Bukovina remained at a stand- " still." [1] The Russians were, however, soon finished with,

---

[1] Ludendorff, II, p. 438.

and the Rumanians had to take over the whole of the active part of the line.   1917. June-Dec.

Then all was quiet on the Eastern Front, except for the capture of the Russian Baltic islands by the Germans in October. The Russians appointed a new Commander-in-Chief, General Kornilov, of whom much was hoped, but he was soon at loggerheads with Kerenski, was relieved of his command on the 9th September, refused to obey the order, marched on Petrograd, and was forced to surrender. Kerenski then appointed himself Commander-in-Chief, and the process was repeated. The Bolshevists, or extreme Communists, seized Petrograd on the 8th November; Kerenski advanced against them with Cossack troops, hesitated, halted for several days, and after a minor reverse fell back. His force immediately dissolved. Russia began to split up; Trans-Caucasia, the Ukraine, and Finland proclaimed their independence, and presently civil war broke out in the valley of the Don. The next Russian Commander-in-Chief, General Dukhonin, was murdered and replaced by a naval ensign of deranged intellect named Krilenko, who was instructed to ask for an armistice. " Now " tell me, is it possible to negotiate with these people ? " Ludendorff demanded on the telephone. " Yes," replied Hoffmann, " it is possible to negotiate. Your Excellency " needs troops, and this is the quickest way to get them."[1] An armistice was concluded at Brest-Litovsk on the 15th December, and on the 22nd peace negotiations began. Showing a glimmer of loyalty which the Allies had hardly expected, the Russian representatives had made it a condition that no German troops, other than those already under orders, should be moved from the Eastern Front. Hoffmann gracefully assented ; he had already issued orders for the despatch to France of all that could be spared of his 80 divisions, and they were even now moving as fast as the railway service could carry them.

Rumania's gallant fight in July and August had been unavailing. She had been granted a respite only because the Germans had decided to move troops to Italy. If she continued to resist it would be only a matter of months before she was overwhelmed, and then the terms imposed upon her would be severe in the extreme. If she parleyed

---

[1] Hoffmann, " Der Krieg der Versäumten Gelegenheiten," p. 189.

now, she might hope for better ones. She also concluded an armistice, the "Truce of Focsani," with the Central Powers, on the 9th December.

In Italy affairs had for some time appeared to be moving to an equally disastrous conjuncture. On the 24th October the Austro-German offensive in the Julian Alps, known as the Twelfth Battle of the Isonzo, was launched. Once more the German contribution was Ludendorff's Central Reserve: surely one of the most effectively employed reserves—considering its minute size in proportion to the forces engaged upon the various fronts on which it operated—to be found in military history. The success of the attack exceeded the enemy's fondest hopes. One Italian Army broke up in complete rout. In less than a fortnight the Austro-German Armies were across the Tagliamento, 40 miles from their starting-point. Their advance continued rapidly to the Piave, which they reached on the 11th November.

The British and French General Staffs had at once realized the seriousness of the situation. Three days after the launch of the attack it was decided to despatch to Italy two British and four French divisions. If the action of the Allies had in earlier moments of crisis been wanting in speed and resolution, it was not so in this case. On the urgent representations of the Italian Comando Supremo, the British increased their contingent to five divisions, and on the 10th November placed General Sir Herbert Plumer in command of that force. The detrainment of the two first divisions began at Mantua next day. On the 12th three French divisions moved from Brescia to Vicenza. Meanwhile, however, the enemy had outrun his supplies. The Italians had to some extent pulled themselves together, and it was they who stopped the enemy on the Piave actually before the Franco-British troops entered the line at the beginning of December. There were to be more anxious moments, but none so critical as those which had passed, and which had caused General Sir Henry Wilson to write in his diary:—" I am coming to the opinion that " we cannot hold the Piave, and that we had better fall " back under cover of rear guards. The loss of Venice " means the loss of the Adriatic, and a serious threat, " therefore, to Salonika and Egypt, but I am afraid that " is coming."

ITALY AND PALESTINE 41

It was the Inter-Allied Conference at Rapallo, on the 1917.
6th November, summoned to consider the crisis, from which June–Dec.
was created the Supreme War Council, the fifth session of
the Conference, held on the evening of the 7th, being
officially considered the first session of the Council. Macedonia was not discussed, except at a meeting of British and
French representatives in Mr. Lloyd George's room, when
the British spoke of rumours of a threatened attack by the
enemy and complained of the lack of news from that
quarter.

Amid all this gloom, Palestine was a bright spot. On
the 31st October the forces under the command of General
Sir Edmund Allenby had struck the first blow, the capture
of Beersheba. By the 7th November the Gaza-Beersheba
line had been rolled up. The British force had then
advanced northward, wheeled into the Judæan Hills on the
19th, and after fierce fighting captured Jerusalem on the
9th December.

Of these events, the Italian defeat, though constituting
a very serious threat to the Allied force in Macedonia, yet
as things turned out affected it comparatively slightly.
The victory in Palestine, on the other hand, had the effect
of hardening the views of the British political and military
authorities against the Salonika venture. They considered
that their preference for Palestine to Macedonia had been
already justified, seeing that the troops which they had
moved from the latter to the former had made possible
General Allenby's great success. Incidentally, that success
had removed any anxiety hitherto felt regarding the situation in Mesopotamia. But Palestine seemed to the British
Government to promise yet richer rewards to endeavour.
They now hoped to be able to drive Turkey out of the war
and perhaps by this means cause the defection of Bulgaria,
which they had given up hoping to do by means of operations in Macedonia. They decided to reinforce General
Allenby still further, by a division from Mesopotamia, and
to make Palestine for the time being the only offensive
theatre of war. Gradually they won over their Allies, if
not to agreement with this opinion, at least to acceptance
of it. After the Battle of Cambrai, the decision was
embodied in a Joint Note by the Military Representatives
on the Supreme War Council on the 21st January 1918. It
was to stand on the defensive on the Western Front, in

Italy, and in the Balkans, and to undertake a decisive offensive against Turkey " with a view to the annihilation " of the Turkish Armies and the collapse of Turkish re- " sistance." That might have been attempted by combined action in Palestine and Mesopotamia; but in February the British Government decided to reduce Mesopotamia also to a defensive rôle, so that the Army in Palestine was now to be the sole striking force.[1]

What happened in Russia and Rumania was also heavy with significance for Macedonia. It will be recalled that at the Calais Conference of the 26th February 1917 it had been decided that only " the co-operation of the Russo-Rumanian " forces against Bulgaria " could justify a major offensive from Salonika.[1] As a fact, General Sarrail had attempted what could only be described as a major offensive six weeks later. But at any rate there was now not the slightest possibility of Russo-Rumanian forces co-operating with the Allied Armies at Salonika. Indeed, there appeared a rather greater risk than formerly of an enemy offensive in Macedonia. Germany was already able to withdraw troops from the Eastern Front; when peace was signed with Russia and Rumania she might be able to withdraw anything up to 50 divisions. Was it altogether incredible that she should seek to drive the Allied Armies of the East into the sea as the next step? Certainly not probable. She had now before her eyes, for the first time since September 1914, the hope of ending the war by obtaining a decision in France. With the United States a cloud on the horizon, she had no time to waste upon side-issues. The tendency was for German units to leave Macedonia, not for reinforcements to arrive there. Still, the risk could not be lightly dismissed. In the following chapters it will appear how insistently the problems of defence obtruded themselves at Salonika during the winter and early spring.

In fine, the events of 1917 on other fronts tended still further to lessen, in the eyes of the Entente Powers and especially in those of Britain, any benefits likely to be drawn from the Macedonian campaign. They did not lessen either its risks or its demands upon their resources of all kinds.

---

[1] " Egypt and Palestine," II, pp. 293–9.
[2] See Vol. I, p. 296.

CHAPTER III.

THE THIRD WINTER.

(Maps A, 1, 2, 3.)

THE RECALL OF GENERAL SARRAIL.

ON the 15th November G.H.Q., which had occupied houses in the Avenue Reine Olga, Kalamaria, for nearly two years, transferred its offices to the buildings of a large orphanage. There was at the moment a prospect that its establishment would be increased and the two corps headquarters abolished, in consequence of the reduction of the force. It was, indeed, fortunate that they were retained; otherwise they would almost certainly have had to be re-established, probably after their commanders and senior staff officers had left the country, when Greek troops were placed under General Milne's orders.

1917.
Nov.-Dec.
Map A.

Another move was the change-over of the 80th and 82nd Brigades between the Struma valley above Lake Tahinos and the Neohori position at the mouth of the river. The 80th Brigade had been on the coast since February 1916, and at the mouth of the Struma since July of that year. During all that time it had been acting in co-operation with the Navy, which maintained a detached squadron of one cruiser and two or three monitors at Stavros and constantly bombarded the enemy's works and communications on the coast. Ties such as seldom can have been knit between the soldier and the sailor in warfare had been established. The Navy's farewell message, from the cruiser *Endymion* (Captain C. M. Staveley), ran :—" Deeply regret " parting with the 80th Brigade after two such happy years " together, and wish them all good luck and a happy " Christmas and a victorious New Year." The last wish, at all events, was to be fulfilled.

The method of the relief is not without interest, as it is an indication of the difficulties on this vast front, with insufficient troops to maintain much more than a screen anywhere except between Lake Dojran and the Vardar. It must, of course, be remembered that time did not press, so that the easiest and safest method was chosen. From the area of one brigade to that of the other was a four days' march. Three camps were established along the route south of Lake Tahinos, the centre double the size of the others, so that troops in course of transfer could meet half-way. Not more than one half-battalion and one battery were allowed to be withdrawn from the Neohori position without replacement. In these circumstances the change-over of the two brigade groups took a month, the first half-battalion of the 82nd Brigade beginning its march on the 10th November and the transference of commands taking place on the 11th December.

Shortly after the 82nd Brigade's move to the coast sector, its commander, Br.-General C. C. M. Maynard, was evacuated owing to sickness and replaced by Lieut.-Colonel R. E. Solly-Flood, hitherto G.S.O.1 at G.H.Q.

The front remained very quiet. There were several small raids during November and December, on the whole successful; but raids on this front, where for long periods they represented, with bombardments by artillery or from the air, the sole activity, become hardly worthy of record in a foreshortened narrative unless they were made on a particularly large scale. One such was carried out on the 20th December by the 2/Cheshire of the 84th Brigade against the village of Butkovo Jum'a, beside the railway, north-west of Lake Butkovo. The village itself was fortified, but to the east of it there was only a slight wire obstacle following the railway.

The plan was based upon the assumption, which could now be confidently accepted anywhere on the XVI Corps front, that something more than a surprise was necessary if prisoners were to be captured in large numbers. The Bulgarian outposts were alert and wary, they knew the ground better than the attackers, and they had no intention of fighting to a finish against superior force. They would disperse to avoid capture, and nothing could prevent them from doing so except forming a cordon round their post as had been done at Homondos and Salmah. In this raid the whole battalion, three guns of the 22nd Battery (18-pdr.), one section of D/CXXX Battery (4·5-inch howitzer), one battery IV Highland Mountain Brigade, a detachment of the 506th (Hampshire) Field Company, a sub-section of the 84th Machine-Gun Company, and a company of the 1/Welch Regiment were placed at the disposal of Lieut.-Colonel A. P. Blackwood, 2/Cheshire. The Welch company was to escort

RAIDS BY BOTH SIDES

1917.
Nov.–Dec.

the mountain artillery, which was to take up a position near the right bank of the Butkovo River, north-east of Starosh. The field artillery was to be established slightly further east in the village of Butkovo, under the escort of a half-company of the Cheshire. Two companies of the battalion were to cut the wire at a level-crossing over the railway east of Butkovo Jum'a, and follow the line until they were north of the village, when they were to assault it from that direction. A half-company on one side and a company on the other were to prevent the enemy from breaking away either to east or west. The distance from Butkovo to Butkovo Jum'a by the route followed was three miles.

The raid was one which its commander could report was "carried out all through according to plan." The attacking party passed between two outposts east of the village which were not much over 300 yards apart without being seen or heard. There was little resistance in the village, where some 30 Bulgarians were killed. Fifty-five prisoners were taken, the casualties of the Cheshire being two officers and 11 men wounded. The loss would have been lighter still but for the explosion of a trip-bomb as the party was returning, which wounded four of the raiders and six of their prisoners. It was an indication that no frontal attack was likely to have succeeded in its object.

The enemy made two raids in considerable strength, on the front of the 66th Brigade at P.4½ and on that of the 65th Brigade at the Mamelon, on the night of the 23rd November. There had been a three days' bombardment of P.4½, and, though the wire had been repaired during the darkness, it was so badly damaged in the end that Br.-General F. S. Montague Bates decided to fill the front trench with loose wire and make the support trench the line of resistance. It was well that he did so; for the attack at night was carried out by two parties, each apparently 75 strong. One party crossed the front trench, but was then stopped. The enemy carried small spades, so evidently meant to hold the position. He appeared to suffer heavily from the artillery barrage and from machine-gun fire, but only five dead were afterwards found. Two prisoners were taken. The 12/Cheshire had 17 casualties, including one man from a detached post missing. At the Mamelon the post of the 9/King's Own was forced to withdraw, and this battalion had four men missing and six wounded.

One important change in the Bulgarian dispositions was noted in the course of December, as a result of the interrogation of prisoners and deserters. For some time the enemy had been holding in reserve about Skoplje the *Mountain Division*, a new formation with an infantry strength of nine battalions, to which three more were subsequently added. He now brought this division into line east of Lake Dojran, relieving the right brigade of the *11th Division*.[1] East of the Vardar there was now no German infantry, the *Jäger* battalions previously on the left bank having been relieved by the Bulgarian *39th Regiment*. From now onwards there was to be a slow but steady withdrawal of German troops, the first—*146th Regiment* and *11th Reserve Jäger Battalion*—to Palestine, and thereafter to France. The Germans felt that they must scrape together every battalion for their coming offensive on the Western Front. It appears to have been an error. A German force of which the infantry numbered about 21 battalions had saved Bulgaria in the autumn and winter of 1916. The presence of such a force on the Western Front would not win the war; its absence from Macedonia in September 1918 probably contributed a good deal to losing it.

On the 13th November 1917 M. Painlevé, President of the Council in France, resigned his office and was succeeded three days later by M. Clemenceau. On the 10th December, after the new President of the Council had been reminded of representations made to his predecessors regarding the command in Macedonia and had thoroughly investigated the case, the Ministry of War telegraphed to General Sarrail that his recall had been decided upon. His successor, General Guillaumat, arrived on the 22nd December, and General Sarrail left for France the same night.

In the official note issued to the public the French Government stated that General Sarrail " had had serious " difficulties to contend with and had rendered great " services." The severest critic of the general's two years

---

[1] As indicated on Map 11, Vol. I, the *Mountain Division* was known to be in Macedonia in May. The brigade of the *11th Division* which it relieved appears, after a rest, to have been moved west of the Vardar and to have entered the line on the *5th Division* front. In August 1918 it returned, relieving the two regiments of the *Mountain Division* in its old sector, while the two other regiments of the *Mountain Division* took over part of the *9th Division's* front between Lake Dojran and the Vardar.

RECALL OF GENERAL SARRAIL 47

of command will agree that both statements were true. It has here been suggested that he did not always take the best measures to overcome his difficulties; but it has or should have been made clear that some of them were insuperable. The greatest, without any doubt, were the uncertainty of the policy which governed the campaign and the conflict of ideas between the Allies whose forces were represented in it. This conflict was above all between Great Britain and France. The Serbians might complain or, as on one occasion, refuse to obey his orders, but their Government and Army were in agreement with his view that a military decision should be sought in the Balkans. The Italians played only a limited part, and it was not General Sarrail but his successor who wrote (after three weeks' experience) that their Government were in this theatre " more con-" cerned with post-war conditions than with the war." [1] Hardly less serious was the very limited support he obtained from France, in regard to which both his successors were more fortunate.

1917. Nov.-Dec.

Of the three ventures undertaken by General Sarrail, the expedition into Serbia in 1915 seems to deserve entry on the credit side, the Battle of Monastir in 1916 belongs there without any doubt, and the offensive of 1917 is with equal certainty a debit. Yet, when one comes to strike a balance, these items are found not to be important enough, big as they are, to establish a plus on one side or the other. In which column it is to go can be settled only after deciding whether the campaign in the Balkans was in itself sound or unsound. By that General Sarrail stands or falls. For, rather than any other soldier or any statesman during these two years, he kept the campaign alive.

If he was right in this, we must add that it appears certain, as circumstances had developed in 1917, that General Sarrail would never have led the Allies to victory in Macedonia in 1918. He had not now a strong enough hold upon any of them. They had all of them requested that he should be recalled; when his recall came, they did not withhold a measure of sympathy, but neither did they repent of their action. So this remarkable figure, with so many elements of greatness, passed from a scene in which he had not been at home.

---

[1] General Guillaumat's Report of the 15th January 1918.

A New Broom.

The new Commander-in-Chief of the Allied Armies was young, 54 years of age, having risen from the command of a division to that of a Group of Armies in the space of three years and having greatly distinguished himself at Verdun. Quiet and decisive, he had a brusqueness of the sort to which military subordinates do not object provided that it is accompanied by reasonableness ; and, though firm in his own opinions, he was ready to hear and to take into account those of others. General Milne reported that within a week he appeared to have got a grip of affairs. He had brought with him an up-to-date and efficient Chief of the Staff, Colonel Charpy, who was shortly afterwards promoted to the rank of general. He also brought a new Army commander to take command of the Armée Française d'Orient. Immediately after his successful operation west of Lake Ohrid, General Grossetti had been obliged to lay down his command owing to illness and had returned to France on three months' sick-leave. His malady was, however, mortal, and he died early in 1918. General Regnault had since then held the command provisionally. The new Army commander was General Henrys. He had been the right-hand man of General Lyautey in Morocco and had not been released by the Resident-General until July 1916, but had become a corps commander ten months after his arrival on the Western Front.

Map 1. The arrival of General Henrys was followed by that of General de Lobit, who was appointed to command a new group of divisions [1] on the left flank. The chain of command and the dispositions from the British left on the Selimli Deresi were then as follows :—

Selimli Deresi to Nonte, 1st Group of Divisions (General Gérôme, later General d'Anselme), consisting of Greek Corps of National Defence (Seres, Crete, and Archipelago Divisions), French 122nd Division, and one regiment 156th Division, directly under the command of General Guillaumat ;

Nonte to the Crna, Serbian Armies (Crown Prince ; Chief of the Staff, General Bojović), consisting of First Army (Danube, Drina, and Morava Divisions), and Second Army

---

[1] The French never formed army corps in Macedonia, though commanders of groups of divisions were given the rank of corps commanders. Their " Groupements " had only operations staffs.

TASK OF GENERAL GUILLAUMAT

(Vardar, Šumadija, and Timok Divisions), under the command of General Guillaumat;

1917. Dec.

in the bend of the Crna, Italian 35th Division, French 16th and 17th Colonial Divisions, directly under the command of General Henrys;

the Crna to the neighbourhood of Lake Prespa, 2nd Group of Divisions (General Regnault, later General Patey), consisting of French 30th, 76th, and 11th Colonial Divisions, under the command of General Henrys;

on left flank, 3rd Group of Divisions (General de Lobit), consisting of French 57th and 156th Divisions, with certain other troops, under the command of General Henrys.

On the 30th December General Guillaumat very frankly read out to General Milne his instructions, signed by General Foch and counter-signed by M. Clemenceau. In these it was laid down that the Allied Armies under his command would be based not only upon Salonika but upon the whole of Greece. Their primary mission was to prevent the conquest of Greece by the enemy, for which purpose they were to maintain the present line from the Ægean to the Albanian lakes and if possible keep in touch with the Italian forces based on Valona. If they were forced to give ground, they were to deny to the enemy access to Greece, particularly to the region east of the Pindus, while keeping possession of the Entrenched Camp. When the defensive organization was complete the possibilities of offensive action were to be considered. The rôle of the Greek Army was to be worked out prior to its taking the field. By precautionary measures taken in agreement with General Ferrero, the Italian commander at Valona, or with the Greek Government, the safety of the naval base at Corfu, on which communications across the Adriatic depended, was to be assured.

These instructions [1] are of the highest importance. The first two paragraphs, in particular, were to give rise to much discussion and even controversy, because they clearly implied that, in the event of a retreat, it was more important to cover Old Greece than to retain Salonika, and that if the Allied forces were really hard pressed they would have to shift their base. The point must be further considered

---

[1] See Appendix 5 for a translation. There is also one of the detailed notes by General Foch accompanying the document.

when we come to study the scheme of defence of General Guillaumat.

The detailed notes of General Foch are equally important. So far as they concerned the British, they are merely explanatory, but with admirable precision and thoroughness, of the broad principles laid down in the preceding document. They called, in short, for a complete examination of the present situation from the point of view of defence, from which the Commander-in-Chief was to proceed to a consideration of the methods and requirements of an offensive. They showed that the French Government had in no way abandoned their intention of attacking eventually in the Balkans.

For the rest, the third paragraph marks the intention to carry out a more sweeping change than appears on the face of it. It had been General Sarrail's theory—based on hard experience and certainly not without point—that the relations between the commander of allied forces and the contingent furnished by his own country must be entirely different to those which he establishes with the other contingents. It is only from the former that he can expect instant and unquestioning obedience; it is only from its commander that he can call for complete acceptance of any orders issued without reference to a higher authority such as the commander's Government; he must therefore keep his hand upon his own contingent, control its rearward services, and if necessary split up its fighting troops, who may be called upon to go where or to do what others will not. This was particularly the case in Macedonia, because certain of the Allies were lacking in rearward services and in heavy artillery. Of the latter the Serbians had little, the Russians and Italians none, so that French artillery had to be allotted to them.

The result of General Sarrail's policy was that the Armée Française d'Orient, which contained the great majority of the French divisions, was not really, in the precise French use of the term, an "Armée," but rather a "Détachement d'Armée," because it lacked certain of the services which constitute an Army—because, if one may so put it, it could not live by itself. Those brief phrases, " providing it with an Army organization and the necessary "services," and "decentralization of the Salonika Base," must therefore be taken to imply a far-reaching change of policy. The French contingent was no longer to be the Commander-in-Chief's personal command.

1918. Jan.

The transfer of the Italian 35th Division to the extreme left of the Allied line, where it would be in touch with the Italian Corps based on Valona and could likewise be based on that port, had long been demanded by the Comando Supremo. General Sarrail had agreed to it in principle, but had not yet carried it into effect. In January 1918 the break-up of the Russian division occurred, and these troops had to be withdrawn. General Guillaumat then found it impossible to spare so strong a force as the Italian—18 battalions, and the only ones in Macedonia always up to establishment—for so quiet and sparsely held a front as that west of the lakes. It has been suggested, but we have no right to conclude that the suggestion had any basis other than the gossip which unfortunately often clouds the relationships of Allies in the field, that he was glad of the excuse not to increase Italian influence in the Koritza area. Even had that been the case, he could have defended his point of view by the argument that he did not want to increase Græco-Italian friction.

General Milne reported that he was in agreement with the views of General Guillaumat, though he did not guarantee that this would always be the case. He felt that there was now a strong and steady hand at the helm. Generally speaking, all that the Commander-in-Chief of the Allied Armies had so far been able to decide was that the front line, being the strongest, was to be the main line of defence, and that in case of necessity the flanks would be refused so that, if forced back, he might continue to hold both Salonika and Northern Greece. He informed General Milne in confidence that he had not the means to secure a success and that the military situation in general was not favourable, but that he would begin the preparation of plans for an advance when an opportune moment arrived.

The general visited the front of the XII Corps on the 3rd January, and that of the XVI Corps on the 9th. These visits were made chiefly so that he should see as much of the country and of the enemy's lines as possible, but were also occasions for an exchange of international courtesies and for a display of ceremonial. Thus, at XVI Corps headquarters the 2/Buffs provided a guard of honour for the visit; the 85th Brigade band played during luncheon;

the massed drums of the brigade were also in attendance; and after luncheon the general inspected another battalion of the brigade, the 2/East Surrey. The visitor was impressed. In his first fortnightly report to the Ministry of War, he noted :—

" Armée britannique :—Équipement, tenue, discipline "impeccables. Moral excellent."

At the same time he reported that the relief of the Russians was in progress, and none too soon. " No illu-" sions," he stated, " must be cherished as to the possibility " of making use of these misguided men." The Serbians inspired him with confidence. As for the Greeks, he was determined that there should be an overhaul of the methods of the French Mission engaged in the organization of the Royal Army, which he hoped would enable a well-trained and serviceable contingent to be placed at his disposal within a reasonable time.

One of the first actions of General Guillaumat was to appoint an Allied Commission, under General Génin, to study the question of the Entrenched Camp, its value as a defensive position, and what fresh work upon its fortifications, gun positions, and communications would be necessary in case it should have to be held in the event of a Bulgarian advance. General Milne appointed his Engineer-in-Chief, Major-General Livingstone, to be the British representative on this commission, subsequently adding the G.O.C.R.A., Major-General Onslow. These old defences had necessarily been neglected since the advance to the Greek frontier, and had not been in all respects completed according to the original plan when that advance took place, but they had not suffered seriously. Though sections of the trenches had fallen in, their cleaning and repair would not require more than a few weeks.

The appointment of this commission was typical of the methods of General Guillaumat, methods which, in fact, he employed for other purposes than that of an examination of the Entrenched Camp. On landing he had been struck unfavourably by a certain aloofness in the relations between French and British General Headquarters, due not to personal antagonism but to lack of confidence and still more to the secrecy in which his predecessor had enveloped his ideas and his plans. The new Commander-in-Chief of the Allied Armies desired to abolish this aloofness and at

THE SPIRIT OF CO-OPERATION 53

the same time to get work done quickly by co-operation, by **1918.** the study in common of questions affecting the Armies in **Jan.** common. For this purpose he appointed joint bodies formed from the " opposite numbers " of the Armies to deal with these questions as they came up. He had perhaps been led to take this step by the success which had always attended such methods in the Allied Railway Commission. The British and French Directors of Railways, Colonel F. D. Hammond and Lieut.-Colonel Delaunay, shared an office building, working closer to each other than to their own staffs. Every problem was discussed by word of mouth, and it was seldom that a letter was sent from one to the other except to confirm an agreement.

General Guillaumat was successful in both his aims, particularly as regards the Entrenched Camp. The president of this commission, General Génin, was an old friend, who could always obtain from him an immediate ruling on any doubtful point, and had the experience of the conditions which he lacked. The commission became more than a consultative, in fact an executive body. By the time its labours were ended the defences of the Entrenched Camp had been greatly strengthened by the provision of concrete machine-gun emplacements for both flanking and barrage fire, of strong and up-to-date artillery observation posts, and of roadways leading back from the present front by which the forces holding it could in case of necessity retire.

One of the most important decisions regarding the **Map A.** Entrenched Camp was on a point which had never been satisfactorily settled hitherto. It concerned a proposed advanced position west of the Seres road, on the line Gnoina–Yeniköi–Rahmanli, which General Mahon had rejected, though its inclusion in the defensive line had been urged by General Sarrail and advocated by General de Castelnau on his visit of inspection in December 1915.[1] This dominant *massif* was in uncomfortable proximity to the British trenches between Aivatli and Dautli, and possession of it would have enabled the enemy to shell the shipping in Salonika harbour.[2] Nevertheless, the British view had

---

[1] See Vol. I, p. 91, *fn.* and p. 92.
[2] In 1918 even a 150-mm. gun could have shelled the harbour at more or less extreme range from here. A 210-mm. gun could have done so well within its range; and a gun of this calibre, which did not require a railway mounting, could have been got into position *via* the Seres road.

always been that it was impossible to hold it as part of the system of defence and that if it were held its garrison would inevitably be cut off and captured. General Guillaumat now decided that this view was correct. The danger that the British would at the last moment be ordered to hold the *massif* was thus removed.

In his first two months at Salonika General Guillaumat was able to accomplish little that was tangible. His hopes of doing so depended in part on fresh drafts from home promised for the French contingent, which would enable him to carry out more frequent reliefs; in part upon measures of reorganization, training, improvement of communications and of medical services, which could only be gradually put into force; in part upon the creation of a " Service industriel " for the exploitation of agriculture, forests, and mines, which likewise would take time to bear fruit. Yet he had already made a contribution of great value to the Allied cause. At a moment far from hopeful from the general point of view he had brought to the Armies a measure of hope based upon the confidence which he himself inspired.

Events of January and February 1918.

Map A.
On the 8th January, after the relief of the Russians, the enemy carried out a small attack on their old front, now held by French troops, and made a temporary lodgment in their trenches. In February he showed greatly increased activity on the Serbian front and that of the Armée Française d'Orient further west. In the latter part of the month there were almost daily raids and bombardments in this quarter, strengthening the belief, unfounded as has been shown, that he was contemplating an offensive.

The liveliness did not extend to the British front, which was quieter than ever. One big raid was carried out on the 25th February by the 83rd Brigade (Br.-General R. H. Hare) against Bursuk and neighbouring villages north of the Butkovo and east of the lake of that name.[1] The 449th

---

[1] On the Austrian Staff Map, the basis of Map A, the Struma is shown quite incorrectly as joining the Butkovo about three miles east of the lake, so that it would appear that it was this river which had to be crossed to reach Bursuk. Actually the course shown on the map is an old one, today a sandy nullah, and the Struma—as can be gathered from Map 2— runs down just west of Haznadar. The river south of Bursuk is therefore the Butkovo.

(Northumbrian) Field Company R.E. put a flying bridge across the river and then threw a pontoon bridge of nine canvas boats and five half-pontoons with superstructure, by which the 2/King's Own crossed. One party of the raiders penetrated as far as a village named Porlida, 2¼ miles from the bridge. A number of the enemy were killed, but only seven prisoners, with a machine gun, were brought in. The casualties of the King's Own, with those of an attached company of the 1/York and Lancaster, were three killed and 16 wounded. The bridge was dismantled after the main body had recrossed; then the covering party was withdrawn by the flying bridge, which was then in its turn removed. 1918. Jan.-Feb.

Work on the defences was pushed on actively. The "River Line," the line of the defence on the Struma, was strengthened by the construction of a number of concrete machine-gun emplacements—18 on the front of the 27th Division. The bunds on the right bank were heightened and thickened to provide as far as possible against the flooding which would follow the melting of the snows in the mountains to the north. Map 2.

Over a year ago General Milne had begun the construction of a second line of defence from Lahana through Kürküt to Lake Arjan.[1] Little military labour being available, the Engineer-in-Chief, Major-General Livingstone, had recruited both male and female labour from the neighbouring villages—some of which were actually inhabited by Bulgarians—with good results. The villagers worked hard under the supervision of the Royal Engineers, and not only dug well but became expert wirers in a surprisingly short time. This line had been extended eastward from Lahana to Ahinos, at the head of Lake Tahinos, but this part of it had no advantage of commanding ground, and it was General Milne's intention to construct when possible another defensive position behind the XVI Corps front, following the crest of the Beshik Dagh. West of Kürküt there was now a double second line of defence, the foremost curving first north-westward to cross the high ground at Vaisili and then running in a general west-south-westerly direction towards Lake Arjan at Dragomir, that in rear running by Sermenli and Yanesh towards the same point. These lines Maps A, 3.

---

[1] See Vol. I, p. 253.

were at their greatest distance (between Vaisili and Yanesh) over three miles apart, while at their termini on the shore of Lake Arjan, north of Dragomir, they approached within 600 yards of each other. They were connected by a switch from Irikli to Yanesh, facing towards the Vardar valley. The rear line was the main one, and, as will be seen when we come to consider General Guillaumat's defensive plans, was to be the " First Position of Retirement."

These defensive positions were strong by nature. The works, though not always continuous, had been carefully sited and in general dug deeply enough to permit of their occupation. Between Lahana and Kürküt, where Major-General Livingstone had employed his natives, the line was particularly good, consisting of a series of natural bastions, with flat ground between them which could be swept by machine-gun fire. These bastions had been strongly fortified, and subsequently provided with curtains by the fortification of the low ground intervening. Elsewhere proposed extensions had been marked on the ground, so that work could at once be put in hand in case of need. Machine-gun emplacements and shelters had been constructed and sites for battery positions and command posts chosen. A continuous wire entanglement had been put up. It was not defences but troops to hold them that were lacking in the British zone.

On the Lines of Communication, at the Base, in the docks and the R.E. Base Park, the fullest possible use had long been made of Mediterranean labour. In January 1918 that rationed by the British amounted to over 16,000 Greeks, nearly 2,400 Turks, 2,000 women, and some 2,000 Maltese, in addition to 3,500 muleteers. In the forward zone a proportion of the necessary work was carried out by British " entrenching battalions," first formed in early 1917 from reinforcements and men returning from hospital to the Infantry Base Depots at Summerhill Camp.

The sortie from the Dardanelles of the *Goeben* and *Breslau* on the morning of the 20th January had a certain effect upon Salonika. Both ships struck mines; the *Breslau* sank and the *Goeben*, after doing a considerable amount of destruction, turned back and was beached at Nagara. At the request of the British admiral General Milne despatched ten aeroplanes to Mudros to assist the naval machines in bombing her. The ship was, however, towed off without being further damaged, and the machines were at once returned.

1918. Jan.

In January British G.H.Q. issued two memoranda on training, which can only be shortly summarized. It was laid down that commanders of formations were responsible for the efficiency of units under their command; that commanding officers were responsible for the training of officers and other ranks in their units; and that schools and classes of instruction [1] had only the object of assisting commanders in these duties. The sole exception to these principles was as regards technical forms of training which could not be fully exploited in units, and for which it was necessary to send personnel to schools.

G.H.Q. was responsible for the Army Training School (Infantry) where 50 officers and 100 N.C.O.'s were to attend courses of a month which would aim at imparting discipline, morale, power of command, and a thorough general knowledge of their duties; the Army Artillery School, formed nearly a year earlier, where 40 officers and 80 N.C.O.'s, suitable respectively for promotion to the command of batteries and for commissioned rank, were to attend courses of a month; the Army Signal School, for training in Morse telegraphy, linesmen's work both for linesmen and for unskilled sappers and pioneers, and also to undertake trade tests for sappers; the Army Anti-Gas School; the Army Lewis-Gun School; and the Base Training Camps for Infantry Reinforcements. The last-named had now become of great importance. As a result of the scheme for economy in man-power there was in progress a considerable transfer of men from the R.A.M.C. and A.S.C. to the infantry, to be replaced by men of lower physical category, or in the case of horse-transport units by native drivers and muleteers. By the 17th January the numbers already ordered to be transferred were 1,182, with a further 1,300 a month for some three months. It was therefore necessary to increase the establishment of the Base Training Camp, to form a second on the same lines, and to extend the courses to seven weeks.

The War Office sanctioned the appointment of an extra

---

[1] Schools were formed on a permanent basis with an approved establishment, primarily to train instructors; classes of instruction were formed temporarily by corps, divisions or brigades to train personnel and instructors as required.

G.S.O.2. on the staff of G.H.Q. to keep in touch with schools and classes of instruction. An Assistant Superintendent of Physical and Bayonet Training was also appointed to supervise and co-ordinate this form of training, with ten N.C.O.'s of the Army Gymnastic Staff under his orders.

The problem of malaria had now come to a head. Owing to the abandonment of evacuation by hospital ship in 1917 there had now accumulated some 15,000 chronic cases, "a population which did little but circulate between "hospitals and convalescent depots with an occasional day "or two of light duty."[1] In December 1917 Sir Ronald Ross, one of the world's greatest authorities on the disease, was sent out to report and to make recommendations. He telegraphed on the 30th to the Director-General of Army Medical Services in London that a minimum of 15,000 should be sent home and replaced by drafts. The exchange should be carried out before the 1st May, because after that date the Taranto–Itea route would be highly malarial, both in Greece and Italy. Many thousands more required in his opinion either leave or transfer to some healthier front.

The scheme was put into force as fast as shipping from Itea to Taranto could be provided. By the end of February, over 5,000, by the end of April over 9,000 officers and men suffering from chronic and relapsing malaria, or who had been severely affected mentally, nervously, or internally by the disease, had been sent home.[2] Owing, however, to the German offensive on the Western Front in March, the flow of drafts to replace these losses speedily dried up.

On the 1st January the Army received a small but welcome reinforcement. The Commander-in-Chief had pointed out, as long ago as September 1917, that the 6-inch howitzers could not be relied upon to smash the concrete shelters and battery emplacements with which the enemy was now liberally provided on the Dojran front, and had asked for even a single 9·2-inch battery. The War Office replied that it could not spare one, but now sent an 8-inch, the 424th Siege Battery from Palestine. Though this

---

[1] "Medical Services: Diseases of the War," Vol. I, p. 283.

[2] In Vol. I (p. 288) mention was made of the decrease in the incidence of the disease in 1918, and it was attributed to improved treatment and greater precautions. It should have been pointed out that this removal of chronic cases, who not only increased the sick rate themselves but infected other troops, was also an important factor, possibly the most important.

howitzer was less powerful and less accurate than the 9·2-inch, it was more mobile, and proved very useful. About the same time twelve Newton 6-inch trench mortars were sent. This was an excellent weapon for the Dojran front. It fired a projectile weighing 50 lbs., was reasonably accurate up to 1,000 yards, and by means of improved mountings was finally given an extreme range of nearly 2,000 yards. It was an efficient wire-cutter.

1918.
Jan.

Another reinforcement of the highest importance consisted of fast aeroplanes, S.E.5a's and Bristol monoplanes. The first of these had been sent in November, and they arrived gradually until a flight could be formed in each existing squadron. No new squadron was formed until the 1st April, the birthday of the Royal Air Force. Then No. 150, a fighting squadron, was formed, with a flight from each of Nos. 17 and 47. In early May a third flight, of newly-arrived Sopwith Camels, was added. The effect was extraordinary. No. 150 Squadron virtually drove the Germans out of the air. In the course of its short career it destroyed 34 hostile machines, captured two, and lost only one of its own above the enemy's lines.

Finally, in January the force received two sound-ranging sections, which had never previously been employed in Macedonia.

The question of the Greek railways outside the Zone of the Armies was a delicate one. The British and French Governments believed that they could assist the Greek mobilization and obtain greater efficiency as regards their own requirements by including the Piræus–Plati line and if necessary the Volos line in the system already worked and controlled by them. Lord Granville, the British Minister at Athens, was therefore instructed by the Foreign Office on the 30th January to approach the Greek Government with the request that the Piræus-Plati line should be placed under the control of the Allied Railway Commission at Salonika.[1] To this M. Venizelos objected strongly. In an identic Note to the British and French Ministers he stated that the present unsatisfactory state of the railways was due to three mobilizations, as well as to lack of fuel and of rolling stock handed over to the Allies, which he had urgently requested them to replace. To put the control of

---

[1] See Vol. I, p. 277.

transport in the interior of the country into the hands of the Allies would offend national sentiment and would not in other respects improve the situation. The Government would endeavour to do so if the Allies would comply with reiterated Greek demands for fuel and material.

The matter was not pressed. The Allies controlled the railway from Plati only as far south as Katerini, on the boundary of the Zone of the Armies, the rest of the line through Athens to Piræus remaining under Greek control. There was doubtless considerably lower efficiency in its working than if the Allies had taken it over, but the question involved the sovereign rights of Greece, and it was impossible to make any further representations to a Government with which they were allied. Towards the end of the war the Greek Government did, of its own accord, allow the British and French authorities an increased measure of control over this line.

CHAPTER IV.

THE SHADOW OF THE GERMAN OFFENSIVE IN FRANCE: MARCH AND APRIL 1918.

(Maps A, 1, 2, 3; Sketch 2.)

Greek Mobilization and Serbian Reinforcements.

As its title indicates, this chapter is primarily concerned with the events and the atmosphere of the months of March and April 1918. It seems, however, desirable where possible to course to a finish a quarry once started. Accordingly, questions such as the mobilization and assembly in Macedonia of the Royal Greek Army, the arrival of Serbian reinforcements from Russia and Rumania, and the defensive plans and offensive projects of General Guillaumat, all of which covered a much longer period, will be dealt with here from beginning to end.

1918.
March.
Map A.
Sketch 2.

In early February General Guillaumat had informed General Milne that in consequence of the withdrawal of the Russian Division from the line he was anxious that the British should again take over the front to the Vardar, that is, resume the defence of the frontage of three battalions on which they had been relieved by General Sarrail three months before. If the British and Greek Governments agreed, he would make up for this by placing at the disposal of the British the 1st (Larissa) Division of the Royal Greek Army, which was then completing its training at Naresh, outside Salonika. The relief of the French east of the Vardar would not take place until the Greek division had been handed over. The British War Office made no objection, and General Milne was quite willing to fall in with the plan. At the same time, he pointed out to the War Office that he would now be returning to the dangerous conditions of the previous autumn, as the French would withdraw their artillery with their infantry from the left bank of the Vardar. He was therefore emboldened to ask whether some or all of the heavy artillery which he had sent to Egypt could be returned.

The Macedonian theatre was looking up in the world, and the very request was an indication of that fact. What is more, General Milne got his batteries—the 320th, 322nd, and 445th Siege Batteries from Egypt and later the 395th from Mesopotamia. These were tractor-drawn 6-inch howitzer batteries, but arrived without tractors, which were sent from home. A heavy group headquarters, the LXI, which had previously served in Macedonia and had been sent to Egypt, was returned. A request for another 8-inch howitzer battery was, however, refused. The reinforcements were sent by the instructions of a new Chief of the Imperial General Staff, General Sir Henry Wilson having succeeded General Sir William Robertson in that office on the 18th February. There is little evidence of the personal views of Sir Henry Wilson on the Macedonian campaign. It was fated that during the remaining nine months of the war he was to have little time to devote to it; but it appears that he was on the whole less opposed to it than his predecessor had been.

The Greek 1st Division, which was to be attached to the British XVI Corps, began its move towards the Struma valley on the 12th March. It was not to be placed in front line immediately, but was to complete its training under the supervision of the corps commander, General Briggs. The French were to supply it with ammunition for rifles, automatic rifles, and machine guns, and for its 75-mm. Schneider-Danglis mountain artillery and 58-mm. trench mortars; also with rifle and hand grenades. Fireworks were thus the only supply carried by ammunition columns which it fell to the British services to provide. They had, however, to provide second-line transport, engineer stores, food, and forage. The infantry of the division consisted of three regiments, each of three battalions; the artillery of only four 4-gun mountain batteries. The field artillery in the Greek Army formed part of corps troops, and none had yet arrived.

The relief of the French regiment between the Selimli Deresi and the Vardar, which took place on the night of the 20th March, and the entry into line of the Greek 1st Division on the front of the XVI Corps involved a turn-over all along the front, almost all the troops changing places. The details need not be given, except that we may glance at the move of the 228th Brigade from the Struma valley to the sector west of Lake Butkovo. This is of interest as showing the curious conditions on this part of the front. The 22/Rifle

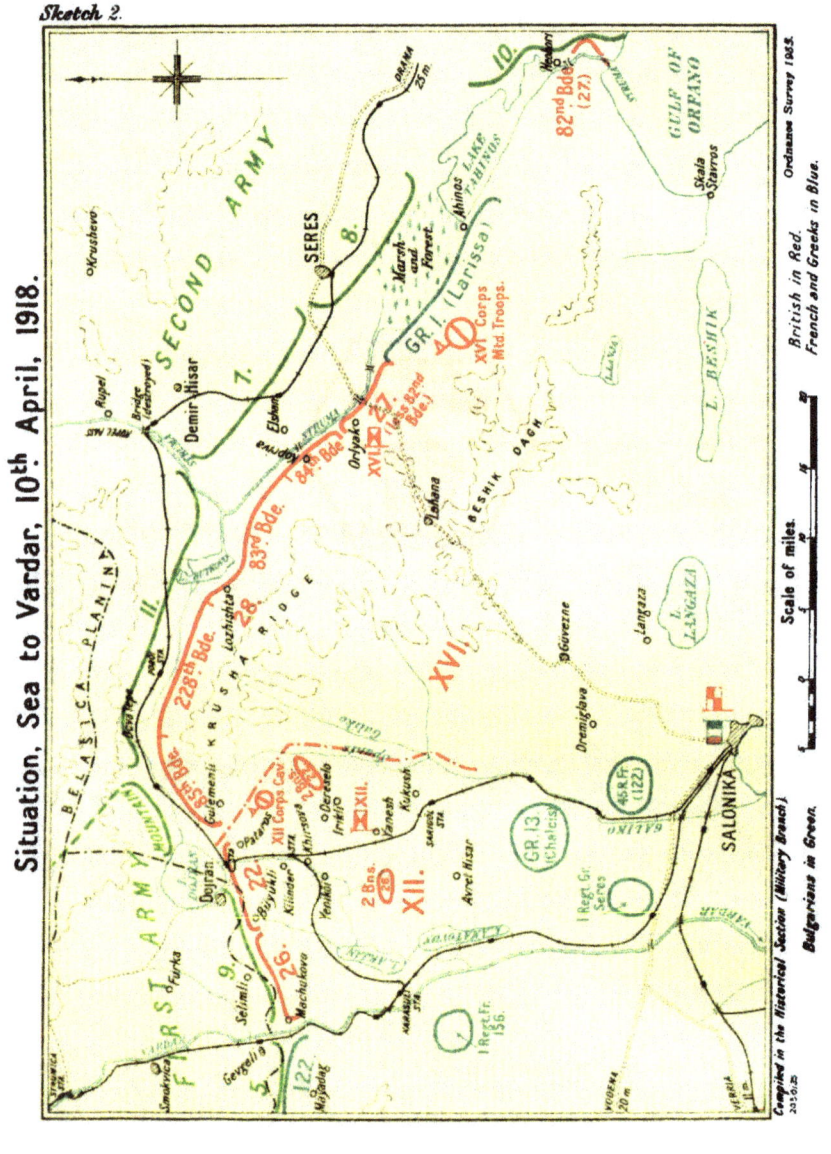

A GREEK DIVISION ON THE STRUMA 63

Brigade, for example, moved in four marches from the hamlet of Turbes, near Orlyak, to Radile, on the Butkovo River. On the last three the battalion was following the British front line, and in many places the route was outside the wire. It moved, of course, by night, a party of scouts going ahead to provide camping grounds screened from observation. On the last night it was actually accompanied by both wheeled and pack transport.

1918. March.

When the reliefs were completed the XVI Corps held the front from the sea to Lake Dojran (having taken over the "Independent Brigade" area from the XII Corps). The dispositions from right to left were :—82nd Brigade at the mouth of the Struma ; Greek 1st Division from Ahinos to Komaryan (the front previously held by the 80th Brigade) ; 27th Division (less 82nd Brigade) from Komaryan to Turbes Island, with the 81st Brigade on the right and the 80th on the left ; 28th Division from Turbes Island to Lake Dojran, having in line from right to left the 84th, 83rd, 228th, and 85th Brigades. The XII Corps held from the south-eastern side of Lake Dojran to the Vardar. Its dispositions were :—22nd Division from the lake to Selimli, with two brigades in line and one in reserve ; 26th Division from Selimli to the Vardar, also with two brigades in line and one in reserve. The Greek division took over its sector on the 26th March, but troops of the 80th Brigade remained in the outpost line and the British brigadier in command until the morning of the 31st.[1]

Except for the lack of heavy artillery, which was, as has been stated, speedily to be remedied, the situation had been slightly eased by the change-over. Nine Greek battalions had replaced three French Colonial battalions east of the Vardar, and though the Greek battalions could not be classed with the French, it appeared that they required only a little further training and some experience of being shot over to make them reliable troops. With regard to the British, however, it was ominous to note how swiftly the sick rate rose when they had to march—and this before there was any sign of hotter weather, there being in fact, a heavy snowstorm on the 27th March.

---

[1] In consequence of this the new dispositions were not completed until the 7th April, because the 80th Brigade could not complete the relief of the 85th Brigade, and the 85th could not complete that of the 79th, until that date.

It was comforting that the 1st (Larissa) Division contained good material, because those that followed might reasonably be expected to contain better. This division had been the first mobilized, at a time when the country was still somewhat unsettled and M. Venizelos had not ventured to call up reservists. Its ranks were therefore filled mainly with young recruits. The commander, General Nider, was a capable soldier of Bavarian extraction. Before dealing with the other divisions it is necessary to say a few words regarding their mobilization.

One of the first acts of M. Venizelos on returning to power in June 1917 had been to ask for a French military mission. This arrived in August and September and consisted of about 150 officers of all ranks and services, divided into three branches: General Staff, Ministry of War, and Training Establishment. At its head was General Braquet, who was appointed Major-General, or Chief of the Staff, of the Army. He was succeeded at the end of the year by General P.-E. Bordeaux, who was given the additional appointment of Inspector-General. General Bordeaux had served under General Eydoux as a member of the French Military Mission between 1911 and 1914, and had inherited the popularity of that well-known soldier.

The mobilization of the Royal Greek Army—so-called to distinguish it from the Corps of National Defence, which was in its inception Venizelist—was carried out with the aid of the Allies in concert, Greece not having the resources to put into the field an army equipped for modern warfare. In December 1917 Great Britain, France, and the United States each voted a loan of £10,000,000 to equip and supply the Greek Army. In February 1918 an inter-allied military commission, composed of British, French, American, and Greek delegates, and assisted by a similar financial commission, was formed in Athens to direct and control the expenditure of this loan. The British military delegate was Major-General R. N. R. Reade, who was elected chairman.

The military commission had to assess the strength of the Army as it mobilized—a difficult matter owing to inaccurate returns—and on this to base its demands for equipment, clothing, transport vehicles, food, and forage, to be purchased in Great Britain, France, locally, or elsewhere. Owing to the difficulties of transport by sea and land, there was constant delay in the despatch of the goods purchased, and also in that of arms, with consequent delay to the mobilization. In fact, up to the date of the Armistice with Bulgaria, the services of the Greek Army were incomplete and a large proportion of its equipment had to be furnished by the Allies on the spot. Roughly speaking, the British were responsible for the supply of food and forage— meat, flour, sugar, rice, tea and coffee, salt, and grain for horses being entirely provided by them for nine divisions, including the Venizelist. It was hoped that less flour and grain would be required after the Greek harvest of 1918 had been garnered, but up to the date of the final offensive the Greek authorities had produced comparatively little from their own resources.

1918. March.

The general situation of the Greek forces was now as follows. There was, first of all, the Corps of National Defence (General Zymbrakakis), consisting of the Seres, Crete, and Archipelago Divisions.[1] This corps had been in line on the right bank of the Vardar for some time and had always acquitted itself creditably. The men were for the most part volunteers; their physique and morale were good; and they constituted probably the best troops Greece would ever put into the field. Of the 1st (Larissa) Division of the Royal Army we have already spoken. Three other divisions had been mobilized: the 13th (Chalcis), which in the course of March moved up to the area of Naresh to take the place of the 1st and complete its training; the 2nd (Athens), which had only just been mobilized; and the 9th (Yannina), which was ear-marked for service in Epirus and would not come under the command of General Guillaumat. The 13th and 2nd were made up of reservists and were likely to be good troops, their physique being excellent. With the 1st Division they formed the I Corps (General Paraskevopoulos), the whole of which was in Macedonia by the end of June.

Now came the question of the three divisions which it had been proposed to mobilize from the Morea, or Peloponnesus, and which were to form the II Corps. This was the quarter of Greece where feeling in favour of King

---

[1] One regiment of the Crete and one of the Archipelago were still, in the early part of 1918, on garrison duty in Athens.

Constantine was strongest. At the British War Office there was for a time some doubt as to whether it were worth while to mobilize these divisions, which it would be hard enough to equip and supply. M. Venizelos, who was extremely lenient towards Constantinist opinion and at the same time bold in confronting it, did not hesitate. He asked the Allies if they wanted the divisions; he would provide them if they did. M. Clemenceau urged that they should be mobilized, and the British Government agreed on the 29th April to furnish their share of food and equipment. They still looked upon the Greeks as potential substitutes for their own troops. In a minute on the supply of the first group of divisions of the Royal Army, dated the 17th April, General Smuts, who had been requested by the War Cabinet—of which he had become a member—to deal with this matter, wrote: " I do not anticipate that these " arrangements will involve much extra strain upon " shipping, because, as the Greek Army becomes mobilized " and draws upon stocks at Salonika, our troops will begin " to be withdrawn from that theatre of war." The irony of the situation was that the Greeks had no intention of replacing Allied troops and that the French had no intention of letting any more British troops go, if they could possibly retain them.

The three divisions from the Morea were therefore mobilized, and without any trouble to speak of. By the end of June the 3rd (Patras) Division had been formed and was moving up to Thessaly, the 4th (Nauplia) was in course of mobilization, and mobilization of the 14th (Kalamata) had begun. In Epirus was the V Corps, consisting of the 8th (Preveza) Division, 3,000 strong, and which it was not intended to bring up to mobilization strength, and the 9th (Yannina) Division. This corps was maintained entirely from Greek resources.

Each division consisted of three regiments of three battalions each (three companies of infantry and a machine-gun company), and two groups each of two 4-gun batteries of mountain artillery. At the disposal of the corps was a regiment of nine 4-gun batteries of field artillery. At that of the Army (Commander-in-Chief, General Danglis) was a cavalry brigade of two regiments with a horse-artillery battery, and two artillery regiments each of nine 4-gun heavy batteries. One of these regiments was armed by Great

THE FRENCH MILITARY MISSION 67

Britain with tractor-drawn 6-inch howitzers,[1] the other by France with 120-mm. guns, also tractor-drawn, each nation carrying out the training of the regiment armed with its own weapons. Until the end of the war the Greek artillery was never fully mobile owing to shortage of horses and tractors.

The aviation services consisted finally of a squadron for each corps, comprising ranging, photographic, and bombing machines, and a protective section. There was a squadron of the same type for the heavy artillery, and one fighting (Army) squadron. The whole of the Greek aeronautical equipment, including the park, photographic section, etc., was French, and all the training was carried out by French officers.

Returns were not accurately rendered, making it difficult to give precise figures. By the end of the war Greece had mobilized some 270,000 officers and men, of whom about 160,000 served in the Salonika war zone, 15,000 in that of Epirus, and the remainder in the interior or in the islands. The fighting strength in the Salonika war zone was finally about 90,000, and the rifle strength, excluding machine-gun companies, 65,000. The most serious weakness was in rearward services, which were never fully organized and the work of which was to the last largely carried out by the British and French.

The services of the French Military Mission cannot be too highly estimated. This was the third Eastern European Army of which France had undertaken the reorganization in the course of the war, in every case with striking success.

It would be unfair to the Serbian Armies to suggest that the work was of quite the same nature in their case as in those of the Rumanians and the Greeks. One may put it that the French had in the Serbian case to assist in the reconstruction of a machine, highly efficient for its own purposes, which had been smashed to pieces. After reconstruction it required no supervision from them. With the Rumanians, they had to reconstruct a less efficient machine, which had likewise been smashed in war, and to supervise

---

[1] The British were unable to provide the Greeks with the modern, long-range 26-cwt. howitzer, and supplied them with the old 30-cwt. howitzer, with an effective range of less than 6,000 yards.

its working when reconstructed. With the Greeks, they had to reconstruct a machine which had been damaged not by warfare but by political strife—and by what can only be described as the kidnapping of a proportion of its personnel and material at Kavalla. Again they had to supervise it after reconstruction, for which purpose they maintained detachments of officers of all arms and services with the higher formations. In all three cases there were grumblings, complaints, and some friction. That was inevitable; the only wonder was that there were not more. An Army which, with the aid of general officers of the type of Generals de Mondésir, Berthelot, Bordeaux, and the last-named's successor, General Gramat,[1] can carry out these tasks with efficiency, and at the same time with tact enough to leave a pleasant memory after war is over and reaction has set in, has good cause for pride. If this impression was weakened by French treatment of Greece after the war, the fault did not lie with the Army.

In general, the Greek soldier appeared to British observers to be brave and dashing but volatile, likely to be better in attack than in defence and to be subject to fits of depression and to political influences if kept too long in reserve or on a very quiet front. Few troops improved more rapidly under active service conditions. The countrymen, especially mountaineers and islanders, were superior to the townsmen, but in general the troops proved themselves second only to the Serbians as marchers. The senior regimental officers, despite the weeding-out of many with Constantinist sympathies, seemed reasonably efficient; the younger easy-going and careless.

The Serbian Armies received in the course of the winter and spring an unexpected and invaluable reinforcement. In the early part of the war the Russians had captured from the Austrian Armies a considerable number of South Slavs—Bosnians, Croats, and Slovenes—many thousands of whom, chiefly Orthodox Bosnians, announced that they were willing to fight against their former overlords. In March 1916 100 Serbian officers under Colonel Kouvaković were sent to Odessa to organize an army corps from these

---

[1] **General Gramat** was the French member of an Anglo-French Mission sent to **Salonika** in May, of which mention is made later in this chapter. In June he succeeded General Bordeaux as head of the French Military Mission in Greece.

troops. Travelling by way of Italy, France, Great Britain, and Petrograd, Colonel Kouvakovič did not reach Odessa until May,[1] but a corps of two divisions was put into the field in time to fight with the highest credit against Mackensen's Army in the Dobruja that autumn. After the Russian *débâcle* in the summer of 1917 it was agreed that the corps should be transported to Macedonia to join its fellow-Slavs.

At the last moment difficulties occurred. The Russians and Rumanians, and their French advisers, protested against the withdrawal of these reliable troops, and there were unfortunate delays, so that after the first two detachments had sailed from Archangel the port was frozen up. These detachments were landed at Cherbourg by British ships and sent to Orange, in the south of France, where they were equipped by the French, and thence transported by the Taranto route to Salonika. At the beginning of January 1918 General Guillaumat reported that 10,000 officers and men had arrived, which would enable the Serbian effectives to be raised to 160 men per company. The Vardar Division was then renamed the Yugoslav Division, and comprised one Serbian brigade of the old division, the other being broken up, and a Yugoslav brigade. All officers down to company commanders were Serbians. The remainder of the corps, numbering some 6,000 men, set off across Siberia in January 1918—after the Bolshevist seizure of power and while negotiations for peace with the Central Powers were in process at Brest-Litovsk—embarked at Port Arthur and Dalny, and reached Salonika in April. About 80 Yugoslavs came all the way from Australia to join.

Morally and materially, the effect was excellent. The Serbians were inspired by the sight of these men of their race who had dared and suffered so much in its cause, had journeyed such vast distances to fight by their sides, and were obviously fine troops. And not only were the six infantry divisions now brought up to a reasonable strength, but the cavalry division was reconstituted, its second brigade, which had hitherto served dismounted, being withdrawn from the line and given horses.

A subsequent visit by Colonel Kouvakovič to Italy was unsuccessful. The Italian authorities declared that the

---

[1] Feyler, Vol. III, p. 30.

majority of their prisoners were Catholic Croats and Slovenes, and that the sympathies of these men were Austrian rather than Serbian. By the time the final offensive was launched in Macedonia not more than a few hundred Yugoslav prisoners from Italy had reached that theatre of war. The rights of the case are difficult to determine ; but French and British officers with knowledge of the circumstances believed that a considerable number of volunteers could have been provided from this source if the Italian Government had cared to back the scheme. Br.-General C. Delmé-Radcliffe, Chief of the British Military Mission with the Comando Supremo, stated on the 7th July that the Serbian Military Attaché in Rome had by that date received 4,000 written applications from men in prison camps who desired to serve. If the men could have been obtained, it was particularly bad luck for the Serbians that they were not, since the 24,000 prisoners whom they themselves had captured and whom they had handed over to the Italians after the retreat to the Adriatic [1] included a considerable proportion of South Slavs.

The Defence Scheme.

Map 3. Hitherto there had been no general scheme of defence for the whole of the Allied Armies of the East, or, at any rate, none had ever been communicated to General Milne ; and he had never been invited to submit an outline of his proposed contribution to any such scheme. That drawn up by General Guillaumat may be said to have been conceived under the shadow of the German offensive on the Western Front in March ; actually he ordered work to be begun upon the scheme eight days before the offensive was launched, but he knew then that it was impending. The fact that the initiative had now definitely passed to the enemy and that he could attack in any European theatre of war made it imperative that the system of defence should be thoroughly organized.

On the 13th March General Guillaumat wrote to General Milne giving an outline of his plans and calling for a detailed study from the British Commander-in-Chief of the conditions on his own front. In this outline no mention was

---

[1] See Vol. I, p. 35.

DISPOSITIONS FOR DEFENCE

made of the intervention of General Guillaumat in the event of an offensive being launched by the enemy, but he indicated in his letter that he intended to make his action felt by the employment of reserves from the less vulnerable parts of the front, to be used not merely as reinforcements but also to carry out counter-offensives.

1918. March.

General Guillaumat began by reminding General Milne of the dual rôle of the Allied Armies laid down in the instructions which he had brought from France: to cover Old Greece and to safeguard Salonika. The front might be considered as comprising three sections: from the Ægean to the Vardar, from the Vardar to the Crna, and on the left the plain of Monastir and the district of the lakes, beyond which the flank was in touch with the Italians in the mountains of Albania. Of these three the centre was the most vital.

For the purposes of defence there were to be three groups. On the east there would be an army of manœuvre holding from the Ægean to the plateau of Gandash west of the Vardar, covering Salonika and providing the garrison of the Entrenched Camp. This would consist of the British Army (and, naturally, though it was not then mentioned, the Greek 1st Division, shortly afterwards attached to this Army) and the 1st Group of Divisions,[1] and would be placed under the command of General Milne. From the plateau of Gandash to the Crna, the centre group would consist of the Serbian Armies under General Bojović. This group would hold its present positions as long as possible so as to cover the Monastir Railway, and if forced out of them would cling to each successive line of retirement, in touch on the right with the eastern group and on the left with the western. On the west there would be a second army of manœuvre under the command of General Henrys, comprising the Armée Française d'Orient of five divisions and the Italian 35th Division. This group had the rôle of covering Old Greece by manœuvring east of the Pindus chain of mountains. Beyond this chain a detachment under its orders would maintain touch with the Italian corps based on Valona and the Greek Yannina Division.

In addition there was to be a general reserve under the orders of the Commander-in-Chief consisting of two French

---

[1] See p. 48.

divisions,[1] one behind the eastern group and one behind the Serbian Armies, and the Greek 2nd and 13th Divisions when ready.

Defence must be active and aggressive. The troops must be disposed in depth so as to permit of the formation of local reserves. Irrespective of these and of the reserves in the hands of the Commander-in-Chief of the Allied Armies, each group should endeavour to have in the event of a general attack by the enemy a reserve of at least one division.

It is unnecessary to describe in detail the three successive lines of retirement laid down for each group, as their significance can be readily gathered from Map 3. It may be pointed out, however, that in the British zone the first line of retirement on the right was to run from the Gulf of Orfano along the heights of the Beshik Dagh to Lahana, not from Ahinos to Lahana. It was, therefore, the line of which General Milne had already contemplated the fortification, in preference to the Ahinos–Lahana line. From Kürküt to Lake Arjan the first line of retirement was to be the rearward of the two lines of defence already prepared in this area, that running through Yanesh.[2]

General Guillaumat laid it down, however, that owing to the vast extent of the theatre of operations the positions of retirement were not to be regarded as parallel lines intended to be occupied successively by the Allied Armies as a whole. On the contrary, if retirement were necessary, it was to be in echelon, the formations less strongly attacked holding on as long as possible to their positions, and not carrying the defence from one position to another without effort to defend intervening ground. This method gave particular importance to the retrenchments or switches running either at right angles or obliquely to the lines of defence. The vital need of being able to manœuvre in a difficult country such as Macedonia made lateral and longitudinal communications equally important. All staffs should have a complete knowledge of the possibilities of

---

[1] It was some time before two divisions were available. The commander of the Italian 35th Division had always refused to broaden his front again after it had been closed up for the offensive of the previous May; nor would the Serbians do so until the Yugoslav reinforcements had entered the line. They then took over some ground in the bend of the Crna.

[2] See p. 55.

movement for the troops of all arms in the zone of each group.

1918.
March.

General Milne thereupon drew up a series of detailed appreciations intended to form part of a fuller defence scheme. At the same time, so that performance should march hand in hand with promise, he accelerated, so far as that was possible, work upon the defences and above all upon the communications. The series of roads leading back to the first line of retirement and thence to the Entrenched Camp (which, practically speaking, was both the second and third position where his front was concerned), already begun under the supervision of his Engineer-in-Chief, Major-General Livingstone, formed the key to the whole system of defence. These roads were suited only to limbered wagons, and would in some cases have speedily been damaged in bad weather, but the enemy was not likely to attack at such a time. Their conversion from the native donkey-tracks even to this standard was extremely valuable. The Seres road remained the only lorry-road on the XVI Corps front, but the XII Corps was better served in this respect, as also in that of lateral communication.

General Guillaumat's outline was the first serious effort made to confront the problem of defence. It could, however, be criticized from two points of view, though it was easier to criticize it than to formulate a better. In the first place, as with every offensive or defensive plan from the arrival of the Serbian Armies to the final victory that was to be so largely due to them, it made very large demands upon Serbian fighting-power. It was upon the Serbians that all hinged. If they broke, the " armies of manœuvre " on the flanks would be in a sorry position. And, west of the Vardar, the final Serbian line of retirement was to be a salient jutting out far in advance of those of the groups on the flanks. Excellent as Serbian fighting qualities had been proved to be in every emergency, there appeared to be a certain risk in depending so completely upon them.

The second criticism, however, was to be much more strongly urged, not by British G.H.Q. at Salonika but by the British Section of the Supreme War Council at Versailles. It was that General Guillaumat was not carrying out the instructions given to him by M. Clemenceau and General Foch. These instructions implied that the defence of Old Greece was more important than that of Salonika and that in the last resort Salonika would have to be abandoned. If that were so, it was necessary to make plans for its evacuation and for the rebasing of the whole force, including the eastern group, upon the ports of Old Greece. General Guillaumat's draft scheme did not contemplate the abandonment of Salonika; in fact, it laid down that the Entrenched Camp was part of the final defensive line and made no mention of any further possibilities.

Immediately after General Guillaumat had been handed his instructions, the British, French, and Italian Military Representatives on the Supreme War Council (at that time Generals Sir Henry Wilson, Weygand, and Cadorna) had addressed a Joint Note to the Council, on the 23rd December 1917. In this they signified their agreement with the sense of the instructions given to General Guillaumat a week earlier, but set themselves to dot the i's and cross the t's on this question, wherein the instructions were, it must be admitted, somewhat ambiguous. The Military Representatives stated that the new Commander-in-Chief's plans "must include, in particular, his arrangements for rebasing "himself on Greece and not only on Salonika, and for the "evacuation of Salonika, should such evacuation be neces-"sary in order to make sure of denying Greece to the "enemy." The Council did not accept this Note; nor was it actually accepted until over five months later, at the session of the 3rd June 1918, by which time the situation had changed considerably.

The British argument was that a retirement to the final line would probably involve the shutting-up of the four British divisions in the Entrenched Camp—which would then have merited in a very ugly sense its nickname of "The Birdcage." Major-General C. J. Sackville-West, British Military Representative from the end of March onwards, strove persistently to enforce the British view— at least that prevailing at Versailles—on this matter, but without success. A full defence scheme was urgently demanded from General Guillaumat, but though he made certain elaborations of his original draft, he kept away 1918. from this question. In May a British and a French general May. officer were despatched to Salonika at the instigation of the Supreme War Council to confer with General Guillaumat as to the possibility of sending reinforcements from Macedonia to France. The British representative, Lieut.-

PROBLEM OF THE ENTRENCHED CAMP

General Sir C. L. Woollcombe, was instructed to approach General Guillaumat on this matter of the possible abandonment of Salonika. At a conference on the 29th, at which General Milne was present, General Guillaumat definitely refused to consider the evacuation of the city or to draw up any plans for it. He stated that if either the Serbians or the Greeks learnt that the question was even being considered, the effect upon them would be very serious indeed. In the second place, he believed that the right group could hold the Entrenched Camp. In the third, the Armies could not be supplied unless it were held. Bases were being formed in Greece at Piræus and Volos, with an advanced base at Larissa, but it would be months before the present front could be supplied from Greece, and in any case these bases would suffice only for the centre and western groups. Lieut.-General Woollcombe obtained from Major-General G. N. Cory, chief General Staff Officer of the British Salonika Army, some notes in which it was calculated that the British would require 95 days to evacuate the base personnel and all stores and 45 days to evacuate the fighting troops and mobile base depots, supposing that sufficient tonnage were available. It was, however, almost certain that the tonnage would be short of requirements.

1918. May.

The matter was never definitely settled, though on the 12th June the C.I.G.S. brought it up at a meeting of the War Cabinet. He went so far as to state that if, as he had reason to fear, there were no proper plans for retirement, "it was "quite possible that there might be a bad disaster to our "troops in that theatre of war." At Versailles the controversy was in progress until it was superseded by that on the possibility of an Allied offensive. One can see in the former some connection with the eternal dispute between France and Britain as to the soundness of the Macedonian campaign ; for it is more than probable that General Guillaumat at Salonika and the French representatives at Versailles parried the British demands because they believed that these would actually lead to the withdrawal of the British contingent. Apart from that, it has been recounted in some detail because it is an interesting problem, though one which, fortunately for the Allies, was sponged off the slate by the subsequent course of the war. It also indicates one of the disadvantages of a council or junta, with no link with the armies in the field, being made responsible for

June.

military policy. Until General Woollcombe came out, General Milne knew nothing of the controversy or of the suggestion that arrangements should be made for the evacuation of Salonika. He had, in fact, been at a loss to understand certain telegrams received from the War Office regarding the construction of bases in Greece.

Nor was General Milne consulted on the subject. He had been glad to have for the first time a reasoned and in his view reasonable defensive policy, and was content to accept the scheme of General Guillaumat, especially when two further Greek divisions were handed over to him. It is true that the prospect of defending the Entrenched Camp with a force which would undoubtedly be battered and depleted before it reached those lines was not such as to arouse enthusiasm, especially in view of the increased range of guns, by the use of superior propellants and stream-lined projectiles, since the camp was constructed. He was, none the less, in full agreement with General Guillaumat that evacuation under pressure was impossible and that no preliminary preparations would make it possible.

Projects of General Guillaumat.

1918.
April.
Map 1.

On the 23rd March, two days after the launch of the German offensive on the Western Front, the War Cabinet decided that none of the four British divisions in Macedonia should be brought to France, because they were saturated with malaria. However, the enormous losses suffered in the ensuing week forced the General Staff to search for troops in every possible direction, and in April it again turned its eyes to Macedonia. For the moment it did not desire to do more than reduce the infantry of the divisions from 12 to 9 infantry battalions, as had been done two months before in France. Eventually, as Sir Henry Wilson indicated in a letter to General Foch on the 12th, it hoped, when more Greek troops were available, still further to reduce the British contingent. The C.I.G.S. sent a similar message to General Milne, who communicated it to General Guillaumat. The French Commander-in-Chief strongly objected to letting any troops go, and it was not until after General Woollcombe's visit that he agreed to the withdrawal of 12 British battalions and to sending home drafts

A MESSAGE FROM GENERAL FOCH

of French troops to the number of 10,000, ostensibly on leave, but actually not to return.

1918.
April.

This question came up when the possibilities of offensive action in Macedonia were once more being considered by the French. On the 1st March General Guillaumat had forwarded to General Foch a report on the subject. For the moment, he stated, there could be no question of a major operation such as the reconquest of Serbian territory or the destruction of the Bulgarian Army. Nor could any offensive in Macedonia lead to a general advance on all fronts unless a definite success on the Western Front or in Italy altered the general situation. All that could be done at the moment was to improve some part of the front, and to harass the enemy so as to immobilize his forces and perhaps even cause him to summon reinforcements. General Guillaumat then considered the possible zones of future action : Monastir and the Crna area with Prilep as objective ; the Dojran-Vardar front with Rabrovo as objective ; and the Struma valley with Seres and Demir Hisar as objective. He concluded in favour of a double operation, on the Vardar and Struma fronts, the former being the main attack. It is of interest to note, in view of what was to follow, that he expressly ruled out of consideration " the mountainous " *massif* between Crna and Vardar, little favourable to an " offensive."

On the 4th April he received a message from France suggesting that Germany might call upon Bulgarian forces to support her offensive on the Western Front. Plans should therefore be made to hold down all the enemy's forces on the Balkan front, and the Allied Armies should be ready to pass to the offensive if circumstances demanded. While preparations were being made, the troops on the whole front should increase their activity in order to harass the enemy, confine his liberty of action, verify his order of battle, and discover his movements. These results should be sought by carefully prepared local attacks by small bodies of infantry, but with the support of the largest possible concentration of artillery. The message, despatched by the Minister of War, but signed by General Foch, who was now Commander-in-Chief of the Allied Armies in France, ended with a demand for reports, especially as to when and under what conditions the Allied Armies of the East would be capable of passing to the offensive. General Guillaumat thereupon asked General Milne for his views, where the British Army was concerned, of the possibilities of an offensive and how long it would take to prepare, and at the same time for a programme for the local actions called for by General Foch.

On the 11th April General Milne sent a full and detailed reply. He had to consider three localities : the mouth of the Struma, the valley between Seres and Demir Hisar, and the Dojran–Vardar front. After balancing the advantages and disadvantages of all three, he concluded in favour of the mouth of the Struma. Here, though communications were not very good, the co-operation of the Navy would be available, the Bulgarian fortifications were less strong than elsewhere, and an attack would strike the enemy's flank in a region where the British could reinforce quicker than he could. The French Commander-in-Chief, however, preferred the Dojran–Vardar front and requested that preparations should be made to carry out if necessary an attack there in from six to eight weeks' time.

There was in London the alarm that always broke out at such moments. The British C.I.G.S., informed by General Milne of the correspondence, wired to General Foch on the 12th April that in his view no useful purpose would be served by an offensive in Macedonia. German troops were being withdrawn thence, and without German support the Bulgarians would not undertake an offensive ; nor would they send troops to the Western Front. The British and French should hasten the arrival of Greek troops, so as to withdraw their own from Macedonia. The Germans were concentrating all their resources in the west, and the Allies could defeat them only by the adoption of a similar policy. General Foch replied through Br.-General C. J. C. Grant, the British liaison officer with him, that operations contemplated in Macedonia were only minor ones for the purpose of retaining the hostile forces there, and that he agreed with General Wilson on the subject of the employment of the Greek troops. As always where Macedonia was concerned, the correspondence tended to revolve round phrases, leaving either side unconvinced by the other and adhering to its own previous ideas.

As to the date suggested by General Guillaumat, however, a definite answer could be given. General Milne wrote on the 17th April that to carry out an offensive action

PROJECTS OF GENERAL GUILLAUMAT

within six weeks was out of the question and that he doubted if it could be done within two months. British troops on the Struma front would have to be relieved, in order to be employed on the Dojran–Vardar front. He understood that the second of the Greek divisions would not be ready for a month and that the third might be still later. **1918. April.**

As it befell, within less than two months of this date General Guillaumat had been recalled; he was, in fact, back in Paris by the 12th June. By that date he had not drawn up a detailed plan of attack, and the document which he addressed to the Ministry of War the day after his arrival was entitled simply " Note on an eventual offensive of the " Allied Armies of the East in 1918." The situation had changed since the 1st March. The departure of German units from Macedonia, the signs of increasing demoralization in the Bulgarian ranks, and the courage and ardour displayed by the Greeks in the brilliant local success against the Skra di Legen all seemed to justify the abandonment of his former caution and the consideration of an action which would be something more than an attempt to improve his position. His project now took the form of a Franco-Greek and British offensive astride the Vardar, an attack by the Greeks on the Struma, and one on the Serbian front. These efforts would possibly be made successively, so that each sector of attack should dispose in turn of the greatest possible resources in artillery, in aircraft, and in transport.

This project was never officially forwarded to General Milne. It formed the basis of the directive subsequently addressed by the Minister of War to General Guillaumat's successor. As we shall see, however, it differed entirely in spirit and in scope from that drawn up and put into force by General Franchet d'Espérey.

OPERATIONS OF MARCH AND APRIL.

During March the British front was quieter than ever, and a successful raid by the 2/Gloucestershire of the 82nd Brigade at the mouth of the Struma was almost the only activity on the ground. In the air, however, British aggression continued, while that of the enemy increased. On the 12th British aeroplanes fired on a train approaching Porna. The driver was seen to jump out; the train then ran off the line, and was bombed. Next day a German **March. Maps A, 2.**

aeroplane was shot down and fell into Lake Tahinos. On the 13th a British machine was brought down into Lake Dojran, the pilot being drowned. On the 20th another German machine was forced down within the British lines and captured intact with its pilot and observer. On the same day a British observation balloon was shot down in flames. On the 22nd there was a successful raid on Drama aerodrome, 57 bombs being dropped and four hangars hit. Many other bombing raids were carried out during the latter part of March and the early part of April.

1918. April. In his letter of the 11th April to General Guillaumat General Milne had, in addition to outlining his suggestions for British action in the event of an offensive, given his plans for the local activity for which General Foch had called. On the XII Corps front this was to take the form of a heavy bombardment followed by raids. On that of the XVI Corps there was room for more extended action, to which, despite all the previous raids in the Struma valley, some originality could still be imparted.

In all the long period during which it had held the line of the Struma the XVI Corps had had very few failures in its minor operations, whether they had been fairly considerable attacks, like the capture of the Karajaköis, Yeniköi, and Bairakli Jum'a, or quite small cutting-out raids. Again and again the Bulgar had been bluffed, outmanœuvred, and outfought in the valley. In some of the villages amusing evidence had been found of the annoyance of the Bulgarian command at being repeatedly tricked. One particular battalion commander's written reprimands and warnings were captured. Twice he had pointed out the dangers of slackness; twice his instructions had been disregarded. Then these instructions were captured in the headquarters of the same company, which had thus thrice been caught napping. The Bulgarians were now about to have a favourable turn of fortune's wheel. Perhaps over-confidence had made some of the British troops forget that they were faced by a crafty enemy, ready to run and fight another day if he did not like the situation but quick to see an opening and determined in exploiting it.

On the 11th General Briggs issued orders that operations were to be begun on the night of the 14th with the object of capturing prisoners both during the advance and subsequently by means of ambushes; and then, when the new position was disclosed, inducing the enemy to believe that the presence of artillery on the left bank of the Struma indicated preparations for a general advance. It was also desired that he should man his forward trenches in front of the Greek 1st Division and so present targets to artillery and aircraft. The Greeks on the right were to occupy the line Beglik, Kakaraska, Salmah, Kispeki, Ada, and Osman ; the 27th Division in the centre Homondos, Kalendra, Topalova, and possibly Prosenik ; the 28th Division on the left Kumli and Ormanli, with possibility of a deeper advance later on. One half of the divisional artillery and as many machine guns as divisional commanders desired might be taken across the river. Six sections of the Corps Heavy Artillery would also cross.

1918.
14 April.

The Greek 1st Division occupied the whole of its objective without meeting resistance except at Salmah. Here, owing to two British guides being wounded by the accidental discharge of a hand-grenade, the company of Evzones [1] sent to occupy the village did not reach it until daylight. The enemy promptly bombarded the place and then launched an infantry attack which drove the Greeks out. A counter-attack was, however, quickly organized, and the Bulgarians were thrown back over the Meander. Reconnaissances by officers' patrols that night led to some sharp fights, and the enemy shelled the villages intermittently, but he made no attack on a large scale. On the night of the 18th, when the British divisions were withdrawn, the Greeks were left out for two days more to gain further experience.

The instructions issued by Major-General Forestier-Walker, commanding the 27th Division, were based in detail upon those of General Briggs. They laid down that the 81st Brigade was to occupy a line from the Greek left at Osman to the Seres road beyond the Belitsa with two battalions, and the 80th from thence to Prosenik with a similar force. Operations were to be divided into two phases, the first of secrecy, concealment, and ambushes ; the second, after the British dispositions had been discovered, of defence and protection from shell fire. As regards the first phase it was laid down that " concealment " being all important, an enemy attack in force being

---

[1] Evzones are Greek Highlanders, who wear the traditional white kilt.

"practically negligible during this period, brigade sector
"commanders are given discretion as to numbers of
"ambushed localities, and as to what proportion of the two
"battalions, to be employed in each sector, will be placed
"in ambush in the front line and concealed in immediate
"support, respectively. . . . In order to effect conceal-
"ment, the troops, whether in ambush or in immediate
"support, will not put up wire entanglement (though a trip
"wire or two, well concealed, is permitted)." When the
second phase began, defence would take precedence of
concealment, but the old works would be employed as far
as possible.

On the right the 81st Brigade's advance and occupation
of the forward line were uneventful. Learning, however,
on the following day of what had happened at Prosenik,
Br.-General Widdrington got permission to begin the second
phase at night, which meant that the works occupied were
dug to full depth, wire was put out in front of them, and
machine guns and Stokes mortars were brought up.

On the front of the 80th Brigade (Br.-General W. N.
Cooke-Collis) the 4/K.R.R.C. pushed out two companies to
the railway. The 4/Rifle Brigade could not, as had first
been intended, also take up a position on the embankment,
as reconnaissance had disclosed that it had crumbled away
and afforded no concealment on this part of the front.
The battalion therefore occupied the outskirts of Prosenik,
likewise with two companies. In each case the leading
companies were disposed as ambushes, either in newly-dug
works or in the old British works of the previous winter.
Those of the 4/Rifle Brigade were some distance apart,
separated by the village, the gap between them being
purposely left in case the enemy sent a party to the village
to collect wood, as he often did. The support companies
of the two battalions were in Kalendra Woods and at
Topalova respectively.

1918. At 5.15 a.m. on the 15th a Bulgar patrol 30 strong
15 April. approached the right of the K.R.R.C. It was fired on, four
of the enemy being killed and five captured. At Prosenik
the presence of the Rifle Brigade companies was apparently
at once detected, for desultory fire was opened upon them
soon after six o'clock. An hour later the enemy sent up
two red lights from the north end of Prosenik and a heavy
bombardment was directed on the village and the railway

OPERATIONS ON THE STRUMA 83

in its neighbourhood. The shelling lasted until 10.15, and 458 rounds were counted. All telephone lines were cut.

1918. 15 April.

The bombardment began again after noon. Under its cover enemy riflemen and bombers closed upon " C," the left company, and by 2.30 p.m. had opened a fire so intense that the men could not put their heads above the parapet. Then came a fierce rush against the left platoon, which attempted to fall back on the next, but was caught in the open, most of the men being shot down. A runner was sent off from battalion headquarters with an order to the company to retire if heavily attacked, but he cannot have reached it. Meanwhile on the right " B " Company was also attacked but held its ground without difficulty, and the company commander did not know that " C " was in any worse case. So far as can be ascertained, it was about 4.30 p.m. when the enemy rushed " C " from the front and right flank and overwhelmed it, only about 16 men escaping. At 5.45 the adjutant, Lieutenant R. Palk, who had come forward, saw the position in the hands of the enemy, and at once ordered " B " Company to withdraw to Topalova. Later in the evening the 4/K.R.R.C. was withdrawn to the Belitsa between Kalendra North and South Woods.

The operations of the 28th Division were of a somewhat different pattern. In this case it was intended that the enemy should learn that there had been an advance; a proportion of the fighting patrols pushed forward to Kyupri and Bairakli were to be withdrawn in daylight to induce him to believe that the whole had retired. The remainder were to lie in ambush for the reconnaissances which he might then be expected to make. Only one battalion each, with detachments of other arms, was here to be employed on the fronts of the two brigades engaged. Another important difference was that, whereas in the case of the 27th Division the artillery did not cross the Struma until the night of the 15th, and therefore not till after the mishap at Prosenik had taken place, in that of the 28th ten 18-pdrs. and two 4·5-inch howitzers were established on the left bank before the operations began.

On the front of the 84th Brigade (Br.-General F. C. Nisbet) the 2/Cheshire moved across Kopriva bridge to Kumli, which it reached at 12.30 a.m. on the 15th. Its orders were to send out fighting patrols to occupy Kyupri and Bairakli before dawn. The Kyupri patrol lost touch with its Lewis guns, waited some time for them, and at 2 a.m. went forward without them. When the guns reached the permanent outpost position the officer in command there would not let them go on, as day was breaking. Kyupri was found unoccupied.

At 8.20 a.m. about 500 of the enemy were seen advancing from the north and on either flank. The outposts were quickly driven in, and the patrol thereupon began a fighting retirement on Kumli. Unfortunately the ground south-west of Kyupri afforded no cover, and though the patrol inflicted heavy loss on the enemy it suffered very heavy loss itself, the casualties being about 60 out of a strength of twice that number.

The Bairakli patrol was first bombarded, then repeatedly attacked. Fighting was at close quarters and was extraordinarily fierce. One platoon beat off five assaults before it was rushed and surrounded at 11.45. Just at this moment an order to withdraw to Kumli was received. The retirement was covered by the support platoon, but the enemy followed up in strength and with great determination, and killed or captured the whole rear guard.

On the front of the 83rd Brigade (Br.-General R. H. Hare) the 1/York and Lancaster with one company of the 1/K.O.Y.L.I. was to cut off any Bulgarians in Dolap Wood, south of Bairakli Jum'a. No enemy was encountered here, but the Gypsy Village on the outskirts of Bairakli Jum'a was found strongly held and could not be entered. Ormanli, where the main line was established and to which the patrols withdrew, was heavily shelled during the day. At one moment the enemy drove in the outposts covering it, but they were quickly re-established.

Thereafter there was quiet on the whole front, except for a certain liveliness on that of the Greeks. British patrols, sent out at night, found no enemy upon the scenes of the recent fighting except at Kyupri, which was occupied by about a company. On the 18th General Briggs ordered the Greek 1st Division to remain in occupation of its advanced line until the night of the 20th; the 27th Division to withdraw at night across the Struma, leaving a detachment to cover the Greek left flank; the 28th Division likewise to withdraw, but to hold on to Kumli for two nights more; and the Corps Artillery on the left bank to be brought in, except for the sections in support of the Greeks.

CAUSES OF A FAILURE 85

The casualties in this unhappy enterprise, from the night of the 14th to that of the 19th, were 349, including 199 missing.[1] The enemy also appeared to have suffered fairly heavily, especially at Bairakli.

1918. April.

General Briggs looked with so much misgiving upon the mishaps which had befallen the 4/Rifle Brigade of the 27th Division and the 2/Cheshire of the 28th that he ordered Courts of Enquiry to examine these affairs and report upon them. In both cases the Court found that insistence in the instructions upon camouflage and concealment had so influenced the minds of company commanders that they had almost entirely neglected protection. Both battalions had dug their trenches deeply, so that the sentries could hardly see out of them, and long grass in any case limited their field of vision to a few yards. At Prosenik there was an observation post at the church, but it seems to have been captured at an early stage. In fact, the two companies here were separated by a large village which gave the enemy a covered approach, and no posts were put out to watch this approach. " C " Company's ambush became nothing more than a trap for the defenders, since they could neither observe nor fight from it.

In the case of the Cheshire it was perhaps errors other than these which were chiefly responsible for the minor disaster. Lack of reconnaissance led to the patrols arriving late (and at Kyupri, as has been shown, without Lewis guns) and being seen by the enemy before they had reached their objectives. Then, in the retirement from Bairakli no

---

[1]

				KILLED	
				British	Greek
Officers	..	..	..	3	—
Other Ranks	..	..	..	19	5
				WOUNDED	
Officers	..	..	..	3	2
Other Ranks	..	..	..	92	26
				MISSING	
Officers	..	..	..	5	—
Other Ranks	..	..	..	194	—

Almost half the Greek casualties were caused by the accidental explosion of grenades, in the use of which they were not yet expert, and this, as has been stated, also accounted for two of the British casualties, guides from the Corps Mounted Troops. The Bulgarians claim the capture of 150 British prisoners and three machine guns—actually Lewis guns (Lon, p. 267).

attempt was made to support the rear guard, which was sacrificed and left to its fate.

There were secondary points in the findings of the Court respecting faulty dispositions, but they need not be gone into here. The main causes of the misadventures of the two battalions were undoubtedly those set out above. It was a lesson learnt at considerable cost.

On the XII Corps front an operation was carried out in the early hours of the 16th April, bold and interesting enough to deserve mention, even though it did not result in contact with the enemy. A party of four officers and 23 other ranks of the 65th Brigade embarked at Dojran Station in four small boats, in each of which were two bluejackets from the fleet, and rowed to Dojran. The object of the expedition was to capture prisoners in the town, but though the party remained some time in it and explored the streets and buildings near the shore, no Bulgarians were seen.

The main operation of the XII Corps consisted of a four days' artillery programme beginning on the 18th April, wire-cutting and bombardment by day and harassing fire by night, particularly on the front of the 22nd Division. The first day's fire was to be directed against O.4, O.5—the works on the Petit Couronné—and O.6, to give the enemy a first impression that this was the threatened portion of the front. On the third day there was to be a small daylight raid on the Petit Couronné, and during the last night two big raids on O.2 and O.3, between that hill and the lake. The bombardment group consisted of the 8-inch howitzer battery, two and a half 6-inch howitzer batteries, and three 4·5-inch howitzer batteries; the barrage group of thirty-four 18-pdrs., which carried out wire-cutting by day. There was also a medium trench mortar brigade, including the newly-arrived Newton mortars. Thirty-four machine guns were employed in harassing fire by night and barrage fire.[1]

---

[1] The Bulgarians state that owing to the intensity and accuracy of the machine-gun fire at night it was impossible to repair the breaches in the defences made by the artillery and mortars, or even to place temporary obstacles in them (Nédeff, p. 167). The grouping of machine guns and indirect fire in accordance with the principles taught at Grantham had only been recently introduced. The war diary of the Machine-Gun Officer of the XII Corps notes on the 6th December 1917 :—" Previously " commanders of formations had opposed this method, preferring to have " guns well forward to fire obliquely along the trenches. These com- " manders are not easily convinced that machine guns can hit their targets " without firing direct and without being at short range. However, they " are now beginning to appreciate the present methods of employment of " the guns."

RAIDS ON THE DOJRAN FRONT

At 8.30 a.m. on the morning of the 20th a brilliant little daylight raid was carried out by a party of the 9/King's Own on the Petit Couronné. Scaling the hill unobserved, the raiders entered the enemy's works, bombed dugouts, and returned with two prisoners, having suffered no casualties.

1918. April.

The two big raids were carried out by the 12/Lancashire Fusiliers of the 65th Brigade (Br.-General G. E. Bayley),[1] two companies against O.2 and one against O.3, simultaneously in the early hours of the 22nd. At O.2 there was a fierce and bitter struggle, the enemy in many cases standing up on the parapet to fire and hurl bombs at the attackers. The leading platoons of both companies entered the trenches but were unable to remain in them. At O.3, on the other hand, the attack was successful, a number of the enemy being killed, though no prisoners were taken.

The losses in the actual raid were 61, but if the whole period of the bombardment be taken into account, they were more than twice as great, the retaliatory fire of the Bulgarian artillery being heavy and effective.[2] A deserter who surrendered in May stated that the enemy had 100 casualties between the lake and the Petit Couronné from the raids and bombardments.[3]

On the Allied front west of the Vardar there was no activity during this period beyond increased artillery fire and some small raids by the French, Serbians, and Italians. The local operations planned by General Guillaumat in response to the demand of General Foch were more considerable in scope than those on the British front, required longer preparation, and were therefore reserved for the month of May.

---

[1] A few days later Br.-General Bayley returned to England for a tour of home duty, Lieut.-Colonel B. L. Majendie succeeding him.

[2]

	KILLED	WOUNDED	MISSING
Officers	1	6	2
Other Ranks	12	104	11

a total of 136.

[3] Nédeff (p. 169) gives the casualties as 52, but he appears to be referring only to the two big raids and not to the whole period of the bombardment, since he mentions no missing, whereas we know that two prisoners were captured on the 20th.

CHAPTER V.

GENERAL GUILLAUMAT'S REHEARSAL.

(Maps A, 1, 3; Sketches 3, 4.)

THE GREEK AND FRENCH OPERATIONS IN MAY AND JUNE.

1918.
May.
Map A.
DURING the month of May the artillery bombardment on the front of the 22nd Division west of Lake Dojran was continued at intervals, and gaps already cut in the enemy's wire were kept open. On the night of the 6th, after bombardment and harassing fire carried out by a powerful concentration of artillery at the disposal of the 22nd Division,[1] but without immediate artillery preparation, a raid was carried out against O.2 by a company of the 11/R. Welch Fusiliers. Every artifice which had been evolved in this type of warfare—which was, of course, only a development of the age-old siege warfare—was employed. In particular, an elaborate system of "blocks," or curtains of fire upon possible approaches, the innermost composed of 18-pdr., trench-mortar, and machine-gun barrages, was placed round O.2 while the raid took place. Body-shields were worn by the attackers; and it is reported that they were useful, very few men being killed and most of the wounded being hit in the legs. The main objective, a large concrete "pill-box," was reached and blown up with gun-cotton, and a number of the enemy were killed with the bayonet in the trenches or with bombs in dug-outs. Once more, however, as so often on this front, the casualties were extremely heavy, amounting to 81, over 50 per cent. of the raiding party.[2]

Otherwise there was no activity on the British front until the last few days of the month, except in the air. Here the R.A.F. celebrated its reinforcement by fast scouts and

---

[1] Bombardment Group: two 8-inch howitzers, six 6-inch howitzers, ten 4·5-inch howitzers; Barrage Group: 28 18-pdrs., five Newton trench mortars, two 2-inch trench mortars; Wire-cutting Group: formed from part of Bombardment Group by day. There were also 22 guns of the 65th and 67th Machine-Gun Companies. Counter-battery work was carried out by XII Corps Heavy Artillery.

[2]

	KILLED	WOUNDED	MISSING
Officers	—	3	1
Other Ranks ..	3	66	8

Sketch 3.

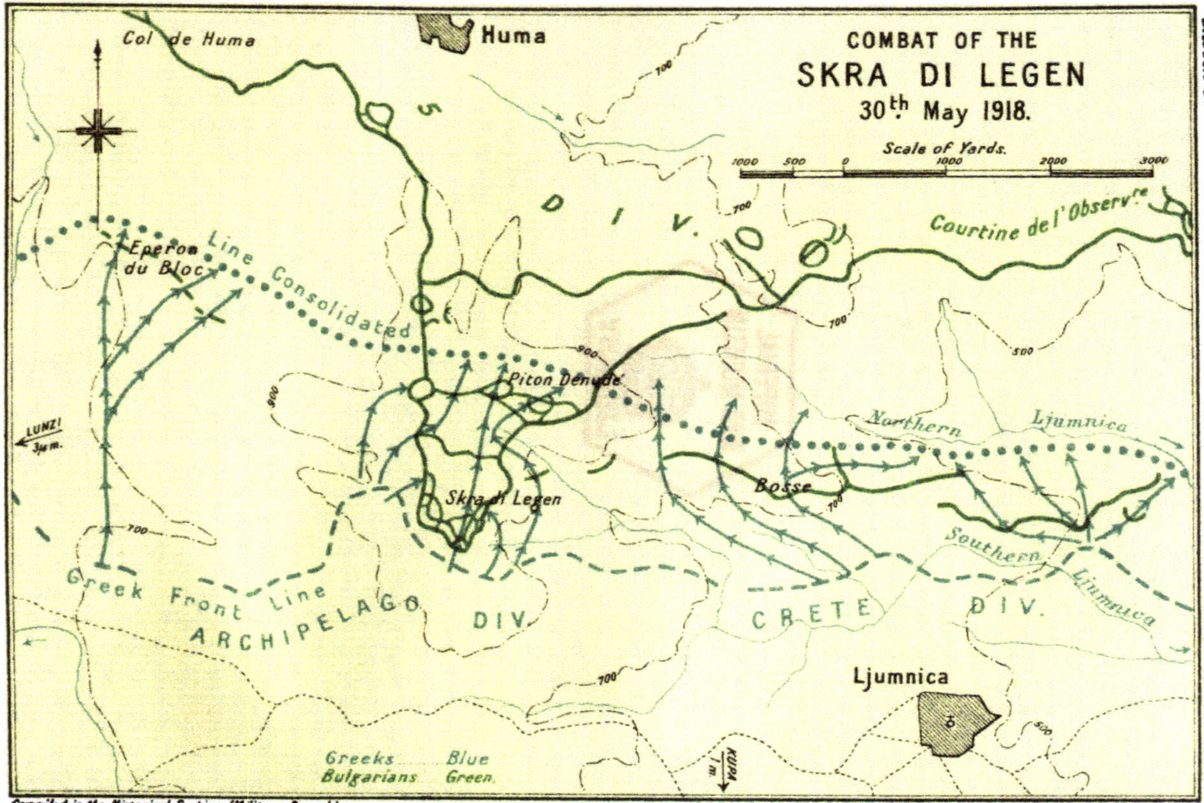

Compiled in the Historical Section (Military Branch).
3050/35.

Ordnance Survey 1935.

COMBAT OF THE SKRA DI LEGEN 89

fighters, which rendered its bombers almost immune from attack, by bombing raids on a scale not hitherto attempted. On the 8th, for example, there was a steady procession of aircraft over Drama aerodrome, 72 machines (including, of course, several which made two or three trips) dropping 4,500 lbs. of bombs. Serious damage was done to hangars and to machines on the ground. On the morning of the 23rd a successful raid was carried out by 27 machines against another aerodrome, that of Hudova. In the course of the month six hostile machines were shot down on the British front—including one by a French aeroplane—and five were driven down out of control without being seen to crash. Two of the latter were certainly destroyed; for they emitted clouds of black smoke as they fell. The British mastery of the air was now fast becoming complete. *1918. May.*

General Guillaumat had for some time been considering an action which would serve as a rehearsal for the offensive which he had in mind, test the quality of his Greek troops and the enemy's powers of resistance, and also gain some valuable ground. He finally decided to capture the enemy's foremost line on a frontage of some eight miles, from north-east of Ljumnica, or Lyumnitsa, to north of the village of Lunzi, three miles east of Nonte. The centre and keystone of this position was a rocky hill named Skra di Legen, which formed a salient in the enemy's line. *Sketch 3.*

By nature the position was extremely strong, and it was well fortified, having rock-hewn shelters impervious to artillery fire, and numerous machine-gun emplacements. The Skra di Legen itself had a precipitous face towards the Greek line, here very close to the enemy. To the west, on the other hand, in front of the Bulgarian position on the Eperon du Bloc, there was a " No Man's Land " of upwards of two miles, which could not be crossed until the dominating height of the Skra di Legen was taken. The difficulties were increased by the indifferent communications in the hilly region about Kupa, which made it an immense task to emplace the heavy artillery and to bring up the supplies and stores of all kinds required for the attack.

The formations which were to carry out the assault were withdrawn at the beginning of April for training. They were the Archipelago Division (with one regiment of the Seres Division in place of one of its own on duty in Athens) and a regiment of the Crete Division. The

90 GENERAL GUILLAUMAT'S REHEARSAL

1st Regiment de Marche d'Afrique was to be in support. The very strong artillery support included one section of the British 424th Siege Battery (8-inch howitzer). Six 60-pdrs. of the 20th and 190th Heavy Batteries also crossed to the right bank of the Vardar to assist in a secondary operation. In order to keep the enemy in doubt as to the precise objective, artillery bombardments and raids were carried out during the days preceding the attack, by the French 122nd Division and the British beyond the Vardar on the right, and by the Serbian Armies on the left. The British began with an intense bombardment on the 28th May on the front of the 22nd Division, which extended next day to that of the 26th Division. Successful raids were carried out by the French and Serbians on the evening of the 28th and by the 7/S. Wales Borderers of the 67th Brigade, against O.3, on the morning of the 29th.

1918.
30 May. The attack was launched at 4·55 a.m. on the 30th May. With splendid dash the islanders of General Joannou's Archipelago Division swarmed up the flanks of the Skra di Legen and captured it. In two further bounds they reached the Piton Denudé, the final objective. To the west they swept across to the Eperon, and were in possession of it by 6.15. East of the Skra di Legen the Cretan troops crossed the Southern Ljumnica and secured the high ridge between the Southern and Northern branches, though here the operation was not completed until the afternoon. Many hundreds of the enemy were captured unprepared and unwounded in their dugouts owing to the fashion in which the leading Greek wave clung to the creeping artillery barrage. The enemy reacted strongly with artillery fire and launched several counter-attacks in the afternoon and during the night, but without success.

The capture numbered 1,812, including 33 officers and a certain number of German specialist troops such as signallers. The Allied losses, all but 136 of which were in the Greek ranks, were 2,795.[1]

General Guillaumat's plan had been as bold as shrewd; for had the attack been a failure the effects upon the

---

[1] Bujac, p. 57, *fn*. The captures are from a brief report by General Guillaumat dated 3rd June. According to Colonel Bujac, these figures do not include wounded prisoners; he states that the total number taken was "about 2,500." He adds that 50 machine guns and 60 trench mortars were taken and that 800 dead were found upon the field.

mercurial Greek troops would have been unhappy. He had 1918.
thought he could rely upon the Corps of National Defence, 30 May.
and it had not failed him. Now he advertised the victory
with the skill of a showman. Greece in particular rang
with the news, which not only filled the Venizelist troops
with intense pride, not only inspired the Royal Greek Army
—and that at a moment when the troops of the doubtful
Morea were being mobilized—but greatly enhanced the
prestige of M. Venizelos. The success also seemed to point
to the possibility of ending the deadlock on the Macedonian
front. Brilliant feat of arms as it was, few actions so small
have made so much stir. If the Macedonian campaign had
been cursed by politics, it had at least shown here how much
a well-planned military action could be made to contribute
to political ends.

No operations could have differed more completely 15 May.
from that of the capture of the Skra di Legen than those Maps 1, 3.
begun earlier in the same month in Albania. General
Guillaumat had reached an understanding with General
Ferrero, the Italian commander at Valona ; and the Italian
authorities, far from attempting to prevent a French
advance south-west of Lake Ohrid, were now prepared to
co-operate. On this mountainous and thickly wooded
front, where there were peaks of over 6,000 feet, still covered
with snow, only small numbers of lightly equipped troops
could be employed. The French striking force consisted
of the 58th Battalion of Chasseurs-à-pied, a battalion of the
372nd Regiment, ten platoons of Albanian Mobile Gendarmerie, three mountain batteries, and a single 155-mm.
howitzer. A mounted detachment of Moroccan Spahis was
employed as advanced guards and for patrol work. The
defenders were Austrians, with a number of Albanian
irregulars.

The French advance, in a general westerly direction,
was made in four columns, the right being on the Devoli
River. The operation began on the 15th May and lasted
three days. The details cannot be given here ; but it may
be said that the whole affair was cleverly handled and completely successful, liaison being maintained by telephone in
most difficult country, the progress of the columns being
reported by aircraft, and supply and the evacuation of
wounded being carried out by pack convoys. The frontage
of attack was about ten miles, but an Italian attack to the

south resulted in the total frontage lost by the enemy being nearly twenty, while the depth of the advance averaged six miles. The French casualties were 133. The line now held was actually considerably shorter than the former one, and the enemy had been pushed back to a safer distance from the Santi Quaranta route.

1918.
June.
The new front was handed over to Annamite and Albanian Tirailleurs, the troops which had done the fighting being withdrawn to Koritza. In June the latter were employed in fresh operations, this time north of the Devoli. Between that river and the basin of the upper Shkumbi there is a great mountain mass known as the Kamia, its central peak rising to 7,054 feet, its flanks superbly clothed with forests of oak and chestnut. The capture of this ridge, not very strongly garrisoned so far as numbers were concerned but defended by numerous machine guns and a fair amount of artillery, was impossible except by surprise. During the night of the 8th the attacking troops of the main column were hidden in a thicket within striking distance of the crest, where they remained all the following day in silence and without fires. Austrian patrols moved about in front, but apparently considered the thicket impenetrable. At midnight the French troops quitted their lair and advanced to the attack on Point 7,054.

The assault was carried out entirely with the bayonet. The half-frozen Austrian sentries gave no alarm, and the majority of the garrison was captured asleep. That was only the first stage of five days' continuous fighting, but it was the decisive one. By the 14th the French line ran from near Udunishta on the shore of Lake Ohrid, across the Shkumbi at Slobinya, and thence southward to the Devoli south of Shinapremte, the average depth of the advance being from five to six miles on a front of 20. Over 400 prisoners, 10 guns, and great quantities of material were captured, and the French casualties did not exceed 50. It was the last operation carried out on the instructions of General Guillaumat, and was, in fact, begun on the day of his departure.

A GREEK CORPS IN THE STRUMA VALLEY.

Map A.
Sketch 4.
On the 5th May General Guillaumat informed General Milne that the 13th (Chalcis) Division of the Royal Greek Army was now ready to be put at the disposal of the British

and that he wished the Naresh training-camp to be cleared as soon as possible so that the 2nd (Athens) Division should use it. He also wrote that the headquarters of the Greek I Corps was now to enter the British area. General Negropontis, commanding the 13th Division, established his headquarters at Nigoslav, and on the 21st the commander of the British XVI Corps, General Briggs, issued orders for the division to place one regiment in the " River Line " between Gudeli bridge and Ahinos in relief of troops of the 1st Division. At the same time the withdrawal to a " Summer Line " was carried out, though, owing to the possibility of an offensive before the winter and Greek powers of resistance to malaria, not on the scale of the previous year. On this occasion there was only to be a thinning out on the middle Struma, where the line of redoubts on the left bank would be maintained. Only on the left of the XVI Corps, above the valleys of the Butkovo and Hoja, would there be a withdrawal from the advanced line.

1918. May.

This withdrawal was not completed until the night of the 2nd June, mainly owing to the vast labour of removing three Greek 150-mm. Krupp guns in Fort Dova Tepe; which was to be evacuated for the first time since the French had occupied it exactly two years before, after the advance from the Entrenched Camp. These guns were in full view of the enemy ; and one of them was on a siege mounting, gun and carriage weighing together $6\frac{1}{4}$ tons. Their removal and replacement by dummy guns made of wood took eighteen nights of hard work.

There was a certain amount of trouble with the Greek Government at this moment. They had got wind of the projected withdrawal to France of 12 British battalions and 10,000 French troops and, as General Guillaumat had anticipated, were seriously perturbed. Moreover, M. Venizelos appears to have known something of the British desire to withdraw more troops when all the Greek divisions had arrived. On the 18th May his Foreign Minister, M. Polites, informed Lord Granville that M. Venizelos had no intention of allowing the Greek troops to be used as stopgaps on a defensive front. Greece had entered the war to assist in carrying out an offensive against Bulgaria, and if there were no offensive M. Venizelos would have to reconsider his position, in case France and Britain, hard-pressed on the Western Front, should be tempted to sacrifice Greece.

The Greek Government were pacified for the time being, but it was clear that any word of the departure of more troops would arouse a storm.

1918. June. The latter part of June saw the whole British XVI and the Greek I Corps on the move. In the first place the Greek 2nd Division (General Contaratos), after a month's training at Naresh, marched into the area of the XVI Corps west of the Seres road. Then, now that General Milne had three Greek divisions at his disposal, General Guillaumat desired that he should send a division across the Vardar and relieve the French 122nd Division on the right or west bank. At the same time the 12 British battalions destined for France were withdrawn from their brigades. These battalions were the 14/King's (Liverpool) Regiment, the 12/Lancashire Fusiliers, and the 13/Manchester from the 22nd Division; the 9/Gloucestershire, 10/Black Watch, and 7/Wiltshire from the 26th Division; the 13/(Scottish Horse) Black Watch, the 4/K.R.R.C., and the 10/(Lovat's Scouts) Cameron Highlanders from the 27th Division; the 2/Northumberland Fusiliers, 3/Royal Fusiliers, and 1/K.O.Y.L.I. from the 28th Division. The great value of the Taranto route was proved by the ease with which their transshipment was conducted, three small French transports sufficing to move them all in little over a fortnight from Itea to Taranto. The battalions were sent without transport, but 120 G.S. limbered wagons and 312 mules were subsequently despatched owing to a shortage in France.

The move proved also how crippled the Army was with malaria. The 14/King's, reaching lorry-head at Bralo on the 18th, the hottest day of June, left 23 officers and men in hospital there. At Itea, the port of departure, six were dropped, at Taranto 67, at Faenza 20, at Genoa four. This total of 120 represented over 14 per cent. of the ration strength on arrival at Bralo. Other battalions, travelling in cooler weather or making different arrangements, carried their sick on with them to France; but one sent 273 men to hospital there within a few days, and all suffered. G.H.Q. in France wired in alarm that the battalions were unfit for immediate service and that systematic treatment with quinine should be carried out on the journey. " Possibly," wired General Milne, " it is not understood in France that " in the whole of this Army malaria is prevalent. Except " when suffering from actual attacks, troops are better

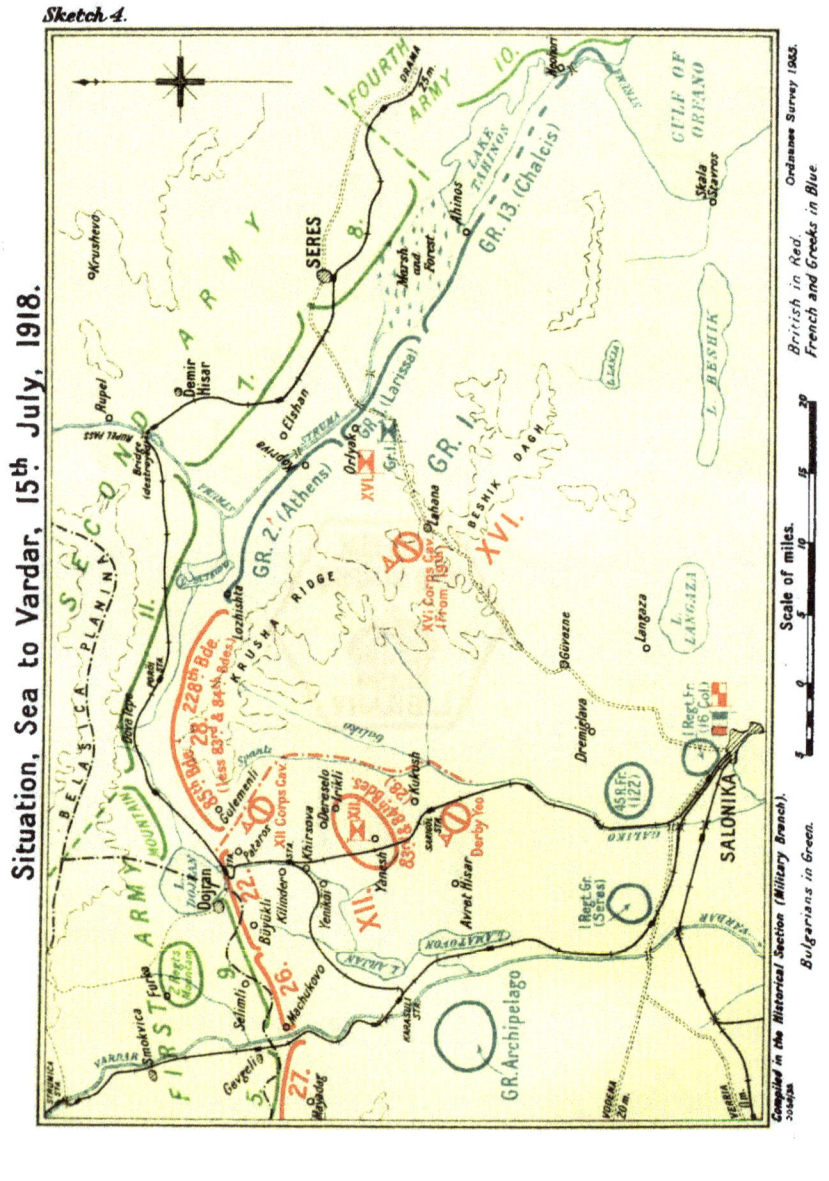

THE INCIDENCE OF MALARIA

"without quinine, as is shown by experience here. . . . 1918.
"My Consultant Physician and D.M.S. do not approve June.
"systematic quinine treatment of all ranks." Eventually it was decided, on the advice of Sir Ronald Ross, that only men who had had an attack within sixty days of their departure should be dosed on their way to France.

What, in fact, the statistics regularly sent home did not show was that the vast majority of officers and men were attacked sooner or later. Perhaps the best of all prophylactics was age. Senior commanders were to a great extent immune from the disease, while their staff officers, who like them had better protection from the mosquito than the fighting troops, generally had to take their turn in hospital. It was also noted that the veterans of the 228th Brigade suffered less than the younger men of other formations.

The battalions sent to France were there given special treatment, which included a liberal diet and rest followed by steady and increasing exercise both in military training and in sport. Moral stimulus was also applied, in the form of lectures explaining to the men that, having been removed from the infected zone, they need no longer fear malaria if they followed the treatment prescribed. The battalions finally took their places in the line, to serve throughout the arduous battles and advances of the autumn without a malarial relapse.[1]

The reliefs necessitated by these withdrawals, by the arrival of a third Greek division, and by the transfer of the 27th Division to west of the Vardar were interrupted by insistent reports that the enemy was contemplating an operation on the Struma. Hitherto the number of Bulgarian deserters had never been large, and those that had come in of late had belonged for the most part to a disciplinary formation on this front, the men in which could hardly be expected to be enthusiastic soldiers. About the middle of June the trickle swelled to a stream, 28 deserters giving themselves up in the course of three days on the XVI Corps front. These men were not criminals, and they all announced that they had surrendered in order to avoid taking part in an offensive or large-scale demonstration—

---

[1] "Medical Services: Diseases of the War," Vol. I, p. 285. It is here stated in error that the battalions from Salonika numbered 22. Probably the battalions of the 10th and 60th Divisions sent to France from Palestine, which had previously served in Macedonia, are included.

as to which, the stories varied—to be carried out between Lakes Tahinos and Dojran. General Briggs thought the tales sufficiently worthy of credence to man his river line, dispose reserve battalions in readiness for counter-attacks, and on the 16th obtain leave from General Milne to postpone all artillery and infantry reliefs for 48 hours. Next day more deserters came in and reported that the operation had been cancelled and the troops withdrawn to their main line in consequence of a mutiny.

The corps commander reported to the Army commander that in his opinion a Bulgarian offensive had really been planned to coincide with the Battle of the Piave, the Austrian offensive in Italy launched on the 15th June, and that it had been abandoned owing to the insubordination of the troops. He considered that a British offensive at an early date was desirable.

All danger being obviously over, the reliefs were continued. The 27th Division handed over its trenches on the middle Struma to troops of the Greek 2nd Division, while its Neohori front on the lower Struma, held by the 82nd Brigade, was taken over by two regiments of the Greek 13th Division. At the same time two brigades of the 28th Division were relieved and disposed in reserve, one to the division, the other to the XVI Corps. The relief of the 27th was completed by the 26th June, and the division then began its move by lorry, rail, and march route to the area of the XII Corps, in which it was now to be embodied.[1] The 143rd and 180th Heavy Batteries and the 127th Siege Battery were also transferred from the XVI Corps to the XII Corps, being replaced by six Greek heavy batteries, three of 120-mm. guns and three of 6-inch howitzers.

1918. July.
By the 9th July the 27th Division had relieved the French 122nd Division, the French commander, General Topart, having exercised command over all British troops as they entered his area until the relief was complete. The new front, known as the "Mayadagh Section," provided a striking contrast to the Struma. From the Vardar to the Ravin de la Bergerie—the boundary with the Crete Division—

---

[1] The 80th and 81st Brigades moved by lorry along the Seres road to Güvezne, where they entrained and were carried to Gümendje on the C.O. Railway, at the point where it crossed the Vardar. The 82nd Brigade travelled by the light railway from Stavros, transferring to the normal gauge at Güvezne. Artillery and transport marched.

it was 8,000 yards long, or about 10,000 along the front-line trench. The whole area consisted of a series of ridges, intersected by deep valleys, at right angles to the course of the Vardar and so very well suited to defence. It was also well fortified, though the foremost trenches had been badly knocked about by bombardment during the action of the Skra di Legen. A curious feature of it was that in Mayadagh and Kara-Sinanci, two very large villages within about a mile of the front line, the French, easy-going in such matters by British standards, had allowed to remain some 2,000 inhabitants, mostly Turks. The divisional front was held by two infantry brigades in line, with one in reserve.

1918.
July.

The Greek I Corps was attached to the British XVI Corps. General Briggs, who now had only one British division and British corps troops at his disposal, was therefore in a position very similar to the commanders of German formations composed for the most part of Bulgarian troops. The Greek corps commander, General Paraskevopoulos, who had established his headquarters at kilometre 61·5 on the Seres road near Bashköi, exercised direct command over his own three divisions and corps troops from the 5th July, but took his orders from General Briggs.[1] General Paraskevopoulos was to have little opportunity to distinguish himself in Macedonia, but as *Archistrategos*, or Commander-in-Chief, he directed the operations in Asia Minor with complete success until forced by the Constantinist reaction to resign in November 1920.

The whole front from the Gulf of Orfano to the Ravin de la Bergerie, a distance of 65 miles as the crow flies, was now in the hands of the G.O.C.-in-C. British Salonika Army, with the following troops at his disposal:—

XVI Corps:—Greek I Corps, 28th Division (with 228th Brigade), XVI Corps Troops;

XII Corps:—22nd, 26th, and 27th Divisions, XII Corps Troops;

Army Troops:—Derbyshire Yeomanry, XVI Corps Cyclist Battalion.[2]

---

[1] It had been the intention of General Guillaumat that the command on the Struma should be handed over to the Greeks, and General Milne had been about to send home one of his corps headquarters. General Franchet d'Espérey preferred that British G.H.Q. should remain in command of this front, and the arrangement was therefore cancelled.

[2] These troops were withdrawn from the XVI Corps and moved across to Sarigöl.

The XVI Corps held the front from the Gulf of Orfano to Lake Dojran, having on its right the Greek I Corps from the gulf to Lake Butkovo, and the 28th Division between Lakes Butkovo and Dojran.[1] From Lake Dojran, inclusive, to the Ravin de la Bergerie was the XII Corps, with the 22nd Division on the right, the 26th in the centre, and the 27th on the left beyond the Vardar. The 22nd and 26th had each a brigade, less one battalion, in divisional reserve, these two battalions being in XII Corps reserve. The reserve brigade of the 27th Division was, on the other hand, entirely at its disposal. All brigades in the British force, with the exception of the 228th, now consisted of three battalions.

The reliefs, entailing long marches and long moves by rail in hot weather, had been trying. The Greek troops had arrived short of many necessities, such as telephone cable, telephones, gas-masks, range-finders, telescopes, and binoculars, and were very short of ammunition. Supply, which the British had to supervise, was complicated by such facts as that the Greek I Corps used three types of small-arms ammunition : Mannlicher for the rifles of the fighting troops and machine guns, Gras for the rifles of auxiliary services, and Lebel for automatic rifles. The British, especially the signal services and the Royal Engineers, worked very hard to assist them and "settle them in" on the Struma. General Briggs was well pleased with the appearance of the two incoming Greek divisions—which, for reasons that have been explained, were superior to the 1st Division. "Smart, and they march well" (of the infantry) ; "a smart body of men ; their equipment was "well put on, and their animals were very well loaded with "the tools, etc." (of the engineers) ; "a well-set-up body "of men, commanded apparently by a first-class colonel" (of the artillery), were phrases in his report after inspecting the 13th Division. This division had, moreover, a number of junior officers promoted after service in the Corps of National Defence—in itself a tribute to the strength of M. Venizelos and his *régime*. The transport was the weak spot. A large proportion of the animals appeared unserviceable, not from condition, but by reason of malformation, age, or lack of size. The Greek engineers were lacking in mechanical

---

[1] The divisional boundaries were, Greek 13th Division Gulf of Orfano to Gudeli, Greek 1st Division thence to Turbes Island above Orlyak bridge, Greek 2nd Division to Lake Butkovo, 28th Division, with two brigades, as above ; two brigades of 28th Division in reserve.

knowledge and at first could not repair a defective pump without British aid.

1918. July.

The general impression made by the Greeks upon the British troops whom they replaced was a favourable one, and good staff work in both the British and French areas minimized the discomforts of the moves. The reliefs were not without their humours. In one case the British brigadier, still in command of his sector, was awakened by the alarming news that almost the whole Greek garrison of a strong point on the left bank of the Struma had marched out rearwards without an explanation. Hurried and indignant enquiry revealed that they were going to dig a communication trench to their post and that the interpreter had forgotten to inform brigade headquarters. Again, a British brigadier, desiring to show the senior officers of the relieving troops over the whole system of defence in one day, found that impossible. "Owing to heat and enormous "thirst of Greek officers, who wanted drinks at every work, "it was only possible to do the first line," notes the unemotional war diary.

During June there was a marked increase in the activity of the Bulgarian artillery on the Dojran–Vardar front. Fire was directed chiefly against the British artillery emplacements and observation posts, and on bright moonlight nights was controlled by aeroplanes. At the time it was impossible to account for this unwonted lavishness in the expenditure of ammunition by the enemy. We now know that it was a measure of policy to encourage the infantry.[1] The Bulgarians apparently flattered themselves that they had "destroyed certain hostile batteries." They accomplished nothing of the kind, and in fact did very little damage. Their most successful bombardment was directed against " A " Battery, CXIV Brigade, of the 26th Divisional Artillery, on the night of the 25th. On this occasion they put one gun out of action, demolished the signal pit, killed the battery commander and three men, and wounded three men. The casualties for the month in the 22nd and 26th Divisional Artillery were nine killed and 12 wounded, and the 22nd had also 19 horses killed.

June.

In the air the successes of the previous month were continued. Eight of the enemy's machines were destroyed

---

[1] Nédeff, p. 170.

on the British front and five driven out of control, while only one British machine was lost. Four aircraft were also shot down by the French.

The troops faced their third summer with fortitude. The total number of convictions by Courts Martial for the month of June was only 111, or 0·067 per cent. of the ration strength of the force. In general the spirit of the troops remained excellent, extraordinarily high in view of the nature of the campaign and above all its stagnation. With increasing heat, sickness showed its usual advance. There were 10,109 casualties from sickness or wounds in the hospitals on the 1st June, and the figure had risen to 13,812 by the 9th July. Thereafter the curve descended, though this was, of course, due largely to the removal of the cases of chronic malaria, and in smaller degree to the departure of 12 battalions. It must be noted also that these figures are those of admissions to hospital only and do not represent by any means all the incidence of sickness from malaria. By June less than 2,000 officers and men certified as chronic malarial cases still awaited shipment. Measures were at last taken to increase the allotment of leave, and not before it was time. There were still 29,000 men who had had no leave for $2\frac{1}{2}$ years, and 2,300 who had had none for three years.

Map 1. The shipping situation had improved in certain respects. For example, the light railway to Stavros, which had been open since early May, had enabled two of the three boats on the Salonika-Stavros service to be dispensed with, one being retained to carry hay to Stavros and bring back timber and charcoal from Stratoniki in the Gulf of Ierisos. Even this one was not regularly available, and sailing boats had frequently to be hired to replace it. Then, again, an increasing proportion of the stores from the United Kingdom was now sent by rail *via* Cherbourg to Taranto, and thence shipped to Salonika. At the beginning of July it was decided to transport a proportion of these stores in open lighters to Itea, by lorry to Bralo, and by rail to Salonika, so that the short cut hitherto mainly used for personnel was now employed for material also. The carrying-power of the railway was, as has been stated, too small to allow this safe and handy route to be used to any great extent for supplies,[1]

---

[1] See Vol. I, p. 276.

about 3,000 tons a month being all that could be dealt with. Over 40,000 tons per week were still being landed at Salonika from British ships for British needs, and at least as much from British ships for the other Allies.[1]

1918. June.

The demands of the Greek Army continued to deplete the labour at the disposal of the British, and it was impossible to replace it on roads and rearward defences by military labour, the troops having more than enough work in the forward zone. It was also a matter of policy to employ civilian labour to the largest possible extent, as it had been found that heavy work greatly increased sickness among the troops. So short had Greek labour become that on some tasks, rearward defences as well as roads, as many women as men were employed.[2] After repeated applications General Milne obtained another 2,000 Turkish prisoners of war from Egypt.

Efforts were made to cut down official correspondence, the enormous growth of which was one of the most curious features of the Great War. Stagnant warfare led inevitably to a large increase in telegrams, letters, returns, and reports. In the month of May XII Corps Signals dealt with over 2,000 messages and packets a day, the total for the month being 67,937. Something could be done to set a limit to *paperasserie*, but very little while trench-warfare continued. The best that could be hoped was that, once active operations were resumed, commanders would be strong-minded enough to jettison the great bulk of it.

In the midst of the reliefs carried out on the British front, for which his instructions were responsible, General Guillaumat was recalled to France. The German advance had made it necessary to place in command of the Paris defences a soldier who would inspire confidence and whose Republican sympathies were as well assured as his military qualities. The French Government also desired to have him at hand in case of any accident to General Foch or General Pétain. On the 9th June he left in great haste and secrecy, unable to await the arrival of his successor—whom

---

[1] As far as can be ascertained, about 75 ships entered Salonika harbour each month, of which about 40 were British. The British also were on the average of larger tonnage than the others, though not more than one-third of them were over 4,000 tons.

[2] The 16,000 Greeks employed, as stated on p. 56, had by June decreased to under 13,000. On the other hand, the number of women had increased from 2,000 to 3,700.

he apparently passed in the train in France—leaving the command-in-chief temporarily in the hands of General Henrys. On the 17th General Franchet d'Espérey arrived, taking over command next morning.

The new Commander-in-Chief of the Allied Armies of the East and future Marshal of France was 62 years of age, seven years the senior of his predecessor. Yet time and his numerous campaigns in Tunisia, Tonkin, China, and Morocco, as well as arduous service in the present war, had dealt with him lightly and had no whit diminished his vigour, activity, incisiveness, or his remarkable grasp of detail. He was also one of the few senior French officers who had a knowledge of the Balkans. Born in Algeria and joining the 1st Algerian Tirailleurs as a 2nd-lieutenant, his service had been almost entirely colonial until his appointment to the command of the I Corps at Lille on the eve of the Great War. His conduct of the command of that corps at Guise resulted in his immediate promotion to that of the Fifth Army, which he led at the Marne. In March 1916 he was appointed to command the Group of Armies of the East, which he afterwards exchanged for the Group of Armies of the North.

General Franchet d'Espérey had to make his way to the confidence of the Allied Armies in face of the feeling of universal regret, so strong as to amount almost to exasperation, with which the departure of General Guillaumat was regarded. In six short months the latter's measures and his moral influence had had an extraordinarily beneficial effect upon his command and upon the relations between the various contingents. And, if the weapon which he had retempered was to be wielded in masterly fashion by another arm, General Guillaumat was not yet done with the Armies of the East. We shall see that the work he had accomplished for them as their Commander-in-Chief was to be continued by services of the first importance, though it was to be in the council chamber that they were to be rendered.

CHAPTER VI.

THE GENESIS OF THE OFFENSIVE.
(Map 1.)

SALONIKA—PARIS—VERSAILLES—LONDON—ROME.

THE reader who has followed the campaign in Macedonia from its inception will agree that its most striking characteristic has so far been the difficulty found by the Allies in reaching a unanimous decision on any problem of military policy. As it had begun and continued, so it was to end. The origins of the final offensive were involved in a curious drama, with scenes shifting from Salonika to the capitals of the three chief Allies and to Versailles, the seat of the Supreme War Council. And the protagonist, the man who more than any other made the offensive possible, was a soldier no longer officially connected with the campaign, General Guillaumat, the former Commander-in-Chief of the Allied Armies of the East and now Military Governor of Paris. That the offensive, in conception and in tempo, was to differ greatly from that which he had advocated, and that the permission of the Allies—their attention riveted upon the tremendous struggle in France—was to be accorded to his plan rather than to that actually carried out makes the affair still more curious. Let us follow its development, not forgetting as we read that in France the tide turned in late July, and that many projects which had seemed impossible in June had taken on another aspect by September.

1918.
June.
Map 1.

It has been said that the seed of the final plan lay in a proposal made to General Sarrail a year before, after the failure of the May offensive, by the Crown Prince of Serbia. We need not concern ourselves with this question; plans are plentiful enough in war, but they depend upon the power to carry them out. General Sarrail's own plan for May had, for that matter, a strong resemblance to that of General Franchet d'Espérey. It is, however, certain that when the latter arrived at Salonika his attention was called to a Serbian project for an attack on the Dobropolje, which was to be the prelude to something more than a local operation such as the recent capture of the Skra di Legen. It appears certain also that the parent of this plan was the ablest soldier of the Balkan countries, the Voivode Mišić, who had hitherto commanded the First Army and now exchanged posts with General Bojović, becoming Chief of the Staff.

General Franchet d'Espérey had come out in haste and without special instructions. A few days after his arrival he received a telegram from the Ministry of War, dated the 22nd June, which informed him that a directive was about to be sent to him by messenger, and that he was to set to work upon a plan on the lines of General Guillaumat's projects. The actual directive was drawn up the same day by the Ministry in consultation with Generals Foch and Guillaumat, signed by M. Clemenceau on the 23rd, handed to a messenger, Commandant Enaux, on the 24th, and delivered by him to General Franchet d'Espérey at Salonika on the 2nd July.[1] It was not communicated to the British, Italian, and American Military Representatives on the Supreme War Council until the 30th June.

The directive [2] began by pointing out that the enemy was exerting all his strength to obtain a decision in France. In the outer theatres, and especially that of Macedonia, it therefore behoved the Allies to assume an aggressive attitude. Germany could now do little for Bulgaria, and that country was passing through an internal crisis. The object of the Allies should be to break through the Bulgarian defences and open to the Serbian and Greek Armies access to their lost territories, and this object could be attained only by an action carried out with all the forces of the Allied Armies. Such an action could, however, be carried out neither immediately nor by means of a single stroke. The general offensive must be preceded by a series of partial ones, spread out over a certain period of time and growing in intensity, all leading to a final decisive period of action. The series of operations, begun so happily at the Skra di Legen and in Albania, should therefore be continued in order to make it possible to launch the general offensive before the autumn.

With the telegram in his hands, General Franchet d'Espérey did not wait for the written instructions. On the

---

[1] Lieut.-Colonel Lepetit: "La Genèse de l'Offensive de Macédoine," in *La Revue Militaire Française*, July 1922, pp. 28 *et seq*. This important article is based upon the documents of the Service Historique.

[2] A translation of the directive is given in Appendix 6.

29th June, after a long examination of the ground from a Serbian observation post, he adopted at Serbian G.H.Q. a plan in which the principal rôle was confided to the Serbian Armies.

We must now turn to the Supreme War Council, which held its seventh session at Versailles on the 2nd, 3rd, and 4th July. Among the matters which it discussed was the campaign in Macedonia, regarding which it passed the following resolutions :—

1918.
July.

" 1. The Military Representatives shall report as to
" the desirability of undertaking an offensive in the Balkans.
" Diplomatic Representatives shall be attached to the
" Military Representatives for this inquiry.

" 2. Pending the result of their inquiry, no general
" offensive shall take place.

" 3. The report of the Military Representatives shall,
" if possible, be decided on by direct communication between
" the Governments concerned, but, in the case of necessity,
" shall come before the Supreme War Council.

" 4. The appointment of the Commander-in-Chief of
" the Allied Armies of the East shall in future be subject to
" the approval of the Governments concerned." [1]

From the point of view of the British representatives this joint resolution marked a distinct step forward in favour of the Macedonian campaign. This step was certainly not instigated either by the Government's military advisers at Whitehall or by their permanent military representatives at Versailles. Major-General Sackville-West's staff was still engaged in urging its objections to General Guillaumat's defence scheme, considering the chances of a Bulgarian offensive in Macedonia with the aid of ten German divisions, and suggesting the possibility of getting Bulgaria out of the war by diplomatic means. A paper on this last subject by Br.-General Sir Hereward Wake, Bart., drawn up on the 3rd July, while the Council was in session, stated that military action was not possible, but that diplomatic or political measures might succeed.

However, when in accordance with this resolution the diplomatic and military representatives met in the Trianon Palace at Versailles on the 11th July, another step forward,

---

[1] That of General Franchet d'Espérey had been made without reference to the Allies. Representations on the subject were made by Mr. Lloyd George to M. Clemenceau in the course of the session.

very small, very cautious, was taken. This time General Guillaumat took part in the session in an advisory capacity. Called upon for his views, he declared his faith in the success of an offensive. The Allies had numbers and quality on their side. As regards the Greeks, it would be a positive danger to leave them idle, since troops and people alike believed that Greece had entered the war to win back her lost provinces in eastern Macedonia. This time the resolutions were as follows :—

"*From the Political Point of View :*

"1. That it is advisable to study the question of a "general offensive in the Balkans with a view to the effect "that may result from it on the Bulgarian situation.

"2. That it is not desirable to carry out this offensive "unless it leads to a victory of more than local importance.

"*From the Military Point of View :*

"That it is advisable to request the Military Repre-"sentatives of the Supreme War Council to examine the "conditions of a general offensive with a view to its probable "results, both as to gain of ground and as to its effect on "the Bulgarian Army.

"The French Government will be requested to supply "to the Military Representatives complete information on "the general offensive in project, as well as on the method "of execution. The question of local operations, as "previously settled, remains unaffected by this resolution."

Lord Robert Cecil, Lord Derby, and Major-General Sackville-West were the British Representatives who put their signatures to this document. The resolution was forwarded on the 18th by M. Clemenceau to General Franchet d'Espérey, with instructions to continue his preparations.

The next move was a request, on the 15th July, by Major-General Sackville-West to the French Section for information on eleven points: front of attack, objectives and limits of advance, forces to be employed, arrangements for concentration, work on communications required, general plan, estimated casualties and reinforcements to replace them, reasons for anticipating that the Bulgarian Army would sustain an important defeat, modifications in transport and equipment considered necessary, possible enemy action which had been taken into consideration, dates of concentration and beginning of operations.

The replies were drawn up by General Guillaumat in a letter dated the 19th July, and forwarded by the French military representative, General Belin, next day. General Guillaumat answered the questions in a broad sense; to some of them he considered a reply impossible. So far as he knew, the main front of attack would be between Lake Dojran and the eastern branch of the Crna, combined with a secondary attack on the front Demir Hisar-Seres-Drama; the objective of the main attack would be the Vardar between Gradsko and Hudova; it would probably be carried out by 12 divisions (two British, two Greek, six Serbian, and two French), leaving six Greek and two French for the Struma attack and two British, one or two Greek, three or four French, and the Italian troops as a reserve; preparations, if commenced at once, would take two months; all work necessary on communications had already been studied and was for the most part in hand; only the Commander-in-Chief of the Allied Armies of the East could give the general plan and methods of attack; heavy losses were not to be anticipated, especially after the rupture of the front; the reasons for anticipating an important Bulgarian defeat had been given at the conference of the 11th; the Armies were already equipped for mountain warfare, but it would be wise to replace the animals which had been somewhat inconsiderately withdrawn;[1] the Bulgarian Army, on its huge front, could find reinforcements only by withdrawing them from other parts of the front, and it could not expect Austrian or Turkish reinforcements—the question of German reinforcements depended on the efforts of the Allies on the Western Front; it ought to be possible to begin operations by the 1st October. Finally, General Guillaumat remarked that the question of the chances of success hardly needed to be put.

It had meanwhile occurred to the American, General Tasker H. Bliss, the military representative of the only great Power in the Alliance which had no particular interest in the Macedonian campaign, to ask for the personal views of the British Commander-in-Chief in that theatre of war,

---

[1] " A very palpable hit! " See Vol. I, p. 283. Horses and mules had been withdrawn from the French contingent also.

who had not so far been consulted. The demand was, of course, made through the British War Office.

General Milne, who had not yet received any instructions from General Franchet d'Espérey, wired on the 22nd July that, with the Bulgarians growing war-weary, the Austrians in difficulties in Italy, and the Germans fully occupied in France, the time might be approaching when Allied offensive action in Macedonia would have far-reaching results. As before, he said that he thought well of an attack at the mouth of the Struma—in which view he had the strong support of General Briggs, his corps commander on that front. His aim would be to capture Kavalla and Drama, roll up the enemy's left, and thus reach the Rupel Pass. He objected to the proposal in General Guillaumat's plan of the 1st March that the main attack should be launched between Lake Dojran and the Vardar,[1] on the ground that there were not sufficient men and guns to drive the enemy from this position without a turning movement elsewhere; but, looking round for a more suitable point, he remarked significantly that the Serbians had always recognized the possibilities of their front. He reiterated the view of nearly two years ago, which was characterized in these pages as the first " note of optimism " struck by a British hand,[2] by proclaiming his belief that if the Bulgarian line were turned or broken their forces would begin to disintegrate. But they would fight stubbornly for their present positions, and the Allied Armies would need to be well supplied with ammunition and well equipped with transport. He summarized his views in the final paragraph of his telegram as follows :—

"Summary. Guillaumat's plans were for local operations only; but in my opinion an offensive here at the psychological moment may have more than local effect and should be prepared for. My general plan would be for Greek Army first to attack enemy in Eastern Macedonia; if successful, they turn his flank; even if unsuccessful, they will compel him to detach troops from centre, thus facilitating subsequent operations there by rest of the Allies. However, the time for taking the offensive in this theatre depends on factors which the Supreme War Council are alone qualified to judge."

---

[1] See p. 77.   [2] See Vol. I, p. 203.

This telegram certainly gave some support to the French case for an offensive. So far, however, it was rather in the air. Now came realities. On the 25th General Milne telegraphed that he had received from General Franchet d'Espérey instructions to prepare for offensive operations during the second half of September,[1] entailing the employment of at least three British divisions, while two Greek divisions would also be allotted to him. The attack would follow and be conditional upon attacks on other parts of the front. The British attack was likely to be successful only if the War Office was prepared "to bring us up to "fighting pitch by sending the necessary ammunition and "reinforcements by the date mentioned." It seemed right, General Milne concluded, that the Allied forces in Macedonia should be prepared to take advantage of the situation in the autumn.

1918. July.

That brought the War Office upon the scene. On the very day, the 25th July, that this telegram was sent, General Sir Henry Wilson had written, in the course of an appreciation of the whole military situation for the War Cabinet:—
" On the whole, I am averse to undertaking an offensive in
" the Balkans, and recommend that we economize British
" troops to the utmost by the gradual substitution of Indian
" units as fast as they can be made available."[2] General Milne was informed that an offensive was undesirable, unless made at a moment when Germany could not reinforce Bulgaria from the Western Front. In September this condition would not exist. And no hope could be held out of reinforcements or ammunition in excess of the usual allotment.[3]

On the 30th Sir Henry Wilson telegraphed a message to M. Clemenceau, pointing out that the Supreme War Council had decided on the 4th that no general offensive should take place pending the result of the enquiry then instituted. Yet the British Commander-in-Chief had been ordered to prepare for one, and had promptly asked for reinforcements and ammunition which were not available. The C.I.G.S. asked to be furnished with the instructions sent to General Franchet d'Espérey. M. Clemenceau,

---
[1] The directive mentioned is given (in a translation) in Appendix 7; General Milne's telegram is given in Appendix 8.
[2] It is hardly necessary to say that the C.I.G.S. desired to "economize" British troops with a view to sending them to France.
[3] This telegram, of the 27th, is given in Appendix 9.

bland because he had the cards in his hand, replied that since the meeting of the Council on the 2nd July he had sent only two telegrams to Salonika. The first was to inform General Franchet d'Espérey of its proceedings; the second to tell him of the meeting of the diplomatic and military commission, which had decided that the question of an offensive should be studied at Versailles, and that preparations should be made at Salonika. He had now wired again, warning his general to await formal permission before he attacked.

1918. Aug. Now came what, so far as Versailles was concerned, was to be the final step. On the 3rd August the military representatives of France, Great Britain, Italy, and the United States met and, after considerable discussion, passed the following resolution :—

" 1. That it is necessary to push on with all speed the " preparations for an offensive in Macedonia on the basis " contemplated, in order to put the Allied Armies of the " East in such a state as to be able to execute it at latest by " the 1st October 1918 (provided that these preparations " do not require any assistance in men or material from the " Western Front, and do not divert any tonnage, now or " subsequently available, which is required for the con- " tinuous arrival at the maximum rate of reinforcements in " effectives and material indispensable to the execution of " the plan for the Western Front approved by the General " Commanding-in-Chief the Allied Armies in France).[1]

" 2. That it is expedient, in principle, to leave the " General Commanding-in-Chief the Allied Armies of the " East free to launch this offensive at the moment he con- " siders most favourable; unless new and unforeseen " circumstances arise which compel the Supreme War " Council to fix the time itself or to abandon the enterprise " altogether."

Forwarding this letter to the War Cabinet on the 5th, Major-General Sackville-West observed that he had signed it because he had been given to understand that an offensive was necessary to maintain the morale and, indeed, the very existence of the Greek Army. He considered it impossible to say what material results the offensive would give. The autumn was not the best time from the British point of

---

[1] The passage in brackets was added at the instance of General Bliss, the American representative. How deplorable it was will appear.

view, owing to the ill-health of the troops, the radical change in organization which would be in progress,[1] and the fact that neither before nor after the attack would reinforcements for the British Army be available. On the other hand, he had been informed that General Foch was anxious that the attack should take place and that it fitted in with his plans. As General Milne had stated that more ammunition was necessary and as the military representatives had expressly stated that no personnel, material, or shipping should be diverted, it seemed probable to Major-General Sackville-West that deficiencies would limit the scope of the operations.

1918. Aug.

Nothing more of importance enough to detain us happened until the 4th September, when a conference was held at 10 Downing Street, at which General Guillaumat acted as advocate for the offensive.[2] Closely questioned by the British Prime Minister, General Guillaumat put his case with marked skill and clarity. He still looked only for a limited offensive, as he showed when he replied in the affirmative to Mr. Lloyd George's question as to whether an advance on Sofia could be considered five or six months hence. The British representatives then withdrew to consult among themselves. Mr. Lloyd George declared that General Guillaumat had convinced him. He considered that the Italians should be urged to attack simultaneously. General Wilson told him that he was in communication with General Diaz on the subject, and that General Sir Edmund Allenby was attacking the Turks in Palestine on the 18th September.[3] Returning to the conference room, Mr. Lloyd George announced :—" The " British Government give their consent to the proposal so " far as it concerns them and the British troops."

Sept.

One more barrier to surmount : the permission of the Italian Government had to be obtained. There was no

---

[1] The change in organization referred to was the projected despatch of Indian troops to replace British in Macedonia, of which something will be said later.

[2] Present, for Great Britain, Mr. D. Lloyd George, P.M. (in the chair) ; Viscount Milner, Secretary of State for War ; Lord R. Cecil, Assistant Secretary of State for Foreign Affairs ; General Sir H. H. Wilson, C.I.G.S. For France, M. Paul Cambon, Ambassador ; General Guillaumat, Military Governor of Paris ; M. de Fleuriau, Counsellor of Embassy.

[3] General Allenby's preliminary attack, above the Jordan valley, was carried out on this date ; his main attack took place next day. The Italians did not attack till more than a month afterwards.

112   THE GENESIS OF THE OFFENSIVE

time to waste. At Salonika General Franchet d'Espérey was on tenterhooks. On the 5th September he telegraphed that all was ready for an attack on the 12th. The enemy was beginning to realize what was brewing. Unless orders to the contrary arrived, the attack would start on the 14th. M. Clemenceau forbade an attack without orders from him. Off to Rome posted the indefatigable General Guillaumat, where again he won his case. On the evening of the 10th General Franchet d'Espérey received a wire from M. Clemenceau that the Italian Government had agreed. " Vous êtes en conséquence autorisé à commencer les " opérations quand vous le jugerez convenable." [1]

General Milne's Problem.

The position of the commander of the British Salonika Army was difficult and anxious. After Mr. Lloyd George and General Sir Henry Wilson, he had the weightiest responsibility for British participation in the attack, because a hostile verdict on the offensive from him would almost certainly have killed it, where the British were concerned. Far from giving such a verdict, he had, as we have seen, twice stated that the Armies of the East should be prepared to play their part. He did not change his views when he saw his own favourite project of a turning movement from the mouth of the Struma set aside because it would have been too far distant from the Serbian front, where the break-through was to take place; when he saw himself committed once more to an attack in that region west of Lake Dojran which he had so much reason to dread.

From the point of view of British prestige alone, a refusal would have put the country, as well as its general and its armed forces in this theatre of the war, in an almost intolerable position. For the best part of three weary years a British Army had been cooped in Macedonia, always playing a minor rôle, always denied by policy or circumstances the chance of striking a real blow, always suffering and waiting. Its position was becoming little short of ignominious, through no fault of its own, while it had none of the comfort or safety which might have been expected to be the results of inactivity. The British Army was the

---

[1] Lepetit, p. 42.

GENERAL MILNE'S PROBLEM

1918.
July.

stop-gap, the trench-holder of the expedition, as the British nation was its milch-cow. To have stood aside now would have been to put the final touch to a general picture so little in accord with all our traditions and professions as to be well-nigh incredible.

Yet that was only half the case. The commander and his troops—perhaps the country also—might have swallowed this last pill, bitter as it was, if prestige only had been in question; Macedonia had afforded good training in overcoming fastidiousness of the stomach. But General Milne saw the touch of genius in the plan of General Franchet d'Espérey. Even here he was, it is true, in the dark. His knowledge of the ground outside his own front was necessarily limited. Success on the main front would depend on factors which it was extremely difficult for a Western European soldier to estimate—the chief being the ability of the Serbian troops to march and fight, almost without supplies, for days, or it might be weeks, in mountainous country. The closest British observer, Br.-General E. A. Plunkett,[1] had, in fact, sent to the War Office a pessimistic telegram on the subject. Yet General Milne did definitely believe in the plan, and, realizing that a subsequent British attack on the Dojran front formed a necessary part of it, he was prepared to make this attack.

In both his telegrams which have been mentioned, and especially in that of the 25th July,[2] he had, however, laid it down that success was not probable unless he were given the necessary means. What he asked for was, first, reinforcements in personnel to bring his units up to establishment; secondly, and still more important, small reinforcements in artillery and a large increase of ammunition, especially chemical shell. What happened was that the British authorities at home gave their approval to the attack but did not supply the means which he declared to be necessary.

General Milne's demands had, in fact, begun immediately after the arrival of General Franchet d'Espérey and before he received any instructions from the latter. In a telegram of the 25th June the British Commander-in-Chief pointed out that the stocks of 18-pdr. ammunition had

---

[1] Br.-General Plunkett, formerly liaison officer with the War Office, had succeeded Br.-General Corkran as British representative with the Serbian Armies.
[2] See p. 109, and Appendix 8.

dropped to little more than half the authorized establishment. The War Office replied that steps would be taken to hasten the arrival of ammunition despatched *via* Taranto and that 15–20,000 rounds a week would in future be sent. Then followed a series of requests, in almost all cases refused. General Milne asked for 8-inch howitzers to be substituted for 6-inch in one of his siege batteries, and for the return of two 6-inch guns sent to Egypt in August 1917. He then sent his Deputy Quartermaster-General, Major-General Rycroft, to London and directed him to represent to the War Office his need for another 8-inch howitzer battery. In none of the three cases had he any fortune.

The situation on the Dojran front was from the artillery point of view a peculiar one. It had appeared to the Commander-in-Chief, himself an artillery officer, and to his senior subordinates of that arm that the failure of the two attacks in April and May 1917 had been largely due to inadequate counter-battery work, that is to say, that the hostile artillery had not been sufficiently neutralized. Now, owing to the excellence of the Bulgarian observation posts on the Grand Couronné and the " P " Ridge, the 6-inch howitzers and 60-pdrs., firing high-explosive shell, could not fulfil this task to the same extent as in France. The former had not the range; the latter had not the accuracy at extreme range—besides being deficient in hitting-power.[1] Neither could be moved further forward without inviting destruction. Hence arose the demand for 8-inch howitzers. One battery had been sent, and invaluable it had proved. The arrival of the two sound-ranging sections, of which mention has been made, had also been helpful. Flash-spotting instruments had been improvised by XII Corps Signals, and a section formed on the corps front from both heavy and field artillery observers. Improved liaison with the Royal Air Force had also been of service. But sound-ranging, flash-spotting, and aircraft observation could avail only to the extent that long-range weapons existed to take advantage of the targets which they indicated. The requirements were not large, because heavy artillery on the enemy's side was not numerous. General Milne would have

---

[1] One concrete casemate, at which 60-pdrs. had been shooting for months, was examined after the Bulgarian retreat. It was surrounded by innumerable 60-pdr. shell-holes and must have been repeatedly hit, but the only apparent damage was a certain amount of chipping.

been comparatively easy in his mind regarding heavy artillery—though not regarding field artillery—could he have obtained the extra 8-inch battery, the substitution of 8-inch equipments for 6-inch in a second battery, and the two 6-inch guns, which was all that he had asked for. He could not get them.

1918. July.

It appeared that this weakness in heavy artillery could best be mitigated by the use of gas shell with smaller calibres for counter-battery work. If the enemy's heavy batteries, frequently in concrete emplacements on the Dojran front, could not be put out of action by high-explosive shell, they could, it was hoped, be effectively neutralized by gas. On the 17th July, two months before the launch of the offensive, General Milne first raised this question with the War Office, asking that his ammunition stocks should be adjusted so that 10 per cent. of that for 4·5-inch howitzers,[1] 40 per cent. for 60-pdrs., and 20 per cent. for 6-inch howitzers should consist of chemical shell. The War Office replied that an endeavour would be made to increase the supply of chemical shell, but that the output of that for 60-pdrs. was too limited for his demands to be met in this case.

Again, on the 2nd August—still six weeks before the offensive—General Milne wired that ammunition in certain quantities was essential by the first week of September, concluding his telegram with the remark that his ammunition reserve was far below the sanctioned establishment, despite his repeated protests. To this the reply was that considerable quantities of ammunition were in a vessel which had sailed to Cherbourg on the 24th July. Further quantities would be sent, but not by any means to the extent of the demands; and no guarantee could be given that it would arrive by September. No chemical shell for 6-inch howitzers was available. Could then, he asked, this nature be replaced by 4·5-inch and 60-pdr. chemical shell? The reply was that it could not.

Aug.

Learning of General Milne's difficulties, General Franchet d'Espérey telegraphed to M. Clemenceau that the British demands for ammunition were fully justified, and that priority in despatch should be given to it. This message, which was forwarded to the War Office on the

---

[1] The supply for 4·5-inch howitzers was to be chiefly lethal shell for use in attack; that for the other natures of the types suitable for counter-battery.

10th August, may have had its effect; for on the 16th the War Office telegraphed that a further consignment of chemical shell, in addition to that already promised and including 10,000 rounds of 6-inch, would be sent *via* Cherbourg and Taranto within the next fortnight. This quantity was afterwards increased to 15,000, the figure demanded by General Milne.

Unfortunately, it was now too late, as the Taranto route was choked with stores. We find General Milne urgently wiring on the 1st September to ask if all or any of the 6-inch chemical shell had been despatched. Telegrams now rapidly succeeded one another; an officer was sent from Salonika to Italy to expedite the supplies on their way; and, to put the matter shortly, a small quantity—apparently 3,000 rounds [1]—of 6-inch shell arrived the day before the attack. It is the recollection of Br.-General Holbrooke, commanding the Heavy Artillery, that the last battery received its allotment at 11 p.m.; the consignment was practically all expended on the first day, and there was very little available on the second, when it was, as events turned out, still more needed. The supply of 60-pdr. gas shell was sufficient to be used in both bombardments; but all through the operation heavy group commanders had to be warned to exercise care, and bombardments for destruction had to be somewhat limited.

The shortage was not the only evil. The 6-inch howitzers, British and Greek, were the most important gas-firing counter-battery weapons, and great accuracy was required to keep the shells within a small area such as that occupied by a hostile battery in action. Though officially informed that 4·5-inch high explosive and gas shell ranged alike, Br.-General Holbrooke had had comparative trials fired behind the lines and had found that this was not the case. He had therefore been anxious to test the 6-inch gas shell in a similar way. That the opportunity was denied him was a misfortune. Nevertheless, the shortage was a worse one; for the counter-battery fire on the first day seems to have been effective. No other nature fully replaced the 6-inch howitzer, as the gas used in the 4·5-inch

---

[1] The figure does not appear in the records. Of two officers attached to the Ordnance Services one states that his personal notes show that the consignment " advised as despatched from home " was 3,000, and the other that he is " very nearly certain " that the number was 2,600.

dispersed too quickly, and it was very difficult to obtain a concentration with so slow-firing a gun as the 60-pdr.

1918.
July.

The Newton trench mortars having proved their value on the Dojran front, General Milne had asked for some more of these weapons. On the 3rd July the War Office promised to send another dozen, but unfortunately they had not arrived when the offensive took place.

General Milne was, therefore, committed to an attack of which he strongly approved in principle—and to which his Government had agreed—though he considered his task between Lake Dojran and the Vardar, if not the heaviest or most important, at any rate the most doubtful as regards accomplishment. His demands for extra long-range artillery had been refused, but at least they had been refused early enough to give him time to reconsider his position. He had decided he could go forward if he received certain supplies of ammunition. But he was given no time when these supplies failed him. Here he was told that his demands would be largely met, and up to the last moment he expected that they would be. When this moment came they had not been met in any sense adequately. But the Franco-Serbian forces had then broken through the enemy's lines, and one of the greatest victories of the war was in prospect. Could he then have refused to play his part? It must be obvious that to have done so then was impossible, if only because it would have been a gross breach of faith. His situation was, however, a cruel one.[1]

We have here only mentioned the question of reinforcements in personnel. General Milne reconciled himself to doing without them, realizing how urgent was the demand on the Western Front. Nor have we dealt with other deficiencies. It may, however, be said that one of the most serious of these, which caused grave anxiety, was in motor tyres and tubes, and in spare parts, such as driving-chains, for lorries.

EVENTS IN JULY AND AUGUST.

While General Guillaumat was pleading the cause of General Franchet d'Espérey and his offensive in the capitals of the Allies there was a diversion in Albania which caused

---

[1] Ammunition supply and expenditure are dealt with in Note at end of Chapter.

some alarm in Allied counsels. The Italian XVI Corps had been reinforced by a brigade from Italy and now consisted of approximately 53 battalions (one-third of which were Territorial militia) and 300 guns. The Austrian *XIX Corps*, which faced it, had only about 24 battalions at the front and 14 on the lines of communication ; and though a small proportion of the Austrian infantry consisted of *Jäger* battalions of good quality, it was largely made up of *Landsturm* or *Honved* troops who were indifferent, or Albanian levies, useful in mountain warfare but not when it came to "push of pike." On the 6th July the Italians began an offensive on a considerable scale. On the left, covered by the batteries of the Entrenched Camp of Valona and the guns of two British monitors, the Italian forces passed round the lagoons and marshes north of that town and captured Fyeri. Further east they occupied all the ground south of the Semeni river, captured Berat, the second town after Elbasan in Southern Albania, and established themselves on the heights to the north-east in the bend of the Devoli river. The frontage of the advance was some 60 miles and the average depth at least ten. Over 2,000 prisoners, 26 guns, and six aeroplanes were captured. The French, whose line, it will be recalled, ran across the Devoli south of Shinapremte, had meanwhile pushed forward till their left was in touch with the Italians at the confluence of the Devoli and the Tomoritsa. They, for their part, had a haul of 700 prisoners.

The Austrians struck back resolutely. Early in August, employing apparently only the troops on the spot, they pressed back the Italian centre to the outskirts of Berat, though the gains on the lower Semeni were retained. Then, on the 22nd, having been considerably reinforced, they launched an attack along the whole front. The Italians held their ground at most points, but General Ferrero, apparently acting on orders from the Comando Supremo, at once decided to abandon nearly all the fruits of the advance and to fall back on the coast to the heights north of the Voyusa. This hasty retreat was completed by the 26th, the French being compelled to draw back their flank to south of Tomoritsa in conformity with it.

Then, indeed, the wires became busy. The Commodore commanding the British Adriatic Force telegraphed to the Admiralty that Valona was in danger and that its capture

ITALIAN OPERATIONS IN ALBANIA 119

by the Austrians would upset the whole situation in the Adriatic and render the maintenance of the Otranto Barrage impossible.[1] Urgent representations were made to the Italian Government on the subject, but they took the matter very coolly. They replied that the offensive had been carried out by General Ferrero on his own initiative and had been extended further than the Comando Supremo desired. They also pointed out that the position at Valona was still rather better than that held in early July, which was the line of the Voyusa, and that then no alarm had been raised for the safety of the port. However, the Comando Supremo transported another brigade to Valona and moved a division down to Brindisi to be at hand in case of need. The defence of the Malakastra heights north of the Voyusa was still a matter of discussion between Great Britain and Italy when the great blow was struck on the Macedonian front. Thereafter the question ceased to have importance.

1918. July.

On the greater part of the British front and that held by the Greek I Corps in the Struma valley, July was quiet even by the standard of that quiet summer. Between Lake Dojran and the Vardar there was, however, a certain activity. The enemy's artillery was fairly lively, and he attempted a number of small raids, in which he had but a slight measure of success.

In the instructions issued by the French Commander-in-Chief on the 24th July,[2] General Milne was directed to maintain artillery activity on the front west of Lake Dojran during the period of preparation, which might be taken as beginning on the 15th August. The object was, of course, to keep the enemy's attention fixed upon this front and to prevent him from transferring any of his artillery from it. As this was where the British would have to attack, they would thus be putting the enemy on the alert to their own disadvantage, though to the profit of the main attack on the Serbian front. However, though on the whole front of the XII Corps there was a programme of harassing fire on the enemy's communications by night, bombardments, wire-cutting, and raids were for the time being confined to the

---

[1] The "barrage" was, of course, a flotilla of destroyers, trawlers, and drifters ; but the Franco-Italian naval forces had then just completed the laying of a barrage-net from Fano Island, north-west of Corfu, to Otranto.
[2] These instructions will be dealt with in the next chapter, when discussing the British plans and preparations.

sectors of the 26th and 27th Divisions astride the Vardar, so as not to alarm the Bulgarians unduly for the neighbourhood of the " P " Ridge, the precise area where the attack would be carried out.

1918.
Aug.
Mention must here be made of a suggestion for the employment of tanks on the British front in Macedonia, because, though it came to nothing and was in any case made too late to have been adopted, it is of interest to note the verdict of the officer sent out by the War Office to reconnoitre and report. Captain D. Mackay, Royal Tank Corps, reached Salonika on the 24th August. In consultation with the General Staff he decided that certain sectors which appeared obviously unsuitable might be eliminated and that he would examine only those portions of the front where the co-operation of tanks might be useful and which afforded possibilities of approach. He therefore confined his attention to the Dojran–Vardar front and the valley of the Struma.

The former he divided into three sectors, the " P " Ridge, the centre—which he dubbed the Selimli Deresi sector—and the Piton des Mitrailleuses sector on the left bank of the Vardar. The first-named was out of the question. " Tanks could not operate on the ' P ' Ridge." The second was more promising, as the approaches were good, and there was just a possibility of capturing the Machukovo Salient by an attack from this direction. The objections were that there would be an advance of a mile and a half in the open, that tanks could not pass through the enemy's line in extended formation, and that the country beyond, along the valley of the Vardar, was unsuitable. The third was again impossible. Again the advance would have to cover a long distance in the open, and this time the tanks could only emerge two abreast. Formation would have to conform to the lie of the ravines, and tanks would have to cross these in file. The gradient of the last hundred yards in front of the Piton des Mitrailleuses was one in two. On the Struma front the tanks could easily overrun the trench line between Savyak and the Struma, but would first have to be moved about 60 miles by road. Even then they could not operate against the main line on the hills in rear on either side of the Rupel Pass. After some general remarks upon the principles of tank tactics Captain Mackay concluded:—" Taken

"altogether, tanks would be faced with too many difficulties 1918.
"to render their employment profitable on the British Aug.
"Balkan front."

If he had said the contrary, they could not have been used, as his report to the War Office was dated the 14th September. There is, however, some comfort in knowing that the heavy loss which was to occur in the attack on the "P" Ridge could not, according to this expert opinion, have been lessened by the employment of tanks, at the stage which they had reached in 1918. The most suitable part of the Macedonian front was probably, not anywhere in the British zone, but between Monastir and the Crna. A battalion of light French tanks was actually sent for use here, but did not arrive until after the Armistice with Bulgaria.[1]

Another question, which likewise did not affect the force—or, in this case, not until the war had come to an end—but which caused a good deal of preliminary work, was that of the despatch of Indian troops to Salonika. It had been decided that "Indianization" of the British Salonika Army should be carried out on an even greater scale than had already been done in Palestine. But in the case of Macedonia the War Office was really looking forward to the year 1919, as the reorganization could not have been completed until the spring. Beginning in November 1918 with 12, a total of 36 Indian battalions would eventually be sent from India. Each infantry brigade would then consist of one British and three Indian battalions, which would enable 24 British battalions from the four divisions to be sent to France. In the field artillery the gunners and gun-team drivers would remain British; the other personnel would be replaced by Indians. In the heavy artillery 75 per cent. of the gunners would be British and 25 per cent. Indian. British mountain batteries and ammunition columns would be "Indianized." Thirteen field companies and seven Army Troops companies R.E. would be replaced by companies of Sappers and Miners.[2] In machine-gun companies the gunners would remain British and the drivers would be Indian.

---

[1] "Étude sur la Guerre de Montagne," p. 63, *fn*.
[2] It would actually, as General Milne pointed out, hardly have been possible for Indian personnel to replace British of all trades in the Army Troops companies, as the Indian sappers were not suitable for the supervision of Greek labour, still less for that of unskilled British labour.

Actually the only "Indianization" which was carried out before the end of operations was the substitution of Indian drivers for British in the ammunition columns. This was completed during July, the surplus British drivers being transferred to the batteries of the divisional artillery. The proposed reorganization did not therefore affect the operations in hand, but it came near to doing so very adversely. For on the 1st September General Milne was ordered to send 221 "selected" officers of all the arms in question to Egypt for preliminary training with Indian troops in the Egyptian Expeditionary Force. They were shortly to have been replaced by a similar number from home. This transference, on the eve of the offensive, would have been a serious matter; it would, for example, have deprived the British contingent of about four per battalion of its best infantry officers just at the moment when their experience and leadership were most needed. Fortunately the War Office cancelled this order three days later, deciding to despatch a sufficient number of officers direct from the United Kingdom to Egypt.

General Milne had been authorized to form divisional machine-gun battalions from the three brigade machine-gun companies in each division. Owing to shortage of officers of the Machine-Gun Corps he was, however, obliged to put off this reorganization, and it did not take place. He was also authorized to increase the number of Lewis guns from 20 to 32 per battalion, and in this case extra guns were sent out from the United Kingdom. Each platoon had now two guns, and, platoons being in almost all cases weak, the organization which appears generally to have been adopted was a platoon of three sections instead of four: one Lewis-gun section, one rifle section, and one rifle-grenade and bombing section.[1]

NOTE.

AMMUNITION SUPPLY AND EXPENDITURE.

As the question of ammunition supply, especially that of chemical shell, for the final offensive has been discussed in this chapter, it seems desirable to give the details here, even though that means anticipating the account of the action. On the 15th September, three days before the attack, the total stocks of chemical shell (excluding smoke) on charge were as follows:—

4·5-inch. how.	60-pdr.	6-inch. how.
17,609	12,082	nil

[1] It is not clear that all battalions received their extra guns prior to the offensive.

AMMUNITION SUPPLY

That is to say, not a round of the consignment of 15,000 rounds of 6-inch, of which 2,000 were shipped from England to Cherbourg on the 2nd, 3,000 on the 3rd, and 10,000 on the 6th, had yet arrived; and there was none in the country.

S.S. *Kashing* reached Itea on the afternoon of the 15th with, so far as can be ascertained, 3,000 rounds of chemical shell for 6-inch howitzers. Unloading was carried out with the utmost haste, the 6-inch gas shells having to be sorted out from the large consignment of all natures on board. They were then taken by lorry to Bralo, and left that station in a special train for Salonika at 3.15 p.m. on the 16th, reaching Yanesh at 2.50 p.m. next day. The last lorry-load to the batteries left Yanesh at 7 p.m. This accords with the recollection of Br.-General Holbrooke that the last battery received its allotment at 11 p.m. on the night prior to the attack. A second ship with a further supply arrived on the 22nd. This ammunition was also rushed to Salonika, but it may almost be disregarded for our purposes, as it was of no importance owing to the nature of the operations from the 25th onwards.

When we turn to expenditure, we find that 2,424 rounds of chemical shell for 6-inch howitzers were expended during the week ending at noon on the 21st. In such returns there must always be taken into account considerable miscalculation and wastage, so that Br.-General Holbrooke's recollection that practically the whole consignment was fired on the first day is not necessarily falsified by this figure.

It has been explained why so much importance was attributed to the 6-inch chemical shell. That for 4·5-inch howitzers and 60-pdrs. was plentiful. As regards ammunition of other types and calibres, the expenditure was high. From noon on the 14th to noon on the 21st the expenditure of all natures (omitting anti-aircraft artillery) by the whole of the artillery of the force was as follows:—

	Shrap.	Reduced Charge	H.E.	Chemical	Smoke
6-inch gun	24	124	674	—	—
8-inch how.	—	—	1,467	—	—
6-inch how.	—	—	16,065	2,424	—
60-pdr.	4,110	7	5,883	13,702	—
4·5-inch how.	—	—	29,687	15,134	1,404
18-pdr.	94,108	8,334	44,297	—	4,790
2·75-inch	Shrap. and H.E. 1,645.	Reduced Charge 1,133			

This works out at approximately 360 rounds per 8-inch howitzer, 420 rounds per 6-inch howitzer,[1] 520 rounds per 60-pdr., 960 rounds per 4·5-inch howitzer, and 790 rounds per 18-pdr. All 6-inch howitzers and all 60-pdrs. except one battery were attached to the XII Corps, while 36 out of 44 (including 12 Greek) 6-inch howitzers and 36 out of 44 60-pdrs. took part in the attack on the Dojran position; but as regards the field artillery it must be recalled that the expenditure of ammunition by the 28th Division (the only British division in the XVI Corps) was comparatively small, so that the 4·5-inch howitzers and 18-pdrs. of the XII Corps must have fired more rounds per piece than is given above, especially on the Dojran front. It was because all the 4·5-inch howitzers in the Army, with the exception of the three batteries of the 28th Division, were concentrated (as will be explained later) on the Dojran front that they fired so many more rounds per piece than the 18-pdrs.

These figures suggest that if the barrage on the XII Corps front was distressingly thin, it was owing to shortage of guns, especially of 18-pdrs., even more than to shortage of ammunition.

---

[1] That is, if, as is almost certain, the expenditure of the 12 Greek howitzers of this calibre is included in the return.

CHAPTER VII.

PLANS AND PRELIMINARIES.

(Maps 2, 4, 5, 6; Sketches A, 5, 6.)

THE STRATEGICAL SCHEME.

1918.
June.
Map 4.
Sketches A, 5.

LITTLE was said in the last chapter of the plan adopted by General Franchet d'Espérey except that the main attack was to take place on the Serbian front and that the principal rôle was to be confided to the Serbian Armies. The omission of detail in that place was deliberate, because the plan could not usefully be described in a few words or without reference to the enemy's communications, upon the lie of which it was based.

As a strategical conception it will without doubt always hold a very high place in the estimation of military students; but the general reading public, which has a big vote in the award of eternal fame to such conceptions, may not find it easy to follow. It is when the main features of the country have a certain regularity and appear to follow a certain broad principle of design that the ideas of the commander who employs them for his purposes stand out most vividly and make most appeal to the imagination. To take instances from the Great War only, there are the campaigns of Falkenhayn and Mackensen in Rumania, a huge plain bordered by the Danube on the south and the Transylvanian Alps on the north and west; that of Sir Stanley Maude in Mesopotamia, where the military situation is dominated by the twisting courses of the great twin rivers; and that of Lord Allenby in Palestine, with its coast plain, its saddle-backed hill-chain, its Jordan depression, and, at right angles to these, its Plain of Esdraelon. All these theatres of war, the last especially, have a superb simplicity. A glance at the map admits us at once to the counsels of the commander; we understand the magnitude of his design, and we realize that if it succeeds the ruin of his opponent is inevitable. In Macedonia, where there is no easily discernible order, where the great ridges and masses of the mountains lie at all angles to one another, the essence of the plan and its effect upon the enemy's fortunes are not so readily to be grasped. Yet in truth it was founded upon the

Sketch 5.

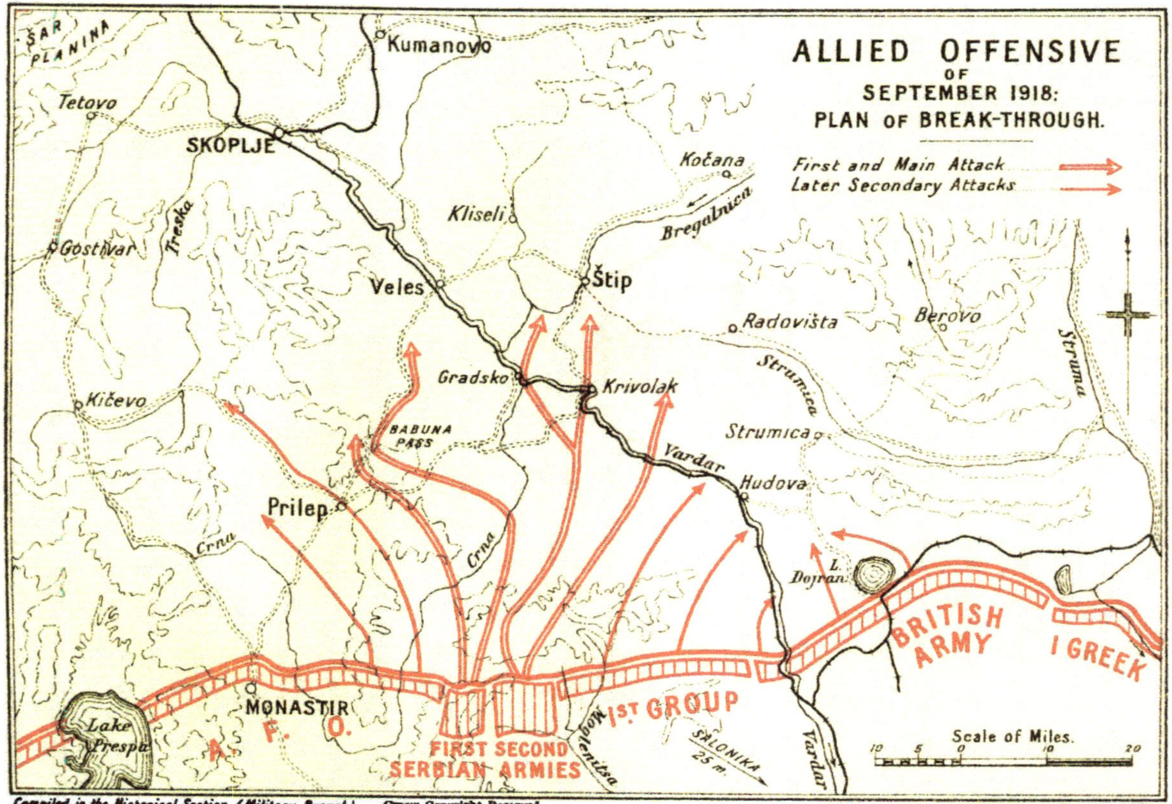

Compiled in the Historical Section (Military Branch)
2050/35

Ordnance Survey 1935.

THE STRATEGICAL SCHEME 125

configuration of the country and the lie of the enemy's communications every whit as much as Lord Allenby's plan in Palestine, and its success made little less certain the complete overthrow of the enemy's forces. Let us disengage the essentials from the tangled complications of the country, and set out the problem and its solution in the simplest terms.

1918.
June.

Behind the long Bulgarian front by far the most sensitive point was comprised by two villages some 10 miles apart and nearly 35 miles from the front line, Gradsko and Krivolak. Gradsko lay at the junction of the Crna with the Vardar, and at that of the light railway from the Monastir front with the main line from Salonika to Niš, and thence to Sofia on the one hand and Central Europe on the other. Through Gradsko ran a road from Skoplje and Veles to Prilep. At Krivolak a road from Štip to Prilep crossed the Vardar. An attacker in possession of Gradsko had only to stretch out his hand in order to seize Veles, 15 miles up the river, where he barred a third road, from Štip through the Babuna Pass to Prilep. Could he force his way another 30 miles up the Vardar, he had Skoplje, and there he barred the Sofia-Kumanova-Tetovo-Monastir road. There were no other approaches to the front west of the Vardar. And if the Vardar valley were cut, the only approaches to that east of the river were the mountain roads from the Strumica valley to Strumica Station and Dojran, the Rupel Pass, and the railway and road from Drama to Seres; Rupel serving only the enemy's left flank and the coast route his extreme left. If Gradsko-Krivolak were swiftly seized, the enemy would be split in two, his main line of communication would be cut, and he would be thrown into almost irretrievable confusion. Moreover, the routes by which the success could most profitably be exploited would be opened up.

How, then, could Gradsko-Krivolak be reached with the requisite speed? At first sight there were only two possible approaches: the valley of the Vardar—to use which it would first of all be necessary to capture the high ground between the river and Lake Dojran—and the Monastir-Prilep road. The former might be ruled out at once from consideration as the area of the main attack. It might be necessary to mount a secondary attack there, but no commander could now put his most fertile, still less all his eggs into that basket. The enemy there was alert, comparatively thick on the ground, and better fortified than anywhere else on the front; he knew that the defence of that part of his line was a matter of life and death for him; there, if anywhere, he would fight to the last, and he had the means to fight. In the Monastir plain and its necessary complement, the bend of the Crna, these considerations applied with only a degree less force. Both fronts had been the scenes of heavy fighting, the attacks on the Dojran front in the spring of 1917 having been repulsed, those at Monastir and in the bend of the Crna in the winter of 1916 having ended in deadlock after initial Allied successes, and those in the latter area in May 1917 having failed completely. That was another argument against choosing either for the main attack now, but it also favoured the chances of a surprise elsewhere.

Immediately west of the Vardar the Bulgarian fortifications were also strong and had a certain depth, while a series of excellent natural defences was provided by the tributaries of the Vardar and the ridges between them, running parallel to the Bulgarian line. Then came the great mountain range of which mention was made so often in the first volume, along which was traced the Serbo-Greek frontier, and the crest of which—except at the south-western end, where the Kajmakčalan had been captured in 1916—was held by the Bulgarians. Various sections of this range had their separate names, but it had also a general title, the Moglena. It averaged over 4,500 feet in height, and its steepness may be gauged by the fact that within two or three miles of the crest there were points in the valley of the Moglenitsa less than 600 feet above sea-level. The attacker would have to climb this wall, having first prepared his attack, emplaced his artillery, brought up his supplies under the enemy's eye. He would have to deal on the crest with defenders ensconced until the latest possible moment in shelters hewn in the rock, shelters which no artillery could destroy. Altogether, it would seem, an unpromising venture.

Yet there was a brighter side to the picture. First of all, the Bulgarians did not expect an attack in this quarter. Their foremost system of fortifications was fairly strong, but their second and third systems were fragmentary and only at one point, the *massif* of the Kozyak, were they likely

THE FRONT OF ATTACK

to prove a very serious obstacle to troops which had pierced the first. The very height and steepness of their mountain line seemed to have made them over-confident that it was inviolable. Secondly, the rivers and ridges behind the mountains, instead of being, as further east, at right angles to the line of advance, ran parallel with it towards the Vardar, and the routes, though with few exceptions only bridle-paths or cart-tracks at best, followed the same course. Thirdly, the south-western and higher portion of the ridge had been captured in 1916, and the great spurs north-east of the Kajmakčalan provided observatories—and, as we shall see, even artillery positions—which were actually higher than the Bulgarian defences. Fourthly, the basin of the upper Moglenitsa, if open to observation, afforded means to supply the front of attack. Vertekop, 25 miles distant, was the broad-gauge railhead of the Serbian Armies, and up to this station the Monastir Railway could be worked to full capacity.[1] From here a 60-cm. line, with a capacity that could be raised to 400 tons a day, ran to Dragomantsi, where it forked, both branches running to within five miles of the front. From Dragomantsi also a series of roads ran fanwise to the lower slopes of the mountains. Supply, in a word, was not easy, but was possible for a really powerful blow on a narrow front. Finally—and this was of great importance—the Allied Commander-in-Chief had at his disposal six divisions of troops hard to match in their fitness for mountain warfare; frugal, tough, and skilful; eager to invade and liberate their own country; led by an accomplished and determined commander who was in some degree the parent of the plan and its enthusiastic advocate. If the mountain barrier and its defences could be carried in one rush, these troops would not easily be stopped short of their objective, provided always that the enemy's reserves could be pinned down upon the rest of the front.

1918. June.

General Franchet d'Espérey decided, in short, to do what the enemy thought was impossible. He would launch his attack on the only part of the front where the frontier-crest coincided with the Bulgarian front line, between the mountains known as the Vetrenik and the Sokol, the peaks of which were six miles apart, under the orders of the

Map 6.

---

[1] Beyond Vertekop extra engines and shorter trains had to be employed. See Vol. I, p. 275.

Voivode Mišić, at whose disposal he would place two French divisions and 80 pieces of heavy artillery, in addition to 84 normally on the Serbian front. The first assault was to be carried out by the Serbian Second Army, commanded by the Voivode Stepanović and consisting of its own three Serbian divisions (Šumadija, Yugoslav, and Timok) and the French 17th Colonial and 122nd Divisions. In handing over these two good divisions to the Voivode Mišić, the Commander-in-Chief stipulated that they were to be employed in first line, for the rupture of the front. On the left of the Second Army the First, under the Voivode Bojović, consisting of the Morava, Drina, and Danube Divisions, with a considerably smaller share than its neighbour of the available artillery, was to await the capture of the heights by the latter before advancing to the attack between the Sokol and the village of Staravina. It has been calculated that the Allied Commander-in-Chief had on the front of the two Serbian Armies massed a three-fold superiority of strength: 75 battalions against 26, 756 machine guns against 245, 580 guns and trench mortars against 146,[1] whereas on the whole front his effectives were almost exactly equal to those of the enemy.

The crests won, the defences of the first position—which averaged about 2,000 yards in depth—overrun, there was to be no appreciable pause. With all possible speed the leading division of the Second Army, covered by a division on either flank, was to press forward to the capture of the second position, on the Kozyak, three miles to the north. On this point General Franchet d'Espérey insisted vigorously, directing that the Serbian orders on the subject should be rewritten. These had spoken of the capture of the Kozyak as part of the exploitation; for him it was rather part of the break-through. It must be carried out automatically according to a programme already drawn up, without its being necessary for the higher command to intervene. Then was to come the exploitation, a rapid advance into the Vardar-Crna loop and upon the objective of Gradsko–Krivolak.

---

[1] Serbian official report. This does not take into account the Bulgarian Army reserve where the infantry is concerned, and in any case there was less disparity in the fighting strengths. The German historians calculate that between the Moglenitsa and the Crna—a wider front than that mentioned above—there were 56,000 Serbians and French against 33,000 Bulgarians and Germans.

EMPLACEMENT OF THE ARTILLERY 129

It is impossible here, in respect of an operation in 1918. which the British played no part,[1] to enter into details of Aug. the preparations. A word may, however, be added regarding the emplacement of the artillery. The problem was a double one. In the first place, it was necessary that a proportion of the heavy artillery should be able to prepare the attack on the Kozyak. In the second, a great proportion of all the heavy artillery available was to prepare the original attack of the Serbian Second Army; but there must be batteries so placed that, by switching their fire, they could subsequently support the First Army. Twelve 155-mm. and 105-mm. guns were hoisted on to the Floka, 3¼ miles south-west of the Sokol. These guns, under the orders of the Colonel commanding the Artillery at Serbian G.H.Q., were first of all to carry out bombardment and neutralization of batteries on the front of the Second Army, and subsequently to support either the Second or the First as required. A second group of two heavy batteries was placed further north on the Belo Grotlo, so as to be able to enfilade the enemy's line from the Sokol to the Dobropolje. As the Floka was 7,756 and the Belo Grotlo 7,020 feet high, these batteries dominated the enemy's position, the peaks of which ranged between the Dobropolje's 6,170 feet and the Vetrenik's 5,153.[2] Yet another group of seven 155-mm. batteries was pushed as far forward as possible up the slopes north of Gorgni Pojar, to take part in the preliminary preparation, and then to support the advance on the Kozyak, with the co-operation of aircraft.[3] General Bunoust, commanding the artillery of the Allied Armies of the East, was attached to Serbian G.H.Q. for the preparation and execution of the attack.

This, then, was to be the principal attack: a decisive Map 4. attack to break the front from the Vetrenik to the Sokol, Sketch 5. followed by rapid exploitation in the direction Gradsko–Krivolak. But the operation was also to comprise a series

---

[1] Except that two 4·7-inch guns (84th Siege Battery R.G.A.) which had long been at the service of the Serbians were employed in the bombardment and that British supply columns, as stated in Vol. I, p. 282, were attached to the Serbian Armies.

[2] These heights are approximate only. The various maps differ considerably.

[3] Feyler, III, pp. 37–40. Colonel Feyler quotes from an official report by Artillery Headquarters of the Armée d'Orient. He gives interesting details of the hoisting of the batteries, by means of tractors and tackle, on to the summit of the Floka. In some cases the work took a fortnight.

of successive secondary attacks. The first of these was to be carried out under the orders of the British Commander-in-Chief, with two divisions of the Greek Corps of National Defence at his disposal, against the enemy's positions on the high ground between Lake Dojran and the Vardar. Its object was to break into the position of the Bulgarian *First Army*, which would already be shaken by the Serbian attack, to hold down reserves on that front, and eventually to clear the railway in the Vardar valley, of capital importance for future operations. West of the Vardar the 1st Group of Divisions was charged with the duty of linking up the main and the Dojran attacks. The second subsidiary attack was to be made on the left flank by the Armée Française d'Orient under General Henrys in the direction of Prilep. Its object was to break the front of the German *Eleventh Army*, whose communications at Krivolak–Gradsko would already be threatened, and to push it in the direction of Albania. Finally, if possible or necessary, an operation was to be carried out in the Struma valley by the Greek I Corps. Then was to come a period of exploitation by the whole of the Allied Armies, " pressed " far enough to liberate the means of communication and " allow regrouping of the forces with a view to further " operations, with decisive objectives."[1]

That constituted the first phase. At its end General Franchet d'Espérey—with a large measure of optimism which had, however, no evil effect upon his scheme—hoped to find his Armies in the following situation, from left to right :—

Armée Française d'Orient : main body in the region of Skoplje with advanced guard about Kumanova and flank guards towards Kačanik and Tetovo ;

Serbian Armies : main body in the area Veles-Štip with advanced guard on the roads leading to Sofia ;

1st Group of Divisions : main body in the area of Hudova and Demir Kapija, holding the crest of the Gradec Planina on the left bank of the Vardar, with advanced guard in the valley of the upper Strumica about Radovišta ;

British Army : main body in the Strumica valley, with advanced guard on the Strumica–Berovo road ;

---

[1] This passage is quoted from General d'Espérey's detailed report on the offensive, of which a copy was afterwards furnished to the British Army.

THE OPPOSING FORCES

Greek Army: main body in the area Demir Hisar–Rupel–Petrić, with advanced guards on the road running up the Struma valley and on that branching off it to Nevrokop.

1918. Aug.

In such a situation the German *Eleventh Army* would be out of action, being either blocked in the corridor from Kičevo through Tetovo or having sought an inhospitable refuge in the mountains of Albania.

For the second phase General Franchet d'Espérey did not at this stage disclose his plans, which in any case depended upon how far the first had fulfilled expectations. He considered, however, that, even if the Germans intervened with reinforcements, the Allies would be in a position to impose their will upon the enemy more easily than in the first phase, and that " distant and audacious goals con-" stituted by the adversary's vital points, Niš and Sofia," might be aimed at.

THE OPPOSING FORCES.

At the beginning of September the Allied Armies of the East consisted of 28 divisions—eight French, six Serbian, four British, one Italian, and nine Greek. One more Greek division, the 9th (Yannina), originally allotted to Epirus, was in course of arrival at Florina. They were divided into four Armies: British Army, under General Milne, which had a total of four British and five Greek divisions, with a sixth Greek division in its rear area ready to be placed at its disposal; 1st Group of Divisions, under General d'Anselme, which had one French and two Greek divisions; Serbian Armies, under the Crown Prince with Voivode Mišić as Chief of the Staff, which had six Serbian and two French divisions; Armée Française d'Orient, under General Henrys, which had five French divisions, one Italian, and one Greek. The Greek Army Command was, it will be seen, not represented, its divisions being split up; but at a certain stage of the operations the Commander-in-Chief, General Danglis, was to take over the Struma front.[1]

1918. Sept. Map 4.

The enemy's front, from right to left, was held by the so-called German *Eleventh Army* under General von Steuben, with two German corps staffs, the LXII and LXI, under each of which were three Bulgarian divisions,[2] and a seventh

---

[1] The Allied Order of Battle is given in Appendix 2.
[2] The German *302nd Division* included in the above was, again, German only in respect of its commander and staff.

Bulgarian division directly under Army headquarters; the Bulgarian *First Army* under General Nerezov, of three Bulgarian divisions; the Bulgarian *Second Army* under General Lukov, of three Bulgarian divisions, and the Bulgarian *Fourth Army* under General Toshev, of one Bulgarian division and some other formations. The last-named Army was comparatively lately-formed, and as it held the coast from the mouth of the Struma to that of the Maritsa it was actually in contact with the Allies only on a narrow front—the sector between the Gulf of Orfano and Lake Tahinos. The German *Eleventh* and Bulgarian *First Armies* formed the *Army Group von Scholtz*, under the command of the German general of that name; the other two Armies were directly under Bulgarian G.H.Q. The Bulgarian Commander-in-Chief, General Jekov, had just entered a nursing-home in Vienna, and his place had been taken by the former *Second Army* commander, General Todorov.[1] The latter had been succeeded in command of the *Second Army* by General Lukov, formerly Chief of the Staff at Bulgarian G.H.Q.

The reserves were in small packets, owing to difficulties of lateral communication, and inadequate in proportion to the total strength, owing to the tendency of the Bulgarians to close up all their forces upon the front—a tendency which General von Scholtz was unable to eradicate. His Army Group reserve of seven battalions and three batteries was where one might expect a German commander of his experience to place it, at the key-point of Gradsko–Krivolak. That of the *Eleventh Army*, 10 battalions and five batteries, was at Prilep and south of the town; that of the *First Army*, nine battalions and some batteries, in the Vardar valley. The *Second Army* had only a single infantry regiment in Army reserve. A curious politico-military scheme was, however, to provide the enemy with another very valuable reserve. The German higher command had been informed that the Greek I Corps was half-hearted in its allegiance to the new Government and that many of the troops hankered after King Constantine. It had therefore decided to send the staff of the *6th Reserve Division*—a division just broken up in France—with six *Landwehr* battalions from Rumania to the Struma front. Here they

---

[1] The Bulgarian Order of Battle is given in Appendix 4.

THE OPPOSING FORCES 133

were to carry out propaganda, with the object of under- 1918.
mining the resisting-powers of the Greeks. By the eve of Sept.
the Allied attack two battalions had arrived and had just
begun patrolling—incidentally, meeting with a most unpleasant reception and discovering that the Greeks had not
the slightest intention of fraternizing. These battalions, and
the others still on the move, were drawn into the main battle.[1]

The strength of the Allies may be taken as 291
battalions [2] and 1,522 guns, and that of the enemy at
302 battalions (including reinforcement battalions) and
1,597 guns.[3] Only three German battalions remained
besides the six on their way, though there were some
Landsturm battalions on the Lines of Communication not
included in the above. The Bulgarians and Germans had
more machine guns than the Allies, but only the German
battalions had an equivalent of the British Lewis gun and
French *fusil-mitrailleur*. The Allied rifle strength was
about 180,000; that of the enemy probably a good deal
higher.[4] In aircraft the Allies had an immense superiority,
about 200 machines to 80.

Except in this one matter, the opposing forces were,
it will be observed, so nearly equal in strength that the
history of war does not furnish many parallel cases. The
Allies had, however, the advantage that the whole of their
force was in contact with the enemy and could be employed
in attack, whereas a considerable proportion of the enemy's
Fourth Army was more or less tied down to coast defence,
between the Struma and the Maritsa. Far more important
still, their troops were better fed and clad and were
altogether in better heart than those of the enemy. Yet
here there has been a good deal of exaggeration, fostered
by German writers who are anxious to find excuses for
defeat. The picture commonly painted represents one side
burning with ardour and the other sunk in dejection,
misery, and disgust with the war. To this it may be

---

[1] "Weltkriegsende an der Mazedonischen Front," p. 67.
[2] The British (War Office) figure is 296 battalions, but it gives the Italians 24 battalions, whereas they had only 19. The Serbian General Staff gives 289 battalions.
[3] These are the Bulgarian figures. The very difficult question of numbers is discussed in Note at end of Chapter.
[4] It is given in the Serbian report as 172,200 and by the British War Office as 204,000, but both these authorities under-estimate the number of battalions.

objected that a very fair proportion of the Allies were burning with fever, which is not conducive to military ardour, and also that in the autumn of 1918 no troops of nations which had endured four years of warfare were untouched by war-weariness. It may also be pointed out that the Bulgarians were by no means at their last gasp, and that they had not reached a depth of despair comparable to that of their Austro-Hungarian allies, or of destitution approaching that of their other allies, the Turks. By the standard of the Turks then preparing to face the great assault in Palestine they were, indeed, well off. Their communications were far better; they were not like the Turks short of munitions. They were short of food, partly through mismanagement, partly owing to German demands upon them, but not nearly so short as the Turks, since they had a rich agricultural and stock-rearing country behind them. Nor were they outnumbered.

There is no doubt that the turning of the tide on the Western Front had depressed the spirits of the Bulgarians. Germany's refusal to hand over to them the whole of the Dobruja had angered them. They regretted their entry into the war and hoped that their new Government, formed that summer by the moderate, M. Malinov, would extricate them from it. Allied propaganda, both within the country and by means of messages sent in various ways across the lines, had had a certain effect in weakening their will to resist. They were weary of German overlordship and chafed against the leadership of German commanders and the predominating power of German staff officers where the command was nominally Bulgarian. There is a story, which comes from both German and British sources, that large numbers of Bulgarian soldiers believed or affected to believe that Germany had made a three years' contract with Bulgaria, that it expired on the 15th September, and that the Army would then be allowed to march home.[1] One

---

[1] This precise date sounds suspiciously like an invention; for it looks as though the 15th had been subsequently chosen merely because it was the day of the attack. The convention between Germany, Austria-Hungary, and Bulgaria was signed on the 6th September 1915, and Bulgarian mobilization began on the 22nd September. Either date would more reasonably be supposed to mark the beginning of the three years' "contract." It may be added that during the retreat east of the Vardar Bulgarian officers told the mayor of Dabilja, near Strumica, that the "contract" expired on the 23rd and that the troops had anticipated its expiration by three days.

need not take very seriously what was possibly only the idle gossip of rest-camp and dugout, but it may well have been symptomatic of Bulgarian sentiment.

On the other hand, where minor operations and raids were concerned, there was no marked falling off to be observed in their courage; as late as the 13th September they issued from their trenches to meet a local French assault north of Monastir and to rout it completely. The number of desertions had actually decreased since the beginning of the year; nor had they ever been numerous considering that there were many Serbians, Greeks, and Rumanians in the Bulgarian ranks. When the offensive was launched the Bulgarians resisted stubbornly on the front of the main attack—standing up outside their trenches to fire and hurl grenades, according to some reports—held up the assault at certain points, and inflicted serious loss upon the attackers. Once their front was broken through they collapsed, as General Milne had long ago predicted they would, and west of the Vardar serious resistance was thereafter met with only at isolated points. On the Dojran front, where their defences were exceptionally strong and were held by the best division in their Army, they fought magnificently, even when their front west of the Vardar was completely smashed. In short, we may allow they were not the men they had been at the time of the Battle of Monastir and the Battle of Dojran, 1917, without attributing to them a deterioration so great as to make them no longer serious foes.

THE BRITISH PLANS AND PREPARATIONS.

The formal instructions of General Franchet d'Espérey were issued to General Milne on the 24th July.[1] After directing that measures should be taken to distract the enemy before and during the main attack, it was laid down that, when this attack had been launched and had made a certain progress, the forces at the disposal of General Milne would be required to drive back the Bulgarians from their positions east of the Vardar and cut their communication with Strumica. For this purpose the " P " Ridge and the heights between it and Lake Dojran must first of all be captured. The best method of doing so would be, it was

---

[1] A translation of the instructions is given in Appendix 7.

136 PLANS AND PRELIMINARIES

suggested, a heavy frontal attack with artillery preparation west of the lake and a surprise flank attack upon the Bulgarian defences on the Blaga Planina, a high spur of the Belašica Planina which ran down to the northern shore of the lake. For the purpose of the attack two Greek divisions, a group of three Greek 6-inch howitzer batteries, and a French armoured train of two 19-cm. guns would be placed at General Milne's disposal. The 2nd *bis* Regiment of Zouaves and the Greek 3rd Cavalry Regiment were afterwards added.

The receipt of these instructions was followed by the correspondence described in the last chapter. As was there stated, the British Government did not give their assent to to an offensive until the 4th September. General Milne, however, began his plans and preparations forthwith, having little enough time even as it was.

1918.
Aug.
On the 14th August General Franchet d'Espérey informed him of the rôle of the 1st Group of Divisions, the link between the forces under his command and the Serbian Armies.[1] During the period of preparation the 1st Group was to take a hand in the harassing of the enemy which was to be general over the whole front. When the attack was launched the Group was to prevent him from moving his reserves and to be prepared for a rapid pursuit should he attempt to slip away. Finally, when the progress of the attacks threatening the enemy's communications had begun to shake him, it was to launch, on the order of the Commander-in-Chief, a sudden attack through Huma in the direction of the Vardar between Miletkovo and Strumica Station.

In the same letter it was stated that the two Greek divisions to be placed at General Milne's disposal would be the Crete and the Seres, from the Corps of National Defence. The former was allotted by General Milne to the XVI Corps and began to concentrate about Gramatna on the Spants stream on the 24th August. The latter was attached to the XII Corps and began to cross the Vardar at Karasuli on the 28th. There was therefore time to give these divisions some training, for which purpose General Franchet d'Espérey lent General Milne the services of a French regimental commander, Colonel Thiry, who had carried out similar

---

[1] A translation of the letter is given in Appendix 10.

MAJOR AND MINOR ATTACKS

work with the troops which captured the Skra di Legen and had a thorough knowledge of Greek methods.

1918. Aug.

On the 17th General Milne submitted to General Franchet d'Espérey the provisional plans drawn up in accordance with the latter's instructions. We may neglect the minor operations to be carried out east of the Vardar during the preliminary period. West of the river, however, there was to be an attack of some importance by troops of the 27th Division on the 1st September. The objective was a strong outpost position, subsequently named from its most prominent feature the " Roche Noire Salient," north of the village of Alchak Mahale. After its capture efforts were to be made to bluff the enemy into the belief that an attack on his lines in rear was being prepared. It was hoped that, prior to the Franco-Serbian attack on the Moglena, the Bulgarian command would be given the impression that a thrust up the Vardar valley was contemplated, and that even after the Moglena attack had been launched it would not dare to move any troops from the immediate left bank of the Vardar for fear that the Allies might undertake an important secondary operation here.

The main British operation would consist of two simultaneous attacks : the principal one carried out by the XII Corps with the Seres Division and the 22nd Division against the defences from Lake Dojran to the " P " Ridge, inclusive ; the second carried out by the XVI Corps with the Crete Division, supported by the 28th, against the crest of the Blaga Planina. The first was to be preceded by wire-cutting and a bombardment in which chemical shell would be employed, and the advance was to be covered by a barrage. It was therefore to have the support of practically all the heavy artillery available and as much field artillery as could safely be withdrawn from the fronts of the 26th and 27th Divisions. The second had to overcome far less formidable defences but had to be preceded by a long advance in the open ; and the artillery allotted to it would be mainly composed of the divisional artillery of the two divisions engaged and five British mountain batteries.[1]

In order that the 22nd Division should be enabled to train for the attack, its two brigades in the line were relieved between the 15th and 17th August : that on the

---

[1] The exact allotment of artillery to the two corps is given in Chapter IX.

right by the 83rd Brigade of the 28th Division, which was transferred by rail and road from the XVI Corps area for the purpose, and that on the left by the 77th Brigade of the 26th Division. Major-General Duncan remained in command of his former front, but with all his own three infantry brigades in divisional or corps reserve and engaged in training for the coming encounter. This training lasted about three weeks and was progressive, starting with squad drill and ending with battalion operations, interspersed with route marches, musketry, bayonet fighting, practice attacks, and consolidation. There were throughout the whole period lectures and "specialist" classes for Lewis gunners,[1] signallers, scouts, and bombers. When the brigades of the 22nd Division moved up to the line again, two battalions of the 83rd Brigade returned to the XVI Corps. Br.-General R. H. Hare, with the 2/King's Own and the other units of the brigade, remained, the brigadier having a special part to play, as a link between the British command and the Seres Division in the coming attack.

The 2nd *bis* Regiment of Zouaves, the three Greek 6-inch howitzer batteries, and the French armoured train were also allotted to the XII Corps. The Greek 3rd Cavalry Regiment was allotted to the XVI Corps.

Map 2. In the Struma valley the Greek I Corps remained for the time being under the orders of General Briggs. General Paraskevopoulos was directed by him to be prepared to push forward his outpost line to include the villages on the Belitsa stream from Beglik Mahale to Prosenik and also Kjupri, the Bairaklis, and Haznadar, and to convert his present line of outposts into his main defensive position. He was also instructed to work out plans for the capture of Seres.[2]

Map 4. On the 31st August General Milne received the Commander-in-Chief's "Instruction Générale pour l'Exploitation,"[3] a document typical of the methods and character of its author. General Franchet d'Espérey went into detail to an extent seldom seen in modern orders, the commander of the 1st Group of Divisions in particular having the action

---

[1] It was during their training that the battalions received their twelve extra Lewis guns.

[2] Like General Milne, General Paraskevopoulos favoured an attack at Neohori and had prepared a detailed plan for one.

[3] A translation is given in Appendix 11. It will be observed that the exploitation referred to is that of the first phase.

of his divisions mapped out in a fashion that left him small discretion in their handling. The instructions, however, display a remarkable breadth of view and a complete mastery of the whole problem in hand. Despite their length, they are, moreover, clear, vivid, and terse. The exposition of the general principles on which the attack was to be conducted contains, in particular, a summary of the essentials in an operation of this type, and of the essentials only.

On all fronts, General Franchet d'Espérey pointed out, the experience had been that tactical success was developed too late because reserves were held too far in rear. In Macedonia the Allies were fortunate because, owing to the comparative weakness of the Bulgarian artillery—comparative as regards length of front, not as regards the artillery of the attackers—reserves could be closed up without risk. (He had himself directed the Serbian Chief of the Staff to revise his dispositions as originally planned in this respect and to close his reserve divisions right up on the leading ones at the foot of the mountains.) Every means that foresight could devise must be employed to ensure that the advance " took off "[1] without delay. The reserves would be used in part to press straight forward, in part to make lateral thrusts with the objects of enlarging breaches and increasing booty. But at every possible opportunity these reserves must be reconstituted, so that commanders might continue to influence the course of the battle. Once the front was broken, extreme boldness would pay large dividends. Every threat to their communications would prey upon the nerves of troops fighting on a front divided up into compartments ; and in this mountainous country the Bulgarian batteries, known to be short of horses, must inevitably be captured if every column pushed on while it could.

" March in several columns to outflank the enemy
" directly one column meets with resistance. Each column
" should be covered by an advanced guard and should keep
" touch with the neighbouring columns. Watch your
" flanks and your rear."

Such were the general instructions. The particular ones concerning the forces under General Milne's command

---

[1] In the original "décoller." The metaphor is taken from an aeroplane rising from the ground.

emphasized the importance of cutting off the retreat of the enemy to the Strumica defile and of clearing the Belašica Planina in order to open up the Vardar valley. They also laid down that the 27th Division on the right bank would cross the Vardar on reaching Pardovica and rejoin the main British forces on the left.

Training and preparation for the attack were carried out in humid heat, the shade temperature twice reaching 100 degrees and the thermometer climbing to over 90 degrees almost every day. As we have seen, every effort had been made that summer to hand over a large proportion of the hard work to civilian labour, and the policy had undoubtedly kept on their feet many soldiers who would otherwise have been in hospital. Now there was no help for it; the troops had to do the work in the forward zone, as civilians could not be employed there and in any case would not have been available in sufficient numbers. The men set about their toil pluckily, but it took heavy toll of their energies.

The engineer work of all kinds was necessarily on a big scale. One very heavy task for which preparations had to be made was that of putting the whole Constantinople Railway between Dojran Station and Demir Hisar into working order at the earliest possible moment. Observation posts of steel or reinforced concrete had to be prepared for both artillery and infantry; new dugouts for command posts and telephone exchanges had to be constructed; concrete emplacements had to be made for batteries which would be situated further forward than in the days of trench warfare; light bridges had to be constructed and placed in position to enable field guns to cross the trenches and watercourses near the front line, so that there should be no delay in the advance of the artillery, and the roads in the forward area had to be prolonged for the same purpose and for the passage of supplies. Water-supply had to be increased by the opening up of springs and the provision of tanks, and where these latter were in the trenches they had to be splinter-proofed. Communication trenches had to be deepened and labelled. Dumps of R.E. stores had to be formed, and wire, pickets, and sandbags had to be made up into loads for pack-mules and carrying-parties. In rear areas the extra traffic on the roads called for unceasing repair.

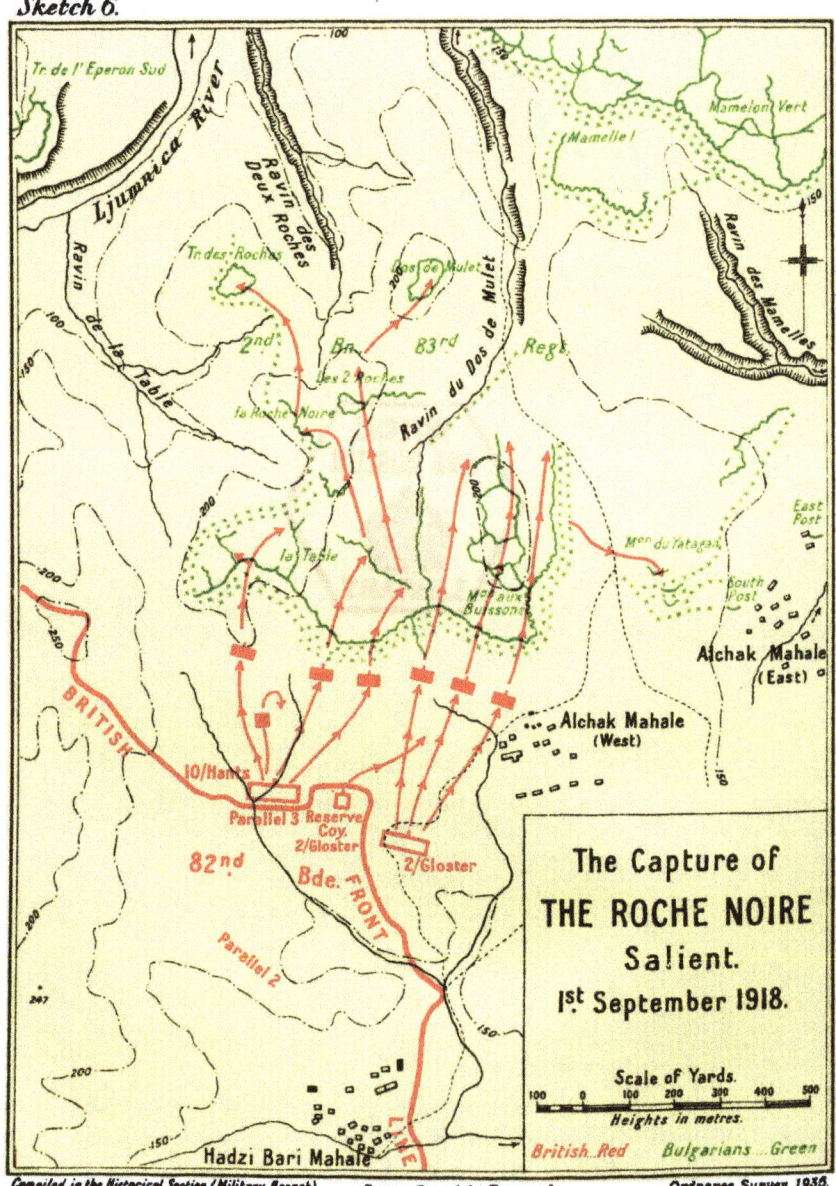

The signal communications in the British zone were now so excellent that there was little to be done beyond strengthening the forward lines and, on the XII Corps front, burying cable to protect it against shell-fire. Pigeons were trained in readiness to be taken forward in the attack, and there were demonstrations with signalling panels for use with aeroplane contact patrols. The 38th Airline Section, attached to XVI Corps Signals, was converted from horse to motor transport, and proved invaluable in the pursuit.

1918. Aug.

The arrival of stores of all kinds and especially of ammunition in unprecedented quantities, their unloading in harbour and transport to railheads, threw upon the dock services and the railways a strain greater than had ever previously been experienced. New sidings at Dudular, the sorting and marshalling station outside Salonika, and at Bralo, the railhead for the Taranto route, were delayed by lack of labour. There was also a shortage of staff owing to sickness at a moment when extra trains were constantly being called for and when every engine and every engine crew were working full time. Trains failed to keep up to their time-tables, and in some cases had to be cancelled for lack of personnel. In the words of Colonel G. D. Rhodes, Director of Railways, the whole railway system was throughout the month of August " on the verge of a break-down." There was worse to come, as it was not until September that the traffic reached its greatest height on both standard-gauge and light railways. Yet, though trains continued to run late, all the essential demands made upon the railways were met. It may be added that when the advance had begun and railhead was moved to Dojran Station the capacity of the line proved far greater than that of the roads beyond.

THE CAPTURE OF THE ROCHE NOIRE SALIENT.

The attack on the Roche Noire Salient was carried out by the 2/Gloucestershire and 10/Hampshire of the 82nd Brigade (Br.-General R. E. Solly-Flood). These battalions had ten days' training, including practice attacks over a full-sized replica of the enemy's position. A sand model was also employed for the instruction of the troops. The Roche Noire Salient formed, roughly, a square of a 1,000 yards on the right bank of the Ljumnica. It jutted out far

1 Sept. Sketch 6.

142 PLANS AND PRELIMINARIES

in advance of the main Bulgarian line and was not connected with it by communication trenches, though three ravines of which the bottoms were screened from view served the same purpose. One of these ravines ran through the salient from north to south, dividing it approximately in half. The position was strongly fortified, with a continuous trench containing machine-gun emplacements and covered on its southern face by a double or triple belt of wire. In the eastern half, on a dominating hummock called the Mamelon aux Buissons, was a big closed work.

The artillery available to support the attack was adequate for so small an operation, though the divisional artillery consisted at the moment of only twenty-four 18-pdrs., twelve 4·5-inch howitzers, and the attached 4-gun Bute Mountain Battery.[1] The heavy artillery was, however, powerful, consisting of 31 heavy guns and howitzers.[2] Three trench-mortar batteries, each of six 6-inch Newton mortars, were also attached to the divisional artillery. Harassing fire and bombardment of selected points having been carried out from the middle of August, the real preparation for the attack, including the wire-cutting, began on the 25th and lasted until the 27th. The last four days prior to the assault were employed in keeping open the gaps already made and in bombardment of the main line in rear.

Experience had shown that the enemy was very alert at night, whereas by day his front line appeared to be empty. The British artillery having cleverly drawn his defensive barrage time after time, it had also been noted that this was not put down until four minutes after it had

---

[1] When the 27th Division crossed the Vardar in June it had brought with it only its XIX and XX Brigades R.F.A. and the howitzer batteries of the I and CXXIX Brigades. The two latter brigades, minus their howitzer batteries, remained on the Struma with the Greek I Corps until mid-August. By the time they were relieved by Greek artillery, plans were far advanced for the attack on the Dojran front, for which they would be required. They were therefore at once attached to the 22nd Divisional Artillery. With the 27th Division there was only the XIX Brigade (three 4-gun 18-pdr. batteries), the XX Brigade (two 6-gun 18-pdr. batteries and one 4-gun 4·5-inch howitzer battery), D/I and D/CXXIX Batteries (both 4-gun 4·5-inch howitzer), and the Bute Battery (four 2·75-inch guns).

[2] One section 424th Siege Battery (8-inch. howitzer), 127th, 396th, and 7th Greek Siege Batteries (6-inch howitzer), 143rd, 153rd, and 180th Heavy Batteries (60-pdr.), two French 19-cm. guns in the armoured train, one French 16-cm. gun, and two French 100-mm. guns. The heavy artillery was all directly at the disposal of the division and commanded by Lieut.-Colonel O. S. Cameron, acting C.R.A.

been called for. It was therefore decided by the divisional commander, Major-General Forestier-Walker, that the attack must take place by daylight, in the late afternoon, and that the troops must be pushed as quickly as possible across no-man's-land in order to escape the barrage. There was risk in keeping the two battalions all day in the British front line, which was in view of Bulgarian observation posts ; had they been discovered they would have been heavily bombarded, and the attack would doubtless have failed. This risk was lessened by screening trenches and approaches some time in advance ; for the rest, the commander counted on the discipline of the troops, who were strictly enjoined to lie low and make no movement. A further difficulty was that, as the British trenches curved abruptly south-east, the Gloucestershire on the right had to move out and assemble in no-man's-land in broad daylight ; otherwise the battalion would have had so far to go that it could not have avoided the barrage. The advance was to begin at 5.30 p.m., but the British barrage was not to descend until six minutes later in the hope of delaying that of the enemy. It had also been arranged that a few rounds of 6-inch howitzer shell with instantaneous fuze should be dropped in front of the objective just before the hour of the assault, in order to create a curtain of dust, the ground being dry as powder.

1918.
1 Sept.

The plan worked well, all the assaulting troops having crossed the 300 yards separating their " jumping-off " line from the enemy's trenches before his barrage came down, with the exception of the reserve company of the 10/Hampshire. This company had for some unknown reason halted for three minutes, and suffered severely. On the right the 2/Gloucestershire captured the Mamelon aux Buissons, meeting with little opposition. On the left the 10/Hampshire had some resistance from bombers to overcome at Les Deux Roches and La Roche Noire. By 6.30 p.m. men of this battalion were seen on the Dos de Mulet and Tranchée des Roches, though, owing to the cutting of telephone wires, casualties among runners, and clouds of dust and smoke, no reports came in from this quarter for over two hours.

The enemy had quickly shortened his fire, which was very heavy and caused far more loss during the period of consolidation than in that of the assault. It had originally been intended to hold the captured position (excluding the Dos de Mulet and Tranchée des Roches, which it had been decided to abandon after the fall of darkness) with only one company from each battalion. As, however, neither battalion had been much more than 350 strong in the attack and both had suffered severely, this could not be carried out.

At 4.30 a.m. on the 2nd the enemy put down a creeping barrage on his lost position, at the same time bombarding the approaches in rear. "C" Company of the Hampshire was then just about to withdraw to the British trenches, but was at once ordered to man La Roche Noire. Just before 5 a.m. the enemy launched a counter-attack on Les Deux Roches and got a footing on the north slope. He was immediately expelled by a counter-attack. Soon afterwards the bombardment died down and the attackers were left in possession of their gains.

The casualties had been considerable, especially in the Hampshire battalion, 298 including those of the artillery and engineers.[1] Sixty-seven prisoners and a machine gun were captured. The courage and endurance of the Gloucestershire and Hampshire had been beyond all praise. They had, it is true, little resistance to meet from the Bulgarian infantry or machine gunners, who had been overwhelmed by the artillery preparation and the barrage. On the other hand they had afterwards to face a tremendous bombardment, as the enemy's artillery was able to concentrate the fire of a great number of pieces upon this small area. On this rocky ground, moreover, it was impossible to dig in to any depth.

During the night of the 1st September the 81st Brigade occupied the enemy's outposts from the newly-captured Roche Noire Salient to the railway in the Vardar valley. Here the enemy's infantry made no resistance. The following night the 1/Royal Scots captured a work on the railway known as Le Crochet. Here again there was no opposition beyond artillery fire, the garrison decamping in haste. The outpost line was then extended to the Vardar, being now level with that held by the 82nd Brigade and within from 300 to 500 yards of the main Bulgarian line.

---

[1]

	Killed	Wounded	Missing
Officers	1	11	—
Other Ranks	37	233	16

THE BULGARIAN EFFECTIVES

NOTE.

THE BULGARIAN EFFECTIVES.

The Bulgarian General Staff has courteously furnished, through H.M. Minister at Sofia, a detailed Order of Battle of the Bulgarian Armies on the 14th September 1918. This includes tables giving the numbers of battalions, machine guns, trench mortars, guns, and squadrons, which are shown in total figures, by Armies, and by divisions, etc. The totals are as follows :— *1918. Sept.*

	Inf. Bns.	Pi. Bns.	M.G.'s	T.M.'s	Guns.	Sqdns.
Eleventh Army [1]	158	8¼	1,575	781	560	18
First Army	67	3	694	599	454	4½
Second Army	44	3	461	124	271	17
Fourth Army	33	2	332	148	312	22
Total	302	16¼	3,062	1,652	1,597	61½

Obviously these figures can be accepted without question, and there would at first sight appear to be no more to be said on the subject. When, however, we find that the estimates made by the Allied Intelligence Services were astonishingly different, we are compelled to give some further consideration to the question. The British (War Office) estimate on the 11th September was as follows :—

Inf. Bns.	Guns.	Sqdns.
267	1,309	36

and this estimate of the infantry is confirmed by Colonel Nédeff, who gives 268 battalions. These differences appear grotesque, but, as regards the infantry, there is not much difficulty in bridging the gap. Analysing the Bulgarian figures, we find included in their total of battalions 18 " composite " battalions, four reinforcement battalions, two Storm battalions, two L. of C. battalions, and one Frontier battalion (gendarmerie). We also find that they include four of the six newly-arrived [2] German infantry battalions, one German reinforcement battalion, and one Austrian battalion, none of which are given by the British. If we add these 33 battalions to the British figure of 267, the total is 300, which is only two less than the Bulgarian figure. And it is probable that the Bulgarian composite battalions as well as those actually labelled " reinforcement " were normally used to supply reinforcements to the line regiments.[3] As regards cavalry, the Bulgarian figure includes squadrons of gendarmerie and military police, which were presumably scattered and need scarcely be counted. The question of the artillery is different. Here, however, the error presumably lies chiefly in the Allies' ignorance of the very large proportion of artillery with the Bulgarian *Fourth Army*. This artillery was obviously intended for coast defence ; the bulk of it never came into action and had no effect upon the battle. The British figures do therefore give a not inadequate estimate of the forces which the Allies had to face, except that the British Intelligence was not yet aware of the arrival of six further German battalions and knew only of the presence of the three already in Macedonia.

---

[1] Including Army Group Troops of the Army Group von Scholtz.
[2] See p. 132.
[3] The British Intelligence knew of their existence but very little else about them.

The Bulgarian rifle strength may be taken as about 200,000, the combatant strength (including staffs, artillery, engineers, signal companies, machine-gunners, pioneers, etc.) as over 300,000, and the ration strength as over 450,000. For a country with a population of about four and a half millions this represents an enormous effort, especially as there were still at least 50,000 troops, mostly of old classes, in the interior, in the Dobruja, and in Northern Serbia.

The large reinforcements subsequently sent by Germany and Austria-Hungary cannot be considered here, as they arrived for the most part only after the Armistice with Bulgaria had been concluded and the Bulgarian Armies had withdrawn from the conflict.

The Dobropolje. (The central peak is the Pyramid. The peak behind the tree is the Kotka South, which masks the Kotka North.)

[*Photographie Boissonnas.*]

CHAPTER VIII.

THE FINAL OFFENSIVE: THE BATTLE OF THE DOBROPOLJE.[1]

(Maps 4, 6 ; Sketches A, 5, 7.)

THE CAPTURE OF THE VETRENIK, DOBROPOLJE, AND SOKOL.

The great Franco-Serbian assault was to be preceded by a single day's artillery preparation. The Commander-in-Chief hoped that this would take place on the 14th September, but he would not have the bombardment begun unless atmospheric conditions were favourable. The bombardment was intended to destroy the whole Bulgarian first-line position, neutralize all batteries covering it, and prevent reinforcements from entering the battle zone. Rather than risk a failure here, he was prepared to wait another day or two. The decision he left to the Voivode Mišić, who was to fix day and hour, and to give the signal from his aery on the Floka overlooking the battlefield. At the hour decided upon by him violent artillery action on the whole front from the Vardar valley to Monastir was to commence.

1918.
14 Sept.
Map 6.
Sketches A, 5.

On the 14th the Voivode waited only until he had seen a fine dawn and then decreed that the preparation should begin within two hours. To the headquarters of all the Armies the message went forth :—" Mettez en route quatorze " officiers et huit soldats," *i.e.*, " fire will be opened on the " 14th at 8 a.m."

All day long the bombardment roared, the mountains re-echoing its thunder and rolling it back into the valley of the Moglenitsa, which was an inferno of noise. For half an hour only, in the afternoon, did fire cease, to permit the French aircraft to photograph the damage. In this task, owing to the gusts of a fierce Vardar wind, they were not very successful. Yet it appeared that the results of the preparation had been satisfactory, and this news was confirmed by infantry patrols after the fall of darkness. Many clean gaps had been cut in the wire and at many points the

---

[1] The French official title. The Serbians call it the Battle of the Moglenitsa.

foremost trenches seemed to be completely destroyed. The enemy's reply had been feeble all the morning, but before dusk he began to bombard the rearward zone of the Franco-Serbian array. That most of his batteries were still intact was also proved by the strength of his barrage next morning, when at 5.30 a.m., in the murk before sunrise, the troops of the Serbian Second Army issued from their trenches and went forward to the assault.

1918.
15 Sept.

The ridge against which they were launched falls abruptly on its south-eastern flank to the western side of the Moglenitsa basin, and its face here, though curved and with some projecting tongues—of which the Vetrenik juts out most prominently from the main mountain mass—has when viewed from a distance a general appearance of regularity. On its north-western flank there is, however, no such steep descent. Behind the Vetrenik, in fact, there is a great spur running due north for a distance of nearly 15 miles to the right bank of the Crna; and after a slight dip the peaks of the Kozyak and the Kučkov Kamen rise actually higher than the Vetrenik itself. The fragmentary Bulgarian second and third systems of defence ran across this spur, and it was upon it that they were strongest.

When the south-eastern face of the Vetrenik–Sokol ridge is examined in detail, the general appearance of regularity disappears. West of the narrow col which links it to the Vetrenik, the region of the Dobropolje is broken and formless. On the southern side of this region is the double-peaked mountain, the Kotka, the northern summit of which was within the Bulgarian lines. The Kotka North, again, is linked by a col, known to the Allies as la Courtine, to a higher peak, the Pyramid of the Dobropolje. Behind la Courtine lies a curious marshy depression, nearly a square mile in extent, the Cuvette du Dobropolje, beyond which the ground rises to the plateau of Kravica. Here the Bulgarian first system of defence deepened, and there was a strong third line north of the Cuvette on the edge of the Kravica plateau and on the Kravički Kamen further east. From the Pyramid the ridge curves south-west and is broken by a deep ravine, beyond which rises the tooth of the Sokol. South-west of the Sokol the heights, mounting steadily to the Kajmakčalan, had been in the hands of the Allies almost exactly two years, and the Bulgarian line ran north-westward on one of the spurs projecting towards the valley of

CAPTURE OF THE VETRENIK

the Crna. The whole mountain face is of majestic beauty, the lower slopes being grass-grown or covered with low scrub, amid which are outcrops of limestone. Occasional coniferous trees overhang the valleys. The bareness of the peaks emerging from the green, by sharpening their outlines, adds to the effectiveness of the picture.

The rupture of the front was to be effected by the French 17th Colonial Division on the right, with the heights of Kravički Kamen, Kravica, and Goliak as its objectives; and on the left by the French 122nd Division, which was to capture the heights of the Dobropolje and the Sokol. On the right of the 17th the Serbian Šumadija Division was to cover its advance by simultaneously assaulting the Vetrenik and capturing the heights north of it. The Vetrenik formed a pronounced salient in the enemy's lines, a salient from which he would by day have been able to look down into the valley where the pursuit divisions, the Timok and Yugoslav, were to assemble. So steep was the southern slope that the position could be assaulted only from the flanks, by way of twisting paths.[1]

On the western slope of the Vetrenik the Serbians swarmed straight up to Point 1570 and captured it, taking 300 prisoners and six guns. On the eastern side the attack went more slowly. It was not till the afternoon that the whole objective was captured and that the Šumadija Division was able to support the 17th Colonial in its assault on the Kravički Kamen.

General Pruneau, commanding the 17th Colonial Division, had decided not to attack in the first instance the Bulgarian line between the Vetrenik and the Bichkiya stream, as the slopes were here particularly abrupt, thickly wooded, and dominated by the peaks north of the Vetrenik. He would contain it during the assault and take it in reverse at a later stage. West of the stream his troops went forward with irresistible determination. By 8 a.m. the second

---

[1] The account which follows is based on the official French report; on Revol, whose book is based on the documents in the archives of the Ministry of War; on the Serbian report; on Feyler, Vol. III; on the official " Étude sur la Guerre de Montagne "; (as regards the 17th Colonial Division) on the official " Historique des Troupes Coloniales "; and (as regards the 122nd Division) on " Une Division française à la Bataille du Dobropolié " by Captain Riniéri. For the 16th and 17th September the German official " Weltkriegsende an der Mazedonischen Front " has also been largely used.

objective on the right, the Kravica, had been stormed, but on the left the 1st Colonial Regiment was short of the Goliak, which was not taken until some two hours later. Now all was ready for the attack on the Kravički Kamen, which General Pruneau had ordered to be carried out from the left flank. Before that could be launched the Bulgarians counter-attacked boldly. The division was in advance of those on either flank and endured an evil two hours. Five times the enemy came on. On one occasion he re-established himself on the all-important plateau of Kravica. The success of the whole affair seemed to hang for a moment in the balance. But the enemy was driven off in his turn and the Kravica was retaken. On the right the Šumadija Division carried the Borova Čuka, which was actually one of the French objectives, removing thus a galling machine-gun nest on the flank; and about 3.45 p.m. a battalion of the 54th Colonial Regiment, again aided by troops of the Šumadija Division, stormed the Kravicki Kamen. So vital did the intervention of the Šumadija Division appear to Br.-General Plunkett, the representative of the British C.I.G.S. with the Serbian Armies, that he wrote in his report to the War Office :—" It is probable that if only Western " European troops had been available the attack would at " this stage have petered out and the whole offensive " movement have failed, as in the spring of 1917."

On the front of the 122nd Division General Topart had formed two columns of attack, as the ravine between the Dobropolje and the Sokol was impassable. The right column, having in the Dobropolje and the Kotka the bigger objective, was by far the stronger, and consisted of two regiments. The attack quickly overran the foremost trenches, despite the stout resistance of the Bulgarians, who stood on their parapets and hurled grenades down upon the heads of the assailants. A flame-thrower accounted for one of their machine-gun detachments in the centre which resisted to the last. The advance was at once continued behind a barrage moving at the rate of 100 metres in four minutes, and the Pyramid was carried by a convergent assault soon after 7.30 a.m. Now came the turn of the battalion in second line, which had to make its way along the ridge bordering the Cuvette du Dobropolje and capture the work on Point 1765 at its north-western corner. This attack was to have been launched at seven behind a fresh

[Photographie Boissonnas.

The Sokol, looking north-west from the heights above Gorgni Pojar. On the left, the slopes of the Belo Grotlo.

barrage, which could be put back half an hour in response to a rocket signal. The battalion (the 1st of the 45th Regiment) was late, but the signal had not been given ; the barrage had therefore moved forward at the hour fixed. Several attempts were made to advance without it, but they were fruitless, except that one company made some ground by following a communication trench along the ridge. Finally, the machine-gun fire grew too hot, and all progress ceased. A fresh bombardment at 10.15 did not break down the resistance of Point 1765 or that of a work, known as the Fortin Bulgare, half-way between it and the Dobropolje. At 11 a.m. another bombardment, directed by an observer from the summit of the Dobropolje, began. This time the field artillery of the second-line division, the Yugoslav, which had gallantly come into action in the open close up to the Dobropolje, took part. A barrage from all the available weapons of accompaniment, Stokes mortars, Brandt guns,[1] 37-mm. infantry guns, and machine guns, was also organized. Under this protection the battalion went on " literally man by man, from rock to rock." At 2 p.m. it took the Fortin Bulgare, and almost immediately afterwards Point 1765 was carried.

1918.
15 Sept.

The Sokol also proved a stiff obstacle. The battalion which was to assault it on the southern face was in touch with one of the Serbian First Army which was to take part in the attack. Meeting intense machine-gun and trench-mortar fire from concrete emplacements which the artillery had not destroyed, the French battalion suffered considerable loss. It fought its way through the foremost trenches, but was then held up 150 yards short of the summit and could make no further progress all day. The Serbian battalion was likewise unable to get forward. General Topart sent up to the Sokol two companies held in divisional reserve, but they did not arrive till dusk and were hardly required. The enemy, thoroughly shaken, had already begun to remove his machine guns. Without their aid the resistance collapsed, and a rush in the dark carried the crest.

Thus on the whole front of the Serbian Second Army

---

[1] General Milne had handed over 12 Stokes mortars to the French a month earlier for this operation. The *canon Brandt* was a little 60-mm. pneumatic howitzer, with a projectile weighing only one kilogram, a range of 400 metres, and a rate of fire of 10 to 12 rounds a minute.

the assault had been successful, the crest had been gained, and the breach in the defences had been opened. It had taken longer than General Franchet d'Espérey had anticipated, but it would be wrong to declare that the operation had fallen behind its time-table, for that would imply a rigidity which was outside his conception. Anyhow, the way was now open for the advance on the Kozyak, while the First Army, freed from observation and flanking fire from the Sokol, could also go forward. This splendid feat of arms had been attended by losses heavy enough, but lighter than might have been expected. The Šumadija Division had about 500 casualties, the 17th Colonial 1,230,[1] the 122nd 790. The 17th Colonial Division had taken over 1,000 prisoners and the 122nd Division 1,400; in all nearly 3,000, with 33 guns, had been captured.

The Voivode Stepanović had not waited for the capture of the Sokol. He had pushed his pursuit divisions right up on to the heels of the two French assaulting divisions, and at 6 p.m. they began to pass through the latter. The drama of the scene, the troops of one nation advancing into the breach made by those of its ally, was heightened by the fact that the frontier here coincided with the position which the French had stormed. It appealed intensely to the emotions of the Serbians. As they marched through the assault divisions and at the same time set foot upon their own soil, men broke from the ranks to shake by the hand and embrace French soldiers, and their columns went forward chanting the *Marseillaise*. The Voivode Mišić directed the Second Army commander to continue the advance during the night so as not to lose contact with the enemy. Following the ridge which led to the Bulgarian second position on the Kozyak, three miles north of the Kravica plateau, the Yugoslav Division moved straight on its objective and was ready to assault it before dawn on the 16th. On its right the Timok Division found the Golo Bilo unoccupied and moved on towards the Topolec ridge, north-east of the Kozyak.

Meanwhile welcome support had appeared on the left flank. The Serbian First Army had accomplished practi-

---

[1] So the French official report and "Historique des Troupes Coloniales," probably including over two hundred casualties suffered in the Bulgarian counter-bombardment and the patrol actions of the 14th; Revol says 912.

THE ENEMY'S SITUATION 153

cally nothing on the 15th. It had originally been intended that its leading divisions, the Drina and Danube, should advance at 9 a.m., by which time the Voivode Bojović hoped that the Second Army would have broken the line on his right. In the afternoon, despite the fact that the Sokol was untaken and that the heavy artillery supporting the main attack was not available to assist him, he had attempted to advance, but had failed completely. However, after the fall of darkness, he tried again, and this time there was little or no opposition on his right. By 10 a.m. on the 16th the Drina Division was over the Gradešnica river. On the left, however, the advance of the Danube Division was contested, the enemy doubtless realizing the urgent importance of maintaining his communications across the Crna. The third Serbian division, the Morava, now went through on the right and found touch with the Yugoslav in front of the enemy's second line of defence.

1918.
16 Sept.

Let us consider the situation as it appeared to the commander of the enemy's Army Group, General von Scholtz. After noon on the 15th the Allied artillery fire had slackened everywhere except between the Vetrenik mountain and the Crna. He could now define the scope of the attack, and soon after nightfall he could estimate the damage. It was very serious, but by no means irreparable. The inner flanks of the Bulgarian *2nd* and *3rd Divisions* had been broken. Owing to the Bulgarian habit of massing their troops on a single line, the losses had been very heavy; and such local reserves as they had had been used up. But the outer flanks were intact and little artillery had been lost. There was no reason why the attack should not be contained if reserves could be moved quickly enough into the breach. And if it could thus be contained, even for 24 hours, it would probably die of inanition, as had many another attack on terrain more favourable than this. He sent what troops he could from his own resources and four battalions from the right of the *LXI Corps* beyond the Crna, placing the broken inner wings of the two Bulgarian divisions and the reinforcements under the orders of General von Reuter, the commander of his reserve. The commander of the *Eleventh Army*, General von Steuben, had already during the afternoon of the 15th ordered a withdrawal to the second line, which ran from the Crna across the heights of the Gradešnica Kossa and the Kozyak to the Preslap. We see now why

154   THE BATTLE OF THE DOBROPOLJE

the Timok, Yugoslav, Morava, and Drina Divisions were practically unopposed during their advance to this line.[1]

THE CAPTURE OF THE SECOND AND THIRD SYSTEMS OF DEFENCE.

Maps 4, 6.
Sketch, 7.
The available accounts of the fighting on the 16th are confused, conflicting, and on the French side scanty. Where the French and Serbian versions differ from the German, it is pretty certain that the latter is correct.[2] The German account is much the more detailed, and it is evident that whereas the German commanders, on ground familiar to the defence but not to the attack, knew at what hour their rear guards left their successive positions, the Serbian command was sometimes unaware of the exact positions of its advanced troops.

According to the French account, the Yugoslav Division set foot on the south-western peak of the Kozyak, Point 1810, at dawn on the 16th, and captured Point 1820 at noon; in the course of the afternoon it was driven from them by a counter-attack, but recovered them before dusk. The Germans state that all attacks on the Kozyak were repulsed throughout the day, and that though the works west of it were captured, a fresh position was taken up on the Ljubinica heights in rear, and all seemed well until after sunset. At 7 p.m., however, the Bulgarians on the Kozyak and the Ljubinica suddenly gave way, and a catastrophe was averted only by the arrival north of the Kozyak of the *13th Saxon Reserve Jäger Battalion*. As has been stated, the German account is probably correct, but from our point of view it does not greatly matter. For, in the course of the night, not only the Kozyak but the whole Bulgarian second-line position from thence to the Crna fell into the hands of the Serbians.

The enemy had, in fact, been forced to the decision to withdraw to his third line, from the western slopes of the Duditsa mountain, across the Blatec Planina, south of Polčište and Bešišta, to the Crna, north of Crbren. This involved the abandonment, on his left, of the trenches about Zborsko, which he still held intact, and, on his right, of the

---

[1] The enemy's dispositions are given in more detail in Note at end of Chapter.
[2] " Weltkriegsende an der Mazedonischen Front."

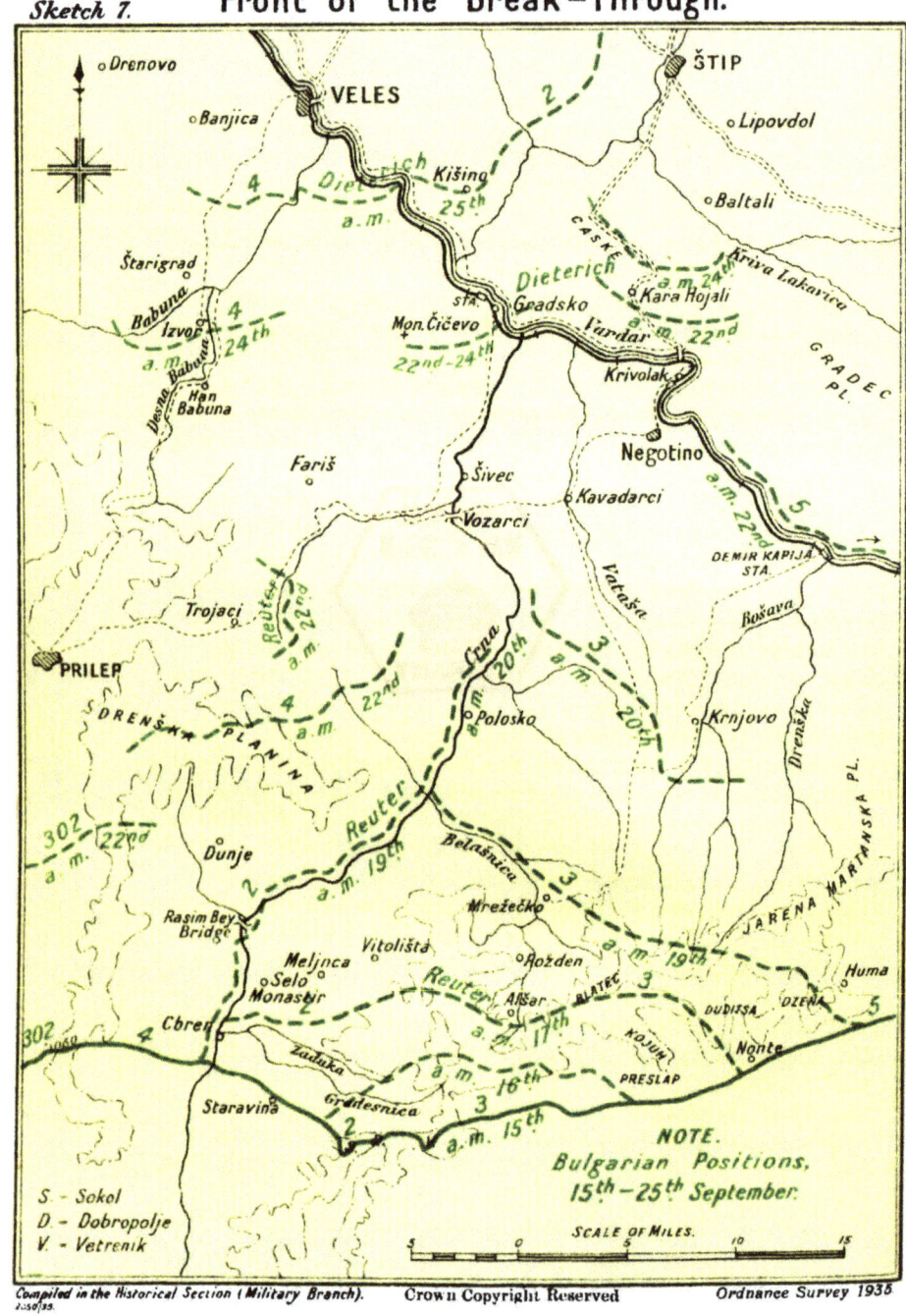

BULGARIAN DEMORALIZATION 155

front line from Gradešnica to the Crna, where the Allies had not yet even attempted to advance. We speak of his decision to withdraw; but where the shattered troops in the centre of the breach were concerned the decision meant only that he put what reserves he could on the new line and determined to stop the fugitives when they fell back to it, as inevitably they would. Pistol in hand, General von Reuter and his staff succeeded in this task. On the ridge north of the Kozyak there was hard fighting before dawn on the 17th, the Saxon Jägers counter-attacking boldly and not retiring until 5.30 a.m., when the Bulgarians on their either hand had already departed. Once again the line seemed fairly well established.

1918.
17 Sept.

The consequence of the withdrawal was that after dawn on the 17th the advancing Serbians met with little or no resistance until in the afternoon they came in contact with the new position, while the extreme right flank of the Armée Française d'Orient had only to overcome the opposition of small rear guards before occupying the villages of Štaravina and Zović. Then followed an incident which bore grim witness to the demoralization of the Bulgarians and to the heights in their hierarchy to which it had ascended. On the Serbian left the blow was struck in air. The trenches in front of it were found empty at 3 p.m. What had happened was that the commander of the *2nd Division*, without orders from the higher command, without informing it or the troops on his left of what he was about to do, and without being seriously pressed by the Serbians, had ordered his troops back behind the Crna. South of Polčište and Bešišta he left a yawning gap, from four to five miles in breadth.

The Serbian First Army thus had a way cleared for it. The vanguard of the Danube Division pressed on to Selo Monastir, which it reached about the fall of darkness, but beyond which it found itself confronted by a strong bridgehead covering Rasim Bey bridge. The Drina occupied Vitolište and Meljnca by nightfall, but was not in touch with the enemy or, in the darkness, fully aware of the gap that had momentarily opened in front of it.

That, however, applied only to the front from the neighbourhood of Polčište to the Crna. Between Polčište and Alšar the enemy clung stubbornly to his third line during the morning and early afternoon, and here the Morava and Yugoslav Divisions were hotly engaged. The central buttress of this position, Point 1737—known to the enemy as the Tribor—was held by the Saxon *Jäger* battalion after its withdrawal across the Kučkov Kamen. Once again the Germans beat off all attacks;[1] but by 5 p.m. the Bulgarians had been driven in on either hand, and the battalion was almost surrounded. In the course of the night it fell back to Mrežečko. Further east the Timok Division attacked the height of Blatec, with the result that the Bulgarians retreated in wild confusion, some battalions already in a state of mutiny. Further east still the extreme left of the 1st Group of Divisions was for the first time on the move. The " Groupement Rondet "[2] occupied Zborsko and advanced on the Preslap.

During the night of the 17th and in the course of the following morning the Bulgarian line fell back behind the Belašnica stream from its junction with the Crna to Mrežečko, and thence to the Dzena mountain. At the junction of the two rivers the line was almost at right angles to that of the troops which had withdrawn behind the Crna. The Belašnica was a considerable obstacle and the Crna a very formidable one indeed. Once more the breach was closed after a fashion. But the barriers placed across it were rotten; for the Bulgarian troops, dejected, wearied out, and in some cases mutinous, could no longer be relied upon. It is not without justice that French historians consider the battle of rupture, the Battle of the Dobropolje, as ending at nightfall on the 17th September. The Bulgarians were not yet in retreat, and on the Crna flank they were with German aid to hold out for two days more. East of the Crna, however, they were to be hustled back so swiftly that the Allied advance thenceforth may fitly be described as a pursuit.

---

[1] The battalion must now have been considerably under 400 strong; its machine guns had not been able to reach it from Dunje; and it had only four light machine guns, with little ammunition. Its part in the action is proof of how much morale and special training can accomplish, even for a handful of men, in mountain warfare. (See " Das Kgl. Sächs. Reserve-Jäger-Bataillon Nr. 13 im Weltkriege," pp. 148–54.)

[2] This consisted of a Franco-Greek force drawn from the 16th Colonial and Greek 4th Divisions. Having received a premature report that the Serbians of the Second Army had reached the upper Poroi west of the Preslap, Colonel Rondet had already attacked on the 16th and had been repulsed.

NOTE.

THE BATTLE FROM THE ENEMY'S SIDE.

The preparations of the Allies had naturally not passed unnoticed by **Map 4.** the enemy, who saw that something was afoot, without realizing the **Sketch 7.** nature of the plan. By the end of August General von Scholtz expected the main attack to take place astride the eastern arm of the Crna, with a secondary attack in the Vardar valley.[1] On the 9th September he pushed forward the Bulgarian *73rd Regiment* and *13th Saxon Reserve Jäger Battalion*, which formed part of his reserve of seven battalions, from the Gradsko area to Prilep and Dunje. At the same time the Army commander, General von Steuben, moved the Bulgarian *53rd Regiment* and a German machine-gun company into close support of the *2nd Division*. To what an extent the enemy was deceived is, however, shown by the fact that on the 14th, in the midst of the bombardment—which, it will be recalled, was general from the valley of the Vardar to the plain of Monastir—he moved the Bulgarian *73rd Regiment* and the *12th Saxon Reserve Jäger Battalion* down to the railhead of the light railway from Prilep, Berance Station, north of Monastir. Later in the day, however, the Bulgarian *16th Regiment* was stationed at Rasim Bey bridge, where it could intervene on either bank of the river.

As has been stated, the Franco-Serbian attack struck the inner flanks of the **Bulgarian** *2nd* and *3rd Divisions*, of which the *2nd* formed part of the *LXI Corps* and the *3rd* was directly under the *Eleventh Army*. From the Sokol to the Vetrenik there were in line four regiments (12 battalions), two of each division. Each regiment had 32 machine guns.

On the afternoon of the 15th General von Scholtz handed over the last of his reserve, sending a German training battalion to the *LXI Corps* and the Bulgarian *49th Regiment* to Alšar, to join the *3rd Division*. At the same time General von Steuben ordered a withdrawal to the second system of defence. General Surén, commanding the *LXI Corps*, despatched the Bulgarian *81st Regiment*, a battalion of the *16th Regiment*, and two batteries from the bend of the Crna to the new line behind the *2nd Division*. General von Reuter, hitherto commanding the Army Group reserve, and a small staff were placed at the disposal of the *Eleventh Army*, to take over the inner flanks of the *2nd* and *3rd Divisions*, and the bulk of the reinforcements. This new force was entitled the "Composite " Division Reuter." It consisted of the left brigade of the *2nd Division* (*10th* and *30th Regiments*), a composite Bulgarian brigade of the *53rd* and *81st Regiments*, the right brigade of the *3rd Division* (*29th*, *32nd*, and *80th Regiments*), the *13th Saxon Reserve Jäger Battalion*, four Bulgarian batteries, some German heavy and mountain artillery, two German mountain machine-gun companies, etc. The units which had been in the fight were cut to ribbons; others were in some cases distant from the front; and all was confusion, so that it was some time before General von Reuter could exercise effective command over the newly-organized formation.

Before he could be said to have done so, on the evening of the 16th, the commander of the *2nd Division*, Major-General Rušev, after the loss of the Kozyak, ordered his troops to retire to the third line, Bešišta–Point 1737. So far as can be gathered from the German account, this withdrawal was rather premature than unauthorized; it was also made without warning to the neighbouring divisions. It necessitated the withdrawal, on the right, of the troops from the Crna to Štaravina—the left brigade of the *4th Division*—behind the Crna and its tributary, the Zaduka brook; and, on the left, of the *3rd Division* to the line Alšar–the

---

[1] "Weltkriegsende an der Mazedonischen Front," pp. 25 *et seq.*

Blatec–Duditsa. General von Reuter's section of this new front, the centre, from Polčište to Alšar, was, thanks to his energy, well established. Until after noon on the 17th he was confident of holding it. But he had reckoned without General Rušev.

The Army commander, General von Steuben, had, as was only right and proper, looked on the black side as well as the bright, and had instructed the commander of the *LXI Corps* that if the line proved untenable, the *2nd Division* would be ordered to retire astride the road from Polčište to Rasim Bey bridge and take up a position on the far bank of the Crna. General Surén did not pass this information on to the divisional commander, whose replacement he had demanded, fearing that it would induce him to retire at once. At midday there came a message from Bulgarian G.H.Q. directing that General Rušev should be replaced by General Niklov. Until the latter's arrival, General von Reuter was to take over the *2nd Division*. However, before he could do so, General Rušev, having apparently learnt of the conditional instructions for retirement from a German liaison officer, suddenly ordered his division back behind the Crna.

Thus was the third position lost; for it was obviously impossible now for the troops on the left of the *2nd Division* to maintain their section of it with this gap on their right. The incident may not have had a vital influence on the course of the battle, because in the then state of the Bulgarian troops the line was bound to break sooner or later. It nevertheless saved the Serbians a fight which might well have been hot, and certainly some delay in their progress, at a time when every hour was valuable to the Allied command.

CHAPTER IX.

THE FINAL OFFENSIVE: THE BATTLE OF DOJRAN.
(Maps 5, 7; Sketches 8, 9.)
THE DOJRAN DEFENCES AND DEFENDERS.

BRITISH airmen, who knew the whole front from the Gulf of Orfano to the plain of Monastir, declared that, as they swept along the Bulgarian line, they could detect at a glance how much stronger it was between Lake Dojran and the Vardar, and especially from the lake to the " P " Ridge, than anywhere else. This sector always struck them as constituting a very fortress, and its numerous deep trenches and thick belts of wire recalled the German defences on the Western Front. Moreover, if the hills west of the lake were not comparable as regards height with the Moglena Mountains, against which the main Franco-Serbian attack had been launched, their formation powerfully aided the defence of the sector. This was fully described in the previous volume.[1] It was there pointed out that the " P " Ridge, well over 2,000 feet in height, ran roughly from north to south at a distance of from 4,000 to 5,000 yards from the western shore of the lake, and that the ground between the ridge and the lake presented from the British lines the spectacle of a rough and irregular series of terraces, slanted north-westward and rising fairly steeply till they culminated in the peak of the Grand Couronné. The original main system of defence here consisted of two lines. The foremost ran from P.4, crossed the Jumeaux Ravine, followed the forward slopes of those buttresses of the Grand Couronné which were known as the Tongue, the Hilt, and the Orb, and ran north-eastward to the lake. The second, roughly parallel to it, started at P.3 and encircled the Grand Couronné itself. On the " P " Ridge there were further strong defences at P.2 and P.1. Between P.4½ and the lake there was an advanced position which crossed the Sugar Loaf, followed the left bank of the Jumeaux Ravine, took in the Petit Couronné and then curved back to the lake shore about 600 yards south of Dojran town. This position was every whit as strong as the main line; but the enemy's

1918.
Sept.
Maps 5, 7.
Sketch 8.

---
[1] Vol. I, p. 304.

commander holding the portion between the Blade and Lake Dojran was empowered to abandon it rather than allow its garrison to be taken prisoner.

In general outline the defences had scarcely altered since the offensive of April and May 1917, but they had been considerably strengthened since then. In particular, the British observers had noted the grim fact that the enemy was using reinforced concrete continuously and energetically. Not only had he constructed numerous dugouts and machine-gun emplacements of this material; he had also emplaced many of his batteries under concrete casemates.

The garrison also was an altogether exceptional force, under a very capable leader, General Nerezov, who had succeeded General Geshov in command of the *First Army* after its reverse at the Skra di Legen. The *corps d'élite* of the Bulgarian Army, the *9th (Plevna) Division*, was still in line; but it had closed up its front, handing over the less important half of it, the Machukovo salient, to the *Mountain Division*,[1] the relief having been completed by the 15th August. The *Mountain Division* was not of anything like so high a quality as the *9th*, but it had put only two of its own regiments, the *67th* and *68th*, into the line, and had taken over from the *9th* the excellent *39th Regiment*, which remained in line immediately east of the Vardar. Of its own other two infantry regiments, the *65th* was now attached to the *5th Division* west of the Vardar, and the *66th* formed part of the *First Army* troops.[2]

The *9th Division* had now four regiments (the *57th, 33rd, 17th,* and *58th*) in line, and the *34th* close up in divisional reserve. The *4th Regiment* was in Army reserve. The division was enormously strong in artillery, having the equivalent of 28 batteries of 122 guns—11 of them German, including a 210-mm. howitzer and two 150-mm. naval guns. On the other hand, there was no Army artillery, except anti-aircraft. In addition to its own 164 machine guns, three German machine-gun detachments with eight

---

[1] Most of the details given below were, of course, known to the British Intelligence. The authorities from which they are here quoted are Nédeff and the Bulgarian Order of Battle furnished by the Bulgarian Military Historical Commission. For the *Mountain Division*, see p. 46.

[2] The *66th Regiment* is shown as *First Army* troops both in the Order of Battle and on Nédeff's map, but is never mentioned by the latter. The point is of some interest, because this was the only regiment on the British front which was afterwards employed elsewhere.

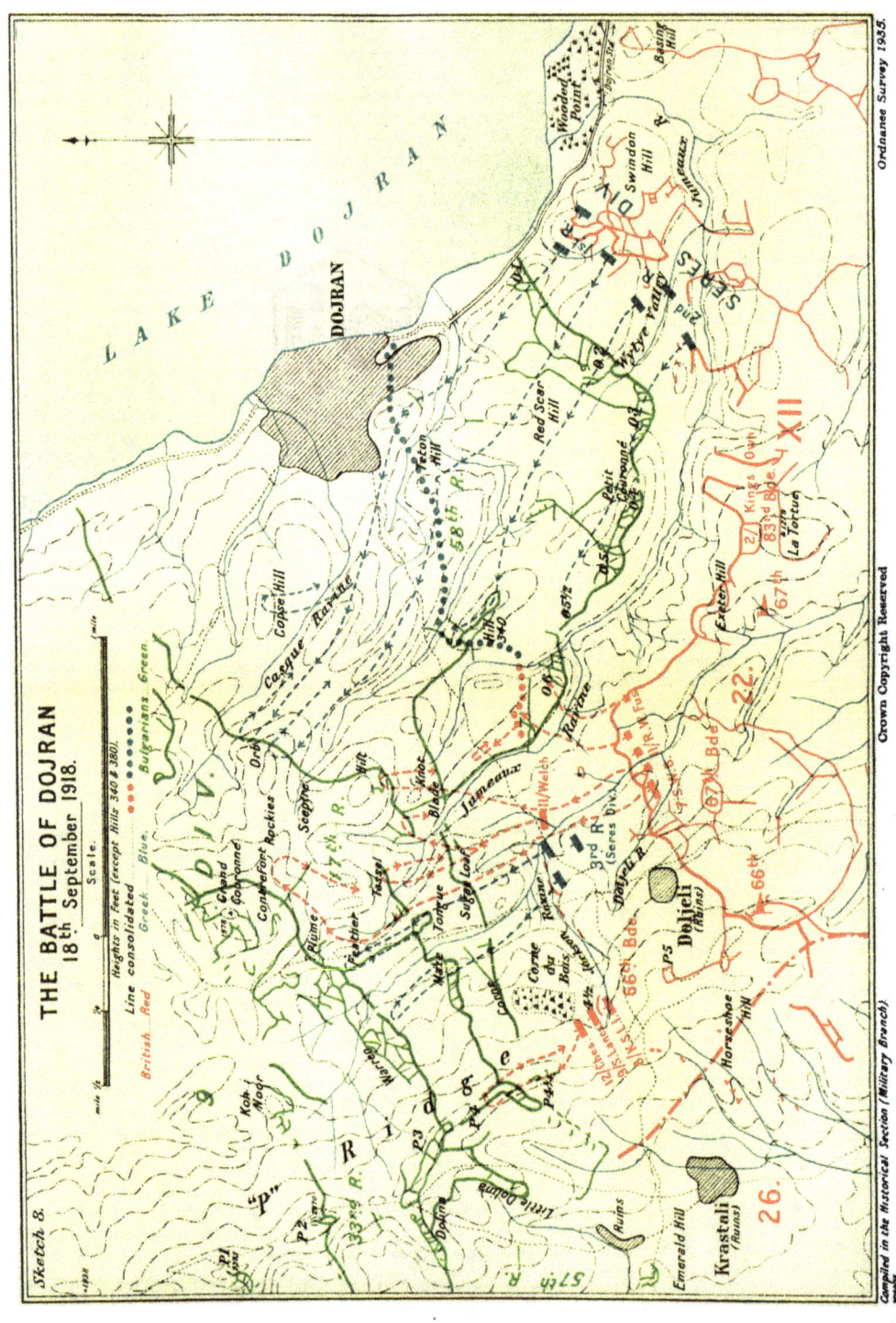

BULGAR MORALE ON DOJRAN FRONT

guns apiece were attached to the *9th Division*. The *Mountain Division* had 16 batteries of 73 guns, including 13 German, and 100 machine guns. From north of Lake Dojran to the Visoka Čuka, a peak on the Belašica Planina known to the Allies as the Signal Allemand—the point where the frontiers of Serbia, Bulgaria, and Greece met, and also that of the junction between the *First* and *Second Armies*—was the *1st Macedonian Brigade*, of six battalions, 24 guns, and 64 machine guns. This brigade belonged to the *11th Division*, which held the Belašica Planina; but as that division formed part of another Army, the brigade had been detached and placed directly under the orders of General Nerezov. The Macedonian troops had for some time had an indifferent reputation, as the numerous soldiers of Serbian nationality among them had no desire to fight for Bulgaria. The brigade had, however, been recently improved by Bulgarian drafts, and it could not have been steadier than it was on the 18th September. Its defences, if hardly comparable to those between Lake Dojran and the Vardar, had been greatly strengthened of late and were now very formidable. The foremost system ran due north along the eastward slopes of the Blaga Planina, a spur of the Belašica. The second line, of disconnected works and trenches, was on the crest of the Blaga, at a height of over 2,000 feet.

1918. Sept.

The Dojran-" P " Ridge position was, we have seen, strong by nature, by reason of the work expended upon it for the purposes of defence and for the protection of the garrison and supporting artillery, of the density of the troops which held it, and of its powerful armament. There were other reasons why it was formidable. Foremost among them, as the Bulgarians fairly claim, must be ranked the high morale of the *9th (Plevna) Division*. The troops believed that their defences were impregnable. In this belief, which had the backing of past experience, they were steadily encouraged by the whole hierarchy of their officers, at the head of which was their able and popular divisional commander, General Vazov.[1] They shared with those of

[1] " General Vazov possessed in the highest degree the power of winning all hearts. He invited regularly to his table all officers who visited him on duty from every part of the sector. . . . In the course of these dinners the 2nd lieutenants used to assure him thus :—the General need not worry ; nothing in the world will induce us to abandon the heights of the Deube (' P ' Ridge) to the enemy." (Nédeff, p. 271.)

THE BATTLE OF DOJRAN

the *Mountain Division*, their neighbour, and also with those of the *5th Division* on the other side of the Vardar, the inestimable benefit of the railway, and were never short of supplies or of ammunition. The *9th Division* had, in fact, been recently completely reclothed, at a time when some of the troops further from the main arteries of supply were in rags. The morale of the artillery was as high as that of the infantry; and gunners were considered " guilty of deser-" tion " if they failed to maintain their fire when it was called for by the infantry, however heavy was the neutralizing fire of the enemy's artillery. Another factor was extraordinarily thorough organization. Elaborate plans and range-tables enabled the artillery to open fire at a moment's notice upon the desired points, every one of which had been carefully registered; and the reserve battery positions had posted up in them all the information and statistics that were kept in the active ones. The system of communication by telephone, flag-signalling, runners, wireless, and pigeons had been perfected, and was linked to the admirable observatories on the " P " Ridge and Grand Couronné. The employment of reserves had been worked out in detail and embodied in the defence scheme.

Map 7.   Such were the position, its defenders, and their means of defence. The Anglo-Greek attempt to break into the fortified area between Lake Dojran and the " P " Ridge was one of which the difficulties and hazards could scarcely be exaggerated. But this time there was to be a new feature in the attack. Simultaneously with the assault of the XII Corps upon these defences, the XVI Corps was to attack those on the Blaga Planina, north of the lake. A single glance at the map will suffice to show the intimate connection of these attacks, seven miles apart though they were. By a similar flank attack across the Blaga the Greeks in the Second Balkan War had turned the Bulgarian position on the heights west of Lake Dojran and forced the defenders to retreat hastily and with considerable loss to the line of the Bajimia.[1] It may, in fact, be said that if the Blaga Planina were captured, a powerful and determined thrust from the south was almost certain to succeed.

---

[1] Oberstleutnant Immanuel: " Der Balkankrieg 1912/13," Vol. V, p. 63.

THE ARTILLERY CONCENTRATION 163

THE ATTACK OF THE XII CORPS—18TH SEPTEMBER.

The object of the attack of the XII Corps, under the command of Lieut.-General Sir H. F. M. Wilson, was to "gain possession of the ' P ' Ridge and neighbouring high "ground, and to exploit this success by all available "means."[1] The troops available were the 22nd Division, the Greek Seres Division, the 83rd Brigade (less two battalions),[2] the 2nd *bis* Regiment of Zouaves, and the XII Corps Cavalry. The artillery to support the attack consisted of 231 pieces, including the Greek—20 mountain guns, 94 18-pdrs., 36 4·5-inch howitzers, 36 60-pdrs., 36 6-inch howitzers, four 8-inch howitzers, three 6-inch guns, and the two 19-cm. guns of the French armoured train.

1918.
18 Sept.
Map 5.
Sketch 8.

This may seem at first glance a considerable concentration, but as the Bulgarian *9th Division* had 122 guns, it represented less than the superiority commonly held to be necessary to support an attack in warfare of this type. If measured by the breadth of the front it was even less adequate. There was one 18-pdr. to about 54 yards, as compared with one to 15½ yards employed by the British Fourth Army (in addition to tanks) in the Battle of Amiens on the 8th August 1918. And, such as the concentration was, it had been made only by denuding the rest of the front of the XII Corps; in particular, that of the 27th Division west of the Vardar had been drawn upon to a hazardous degree. Practically all the heavy artillery which had supported the attack on the Roche Noire Salient had been brought across the Vardar, leaving only four Greek 6-inch howitzers and two British 60-pdrs., though a small amount of French heavy artillery was available to assist in case of need. Another Greek 6-inch howitzer battery and another section of 60-pdrs. were on the left bank of the Vardar covering the left of the 26th Division. One 6-inch gun of the 43rd Siege Battery and one 60-pdr. battery were with the XVI Corps; the " Detached Section " (one gun) of the 43rd Siege Battery [3] was with the Greek I Corps in the Struma valley. Otherwise all the British heavy artillery in the force together with four Greek 6-inch howitzers had

---

[1] XII Corps " Instructions for the Preparations for Attack " are given in Appendix 12. 22nd Division Order No. 120 is given in Appendix 13.

[2] See p. 138.   [3] See p. 13, *fn.*

been concentrated to take part in this attack. With regard to field artillery there is a similar tale to tell. In addition to the 18-pdr. batteries of the 27th Division already attached to the 22nd,[1] the three 4·5-inch howitzer batteries of the 27th were brought across the Vardar, single guns being left in the old battery positions until the last possible moment. All three 4·5-inch howitzer batteries and 22 18-pdrs. from the 26th Division were also allotted to the attack.

Every gun that could be found, consistently with the barest margin of safety on the passive parts of the XII Corps front and with the very minimum of support for the attack of the XVI Corps, had thus been concentrated to fire on the area between Lake Dojran and the " P " Ridge. How near to the bone the artillery defence had been scraped is apparent when we consider that the enemy actually contemplated a counter-offensive astride the Vardar after the failure of the British attack on the 18th September. If he had launched this at all, he would have done so before the artillery could have returned to its normal defensive positions.

The Seres and 22nd Divisions were to be concentrated on a narrow front, from Lake Dojran to Horseshoe Hill— the southern end of the " P " Ridge. On the right the Seres Division, less one regiment, was to capture the advanced line between the lake and the Petit Couronné, and, detaching a special force to deal with the latter, to advance straight to the line Dojran Hill–Hill 340. Leaving sufficient strength on that line to consolidate and hold it, the division was then to continue its advance without pause to the Orb, one of the spurs of the Grand Couronné and within the second line of defence. If the progress of the 22nd Division had not by then made such an attack unnecessary, the Seres Division was then to thrust north-westward against the Grand Couronné itself, in conjunction with a north-eastward thrust by the 22nd. Br.-General R. H. Hare, commanding the 83rd Brigade, was to be responsible for conveying and interpreting the orders and instructions of General Wilson to the Greek divisional commander. As the latter lacked experience of warfare of this nature, Br.-General Hare worked for the most part with the Greek Chief of the Staff, Commandant Aftonides, a highly efficient staff officer, with

---

[1] See p. 142, *fn.* 1.

THE ARTILLERY PREPARATION   165

whom he communicated in French. British liaison officers 1918. were also attached to each of the three Greek regiments to 18 Sept. act in a similar capacity.

The attack on the left was to be carried out by the 22nd Division with a regiment of the Seres Division attached. It was to be directed successively against the three lines of defence and the further defences of the " P " Ridge in rear of them.

Between the two attacks the troops of the 83rd Brigade —the infantry of which amounted, as we have seen, to one battalion only—were to carry out a demonstration from the trenches north of La Tortue, in order to force the enemy to include this part of the front in his defensive barrage. At the same time the 26th Division on the left of the 22nd was to carry out a small subsidiary attack against certain Bulgarian outposts.

In order not to alarm the enemy unduly, previous artillery activity was to be limited to a period as short as possible. The preparation would consist of two days' wire-cutting, the wire within effective range of 18-pdrs. being so far as possible destroyed by them and by trench mortars, and gaps being cut in that more distant by 4·5-inch howitzers. The following night, which was that preceding the day of the assault, would be devoted to bombardment of certain areas and neutralizing fire with chemical shell directed against the enemy's battery positions. The assault was to be covered by a creeping barrage of 18-pdrs. moving approximately at the rate of 100 yards in two minutes with 100-yard lifts, each gun firing four rounds a minute. The 4·5-inch and 6-inch howitzers were meanwhile to fire on carefully chosen points in rear. The right attack barrage and infantry attack were to start at the same hour as those of the left ; but, as the former had a far greater distance to cover, their advance would be echeloned in rear until they drew level with those of the left on the final objective.

The guns of the two machine-gun companies of the 22nd Division [1] which were to take part in the attack were divided between " forward " and " rearward " tasks. The former were to go forward with the infantry and take up

---

[1] That is, one to each brigade in the attack. The Greek regiment attached had its own machine guns, which were at the disposal of its commander.

positions on or in rear of the final objective when captured. The latter had, first of all, the duty of keeping open the gaps in the wire during the two nights preceding the attack, and subsequently of firing overhead barrages during the advance of the infantry.

The co-operation of the Royal Air Force with the XII Corps was to be carried out by two flights of No. 47 Squadron : " C " Flight doing artillery work from Yanesh aerodrome, and " B " providing contact patrols and reconnaissance machines from Hajarli. " C " Flight No. 17 Squadron was to carry out similar duties for the XVI Corps, while No. 150 Squadron at Kirech was responsible for the protection of all artillery and contact machines. "A" and " B " Flights, No. 17 Squadron, at Ambarköi, were detailed for bombing and machine-gun fire within four miles of the front, at the request of either corps ; and " A " Flight, No. 47 Squadron, was at the disposition of the Army for strategical reconnaissance and bombing beyond the four-mile limit. One balloon section was at the disposition of each corps, No. 26 at that of the XVI Corps and No. 27 at that of the XII Corps.

At the beginning of September there was an outbreak of influenza—the very severe form then prevalent almost all over the world and known popularly as " Spanish " influenza—in the 65th Brigade, so serious that, by the 7th, it was decided that these troops would not be able to take part in the operations. The brigade was therefore replaced by the 77th Brigade of the 26th Division and retained in Army reserve at Kirech. There was, fortunately, time to withdraw the 77th for a few days' training. There was also sickness in the General Staff of the XII Corps, very disturbing at such a time. During the preparations for the attack the senior General Staff officer was changed no less than four times.[1]

On the 12th September General Milne outlined to the

---

[1] On the 11th August Lieut.-Colonel P. L. Hanbury, G.S.O.1 at G.H.Q., who was acting as B.G.G.S. of the corps during the absence on leave of Br.-General F. G. Fuller, was admitted to hospital. His place was taken by Lieut.-Colonel T. G. G. Anderson, G.S.O.1 of the 22nd Division, until the 20th, when Lieut.-Colonel Hanbury came out of hospital. On the 23rd Br.-General Fuller returned from leave and resumed his duties. On the 15th September he went down with sand-fly fever, and Lieut.-Colonel Hanbury took over the post for the third time. Br.-General Fuller returned to duty on the 26th. These were not the only cases of sickness in the staff just before the attack.

DOJRAN TO "P" RIDGE FROM

PITON DES ZOUAVES

L'Imperial War Museum Photograph.

corps commanders their future action in the event of the initial operations being a complete success. The first object was to regain touch between the two corps north of Lake Dojran, in the neighbourhood of Hasanli. Next, the XII Corps, rejoined by the 27th Division, which would by then have crossed the Vardar, was to press forward as rapidly as possible to Strumica, while the XVI Corps cleared the Belašica Planina from west to east.

1918.
18 Sept.

The attack was launched at 5.8 a.m. on the 18th September. It was a fine day, and when the sun was well up became intensely hot, but by that time the business was decided. The British troops were determined, but they cannot have felt very sanguine; nor can memories of former failures against these defences have been wholly absent from their minds. All the battalions were weak, taking into action an average of 450 all ranks, including headquarters. They could do no more than give of their best, and that they did. The Greeks, to whom the grim associations of the region meant nothing, whose ranks were better filled, and whose bodily fitness was higher, went forward into the inferno with perhaps brighter hopes of success but with no stronger resolution.

The Seres Division (General Zymbrakakis) advanced with great dash and at once overran the enemy's first line between the Petit Couronné and the lake. By 6 o'clock it was reported that the 1st Regiment on the right had Dojran and Teton Hills; one hour later that the strongly-fortified Hill 340, where the garrison resisted stubbornly, had been taken by the 2nd Regiment and that already there were about 700 prisoners. The 1st Regiment, throwing out a flank guard on the right to seize and hold Copse Hill, then pushed straight forward to the Orb, and carried it, despite much stiffer resistance than had yet been encountered. The regiment had thus broken into the enemy's main line. It was a fine feat of arms, but unfortunately it was partly in vain. The failure of the attack on the left and heavy loss suffered by the battalion which captured the Orb, coupled with the enemy's counter-attacks, forced the Greeks to fall back to Marrow Hill and the Garter. The divisional commander, considering that it was impossible to hold this line, ordered the regiment to withdraw to that of Dojran and Teton Hills. Here at 4 p.m. it established contact with the 2nd Regiment on Hill 340. Towards evening the enemy showed some intention of trying to recover this line also, but, being met by a smart fire and finding the three hills strongly held, he quickly desisted.

The attack of the 22nd Division (Major-General J. Duncan) was made in three columns, each of the value of an infantry brigade : on the right the 67th Brigade (Br.-General A. D. Macpherson), in the centre the 3rd Regiment (Colonel Pagos) of the Seres Division, and on the left the 66th Brigade (Br.-General F. S. Montague Bates). Owing to the nature of the ground their dispositions differed. The task of the 67th Brigade was extremely complicated, especially perhaps that of the right battalion, the 11/R. Welch Fusiliers. Two companies, making their way down Claw and Snake Ravines, were to capture O.6, one of them afterwards supporting the attack on the Hilt. The other two, moving up further west, were to cross the Jumeaux Ravine south of the Hilt and assault that hill at 30 minutes after zero. The centre battalion, the 11/Welch Regiment, was to form up on the lower slopes of the Fang and capture the enemy's trenches between the Jumeaux Ravine and the Sugar Loaf. Passing through this line and crossing the Jumeaux Ravine, two companies were to capture the Knot, while the other two took the Tassel. The 7/S. Wales Borderers had no part in the capture of the front-line defences. It was, in fact, to follow the leading battalion of the Greek 3rd Regiment over the Sugar Loaf and the Tongue ; then to cross the Jumeaux Ravine, break into the defences of the Grand Couronné at the point known as the Rockies, and capture the summit, as well as the spur called Le Contrefort. The Greek 3rd Regiment had a no less grim but a less complicated programme. Its zone of operations was naturally divided into two by the Vladaja Ravine, and it was to advance on a two-battalion frontage, breaking through the three successive trench-lines in front of it and finally capturing the Koh-i-Noor. The 66th Brigade had on the " P " Ridge space only to deploy one battalion at a time. In its case the 12/Cheshire was to capture P.4¼, P.4, P.3, and the last-named's off-shoot, Little Dolina. The 9/S. Lancashire was to follow the Cheshire to P.3, and there pass through it to capture Dolina, the next spur of the ridge beyond Little Dolina. Finally, the 8/Shropshire Light Infantry was to capture P.2 with two companies, one of which was to push on and take P.1.

ATTACK OF 22ND DIVISION

The difficulties attending such movements would have been great enough had every obstacle been blasted from the path of the troops who had to carry them out. There was, however, no question of this being done, except possibly in the case of the foremost defences. After passing through them the advance would be confined to a limited number of gaps in the wire varying from 25 to 100 yards in breadth.[1]

The attack of the 22nd Division went at first promisingly enough behind its thin 18-pdr. barrage—52 guns on an initial frontage of nearly 3,000 yards.[2] On the front of the 67th Brigade the company of the 11/R. Welch Fusiliers, directed against the southern face of O.6, entered the work without serious opposition by 5.18 a.m., beat off two counter-attacks, and got into touch with the troops of the Seres Division on the right. The second company likewise entered the work, at the western corner, but in its case there was very heavy loss, every officer and non-commissioned officer being put out of action. In these circumstances the best troops often fail, but here a private soldier, Private D. Roberts, collected the men who were left and led them forward in the direction of the Hilt in accordance with the orders. The incident is recorded only as proof of the standard of discipline and devotion to duty in the battalion. It had no effect on the action; for the remnants of the third and fourth companies were met retiring from the Hilt. They had passed through the first belt of wire, but had then run into a pocket of gas left by the British bombardment and had been obliged to put on their respirators. They met with stout opposition on the Hilt, and the comparatively few men who reached the trenches were expelled by a counter-attack. In the centre the 11/Welch captured the Fang in the first rush and reached its final objectives, the Knot and the Tassel; but only a handful survived at

---

[1] For example, the 67th Brigade on the right was to have one gap in the defences of the Hilt, one in those of the Knot, and two in those of the Tassel. On the slopes of the Grand Couronné two gaps were to be cut at the Rockies.

[2] There were in all, as stated, 94 18-pdrs. Of these 42, under the command of Lieut.-Colonel R. W. Bourchier, formed the barrage for the Seres Division, and 52, under the command of Br.-General H. E. Carey, C.R.A. of the 22nd Division, that for his own division. The dispositions and chain of command are shown in Note I at end of Chapter. The frontage of the 22nd Division's barrage was about 2,800 yards in the first instance because the troops attacking O.6 had to be supported. After the capture of O.6 the frontage narrowed to about 2,100 yards between the Hilt and P.4.

either point, and in each case it was driven out. The 7/S. Wales Borderers crossed the Sugar Loaf and the Tongue with hardly any loss, made its way up the Feather amid a dense cloud of smoke and dust which probably hid it from the view of the enemy, and actually assaulted the defences of the Grand Couronné at the Rockies. Here, however, the battalion was under the enemy's eyes and isolated into the bargain. Terrific machine-gun fire from three sides simply cut it to pieces. The few survivors withdrew, leaving behind them many wounded. Among these was the commanding officer, Lieut.-Colonel Daniel Burges, wounded for the third time, whose skill had brought his men thus far though every landmark was obliterated by dust and smoke, and whose heroism had constantly heartened them in their desperate endeavour. Lieut.-Colonel Burges was awarded the Victoria Cross.

The Greek 3rd Regiment went forward with no less gallantry. The Sugar Loaf was quickly overrun, and the attack moved on through a storm of fire to the assault of the next line. Here again there was a triumph. The Tongue and the Maze, on either side of the Vladaja Ravine, were captured. On the regiment went again. But now losses were thinning out the waves of assault and slackening their momentum, while ever the enemy's fire grew hotter. A few men actually penetrated the next line on both sides of the ravine at the Feather and the Warren, but were at once driven out. More, the enemy launched a strong counter-attack, which the Greeks, unsupported by artillery, were unable to withstand, and at about 10 a.m. the Bulgarians recaptured the Tongue. For some hours longer the Sugar Loaf was held, but even this had eventually to be abandoned, and was reoccupied by the enemy early in the afternoon.

In the attack of the 66th Brigade on the "P" Ridge the 12/Cheshire, meeting with unexpected delay in the capture of P.$4\frac{1}{4}$, lost the barrage, which moved on up the ridge; and it may be said that from this moment the prospect was hopeless. Desperate fighting went on about P.4, which was penetrated momentarily on the left centre. Cross-fire from other parts of the work at once annihilated those who had made an entry. The attack was renewed, but this fresh effort met with a like fate; the commanding officer, Lieut.-Colonel the Hon. A. R. Clegg-Hill, was killed; and the battalion simply disappeared. The 9/S. Lancashire, following up and with no avenue of approach other than the narrow ribbon of the " P " Ridge, was stopped in its turn by a blast of frontal fire from machine guns in P.4 and of flanking fire from the garrison of Little Dolina, and speedily lost nearly two-thirds of its effectives. Its commanding officer, Lieut.-Colonel B. F. Bishop, was also killed. The third battalion, the 8/King's Shropshire Light Infantry, arrived on the scene before the slaughter was over and found itself under a trench-mortar and machine-gun barrage about P. $4\frac{1}{4}$, while ahead of it the ridge was so congested with men that it was impossible to get through. Lieut.-Colonel J. D. B. Erskine therefore withdrew his battalion—which had lost over one-third of its strength, but might count itself fortunate by comparison with the others—and reorganized it in disused British trenches in Jackson Ravine. The Bulgarians counter-attacked P.$4\frac{1}{4}$ simultaneously with the Tongue, and with like success. The remnants of the three battalions were gradually collected by Lieut.-Colonel Erskine in Jackson Ravine.

1918.
18 Sept.

The attack of the two divisions had thus resulted in the capture of the foremost position and the intermediate position from Dojran Hill to Hill 340 by the Seres Division, but only of O.6 by the 22nd Division. The Seres Division had taken 683 prisoners and the 22nd 94. In the Seres Division's assault the losses had been comparatively light; in that of the 22nd and the attached Greek regiment they had been very high. All three battalions of the 67th Brigade had virtually ceased to exist: The 11/R. Welch Fusiliers came out of action with three officers and 100 other ranks unwounded; the 11/Welch had its commanding officer and 40 other ranks, practically all signallers and runners, left; the 7/S. Wales Borderers had one officer (slightly wounded) and 55 other ranks, of whom 30 subsequently went to hospital with gas poisoning. The 3rd Regiment of the Seres Division had 1,232 casualties, its losses far exceeding those of the British on either flank, but only because it was so much stronger in effectives. The casualties of the 66th Brigade were 857, the 12/Cheshire and 9/S. Lancashire having been cut to pieces, while the 8/King's Shropshire L.I. had a loss of 166.

At 9 a.m. the 65th Brigade, which was in Army reserve at Kirech and isolated owing to sickness, was put at the disposal of Major-General Duncan; and an hour later the

2nd *bis* Regiment of Zouaves was also handed over to him. General Wilson, however, informed General Milne that, owing to the difficulty of assembling troops, he was against another attack that day. He had ordered the 27th Division to hold its reserve brigade in readiness to cross the Vardar to act as a reserve on the left bank, but, learning soon afterwards that a regiment of the Greek 14th Division had been placed at General Milne's disposal by General Franchet d'Espérey and was to move up to Chugunsi, he cancelled this order. At 5 p.m., in accordance with General Milne's instructions, he issued orders for the attack to be renewed on the morrow. General Milne had received from General Franchet d'Espérey a message to the effect that every effort must be made to profit by the break-through on the Serbian front.

At zero hour the 79th Brigade (Br.-General A. J. Poole) of the 26th Division had carried out a minor but costly diversion on the left of the main attack. A company of the 8/D.C.L.I. captured Flatiron Hill with nine prisoners, and a company of the 12/Hampshire established itself on White Scar Hill. After the break-down of the main attack the enemy was able to switch his fire on to these positions. In view of the fury of his bombardment, they were eventually abandoned. The casualties of the brigade in this affair numbered 112.

The Attack of the XVI Corps—18th September.

Map 7.
Sketch 9.
Until the 12th September General Briggs, commanding the XVI Corps, had been responsible for the whole front from the Gulf of Orfano to Lake Dojran, as the Greek I Corps in the Struma valley was under his orders. His own XVI Corps consisted of the 28th Division (less headquarters, one battalion, and the machine-gun company of the 83rd Brigade), the 228th Brigade, which had so long been attached to the 28th Division that it was now regarded as forming part of it, the Crete Division, the Surrey Yeomanry, and the Greek 3rd Cavalry Regiment. His corps artillery comprised only one 6-inch gun of the 43rd Siege Battery, the 190th Heavy Battery, and the IV Highland Mountain Brigade, less the Bute Battery, which was with the XII Corps.

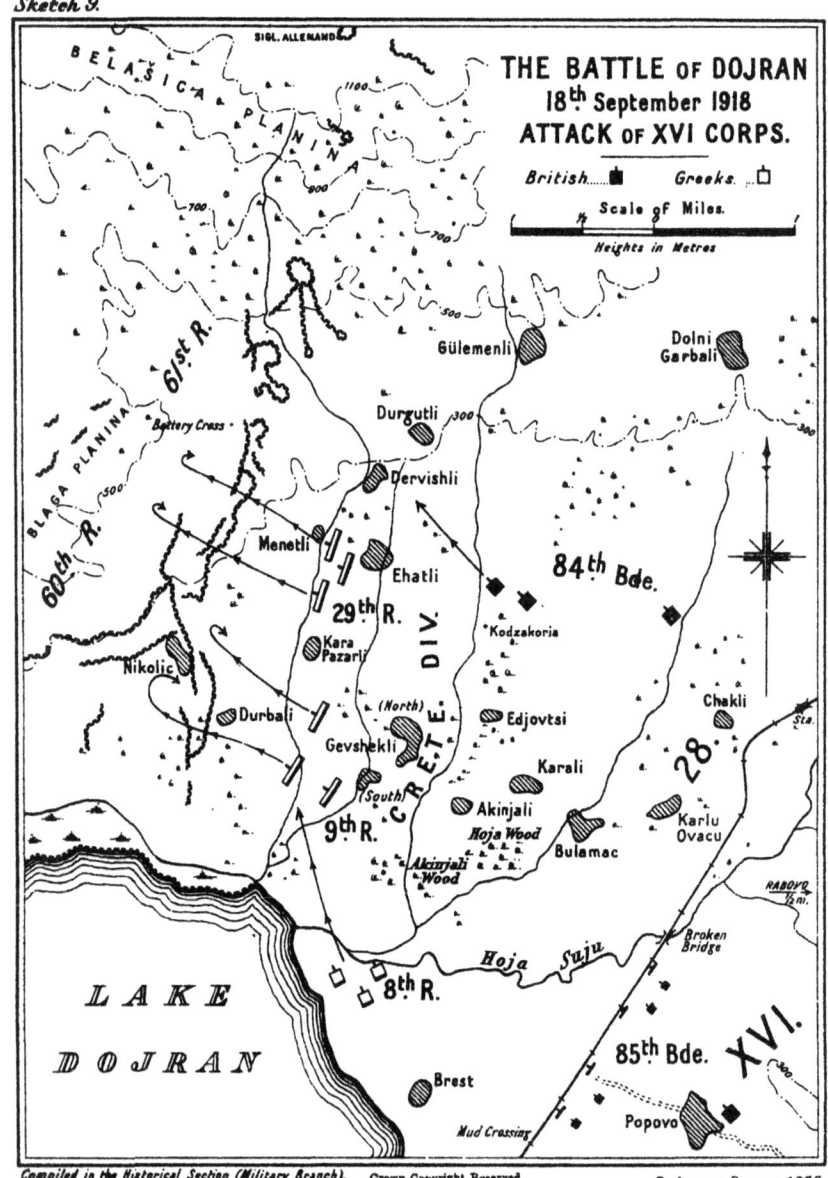

DISPOSITIONS OF XVI CORPS

On the 8th the Greek I Corps had, in accordance with orders from General Briggs, occupied the villages of Kara Orman, Kakaraska, Salmah, Ada, Homondos, Kalendra, Topalova, Kumli, and Haznadar as outposts, in order to give the enemy the impression that an offensive in the Struma valley was in preparation. The advance had not been seriously opposed, but had led to some skirmishing and artillery fire. On the 12th the Greek I Corps had been placed directly under British G.H.Q., so that General Briggs should be able to give undivided attention to the attack which was being prepared on his extreme left flank.

1918.
18 Sept.

This attack, of which the object was to capture the Bulgarian defences between the Belašica Planina and Lake Dojran, involved a long approach march up to an entrenched position and was thus of a type commoner in old wars than in the present, though its like had been witnessed on the Russian front and in the outer theatres. The defences of the XVI Corps were on the forward slopes of the Krusha Range, and the enemy's position on the Blaga Planina was at its nearest point $4\frac{1}{2}$ miles away. The intervening plain was flat as a table and, though wooded and cut by many streams, not difficult to cross; but the attacking forces had to descend from the hills by donkey-tracks. For wheeled vehicles there was available one road from Karamudli (the railhead, on the light railway, for the attack) by which columns could debouch into the plain at Popovo. The 286th Army Troops Company, with the 95th Labour Company and Macedonian workmen, under Br.-General H. L. Pritchard, Chief Engineer of the corps, had slightly widened and greatly improved this road during the days preceding the attack, but it was still narrow and, into the bargain, steep and winding.

While the attack was taking place, General Briggs had to hold a front of about nine miles from west of Lozhishta to Pangarasli, in the " Summer Line " defences high up in the Krusha hills. This line was to be occupied by the 228th Brigade on the right in its old sector, and on the left, from the Todorovo Reka, by the two battalions of the 83rd Brigade, the 1/York and Lancaster and the 2/E. Yorkshire, which were formed into a composite brigade under the orders of Lieut.-Colonel A. A. W. Spencer. The very minimum of artillery was allotted to these formations: to the 228th Brigade, the 22nd Battery, two sections of the 118th Battery, and one mountain battery borrowed from the Greek I Corps; and to the Composite Brigade, one section of the 118th. For the purposes of the attack, including the necessary corps reserve, he had thus at his disposal the Crete Division (three infantry regiments and 16 mountain guns), the 84th and 85th Brigades, the III, XXXI, LIV Brigades R.F.A. of the 28th Division, D (the howitzer) battery of the CXXX Brigade,[1] the III Mountain Artillery Brigade, which was attached to the 28th Division, and his corps artillery already specified: a total of one 6-inch gun, four 60-pdrs., 12 4·5-inch howitzers, 36 18-pdrs., 20 British 2·75-inch mountain guns, and 16 Greek 65-mm. or 75-mm. mountain guns.

The attack was to be carried out by the Crete Division under the command of General Spiliades, with two regiments, the third, with the IV Highland Mountain Brigade R.G.A. attached, being held in reserve north of Brest. The 84th Brigade (Br.-General F. C. Nisbet), with the III Mountain Brigade R.G.A. (less one battery) attached, was to protect the right of the Crete Division, moving in close support, and prepared to link the ground gained with the main "Winter Line," into which the 228th and Composite Brigades were to advance if the attack was successful. The 85th Brigade (Br.-General K. M. Davie), with one battery III Mountain Brigade R.G.A. and the 23/Welch (Pioneers) attached, was to be in corps reserve, and to take up a position with its two leading battalions on the railway and the other two in the foot-hills east of Popovo. The cavalry also was to be in corps reserve on the eastern shore of Lake Dojran.

The method adopted to bring this considerable force of infantry and artillery down from the hills into the plain, which the leading regiments had to cross before assaulting the enemy's position, was as follows. The Cretan 29th and 9th Regiments were to assemble on the night of the 16th at the foot of the ridge in the villages of Rabovo and Popovo respectively, and to remain there concealed throughout the 17th. By night they were to be led by British guides to a position on the railway, with right on Chakli Station. Thence they were to advance at 3 a.m. on the 18th, and rush in silence the little Bulgarian outposts in the maze of woodland and villages of which Akinjali was the centre.

---

[1] This being the brigade to which the 22nd and 118th Batteries, mentioned above, belonged.

ATTACK OF CRETE DIVISION

The capture of these was to be announced by rockets bursting into gold and silver rain. The two Greek regiments were then to be prepared to advance against the Bulgarian trenches from the point known as Battery Cross to Lake Dojran, supported by their own mountain batteries, two to each regiment.[1]

1918.
18 Sept.

Meanwhile the British field artillery would have moved down through Popovo. It was to be divided into four groups, one consisting of the three batteries of 4·5-inch howitzers, grouped under the headquarters of the CXXX Brigade, and the other three of the 18-pdr. batteries of the three field artillery brigades. As soon as possible after the Greek infantry had captured the outposts, the field artillery was to advance to positions in the neighbourhood of Akinjali, and, with the aid of the heavy artillery in the hills and the mountain artillery, carry out a bombardment of half an hour, the heavy artillery endeavouring to neutralize Bulgarian batteries, the 4·5-inch howitzers firing gas shell, and the 18-pdrs. firing shrapnel. At the end of this bombardment, the Greeks were to assault the main line. It was, however, pointed out to General Spiliades that he would not be able to rely entirely for the cutting of the wire upon his mountain artillery, and that the troops must be ready to cut gaps for themselves.

As soon as the Greek regiments had left the railway line, the 84th Brigade Group was to assemble at Chakli Station; when the Greek signal was seen it was to advance to a position north of Kodzakoria Wood in order to cover the Greek right flank.[2] At 6 a.m. two battalions of the 85th Brigade were to line up on the railway between Broken Bridge and Mud Crossing.

The two Greek regiments went forward quietly in the darkness. At 5 a.m. the 84th Brigade (Br.-General F. C. Nisbet) began to move across the plain in echelon, the 2/Cheshire leading; and the 2/Buffs and 2/East Surrey of the 85th Brigade (Br.-General K. M. Davie) began to move up to the railway. The Greek rocket-signal was fired at 5·32, the enemy having abandoned his outpost positions without serious resistance. Meanwhile the forward movement of

---

[1] XVI Corps " Plan of Operations of the Cretan Division " is given in Appendix 14.

[2] Actually, the leading battalion left the station at 5 a.m., half an hour before the rocket was fired.

the British divisional artillery had not taken place without some slight hitches. The head of the long column had passed Popovo Peak at 2 a.m., but the XXXI Brigade R.F.A. was a quarter of an hour late in starting owing to the blocking of the road. By the time the railway was reached, the rocket had already gone up, and the batteries had to cross the plain in daylight. The 62nd Battery of the III Brigade, trotting towards Akinjali Wood, was shelled so heavily that it had for a short time to take cover in Hoja Wood, but reached its position in time to come into action soon after the 18th Battery, which fired its first round at 8 a.m. The bombardment group had opened fire at 6.48, the XXXI Brigade at 7, and the LIV Brigade, which was also shelled as it crossed the plain, at 7.30 a.m.

By 7 a.m. the Greek 29th Regiment on the right was in the ravine west of Kara Pazarli and Dervishli, and the 9th Regiment on the left was west of Gevshekli. The 2/Cheshire had reached Kodzakoria Wood, where it was being shelled by the enemy.

Liaison was bad, as was to be feared with troops of different nationalities, unused to each other's methods and actually seeing each other for the first time. General Spiliades went forward soon after 6.30 and established a command post in Akinjali in order to be in close touch with his troops; but he did not inform Br.-General P. P. E. de Berry, C.R.A. of the 28th Division, of his move, and there was no touch with him thereafter. Communication between the Greeks and the field artillery brigades was also defective or in some cases non-existent; and owing to the cutting of telephone wires by the enemy's artillery these brigades had themselves to rely largely upon the helio to communicate with the rear.

The first Greek attack seems to have begun between 7.30 and 8 a.m., before the artillery preparation was complete. The enemy's line was breached at one point, south of Nikolic, but the small detachment which got in could not maintain its ground. The commander of the 9th Regiment, Colonel Minis, became a casualty, and there was some confusion. General Spiliades then moved up a battalion of the 8th Regiment to the support of his left flank. In order to cover the Greek right more effectively, the 2/Cheshire advanced to Dervishli, reaching that village at 1.5 p.m. The 28th Divisional Artillery was placed directly

WITHDRAWAL OF CRETE DIVISION 177

at the disposal of General Spiliades, who ordered it to carry out a fresh bombardment from 2.30 to 3 p.m. It appears that this order did not reach all the batteries, and, though some came into action when they saw the Greeks move forward, the volume of fire was distinctly less than that of the earlier bombardment.   1918.
18 Sept.

A serious accident ruined the prospects of the second attack. Just as it was about to be launched the enemy's artillery set fire to the long, dry grass on the front of the 9th Regiment. Fanned by the wind, the flames spread swiftly, and the foremost companies, already highly tried, reeled back scorched and choking. Thus only the 29th Regiment went forward. Despite the enemy's fire and the fact that few gaps had been cut in the wire, it penetrated the trenches and made some progress up the hill. Heavy fire from both flanks forced it out again, and soon after 4 p.m. the whole division began to withdraw. Again the British seem to have had no information as to what was happening for several hours. It was not until 8 p.m. that the 84th Brigade received orders to fall back to the line of the railway, and not until 11.30 that the brigade major ascertained that the Greeks had withdrawn. The divisional artillery was directed at 8.30 to withdraw to the line of the Hoja, and the 85th Brigade to hold an outpost position through Akinjali Wood and village. Owing to orderlies losing their way in the dark, these new dispositions were not completed until 4 a.m. on the 19th. The 1/Welch of the 84th Brigade took up a position at Chakli in touch with the troops of the 85th.

The British casualties were very small, less than 100 in all, over half of them being in the field artillery, which had been heavily shelled all day in the open plain. The loss in horses was, however high, about 100 belonging to the divisional artillery alone being killed. The Crete Division's casualties were not far short of 800. It was feared that many of the Greek wounded had perished in the flames, but this can hardly have been the case, since there were only 106 recorded as killed and 37 missing, a comparatively small proportion of the total loss.[1]

On the 20th General Briggs was directed to withdraw the Crete Division to its camps at Kürküt and Gramatna for rest and reorganization.

---
[1] Bujac, p. 143, *fn*.

The Attack of the XII Corps—19th September.

1918.
19 Sept.
Map 5.
Sketch 8.

The attack between Lake Dojran and the "P" Ridge had to be renewed. The two regiments of the Seres Division under the command of General Zymbrakakis could be employed again, but the 66th and 67th Brigades and the 3rd Regiment of the Seres Division were all reduced to shadows. The two British brigades were fit only to hold the line through which the attacking troops were to pass, and even for this purpose it was thought advisable to place two companies of the 9/Border Regiment (Pioneers) at the disposal of each; the Greek regiment was withdrawn. For his second attempt Major-General Duncan had at his disposal the 77th Brigade, detached from the 26th Division and in reserve on the previous day, the 2nd *bis* Regiment of Zouaves, and, as sole representative of his own infantry, the weak and sick 65th Brigade.[1]

This time a rather different method was to be adopted, in view of the difficulty of pushing one column right up the "P" Ridge against five successive objectives and the fact that the failure there on the 18th had been the most complete.[2] Now, the attack directly up the ridge was to be carried only as far as P.4, by one battalion of the 65th Brigade. This had the additional advantage that fire could be maintained on P.3 rather longer than on the previous day. The remaining battalions were to be held in reserve, but were to assemble in Jackson Ravine 20 minutes after zero. The central column, the 2nd Zouaves, after capturing the trenches known as the Warren in the third line, was to turn westward up a spur of the ridge and capture, first, P.3, and then Dolina and Little Dolina. It was a very difficult operation, especially for a commander and troops not acquainted with the country. On the right the 77th Brigade was to capture in turn the Sugar Loaf, the Knot and the Tassel, the Rockies and the Plume. Another change in method was that the troops were to be reorganized on this line, and the capture of the Grand Shoulder, the Koh-i-Noor, and P.2 was to be a separate operation.

---

[1] XII Corps Order No. 33 is given in Appendix 15.
[2] It has appeared unnecessary to provide a special map or sketch for the operations of the 19th, as they can so easily be followed on Map 5 and Sketch 8.

DOJRAN TO "P" RIDGE FROM

PITON DES ZOUAVES (Map 5).

ATTACK OF SERES DIVISION

In order to strengthen the artillery supporting the 22nd Division, 12 18-pdrs. which had on the 18th taken part in the barrage of the Seres Division were now transferred to the left barrage, the pace of which was to be reduced. The 8-inch howitzer battery was transferred from the East to the West Bombardment Group, and was now to fire on the " P " Ridge. There was still available chemical shell for use with 60-pdrs. and 4·5-inch howitzers, but, as has been stated, little or none for the 6-inch howitzers.

1918.
19 Sept.

On the face of it the prospects of success were not very bright ; and yet they were rather better than on the 18th. The enemy had had a severe shaking then, and on the right he had lost his foremost line of defences—his two foremost lines if we count, as we very well may, Dojran Hill to Hill 340 as a line of defence. What would have been the fate of the attack had there not been a disastrous hitch at the very outset is a matter for speculation ; it seems probable that it would at best have been a partial success. As it happened, the issue was in great part decided before ever the barrage dropped.

On the right flank the Seres Division, despite losses and fatigue, again fought extremely well. Once more the Hilt was carried, though only after the first assault had broken down. The Orb was apparently taken likewise, and— according to some reports, though this is doubtful—small bodies of Greeks were seen advancing up the slopes of the Grand Couronné. But again flanking fire held up the advance, and again strong and determined counter-attacks retook the Hilt, this time after savage hand-to-hand fighting. By 10 a.m. at latest the two Greek regiments were back behind Dojran Hill and Hill 340, which had been occupied prior to the attack by the 2/King's Own.

As the companies of the 12/Argyll and Sutherland Highlanders, destined to form the left of the 77th Brigade, made their way up to their position of assembly in the Vladaya Ravine they came upon men of the 2nd *bis* Zouaves lying in the Doljeli Ravine, completely blocking the footway, so that the Highlanders had literally to walk over their bodies. What had happened was this. The regimental commander, Lieut.-Colonel Boré-Verrier, had disregarded Major-General Duncan's suggestion that he should move his two battalions which were attacking in first line, one by the Volovec track and another by a bridle-path just west of it, and decided to move both by the Volovec track as being the wider, leaving the bridle-path to the supporting battalion. Both columns were supplied with guides by the British, one officer being with each, in addition to N.C.O.'s of the 66th Brigade. The column was to leave the Pillar at 2 a.m. One battalion was 25 minutes late, though this delay was reparable, as there was still ample time. Crossing the Doljeli Ravine, the main column on the Volovec track came under artillery fire, one battalion suffering, according to the regimental commander's subsequent report, over 50 casualties. The battalion then lay down or scattered into Doljeli village, communication trenches, and the neighbouring orchards. The battalion commander was wounded, and his successor, on being informed by the British officer with him that he could not advance in artillery formation owing to the British wire, declined to advance in column until the shelling of Jackson Ravine had stopped. He and his men apparently believed that the fire with which they had been assailed was expressly directed upon them and that they were in full view, though the British officer assured him that it was only harassing fire at a venture. It was now 4.30 and the assembly was to have been completed by 4.45. In short, no more than a handful of the Zouaves ever went forward to Jackson Ravine, their place of assembly, and the regiment took no part whatever in the attack.

The battalions of the 77th Brigade pushed on and reached their positions of assembly in time. The Argylls and Scottish Rifles were both affected by gas in Vladaja and Jackson Ravines, not recognizing it at first owing to the smoke and fumes of lyddite, and so not putting on their respirators quickly enough. At 4.50 the brigade commander, Br.-General W. A. Blake, received a message from Major-General Duncan that the French on his left were in some confusion and that if the Argylls found themselves unsupported on their left they were not to go beyond the Tongue. Every effort was made by telephone, visual signalling, and runners sent out in pairs to get this message through, but though visual signalling was apparently successful, the message being acknowledged by the signallers of the Argylls, it does not seem to have reached the commanding officer.

The objectives of the 11/Scottish Rifles were the Fang,

ATTACK OF 77TH BRIGADE

the Knot, and the trenches below the Tassel, and, finally, the Tassel itself. The Fang was captured without difficulty. The company which was then to swing right against the Knot found it impossible to enter that work, largely owing to flanking fire from the Hilt, which had not yet been taken by the Greeks on the right. This company therefore followed those which were now leading against the trench between the Tassel and the Tongue. This trench was captured; but all efforts to take the Tassel failed. Nor was the trench between the Tassel and the Tongue held for more than a quarter of an hour. Finding it untenable, the remnants of the battalion moved to its left and joined the other two battalions, which were now on the Tongue.

1918.
19 Sept.

The 8/R. Scots Fusiliers in the centre captured the Sugar Loaf, but lost heavily from the enemy's fire in crossing it. In fact, the Bulgarian artillery fire was according to all evidence hotter on this than on the preceding day, probably on account of the lack of 6-inch howitzer gas shell for the British bombardment groups. The Tongue was captured conjointly by this battalion and the 12/Argyll and Sutherland Highlanders. Heroic efforts by the latter battalion to reach the final objectives were unavailing; indeed, seeing that its left flank was uncovered by the defection of the Zouaves, they had never the remotest chance of success. The remains of all three battalions were now on the Tongue, under the command of Lieut.-Colonel Falconar Stewart of the Argylls, and were the target for a great proportion of the enemy's artillery, as well as trench mortars and innumerable machine guns in adjoining works and trenches. The Greeks on the right had captured the Hilt, but had lost it again, so that the force on the Tongue had both flanks in the air. Three successive counter-attacks were beaten off. In the third, men of the Scottish Rifles, having no ammunition left, hurled captured stick grenades and even boulders at the enemy, then charged him with the bayonet and drove him off.

Meanwhile Br.-General Blake had realized that the Zouaves had made no move. He made efforts to telephone a message to divisional headquarters asking for a heavy-artillery barrage to be put down on the " P " Ridge, but was unable to get through for a quarter of an hour. When this fire was opened, soon after 10 a.m., it had a certain effect. He had also had several messages from the Tongue with urgent demands for ammunition, and had sent some forward on mules. Unfortunately there was delay here, the dumps not having been established far enough forward, and the ammunition party did not arrive until after Lieut.-Colonel Falconar Stewart had given the order to withdraw, at about 10.30 a.m. A number of mules were hit by the fire of the enemy, who had by now pushed well forward on the flanks of the Tongue.

It appears, indeed, certain that but for Lieut.-Colonel Falconar Stewart's order, the Bulgarians would within a very short time have killed or captured every man of the three battalions on the hill. Even as it was, the 12/Argyll and Sutherland Highlanders, bringing up the rear, was charged by the enemy, who suddenly emerged from the curtain of smoke surrounding the position and was in the midst of the British troops before they realized what had happened. After hand-to-hand fighting they shook themselves clear, but a number fell into the hands of the enemy. Lieut.-Colonel Falconar Stewart was killed or mortally wounded.

Once again the losses had been very heavy, those of the 8/R. Scots Fusiliers 358, those of the 12/Argyll and Sutherland Highlanders 299 (out of 517 all ranks in action), and those of the 11/Scottish Rifles 228. The 12/Argyll and Sutherland Highlanders was afterwards honoured by having bestowed upon it, as a battalion, the French Croix de Guerre, a signal and, for British troops, a very rare distinction which it shared with the 12/Cheshire of the 66th Brigade and the 7/S. Wales Borderers of the 67th, in respect of the attack of the 18th September.

The 65th Brigade (Br.-General B. L. Majendie) was, if all went well, to employ only one battalion, the 9/King's Own (Royal Lancaster), in the assault, to capture P.4¼ and P.4. This battalion came under the same bombardment as had fallen upon the Zouaves near Doljeli village, and, like their leading battalion, had its commanding officer, Lieut.-Colonel B. A. Jackson, wounded. Here, however, the resemblance ended. The battalion pushed on under the command of Captain C. M. Whitehead, and deployed 200 yards from P.4¼, its first objective.

The divisional commander, Major-General Duncan, had learnt from the British liaison officer, who had telephoned from the nearest point at 4.45 a.m., that the Zouaves had

ATTACK ON "P" RIDGE

been checked and were in some confusion. Major-General Duncan had at once sent an order to Colonel Boré-Verrier to move the regiment forward. Zero being at 5.15 and the barrage being timed to lift off P.4¼ at Z+20 minutes, or 5.35, he considered that there was still time to delay the attack of the King's Own, and to stop it altogether if the Zouaves did not advance. He therefore telephoned to the nearest point, which was the headquarters of the 66th Brigade at Pillar Hill, a message which was taken personally by Br.-General Montague Bates :—

"O.C. 9th King's Own.—The barrage will lift at Z+40 "off P.4¼ and Z+48 off P.4 instead of Z+20 off P.4¼ and "Z+28 off P.4. If you find the French have not attacked "the Corne you will not deliver your attack at all, but stay "in Jackson Ravine until further orders." [1]

So far as can be ascertained, this message was telephoned at 5 a.m., so that there was 35 minutes for it to reach the King's Own before the hour at which the barrage was to have lifted according to the table. Br.-General Montague Bates recalls that six separate copies were given to six trained runners. Even if the message did not arrive in time, Major-General Duncan considered that the fact that the barrage had not lifted would be obvious, and that the assault would be delayed until it did. It can safely be said that by September 1918 there were few battalions which would have attacked—or could have been induced to attack—through their own barrage. Here, unfortunately, on the one hand no runner reached the King's Own, in darkness and through a hostile barrage, in time, and on the other hand this was a battalion of exceptional devotion, which acted on the principle :—

> Theirs not to reason why,
> Theirs but to do and die.

The situation was made worse because the 424th (8-inch howitzer) Siege Battery, which on the 18th had been firing on distant objectives, was to-day taking part in the barrage on P.4¼ and P.4, as it was thought that this was the one hope of putting the infantry in. At 5.45 Br.-General Majendie was informed verbally by the headquarters of the 66th Brigade that the message had been sent to the King's

---

[1] The message is given in slightly different form in the War Diary of the 22nd Division. This is the version preserved by Br.-General Bates, which he read over to Major-General Duncan, and which he despatched.

Own, but that the brigade major feared it would be too late. It was too late.

The 9/King's Own waited exactly two minutes, then, finding that the British barrage did not lift, went straight through it and captured P.4¼. The battalion does not seem to have suffered heavy loss at this stage. It then moved forward on P.4, being now under Bulgarian artillery fire and raked by machine guns both from its objective and from the Grand Couronné. It could still, however, give an account of itself; and when the Bulgarians in P.4 stood up to fire they were at once driven down by the Lewis guns. By 5.43 the King's Own was again close to the British barrage. Two attempts were made to go through it again, but on each occasion a salvo of 8-inch shell fell amidst the battalion, and this time there were heavy casualties from the British fire. About ten men got into an advanced work not under the barrage, the rest of the battalion lying down and firing at the enemy and being now assailed with bombs in addition to machine guns and artillery. To encourage his men Captain Whitehead, though wounded, was standing up firing at the enemy with a rifle.

When the barrage did lift the machine-gun fire increased still further, and the battalion was now so weak that there was no impetus to carry it forward. Seeing that to remain where he was invited useless slaughter of his men, Captain Whitehead, wounded a second time, gave the order to withdraw. Passing through a heavy barrage which caused further losses, the battalion reached its assembly trenches at 6.15. Its casualties were 233, including one officer and 29 other ranks wounded but remaining at duty.[1] Twenty minutes after its return it received Major-General Duncan's message.

At 5.46 a.m. Major-General Duncan had had from an artillery officer an incorrect report that the leading French battalion was advancing. He then instructed Br.-General Majendie to move forward a second battalion to support the French in their attack on the Warren, and later, if necessary, to support the left of the 77th Brigade. The brigadier's message, sent off at 6.30, did not reach the 9/East Lancashire until 7.20. The commanding officer,

---

[1] The number of officers and other ranks who went into action is not recorded in the case of this battalion, but like all the battalions of the 65th Brigade it was weaker than the average owing to sickness.

Lieut.-Colonel J. A. Campbell, was in an unhappy situation, as he knew that the troops he was supposed to support were actually in disorder some distance to the rear. In the din it was impossible to issue an order, so, shouting into the ears of his company commanders instructions to follow him in a certain artillery formation, he led the battalion forward from Jackson Ravine within ten minutes of receiving the message. In front of the Corne the leading platoons came up against uncut wire, and two gallant attempts failed to penetrate it. Lieut.-Colonel Campbell, himself four times wounded, thereupon withdrew his battalion, which had suffered 118 casualties.

Just after 11 a.m. the corps commander, Lieut.-General Wilson, telephoned to General Milne that in his view the losses which would be entailed by launching fresh attacks on the " P " Ridge and Grand Couronné would not be justified. General Milne bade him not renew the attack. The 65th and 77th Brigades were therefore withdrawn at night by Major-General Duncan, while the 3rd Regiment of the Seres Division returned to its own command. General Wilson promised to relieve this division as soon as possible. On the front of the 22nd Division the 66th and 67th Brigades remained in line, though none of their own battalions were put in the foremost trenches, which were held by each brigade with two companies of the 9/Border Regiment and a battalion of Zouaves.

So, the attack had failed everywhere, not a yard of ground beyond what had been taken on the 18th having been won, though the gains of that day had been retained. There is no record of the number of prisoners captured, except the statement that they were " nearly 1,000 " in the two days. It would thus appear that about 200 were taken on the 19th, almost all by the Seres Division.

In the two days the losses of the 22nd Division, plus the attached 77th Brigade and the portion of the 83rd which was also attached, were 165 officers and 3,155 other ranks. It is only by recalling the low effectives of the infantry battalions that one can realize the crushing nature of these casualties. More than one battalion lost over 70 per cent of the numbers which went into action. Such losses in a rout are by no means unknown in military history, but in an attack they must be very rare; it is doubtful if they were exceeded at Spottsylvania or Fredericksburg.

186   THE BATTLE OF DOJRAN

Adding the casualties of the heavy artillery, of units of the field artillery other than those of the 22nd Division, and the 112 casualties suffered in the raid of the 79th Brigade of the 18th,[1] the total for the British troops of the XII Corps was 176 officers and 3,313 other ranks. The Greek Seres Division, including the regiment attached to the 22nd Division, had casualties amounting to 173 officers and 2,578 other ranks. This makes the total of the losses in the XII Corps 349 officers and 5,891 other ranks. The British losses in the XVI Corps were only one officer and 85 other ranks. Those of the Crete Division were, however, fairly heavy: 44 officers and 733 other ranks. The total Allied losses in the battle, less those of the Zouaves, which are not known,[2] were therefore 394 officers and 6,709 other ranks. Of this total over 500 captured by the enemy were very quickly released.

The Bulgarian losses between Lake Dojran and the " P " Ridge were 83 officers and 2,643 other ranks, including prisoners, from the 16th to the 19th September inclusive.[3] Those of the brigade on the Blaga Planina are not known, but it is improbable that the enemy lost more than 3,000 all told.

* * * * * * *

In commenting upon the attacks of the XII Corps we may confine our attention to that of the 18th September, because on the 19th the failure of the Zouaves to reach their positions of assembly made the task of the British troops impossible. It is evident that the 22nd Division's lack of success was due more to machine-gun than to artillery fire, heavy as was the latter and quickly as the enemy switched it on to his own works when they had been overrun. The British 18-pdr. barrage was far too thin; neither this moving curtain of fire nor the concentrations of 4·5-inch and 6-inch howitzers in rear of it prevented numerous machine guns from coming into action. In the view of one senior British artillery commander a creeping barrage was unsuitable against this position, where it was partly wasted on ground which could be seen to be without

---

[1] Other casualties of the 26th Division on the 18th are not included, though they were higher than the average of trench warfare and due to the increased activity of the Bulgarian artillery.

[2] The total number of French wounded admitted to British casualty clearing stations for the whole month was 155.

[3] Nédeff, p. 256.

DIFFICULTIES OF THE TASK

defensive organization. He would have preferred a con- 1918.
centration on trenches and points such as re-entrants and 18 Sept.
heads of spurs, where machine guns were known or suspected
to be emplaced, with a barrage on a small scale on ledges
which were defiladed by their lips from the British observers.
It must not, however, be forgotten that it was owing to the
lack of artillery of sufficient calibre—such as 8-inch or
9·2-inch howitzers—to destroy the works and emplacements
in the preliminary bombardment that the enemy's machine
guns remained in being. The obliteration of the rock-hewn
trenches was in any case an impossibility. The gas shell
was on the whole effective, though the meagre supply of
6-inch shell of this nature had caused the gas-bombardment
in the programme to be reduced. It is known that some of
the defending battalions fought in gas-masks, and the
Bulgarian historian states that, on the front of the Seres
Division at least, the defensive barrage and counter-
bombardment were not at full force because the detachments were delayed by having to work in semi-darkness
with their masks on.[1] It had been hoped that, as the
Bulgarians were unaccustomed to gas shell, their protective
measures would be incomplete and would break down;
but, according to the Bulgarian historian—whose statement
is supported by the course of events—the discipline and
training of the *9th Division* were as high in this as in other
respects, and proved equal to the test.[2] The British wire-
cutting was excellent; except at the Corne on the 19th,
there is hardly a mention of this obstacle in the reports,
though doubtless bunching at gaps contributed in some
degree to the losses. The barrage on the " P " Ridge
moved too fast on the 18th, as was recognized when it was
slowed down in the following day's programme. There
were, however, no complaints on this score from the
remainder of the front.

Though fit men are no more impervious to bullets than
sick, the bad health of the British infantry must have
affected their activity. The ground made no concessions to
fever-stricken and worn-out troops. Nor was it only the
infantrymen who were in that case. The artillerymen, who

---

[1] Nédeff, p. 235.
[2] Nédeff, p. 279. Colonel Nédeff also mentions here that preparations
had been made to meet a tank attack, " tank-traps " having been dug
and anti-tank guns installed.

had been subjected to great strain in preparing new battery positions and bringing up ammunition night after night, were no better off. On one occasion a field artillery brigade was ordered to fire smoke shell on the " P " Ridge. Br.-General H. E. Carey, C.R.A. of the division, criticized the slow rate of fire, and was told by the commanding officer that men were lying, completely exhausted, across the trails of the guns. The Greeks did not suffer in this respect, but the Seres Division—except for one regiment for a very short period nearly two years earlier—had never been in contact with British troops and knew nothing of their methods. Here, with short warning, not only was the division called upon to take part in an assault on a front which it had never seen, under British orders and almost entirely supported by British artillery, but one of its regiments—which would have been useful to exploit its success—was separated from it, incorporated in a British division, and launched to the attack with a British brigade on either side of it.

The reader may be tempted to compare adversely the methods of the 22nd Division on the 18th September with those of the French 17th Colonial and 122nd Divisions between the Vetrenik and the Sokol on the 15th. He may note that the 17th Colonial's capture of the Kravički Kamen, an objective no more distant than the Grand Couronné, was completed after the enemy had counter-attacked five times and after the advance had been held up for hours. He may recall that the attack on Point 1765 by the 122nd was a separate operation, undertaken by a mixed force, a battalion of infantry closely supported by Stokes mortars, a 37-mm. infantry gun, and two Brandt guns, after repeated re-bombardment by heavy and field artillery. He will have observed, even from the short account given here, that the French troops halted when they encountered devastating fire ; their weapons of close support concentrated in turn upon each centre of resistance ; then the infantry went forward again step by step, section by section, employing manœuvre, infiltration, mutual support between battalions, and the seizure of important tactical points. Despite the necessity for speed and the reiterated instructions of their Commander-in-Chief that the operation should be carried through in the shortest possible time, they took nearly all day to conquer a system of defence no deeper than that

facing the British, where the fate of the attack was virtually decided in a period to be measured by minutes ; but their deliberate methods succeeded completely in the end.   1918.
18 Sept.

The conditions were so different that these comparisons are hardly profitable. The French attack was a mountain operation, where, once the front line had been overrun, cover was available, and where it was generally possible for supports and ammunition carriers to scale the steep slopes without greatly exposing themselves. The main British attack between the Grand Couronné and the " P " Ridge was an advance into a defile, completely exposed on both flanks.[1] Progress step by step, reorganization followed by resumption of the advance were out of the question unless the hostile artillery were neutralized, the observation posts blinded, the machine guns put out of action.

In view of what happened on the front of the Seres Division, it is reasonable to suppose that the shifting of the main weight of the attack to the shore of Lake Dojran would have given it a better chance of success. Memories of April and May 1917 were discouraging to such a scheme. It also seems clear that, prior to the assault of the 18th September, the British underestimated the quality of the Greek troops, whose dash and drive astonished them. Had the capabilities of the Seres Division been fully realized it is possible that an effort would have been made to allow it to go into action with all its three regiments, in which case its rôle could have been proportionately enlarged. A comment on the whole battle made by one of the British liaison officers is, though it may be described as speculative, worth pondering :—

" Had the Cretan Division been available to leap-frog
" us on this first day at the third objective, I believe the
" whole Grand Couronné spur could have been captured,
" particularly if smoke shell had been used.

" I think the two great mistakes were :—

" (a) in the fifth year of the war sending the Cretan
" Division to attack on the right of Lake Dojran against
" practically uncut wire, and,

" (b) in wasting troops on the left against the almost
" impossible ' P ' Ridge, when a heavy concentration on
" the right might have been made from Petit Couronné

---

[1] See the panoramic photograph facing p. 178.

"to the lake, with only demonstration-attacks westwards towards 'P' Ridge."

The commander of the Armée Française d'Orient, General Henrys, who went over this battlefield some months later, declared that it was the "most terrible" position to assault that he had ever seen. A frontal assault with the resources available really had one hope only: that the spirit of the enemy would be weakened by bad news from west of the Vardar. This was not the case.

Of the attack of the Crete Division against the Blaga Planina there is less to be said. Its prospects of success were perhaps no brighter than those of the main attack, in view of its meagre artillery support. On the other hand, success, if attained, would have had a decisive effect upon the fate of the whole Battle of Dojran, while in the event of failure it was not to be anticipated that the casualties would be very heavy. It was a bold stroke, the difficulties of which lay in communication almost as much as in the strength of the defences or the resistance of the enemy. The argument against the employment of the Crete Division is, however, stronger even than against that of the Seres, because there were in the Struma valley three Greek divisions largely trained under the British corps commander's eye and thoroughly versed in British methods. Like the Seres Division, the Crete Division had been handed over to General Milne by General Franchet d'Espérey, expressly to take part in this operation, because it represented the flower of the Greek forces; but it is by no means certain that one of the divisions of the Royal Greek Army would not have had more success in the attack on the Blaga Planina. General Briggs would infinitely have preferred to employ one of these divisions, but General Milne was prohibited by his instructions from allotting any of them to this attack.

One outstanding success, at least, the Anglo-Greek attacks had had. They had pinned down the strong concentration of Bulgarian infantry and artillery between the Vardar and Lake Dojran and drawn in the reserves. Only one regiment, the *66th*, from that front subsequently came into action against the Serbians. It has sometimes been suggested that a less whole-hearted assault would have had the same result, but this is unlikely in the extreme. The Bulgarians, with their excellent observation posts, were in a position to distinguish at once between a demonstration and a genuine attack.

NOTE I.

XII CORPS: ARTILLERY DISPOSITIONS AND CHAIN OF COMMAND IN ATTACK OF 18TH SEPTEMBER 1918.

Br.-Gen. H. D. White Thomson,
G.O.C.R.A. XII Corps, H.Q. Yanesh.

┌─────────────────────────────────┴─────────────────────────────────┐

Br.-Gen. H. E. Carey, C.R.A. 22nd Divn., H.Q. Chugunsi.

Br.-Gen. P. L. Holbrooke, B.G. Heavy Arty., H.Q. Vergetor.

Lt.-Col. R. W. Bourchier, H.Q. Border Hill.

Gray's Group (52 18-pdrs.), H.Q. Pillar Hill.
- Sub-Group Lt.-Col. W. K. Gray (18 18-pdrs.).
- Sub-Group Lt.-Col. W. F. Parsons (18 18-pdrs.).
- Cottrell's Group, Lt.-Col. R. F. Cottrell (16 18-pdrs.).

Attached:—
Bute Mountain Bty.
1 Greek 65-mm. Bty.
1 6-in. Trench Mortar.
2 2-in. Trench Mortars.

¹ Centre Counter-Battery Group.
Lt.-Col. I. S. Cobbe, H.Q. Mort Homme.
(16 60-pdrs.)

West Bombardment Group, Lt.-Col. H. E. Molesworth, H.Q. Chugunsi.
- 4·5-in. How. Sub-Group, Lt.-Col. G. H. Gordon. (20 4·5-in. hows., 20 6-in. hows.)

3 6-in. Guns.
2 19-cm. Guns on Railway.

East Bombardment Group, Lt.-Col. H. B. Mayne, H.Q. The Shell.
- 4·5-in. How. Sub-Group, Lt.-Col. J. E. Cairnes. (16 4·5-in. hows., 16 6-in. hows., 4 8-in. hows.)

¹ Right Counter-Battery Group.
Lt.-Col. B. B. Colbeck, H.Q. The Shell.
(20 60-pdrs.)

Naper's Group (42 18-pdrs.), H.Q. Piton du Bout.
- Sub-Group Lt.-Col. L. A. D. Naper.
- Sub-Group Lt.-Col. A. P. Heneage.

Attached:—
Lt.-Col. Parnourias (3 Btys. Greek 75-mm.).
1 1 6-in. Trench Mortars.
2 2-in. Trench Mortars.

---

¹ The Left Counter-Battery Group consisted of the XX Brigade R.G.A. of eight Greek 6-in. howitzers and four British 60-pdrs. It was, as described on p. 163, distributed astride the Vardar and unable to fire on the front of attack.

THE BATTLE OF DOJRAN

NOTE II.

THE DISPOSITIONS OF THE ENEMY.

From the " P " Ridge inclusive to Lake Dojran the Bulgarians had in line the *33rd, 17th,* and *58th Regiments,* the first and third of these consisting of three battalions and the second of four battalions, and each having 32 machine guns. The *33rd,* with the regiment on its right, the *57th,* formed the *3rd Brigade* ; [1] the *17th* and *58th* formed the *1st Brigade.* The *34th Regiment* (four battalions) was in divisional reserve, which also comprised the composite battalions attached to the *33rd* and *34th Regiments.* The *4th Regiment* (four battalions), which formed part of the *9th Division,* was in Army reserve, but was placed at the disposal of the divisional commander in the course of the 18th September, with the exception of one battalion which was handed over to the *Mountain Division.* These reserves were fully utilized on the 18th, no less than three battalions being moved to the defences of the Grand Couronné. One battalion of the *34th* was despatched in the evening to Nikolić, to the assistance of the *1st Macedonian Brigade,* opposed to the XVI Corps. The battalion was, however, not engaged, and returned next day. By the evening of the 18th the Army Commander, General Nerezov, had handed over all his reserves,[2] and those at the disposal of General Vazov, commanding the *9th Division,* consisted only of the two composite battalions and his divisional cavalry squadron. Yet it is impossible to criticize the dispositions. In view of the difficulties of movement, especially lateral, each brigade and regimental commander had to have under his hand sufficient troops to launch strong counter-attacks. The fact that the reserves were thus parcelled out does not imply that the principle of defence in depth was neglected.

All the Bulgarian counter-attacks were, as we have seen, successful, except that launched against Hill 340 on the afternoon of the 18th, and this never really developed. General Vazov then decided that the recapture of the whole advanced position between O.1 and O.6 could be carried out only at the price of very heavy loss, and ordered the attempt to be abandoned and the main line to be held at all costs.

In the course of the two attacks by the troops of the XII Corps the Bulgarians claim to have captured 543 prisoners—not specifying how many were British and how many Greek—67 machine guns, and 145 Lewis guns or *fusils-mitrailleurs.*

---

[1] That is to say, the *3rd Brigade* of the *9th Division.* The Bulgarian brigades were not numbered consecutively as in the British Army.

[2] But see p. 160, *fn.* 2.

CHAPTER X.

THE FINAL OFFENSIVE: THE EXPLOITATION.

(Maps A, 1, 8, 9; Sketches A, 7.)

THE EXPLOITATION WEST OF THE VARDAR, 18TH–21ST SEPTEMBER.

THE 18th September, the day on which the Anglo-Greek forces threw themselves against the Dojran defences, was marked not indeed by any pause but by a slight slackening in the great battle west of the Vardar. The left of the enemy's *Eleventh Army* was withdrawing behind the Belašnica, and the Crna south of the confluence, employing the *massif* of the Dzena as a pivot. The Serbian Armies were pressing on at their best pace, and though few troops could have attained as good a one, it was not fast. On the front of the Second Army the Timok Division was advancing over the Blatec heights; further west the Yugoslav Division drove the enemy's rearguard out of the flaming village of Rožden and halted at night with its head at Mrežečko, in front of the new Bulgarian line. On its left the Morava Division of the First Army also closed up to the Belašnica; and the other two divisions, the Drina and Danube, moved against the Crna. Before nightfall they reached the bank, except at Rasim Bey bridge, where the enemy held a strong bridgehead. The 1st Group of Divisions slightly enlarged the breach on the right, a Franco-Greek detachment capturing Nonte at night.

1918.
18 Sept.
Map 8.
Sketches A, 7.

Nevertheless, the breach, 30 miles wide and in the centre some 18 miles in depth, was becoming a pocket, such as had lately proved so dangerous to the attacker on the Western Front. Undoubtedly its shape influenced the German commanders in their next important and, as it proved, disastrous decision. Let us again glance at the situation as it appeared to the *Glavha Kvartira*—Bulgarian General Headquarters—and to Generals von Scholtz and von Steuben.

During the Anglo-Greek attack at Dojran that morning General Nerezov, the Bulgarian *First Army* commander, had gone forward to the trenches to encourage the troops in support and see what he could of the situation with his own eyes. He found it good; the troops were confident, and the enemy's attack was broken. He therefore had a message telephoned to G.H.Q., urging that a general attack should be launched by the *Second Army* on the Struma. If this were done, he for his part was prepared to pass to the offensive with his *First Army*.[1] The advice was daring in the extreme, but it may well have been the soundest that could have been tendered at this moment. If a convergent advance in the direction of Salonika, not only by the *First* and *Second Armies* on the east, but also by the unbroken right wing of the *Eleventh Army* on the west, had made even limited progress it would have set the Allies a difficult problem to solve. At any rate, when the acting Commander-in-Chief, General Todorov, drove to Prilep for a conference that afternoon, he had been won over to the project.

He found the Germans unwilling to risk so bold a stroke. The conference was held at the headquarters of General von Steuben, General von Scholtz, the Army Group commander, being represented by his Chief of the Staff, Colonel Graf von Schwerin. All the commanders were sufficiently impressed by the danger of the situation. Scholtz himself had first appealed to German *Oberste Heeresleitung* for reinforcements on the 16th, the day after the launch of the Franco-Serbian attack; on the following day Todorov had asked for at least six German divisions.[2] All that *O.H.L.* had so far promised was a composite German brigade; there had also been talk of one Austro-Hungarian division. A grand counter-offensive in the direction of Salonika seemed to the Germans impossible; they did not consider that they had sufficient troops or that they could horse sufficient batteries and supply columns for a general advance.

On the other hand, they were averse to any considerable withdrawal, the official excuse for their view being that the abandonment of Ohrid, the capital of the Bulgarian Tsar

---

[1] Nédeff, p. 225.
[2] "Weltkriegsende an der mazedonischen Front," p. 48. Lieut.-Colonel T. G. G. Heywood, G.S.O.1 Intelligence at British G.H.Q., who carried out a special mission to Sofia between the 6th and 10th October, was there shown a telegram from Field-Marshal v. Hindenburg. This telegram was addressed to General Todorov and referred to one from him dated the 16th. It was, however, actually a reply to the demand of General v. Scholtz, not to the much bigger demand of General Todorov, which according to the German evidence was sent on the 17th. The Field-Marshal's telegram is given in Appendix 16.

THE ENEMY'S PLAN 195

Samuel at the beginning of the eleventh century, would have 1918.
had an unfortunate moral effect upon the Bulgarians, who 18 Sept.
regarded the little city with veneration. Here again,
though it is stated that Tsar Ferdinand himself was strongly
opposed to giving up Ohrid and Resan, the Germans seem to
have been at odds with Bulgarian G.H.Q. At least, arguing
after the event, Bulgarian critics aver that, in default of the
grand counter-offensive, a big withdrawal to the line Tetovo–
Skoplje–Štip–the Plačkovica mountains and the Ograźden
mountains (north of the Strumica valley) would have been
the best and most courageous policy.[1] It would certainly
have caused some embarrassment to the Allies. For the
reason cited above, and perhaps also because the big withdrawal would have involved loss of contact with the
Austrians in Albania or forced the latter to fall back, the
German commanders were in favour of a smaller rearward
movement. There was, into the bargain, the fascination of
that pocket. Would not its maintenance induce the enemy
to pause before plunging in deeper, when every step forward
brought a more serious threat to his flanks? And if a
general counter-offensive was impossible, local operations
against the sides of the pocket might be feasible later on,
and very profitable. The final decision, to which General
Todorov was brought round, was that if any further withdrawal on the battle front took place the *Eleventh Army*
should bend back across Hill 1248, north-west of Monastir,
but hold on to its positions from thence westward. Meanwhile the battered Bulgarian *3rd Division* would be propped
up as soon as possible by the German *Landwehr* troops
originally destined for the Struma valley and all other
available reinforcements.[2]

At first glance the decision looks sound; on closer
examination it appears doubtful in the extreme. To begin
with, the danger of the pocket is very much slighter in
mountainous country than in plains. The great experts in
mountain warfare, such as Bourcet, have shown that the
time factor here favours the attacker, so much so that,
despite appearances, the offensive has the advantage over
the defensive. The attacker has already chosen a direction
conforming to the general run of the communications. The
defender, obliged to split up his formations and keep them

---
[1] Bujac, p. 123.
[2] " Weltkriegsende an der mazedonischen Front," pp. 47 *et seq.*

closed up to the front, can seldom collect within the necessary limits of time forces sufficient for a powerful counter-offensive at the most suitable point.

Nor does the decision provide an answer to the most urgent question: What is likely to be the scheme of the enemy's Commander-in-Chief? Such danger as there was in a deep pocket both General Franchet d'Espérey and the Voivode Mišić were determined to avoid. The Commander-in-Chief's directive to his Serbian lieutenant had assigned to the Second Army Demir Kapija and Negotino as objectives, upon each of which two of its four divisions [1] were to advance. But the First Army was to capture the bridges over the Crna at Rasim Bey and further north, establish a bridgehead beyond the river, and subsequently co-operate with the Armée Française d'Orient in an attack in the direction of Prilep, which would constitute a grave threat to the right of the *Eleventh Army* if it continued to cling to its positions north of Monastir. Far from plunging bull-headed into the breach, the First Army was swinging outward in order to enlarge it. It would batter away at the Crna crossings until it had secured a passage. Even though there was no such risk as the Germans had recently incurred on the Marne, that was the best means to avoid being "pocketed," so far as the western side of the breach was concerned.

The eastern side was another matter. Had the Anglo-Greek attack of the 18th been successful, there would have been small need to worry about that; but it had failed, and as we know, the second attack on the 19th was to fail also. Nor was the 1st Group of Divisions west of the Vardar strong enough either in men or in guns to launch a general attack. It could, however, thrust at the great buttress on which the enemy's line had swung back, the *massif* of the Dzena, which rose at its highest point to nearly 7,000 feet. The capture of this mountain mass would cover the advance of the Serbian Second Army, decrease the risk of a successful counter-attack on this flank, and afford an opportunity to turn the strong Bulgarian main line about Huma. General d'Anselme was ready to launch this attack on the Dzena on the morning of the 19th.

---

[1] That is, Timok and Šumadija on the right against Demir Kapija; Yugoslav and 17th Colonial on the left against Negotino. The 122nd was now in reserve to the Allied Armies.

It was a neat and skilful little mountain operation, carried out in five columns by a Franco-Greek force of troops drawn from the French 16th Colonial and the Greek 4th Divisions, under the orders of Colonel Rondet. On the right, a flank guard of two Greek battalions under Lieut.-Colonel Kourospoulos, moving off 24 hours after the others, marched round the southern slopes. A second column of one French and one Greek battalion under Lieut.-Colonel Savin attacked the Dzena frontally from the direction of Nonte ; a third, of a single French battalion, acting as left flank guard to the above, set out to cross the slopes of the Duditsa mountain with the Jarena, the col connecting the Duditsa and the Dzena, as objective. A fourth Franco-Greek column of two battalions under Lieut.-Colonel Pérès, which was already established on the Preslap, advanced north-eastward, to capture the Kojuh and then move against the Jarena from the south-west. On the extreme left a fifth all-Greek column of two battalions under Lieut.-Colonel Gargalides began a turning movement round the western and northern slopes of the Duditsa with the object of coming upon the Jarena from the rear.

The operation lasted two full days ; it was, in fact, not really completed until the morning of the 21st, when the Bulgarians had withdrawn. But throughout those two days the encircling columns were always edging forward, and by nightfall on the 20th, after a bombardment from the plain directed by wireless against the summit of the Dzena, the Savin column had established itself thereon, and that of Lieut.-Colonel Pérès was astride the Jarena.

Meanwhile the Voivode Stepanović had progressed steadily. On the 19th his Timok Division, covering its right rear towards the Dzena, pressed boldly due north between the Drenska and Bošava streams ; the Yugoslav broke the enemy's line on the Belašnica, where, according to the German report, the Bulgarian *3rd Division* made very little resistance. The First Army hammered at the line of the Crna between the Belašnica and Rasim Bey, but failed to establish a bridgehead anywhere, the few small bodies which managed to cross being pinned to their ground or driven back by counter-attacks. At Rasim Bey the enemy still held the right bank. That evening, perhaps, afforded him, if he had the heart, his last chance of preventing the Serbians from completely overrunning the Vardar-Crna loop. Despite the energy and endurance of the Second Army, the pressure cannot have been really severe. The Timok and Yugoslav Divisions were inevitably strung out over bad roads; the Šumadija and 17th Colonial were being held far in rear by the Voivode Stepanović, because he could not otherwise feed them. On the enemy's side the Bulgarian *66th Regiment*, from *First Army* reserve,[1] was on the march to Kavadarci, and two battalions of the German *12th Landwehr Regiment* were expected at Krnjovo, the most threatened point. Certain other reinforcements, including a battalion of German heavy artillery, were on the move. On the other hand, the Bulgarian *3rd Division* was virtually in dissolution, despite the personal intervention of the heir to the Bulgarian throne.

From now onwards Prince Boris, hurrying from point to point in a light lorry which he drove himself, was present wherever the risk of a break-through was greatest, encouraging the troops and displaying qualities of energy, gallantry, and coolness which were to endear him to his people and, within the next few days, to preserve for him the throne on which he now sits.

1918.
20 Sept.
Onward struggled the Second Army on the 20th, the Yugoslav Division crossing the Vataša stream and driving the Bulgarians before it in the direction of Kavadarci. The First Army towards nightfall at last established strong detachments on the left bank of the Crna. On its left the 11th Colonial Division of the Armée Française d'Orient won a bridgehead over the river west of Selo Monastir. The capture of the Dzena by the 1st Group of Divisions has already been recorded.

The enemy was making a last stand to cover the Vardar railway. The *66th Regiment*, not yet engaged and in good case, had reached Kavadarci; the two *Landwehr* battalions had arrived at Krnjovo, from which, however, they had quickly to retreat. General von Scholtz had decided that in the event of further progress by the Serbians he would make a big withdrawal. The *Eleventh Army* would, in accordance with his previous decision, hold its positions between Lake Prespa and Monastir, but would abandon the line of the Crna and take up a new one roughly following the Monastir-Prilep road up to Topolčani and thence due

---

[1] See p. 160.

THE SERBS REACH THE VARDAR 199

eastward across the Crna. But the hitherto victorious *First Army*, which had lost no ground except the strip on the shore of Lake Dojran, would have to make a considerable retirement in order to preserve any semblance of contact. The new line was to run across the Vardar-Crna loop south of Kavadarci to the Vardar at Strumica Station, then eastward behind the Bajimia—the stream which had provided so welcome a stage in the French retreat of December 1915 [1] —to the Belašica Planina. The breach which had been 30 miles wide on the 18th September would now be over 70.

1918.
20 Sept.

The issue of the order was put off from hour to hour at the instance of Prince Boris; but bad news was still coming in, and at 4 p.m. General von Scholtz decided to wait no longer. The order went out to the two Armies, which were bidden to commence the withdrawal that night. But it was not the order originally drafted; for already the Serbians were on the outskirts of Kavadarci, which, in fact, the Yugoslav Division occupied that evening. The *First Army* could no longer hold the heights in the Vardar-Crna loop; it must get behind the Vardar right up to Gradsko. Thus, not only was the railway below Gradsko abandoned, but the Sofia-Štip-Prilep road, which crossed the Vardar at Krivolak, was on the point of being cut.

And so, before dawn on the 21st, the Serbians, looking down from the high ground into the valley of the Vardar, saw the glare of burning villages and depots, while ever and anon the crash of an explosion came to their ears as the enemy blew up an ammunition dump. Down into the valley marched the troops of the Second Army. That evening the heads of the columns reached the river: the Timok Division in the neighbourhood of Demir Kapija, the Yugoslav towards the confluence with the Crna. On all that front the enemy was behind the formidable barrier of the Vardar.

21 Sept.

On the wings the withdrawal was slow and even deliberate, but already General d'Anselme was beginning to push his left eastward from the Dzena to outflank the rest of the Bulgarian line between that point and the Vardar, and was prepared to launch a strong attack on Huma next day. On the left Bulgarian columns were seen moving northward from the Crna bend towards Prilep.

---

[1] See Vol. I, p. 73.

Here French and Greek patrols found the positions abandoned. The Italian 35th Division rushed the notorious Côte 1050, from which the enemy had looked down upon its troops for two years, and scattered the Bulgarian rear guard in flight. The Italian troops knew only too well the strength of that fortress, the equivalent on their front of the Grand Couronné on the British, but even they were amazed by the size of the chambers on the northern flank of the hill, hewn out of solid rock, absolutely impervious to artillery fire, and lit by electricity.[1] Even west of the bend there was progress on the immediate right bank of the Crna ; but west of Monastir the enemy's line held firm, and the French fighting patrols could nowhere get a footing in it.

That the Allied Commander-in-Chief had no intention of burying his troops in a pocket he showed by a new general instruction issued on the afternoon of the 21st.[2] " We have now," he wrote, " to widen the breach made in " the enemy's array and to complete our success." The Serbian Second Army would halt its main body on the Vardar between Demir Kapija and Gradsko, establishing on the left of that front a strong bridgehead from Krivolak to Gradsko. The bridgehead would be on the left because, as we remember, Krivolak–Gradsko was the goal of the first stage of the operations, the nodal point of the routes from Prilep into the heart of Bulgaria by the valley of the Bregalnica and into the heart of Serbia through Veles and Skoplje. Meanwhile the right of the Army would aid the 1st Group of Divisions to reach the Vardar and in its turn establish a bridgehead about Hudova (Strumica Station). The First Army was directed to " operate in the direction of " Prilep and north-east of that town in order to outflank " the enemy's successive positions of retirement and to " facilitate the advance of the Armée Française d'Orient."

The Armée Française d'Orient, for its part, was to progress in the direction of Prilep in the manner indicated in the " General Instructions for the Exploitation " issued on the 21st August.[3] It was not to launch a grand attack

---

[1] Villari, p. 235.
[2] This instruction, unlike others referred to, does not appear to have been preserved among the British documents. It is here taken from General Revol, who, though he does not quote it quite in full, does quote textually the most important passages, so that reference to the French Historical Service has not appeared necessary.
[3] See Appendix 11.

until its artillery had been returned to it, unless signs of withdrawal seemed to call for action earlier. Now, the instructions to which allusion was made had laid down a great programme for the Army. It had been directed, first of all, to "operate in the direction of Prilep, in touch "with the Serbian First Army, so as to break the enemy "array west of the Crna or at least force him to retreat." Then it was to take as objective the important road-junction of Kičevo (where a road to Prilep branched off from the Skoplje–Tetovo–Gostivar–Monastir road) "so as "to manœuvre out of position the Bulgarian forces still in "the region of the lakes." And then its rôle was to be the grand, the predominant one: "becoming the marching "wing of the Allied Armies, the A.F.O. will continue its "movement, its left thrown forward, so as to attain at the "end of the First Phase the line Veles–Usküb (Skoplje)."

1918.
21 Sept.

The Army could not, however, completely fulfil this rôle while the enemy held on to his positions from Hill 1248 westward. And the enemy was holding on precisely to secure his communications through Kičevo, because he has first of all to feed, then to withdraw, something like four divisions by a road following a winding course to Skoplje, and dared not risk jambing this corridor. General Franchet d'Espérey, for some reason not clear,[1] but possibly because he thought that by not hurrying the enemy he would have the better chance of blocking him at Skoplje, sent no order to General Henrys to widen his zone of advance by an attack north-west of Monastir, and General Henrys, while exercising continual but ineffective pressure, did not launch one. His right, of course, in front of which the enemy had retired, was in motion and was swinging westward towards the Monastir–Prilep road. By such means General Henrys doubtless hoped to cut across the line of retreat of the enemy between Monastir and the lakes. He had, as appears from the instructions quoted above, a double rôle, first, to operate towards Kičevo, and, secondly, to march on Skoplje. We shall see that General Franchet d'Espérey did not agree with his conception of the relative importance

---

[1] Not clear to the most instructed commentator. General Revol (p. 79) writes:—" Franchet d'Espérey lui-même prescrit qu'elle (l'attaque) "'n'aura lieu qu'après la réunion de tous les moyens.' Cela manque de "précision; cela permet d'attendre. Et l'armée française d'Orient "attend."

THE PURSUIT ON THE BRITISH FRONT, 21ST–24TH SEPTEMBER.

**1918.
19 Sept.
Maps A, 9.**

The evening of the 19th was marked by a pause of grim significance on the British front. Between Lake Dojran and the Vardar especially there was a silence of exhaustion, the artillery on both sides being worn out by day after day of almost continuous bombardment. What was to be the next move? A letter from General Franchet d'Espérey, which came in to British G.H.Q. at 6.45 p.m., answered that question. Although the attacks on either side of Lake Dojran had not accomplished what had been hoped, yet they had tied down a great proportion of the enemy's forces. Meanwhile the Serbian advance was threatening his communications in the Vardar valley, and the 1st Group of Divisions was about to begin manœuvring by its left towards the river. The immediate object of the forces west of the Vardar would now be to drive the enemy to the left bank all the way down from the river's confluence with the Crna to the present front line. For this purpose General Milne was requested to place the 27th Division temporarily under the orders of General d'Anselme, commanding the 1st Group of Divisions, and to reinforce it with artillery from the left bank.

General Milne at once agreed to these measures. At the same time he pointed out to General Franchet d'Espérey how difficult was his situation. Owing to very heavy losses and lack of reinforcements, the 22nd Division and one brigade of the 26th were incapable of further action unless first withdrawn into reserve. The two Greek divisions must likewise be given a rest. The Seres Division would not be fit to fight again for some time to come; but the Crete Division could soon resume active operations, and if withdrawn to the Kürküt area could be quickly moved up again. It would be necessary to use the Greek 14th Division to replace the most exhausted formations of the XII Corps and to retain the 2nd *bis* Zouaves for a few days longer.

Of reinforcements there was no hope. General Milne, in a personal telegram of the 20th to General Sir Henry

Wilson, made a strong appeal for his formations to be brought up to strength as quickly as possible either by British drafts or by the long promised Indian troops. He pointed out that his four divisions really represented only the value of two, hardly even that, because skeleton divisions were extravagant to maintain and gave a false impression to the Allied command, so that tasks beyond their powers were likely to be assigned to them. The C.I.G.S. replied next day that British drafts could not be found, but that the movement of the Indian battalions would be hastened and that he hoped the first six would reach Salonika about the third week of October. He remarked that, to his knowledge, no suggestion had been made of continuing the operations with the Anglo-Greek force, the action of which was to have been limited to that already undertaken. This telegram was sent before the C.I.G.S. had learnt of the Bulgarian retreat east of the Vardar; it was, of course, then obvious that the British Army must take part in the pursuit.

1918. 20 Sept.

Yet the bald truth is that the War Office and the British Section of the Supreme War Council had never liked the offensive and were now surprised by its development. Even the French General Staff was half-hearted on the subject ; on the 21st it actually considered the possibility of withdrawing more troops from Macedonia, in anticipation of which the Commander-in-Chief must give thought to measures for " limiting his offensive and stabil- " izing his new front." [1] As late as the 25th, when the Allied Armies were well on their way to a decisive success, the British Section of the Supreme War Council telegraphed to the C.I.G.S., asking to be informed of the scope of the operation, whether any reinforcements had been promised to General Franchet d'Espérey, and, if so, where they were to come from. Unless Bulgaria sued for peace, it appeared that the Allies would either have to fall back to their old line and abandon their gains or find a new line of defence, which would almost inevitably be longer than the old and require more troops for its maintenance.

General Franchet d'Espérey had, in fact, taken upon his shoulders the real responsibility for Allied military policy in the Balkans. The scheme upon which he had

---
[1] Larcher, p. 232. This was an appreciation on which no action was taken.

embarked was not that to which the Allied Governments had been induced to give their approval, and he had of set purpose been vague regarding its scope. As it proved, it was most fortunate that he was left uncontrolled; otherwise it is improbable that he would have been able to win a complete victory. And in the Balkans at this time a victory incomplete would have been hardly a victory at all.

*   *   *   *   *   *   *

On the morning of the 20th General Milne directed General Briggs to withdraw the Crete Division at once to Kürküt and neighbouring camps. He directed General Wilson to withdraw the 22nd and Seres Divisions as soon as reliefs could be arranged, and placed at his disposal for this purpose the Greek 14th Division of two regiments,[1] and the two battalions of the 83rd Brigade which had temporarily formed part of a composite brigade on the XVI Corps front. All the field artillery batteries of the 27th Division now east of the Vardar were to return to their division at once, and in addition the XX Brigade R.G.A. (three 60-pdr. batteries), the XXXVII Brigade R.G.A. (three 6-inch howitzer batteries), and the Bute Mountain Battery were to be moved to the west bank at the earliest possible moment.

General Wilson could not relieve the 22nd and Seres Divisions until the battalions of the 83rd Brigade and the Greek 14th Division had arrived. The British battalions, moving by lorry, rejoined their brigade on the afternoon of the 21st, and the brigade was ordered to relieve the Seres Division on the night of the 22nd. At noon on the 21st the 27th Division came under the orders of General d'Anselme.

1918.
21 Sept.
That morning had brought the first signs of the retreat, loud explosions being heard between 8 and 8.30 a.m., and the Royal Air Force observing considerable movement northward on both banks of the Vardar. By early afternoon this movement had developed, and then British aircraft began to bomb with terrific effect long columns of transport. The aircraft flew over the columns in relays, dropping bombs upon them and then returning to their aerodromes for another load. In some cases they swooped down to within fifty feet of the ground, to rake troops and

---

[1] For the arrival of the first regiment of this division, see p. 172. General Franchet d'Espérey now sent a second.

transport with machine-gun fire. The target was an extraordinary one. There is in existence a set of aeroplane photographs which show a solid stream of transport, for the most part double-banked, between Valandova and the Rabrovo cross-roads and also south and east of the latter point, with bombs bursting in its midst. At the crossroads it can be seen that the columns are completely blocked by the bombing and are in a congested mass, unable to make their way northward towards Kosturino.

1918.
21 Sept.

General Wilson issued instructions that all defensive work should cease and that the troops should be given as much rest as possible with a view to an advance. He ordered the 26th Division to occupy the Machukovo Salient, and placed the Greek 14th Division (Colonel Orphanidis) under its orders. He closed up the cavalry at his disposal, the Derbyshire Yeomanry and the Lothians and Border Horse, and sent a squadron of the latter across the Vardar to rejoin the 27th Division, to which it had previously been attached. The French armoured train was, by order of General Franchet d'Espérey, transferred to the 1st Group of Divisions.

Thus, the great moment, awaited for three years and mocking all hopes, till many had ceased to believe that it would ever come, had come at last, but very awkwardly for the Anglo-Greek Army. On the front of both the XII and XVI Corps reliefs were in progress, with the object of withdrawing the most exhausted and depleted formations for rest and reorganization. On that of the XII Corps they were never actually to be completed, except in the case of the Seres Division ; on that of the XVI Corps it was to be necessary to countermand them, the Crete Division being brought back before half of it had reached its camping ground. Of the twelve British brigades—not counting the 228th, which was incapable from its constitution of great exertion—only seven could be reckoned as fresh, and of these two belonged to the 27th Division and three to the 28th, both of which had been very heavy sufferers from malaria. The fittest troops were probably the 78th and 79th Brigades of the 26th Division. Influenza, which had so heavily attacked the 65th Brigade, had extended its ravages to many other formations ; certain technical units such as signal companies and sections, wherein practically every man formed an important cog in the machine, were especially hard hit. The next week was to be a nightmare to many men, who had to march and sometimes fight—though there was no really heavy fighting—when they ought to have been in hospital or at least in a medical rest-camp.

The newly-arrived Greek division, the 14th (Kalamata), consisting of two infantry regiments only and without artillery, was not fully trained, but it was fortunately fresh and vigorous. It was also well led, Colonel Orphanidis—with exhortation and impulsion from General Briggs, which were never lacking—being the most efficient and energetic Greek divisional commander with whom the British had worked. It was to do excellent service in the pursuit. The Crete Division, though it did not receive its promised rest, proved that it was fit for more work and of a most difficult kind.

1918.
22 Sept. During the night of the 21st the 26th Division pushed out two battalions which occupied the enemy's front-line trenches in the Machukovo salient. Before morning reports came in from the whole of the XII Corps front that the patrols sent out had either not found contact with the enemy or had been opposed only by very weak rear guards. The Seres Division was ordered to occupy the Grand Couronné, but to go no further, as it was not fit to take part in a pursuit and was to be relieved as soon as possible by the 83rd Brigade. At 7.10 a.m. on the 22nd General Wilson ordered the 22nd and 26th Divisions to concentrate and prepare to advance. The patrols of the 22nd had by now entered the trenches of the second line ; the 2nd *bis* Zouaves was occupying the Koh-i-Noor and P.2, and the 26th Division had patrolled from Boyau Hill a full mile along the enemy's front line, which here ran due north. From the " P " Ridge it could be seen that the enemy had withdrawn as far as the Blaga Planina and its western extension, the Kara Bail Ridge. Again, as soon as it was light, the Royal Air Force had begun to bomb the Bulgarian transport thronging the roads northward, especially the main road from Dojran which entered the Strumica valley by the pass at Kosturino. Terrible execution was done ; horses and bullocks were stampeded when they were not hit ; and inextricable confusion was caused in the columns. The German aircraft, active until the 20th, now hardly put in an appearance. As the officer commanding No. 16 Wing, Lieut.-Colonel G. E. Todd, remarked in a

letter to Major-General W. G. H. Salmond, " they must have "realized that it was all up with the Bulgars, and consequently packed up and cleared off."

From General Franchet d'Espérey there came at noon an exultant telegram that the enemy was in retreat on the whole front from Monastir to Lake Dojran, and that the retreat must be turned to a rout by an unceasing and resolute pursuit.[1]

It will be recalled that it was General Milne's original intention that his two corps should reunite north of Lake Dojran in the neighbourhood of Hasanli. That, however, had been before both had failed in their attacks. The situation was now rather different. On the front of the XVI Corps the enemy would certainly cling to the crest of the Belašica Planina till the last possible moment. To storm these mountains frontally was impossible. The XVI Corps could therefore from its present position take part in the pursuit only by crossing the Blaga Planina. But that ridge was still held by the enemy, and could more easily be taken from the rear, by means of an advance west of Lake Dojran. Moreover, west of the lake there were several roads leading northward, that through Kosturino to Strumica being, so far as was known, a good one.

General Milne therefore decided to alter his dispositions. He would bring the headquarters of the XVI Corps over to the left flank and place under General Briggs's orders the two left-hand divisions, the Greek 14th and British 26th, and the Derbyshire Yeomanry; also the 27th Division as soon as it crossed the Vardar and returned to the British command. General Wilson, commanding the XII Corps, would retain under his orders the 22nd and Seres Divisions,[2] and the 2nd *bis* Zouaves; he would take over the 28th Division (of which the 83rd Brigade was already under him), the Crete Division, less artillery and one regiment,[3] and the 228th Brigade east of Lake Dojran. The 28th Division

---
[1] See Appendix 17.
[2] The Seres Division was shortly afterwards handed over by General Franchet d'Espérey to the Greek I Corps to relieve the 1st Division in the Struma valley, in order to place a fresh division in reserve to the Allied Armies. The relief had not yet taken place when the Armistice was concluded.
[3] By orders of General Franchet d'Espérey, the Cretan 29th Regiment and the mountain artillery of the division were moved to Bohemitsa, on the right bank of the Vardar, as reserve to the 1st Group of Divisions. They were not actually required, and rejoined their division on the 27th.

would, however, be relieved as quickly as possible by the Cretans, and, leaving one of its artillery brigades with them, march round the southern shore of the lake in order to take part in the pursuit on the western side. The XVI Corps would then become the marching wing of the Army, its objective being the Strumica valley, where it would be behind the Belašica Planina. The XII Corps would clear the Blaga Planina from the south-west and advance as far as the dominating height of the Višoka Čuka, or Signal Allemand, on the Belašica Planina. The Crete Division, east of Lake Dojran, would cross the plain and work its way up the slopes of the Belašica Planina, thus co-operating with the XII Corps, the advance of which would in turn make the scaling of these precipitous heights by the Cretans possible.

In the course of the 22nd the 83rd Brigade and the 2nd *bis* Zouaves, both attached to the 22nd Division, pushed forward and occupied without opposition the villages of Kara Ullar and Hamzali. The field companies of the division made the Dojran-Volovec track through the bombarded area fit for the passage of guns. On the front of the XVI Corps the 26th Division occupied a line from Dugout Hill, through the little town or large village of Stojakovo to a hummock on the bank of the Vardar known as the Table de Bogorodica. The Greek 14th Division was at nightfall moving up to fill the four-mile gap between Hamzali and Dugout Hill. The heavy artillery on the Dojran-Vardar front was divided between the two corps: the LXXXII Brigade R.G.A. (20th and 196th Heavy Batteries, 132nd and 320th Siege Batteries) to the XII Corps; the LXXV Brigade R.G.A. (188th and 192nd Heavy Batteries, the 130th Siege Battery) to the XVI Corps.[1]

The orders issued by General Milne for the 23rd were as follows. The advance was to be continued with the greatest

---

[1] The XX and XXXVII Brigades R.G.A., comprising three 60-pdr. and three 6-inch howitzer batteries were moving across the Vardar to rejoin the 27th Division. The 190th Heavy Battery and one 6-inch gun of the 43rd Siege Battery remained east of Lake Dojran, where on the following day General Spiliades, commanding the Crete Division, assumed command of all troops, including the 228th Infantry Brigade. The commander of this brigade, Br.-General W. C. Ross, was directed to carry out the same functions at the headquarters of the Crete Division as Br.-General Hare had at that of the Seres Division during the attacks of the 18th and 19th; that is, to convey and interpret the orders of General Wilson to General Spiliades.

ENEMY'S RESISTANCE ON BAJIMIA 209

possible speed ; the XII Corps was to clear the Blaga Planina and the Kara Bail spur ; the XVI Corps to secure the high ground at Casandule overlooking the valley of the Bajimia and the road bridge between Mravinca and Miletkovo. The boundary was the main Cinarli-Dedeli road, inclusive to the XVI Corps.[1]

1918.
23 Sept.

The heat, the fatigue of many of the units engaged, and the bad state of the roads made the advance of the XII Corps on the 23rd a slow one. On the right the 83rd Brigade (Br.-General R. H. Hare), which had concentrated at Kara Ullar with advanced guard at Hasanli, advanced up the steep slope of the Blaga Planina, two battalions in line and the XII Corps Cyclist Battalion covering the right flank. The opposition was very slight and came only from single snipers, but the brigade did not reach the crest until 9 p.m. The 2nd *bis* Zouaves had some trouble with a small rear guard on the Kara Bail, but cleared the ridge during the night. One field artillery brigade of the 22nd Divisional Artillery came into action in support of each formation, though they found few targets ; the other two were held in rear for the time being so as not to congest the tracks.

On the front of the XVI Corps the Derbyshire Yeomanry, moving forward from Stojakovo, rode through Bogdanci and reached a position north-west of Furka, where it came under the fire of mountain artillery. It was evident that the enemy was holding the high ground south of the Bajimia in some strength, there being half a dozen mountain guns in action about Casandule. Fire was opened by the advanced sections of field artillery, and bodies of Bulgarians were seen falling back in confusion across the Bajimia, but they still apparently held the south bank at nightfall. The head of the Greek 14th Division, which had started in rear of the other troops, got no further than Furka ; the 78th Brigade (Br.-General G. H. F. Wingate) of the 26th Division occupied the Schwarzberg, half-way between Bogdanci and Casandule. The heavy artillery was far in rear, three 6-inch howitzer batteries having managed to reach Stojakovo, nearly ten miles distant from the Bajimia.

Only a handful of stragglers and half a dozen abandoned guns had so far been captured, but immense quantities of

---

[1] See Appendix 18.

stores of every kind had been found, sometimes half-burnt but more often intact. The quantity and quality of the Bulgarian supplies, the size of the ammunition dumps, and the excellent equipment of the headquarters were, indeed, a matter of astonishment to the British troops. There was certainly on this part of the front no evidence of the penury of which many deserters had spoken.

General Milne was anxious to hasten the advance. There were, he considered, more columns on the roads than were required to deal with the very slight resistance of the enemy, and their number was in itself a check to progress. The time had now come, he pointed out, for the bold employment of advanced guards with a few light guns; behind them the columns should not deploy unless forced to do so by opposition more serious than had yet been met with. His orders for the morrow were that the XII Corps should clear the remainder of the Blaga Planina and occupy the Višoka Čuka, or Signal Allemand, on the Belašica Planina, and that the XVI Corps should continue its advance on the Kosturino defile, the gate to the Strumica valley, reporting its progress to General d'Anselme, commanding the 1st Group of Divisions, and establishing touch with his troops when they crossed the Vardar.

1918.
24 Sept.
General Wilson thereupon ordered the 22nd Division to push forward an advanced guard to the Signal Allemand, and the Crete Division to advance its left regiment to the neighbourhood of Nikolić, whence it was to endeavour to get touch with the 22nd on the Belašica Planina. The advanced guard of the 22nd Division consisted of the 65th Brigade (Br.-General B. J. Majendie) with the Surrey Yeomanry, the C Brigade R.F.A., and a section of the 100th Field Company R.E. attached. The 83rd Brigade and the Zouaves were to remain on the objectives already reached.

The 65th Brigade, having moved to Kara Ullar on the evening of the 23rd, set out at 7 a.m. on the 24th, preceded by the Surrey Yeomanry, and reached the outpost line of the 83rd Brigade on the Blaga Planina at 10 a.m. It was no easy task that the brigade had before it. The distance from the outpost line to the Signal Allemand was $4\frac{1}{2}$ miles as the crow flies, but that figure by no means represented the difficulties of the advance. Fair but steep and winding tracks ran along the Blaga Planina as far as the abandoned Bulgarian defences on the crest, but from thence forward,

LEFT BANK OF BAJIMIA CLEARED

up the craggy slopes of the Belašica Planina to the Signal Allemand, there were only bridle-paths. The Surrey Yeomanry, pushing on ahead, was shelled by several batteries on the Belašica Planina and was soon obliged to dismount and continue the advance on foot. The advanced guard of the 65th Brigade reached a point known as Zeus Junction on the Blaga, and at 2 p.m. pushed a post forward to Asser Junction. At nightfall it was learnt that the Yeomanry, whose horses were completely exhausted and without water, had been forced to abandon the advance and was returning to camp. The Crete Division on the right had made little progress north of Lake Dojran.

1918.
24 Sept.

In the evening the 83rd Brigade was withdrawn from the Blaga Planina to Černište, there to await the arrival of its own division, the 28th, which was now marching round the south side of Lake Dojran. The leading brigade, the 85th, reached Černište late that night, the 84th halting at Dojran.

General Briggs, who had established advanced headquarters at Stojakovo, ordered the Greek 14th Division to continue the advance on Kosturino and the 26th to seize the heights north of the Bajimia Dere. The Derbyshire Yeomanry, which had reached the neighbourhood of Furka on the evening of the 23rd, led the advance. The regiment now found it possible to push patrols across the Bajimia to Tatarli, Valandova, and Rabrovo on the northern bank, all these villages being clear of the enemy. In Rabrovo 50 British wounded and about twice as many Bulgarians were found in a hospital. The Yeomanry was pretty heavily shelled, and its main body did not cross the river, taking cover for the night in the bottom of the valley near Čestovo. The two Greek regiments and the 78th and 79th Brigade of the 26th also reached the left bank of the Bajimia.

As will shortly be recorded, the leading brigade of the 27th Division, the 80th, crossed the Vardar at Pardovica during the day and moved to Bogdanci. The 143rd Field Company R.E. with 100 men of the 96th Labour Company set about repairing, with captured material, the burnt wooden bridge at Gjavato.

Thus, none of the day's objectives had been reached. On the right a long, weary, and stony way to the Signal Allemand still lay ahead, and that peak was actually not to be occupied until the early hours of the 27th. On the left there were no troops except cavalry outposts beyond the Bajimia. The main bodies of the Greek 14th Division and of the 78th and 79th Brigades had, however, covered the best part of ten miles, and, owing to the state of the road as far as Bogdanci, their transport was not in all cases able to follow them so far. The troops of the 78th had, in fact, to eat their iron ration next day. A heavy strain was thrown upon the resources of the 26th Division because its transport had to carry rations for the Greeks, and the attachment to the division of the 798th Army Horse Transport Company and 50 carts of the 3rd Indian Mule Corps did not entirely overcome the difficulty. The Greeks, hardy souls, could go on so long as they had a crust to gnaw, and appeared quite capable of dealing with the opposition likely to be met; but if, as was possible, it came to a fight for the Kosturino defile, it was advisable that the 26th Division should be up. In like circumstances, Marlborough, during the advance to Blenheim, wrote that the British and Dutch could not continue to march without food, and that the Germans, who hardly expected such a luxury, could not march without them.

Nemesis had been long in exacting retribution for a dangerous economy by the home authorities, but she was doing so now. For the first time since the divisional transport had been cut down in the spring of 1917 the abandonment of the old scale known as " Salonika 4 " was seriously felt.[1] And, if it be admitted that the trouble arose also in the rearward echelon of supply, the lorry columns, it must be said that here also deficiencies, in items such as tyres and spare parts, all of which had been demanded in good time, made their unhappy contribution.

The Passage of the Vardar.

1918.
Sept.
Maps A, 9.

Nothing has been said of the 27th Division west of the Vardar since its capture of the Roche Noire salient at the beginning of September. It had gone through a difficult and somewhat dangerous period during the preparations for the attack on the Dojran—" P " Ridge defences. The heavy artillery attached to it and its own 4·5-inch howitzers had been gradually sent across the Vardar until, from the 13th September onwards, four Greek 6-inch howitzers, two

---

[1] See Vol. I, p. 282 and (for the divisional train) pp. 380–3.

TASK OF 27TH DIVISION

60-pdrs., and 24 18-pdrs. were all the artillery remaining on the divisional front. All the time the division had to maintain activity sufficient to prevent the enemy from discounting the possibility of an attack on the right bank of the Vardar. Major-General Forestier-Walker's instructions were to harass the Bulgarians continuously, but not to attack the powerfully-fortified Džeovo ridge, south of the Ljumnica river, while it was held in its present strength. If the enemy withdrew, the division was to pursue him to the Vardar at Pardovica, in liaison with the 1st Group of Divisions, and to cross the river there.

1918. Sept.

Major-General Forestier-Walker directed that there should be a great deal of bustle and obvious signs of preparation. The patrolling of the infantry was to be aggressive; gaps which had been cut in the enemy's wire in the early days of the month when the artillery was plentiful were to be kept open; the remaining guns were to carry out registration from new positions; "jumping-off" trenches were to be dug and partially concealed; roads were to be screened, but the enemy was to be allowed to see a fair amount of lorry traffic upon them by day; a large dummy camp was to be pitched, as if in preparation for the arrival of reinforcements. But, in dealing with a wily foe, it was necessary that there should be no exaggeration; for example, the camouflage of new trenches had to be insufficient to hide them, but not blatantly so. All that the junior officers and the rank and file were told was that preparations were being made for an attack on the Džeovo ridge; and there was, in fact, a possibility that the division would be ordered to carry this out. All these ruses had a certain value, but undoubtedly the most important and valuable measure from the British point of view was that already taken, the capture of the Roche Noire Salient. No inducement to the enemy to hold his front in full strength could have been greater than the memory of that blow and the prospect of its being repeated.

There were several raids during the period of waiting. In the early hours of the 11th a party of Bulgarians rushed a listening post of the 82nd Brigade on the recently captured Tranchée des Roches. On the mornings of the 12th and 14th the 81st Brigade successfully raided the enemy's trenches. In the former case the 2/Cameron Highlanders entered a work on a hummock known as the Mamelon de

Džeovo; in the latter the 1/Royal Scots surprised a post at the "Arbre Plumet" in the Vardar flats. Again, on the night of the 19th, after the attacks east of the Vardar were over, the Camerons raided the Mamelon Vert. In each case a prisoner was captured for the purpose of identifying the formations in line and a number of the enemy were put out of action, but the British casualties amounted in all to 37. The enemy's artillery was active, especially on the morning of the 18th, when the attack east of the Vardar was launched.

1918.
21 Sept. During the night of the 20th the 80th Brigade relieved the 82nd in the Roche Noire or left sector. At noon on the 21st the division came under the orders of General d'Anselme, commanding the 1st Group of Divisions. That evening large fires were seen burning in the town of Gevgeli; numerous explosions were heard; and the Royal Air Force reported that between 6 and 7 p.m. the roads leading to the bridges at Pardovica and Miletkovo were packed with transport. The enemy was undoubtedly crossing the Vardar.

22 Sept. During the night the 81st Brigade (Br.-General B. F. Widdrington) pushed its patrols to the right bank of the Ljumnica, and at dawn on the 22nd scouts and officers' patrols found Gevgeli clear of the enemy. The pursuit here began more quickly than on the left bank of the Vardar, and by 5 p.m. the 81st Brigade held Gevgeli and the high ground north-west of it, while the 3/K.R.R.C. of the 80th (Br.-General W. J. N. Cooke-Collis) was keeping touch with the right flank guard of the Archipelago Division as it advanced through Gurincet and Negorci. The artillery moved forward, and the 82nd Brigade, in reserve, closed up to Alchak Mahale. On the 23rd the 80th Brigade moved on Pardovica, and by noon all four field artillery brigades were across the Ljumnica. Though there was no opposition, a slight pause was now necessary. Traffic had to be cleared off the Mayadag–Gevgeli–Pardovica road to allow the bridging train through, the road-bridge at Pardovica having been, as was inevitable, blown up by the enemy. The 80th Brigade therefore bivouacked half-way between Negorci and Pardovica, resuming its march to the Vardar in the early hours of the 24th. The division had been returned to the British command at midnight.

The bridging train had long been prepared. The equipment of one division being quite insufficient, that of the 26th Division and two pontoon wagons of the 22nd had been borrowed, and the whole train had been parked at Drevenon. The personnel, consisting of the 501st (2/Wessex) Field Company R.E. under the command of Major R. B. Pitt, had repeatedly rehearsed their work. The site of the proposed bridge had already been decided on, and aeroplane photographs which showed the sandbanks and shallows of the river—very low at this season—having been taken, it had been possible to calculate the length to be supported on pontoons and that to be carried on trestles and piles.

1918.
22 Sept.

The train left Drevenon at 11.30 p.m. on the 22nd. After a march of 24 hours, during which the whole of the mile-long column was hardly ever moving simultaneously owing to stoppages caused by the snapping of traces, the break-down of vehicles, the exhaustion of the horses, the necessity of repairing bridges over nullahs, and above all by the blocking of the road by heavy artillery which could not climb the hill at Mayadag, a halt was called in Gevgeli. By this time the horses were in a lamentable state, and the train could scarcely have proceeded had not the field artillery provided 44 teams to take it on.

23 Sept.

The train drew up at the site at 4 a.m. on the 24th. By now the head of the 80th Brigade had arrived, and all the time the work was in progress fresh units and transport were closing up, all eager to cross. The shallows were bridged with the aid of infantrymen who spread out across them to act as a human conveyor and floated from hand to hand the rectangular boxes which were to serve as piles.[1] The bridge, over 500 feet in length and consisting of twelve pontoons, twelve Weldon trestles, and three improvised trestles designed by Major Pitt, was completed in about five hours, a very fine feat by men who had had no sleep for two nights and no food except their haversack rations, eaten on the move, for 36 hours.

24 Sept.

In the course of the day the 80th Brigade with the XIX and CXXIX Brigades R.F.A. and the Bute Battery crossed the river and moved to the neighbourhood of Bogdanci. The 81st Brigade, having halted some hours, reached Pardovica at 5 p.m. and bivouacked on the right bank.

---

[1] These rectangular boxes consisted of 10-inch by 1¼-inch planking, with a heavier sole-piece nailed to one end. After being floated into position they were set upright, filled with stones or sand, and then cut off at the requisite height above the water.

The bridge could not carry heavy artillery, and Major-General W. H. Onslow, Major-General Royal Artillery at G.H.Q., had directed that the 60-pdr. and 6-inch howitzer batteries of the XX and XXXVII Brigades R.G.A. should return to Karasuli. Br.-General V. Asser, C.R.A. of the Division, had, however, found a ford west of Pardovica by which he believed a crossing would be practicable, and he obtained Major-General Onslow's permission to make the attempt. Before noon next day all the 60-pdrs., one 6-inch howitzer battery, and one four-wheel-drive lorry had crossed. The LXVI Brigade R.G.A. (two 6-inch howitzer and two 60-pdr. batteries) had been sent to Stojakovo by Major-General Onslow to await orders from Major-General Forestier-Walker in case the heavy artillery on the right bank was unable to cross.

Simultaneously with the 27th Division, but having, of course, a considerably greater distance to cover, the 1st Group of Divisions had marched towards the Vardar. On the right the Archipelago Division was directed on the river between Pardovica and Miletkovo; in the centre the 16th Colonial Division and the Greek 4th moved on the line Miletkovo–Davidovo; on the left the mixed detachment of Colonel Rondet covered the flank and kept touch with the Serbian Second Army on the Marianska Planina. The Second Army in its turn spread out along the river on the 22nd from Demir Kapija to the confluence of the Vardar and Crna, getting small detachments across at certain points and capturing a considerable quantity of rolling stock loaded with flour, petrol, and salt. On the 23rd the Second Army pressed forward on the left bank. The Timok Division, having won a little bridgehead overnight at Demir Kapija, fought its way up the spur of the Gradec Planina which here ran down to the river, while the Yugoslav, aided by the Cavalry Division, crossed north of Krivolak and captured the heights of Kara Hojali. The 1st Group of Divisions closed up to the river, but had no troops across it until the 24th, and was unable to establish a bridgehead until next day at Strumica Station, where a bridge was found more or less intact.

The Widening Breach, 22nd–24th September.

By the night of the 21st September the Allied Armies had already gained a considerable victory, but were still far from a decision. The number of prisoners captured was, indeed, so far remarkably small, somewhat over 5,000 ; and the enemy had probably suffered more heavily by the loss of guns, many of which lay at the bottom of ravines and had not been counted, or in some cases even discovered. The dispositions of the opposing forces bore a remarkable resemblance to those of mid-November 1915, when the French had advanced into the Vardar–Crna loop, if whole divisions are substituted on the map for regiments on either side.[1] But then the Bulgarians were flushed with victory, and the resources behind their troops engaged upon the Vardar and Crna were almost limitless, or limited only by the difficulties of communication. Now the enemy was oppressed by defeat, war-weary, dispirited, and in the case of some units incapable of resisting a serious attack. Nevertheless, the situation was not yet entirely satisfactory from the point of view of the Allies. General Franchet d'Espérey was already looking towards Skoplje, but before he could launch an arrow upon that target he must enlarge the breach already made in the enemy's lines, win room for manœuvre outside the Vardar-Crna loop, and further stretch the straining arc in which the enemy's forces lay.

1918.
22 Sept.
Map 8.
Sketch 7.

We have already mentioned the advance to the Vardar of the 1st Group of Divisions, including the British 27th Division, and the closing up to the river of the Serbian Second Army. On the 22nd good progress beyond the Crna was made by the First Army, which by evening had its advanced guards on a line from the bank north of Šivec to Hill 1250 on the Drenska Planina, nine miles west of the river. The bridge at Vozarci, captured intact, was a useful link between the two Armies. The 11th Colonial Division, supported by the 3rd Greek, got astride the Selečka Planina, and on its left the Italian cavalry reached Kanatlarci. Prilep was obviously about to fall. Meanwhile a number of heavy batteries which had helped to open the breach at the Dobropolje had been transferred to new positions about Monastir, and preparations were being made for a thrust here.

General von Scholtz had now to make a choice between withdrawing his right wing and seeing it driven into the Albanian mountains, and, stubborn as he was, he decided

---

[1] See Vol. I, Map 4.

on the former alternative. Was he even in time ? Would the *LXII Corps* on the right be able to get through Tetovo to Skoplje before the Franco-Serbian troops reached that town ? Was even the *LXI Corps* certain to reach Veles by the Babuna Pass ? If all went well something, perhaps a good deal, might be saved from the wreck; for the withdrawal would take him closer to reinforcements which he now knew to be on the road. Yet it was going to be a near-run thing, and the prospects of the *LXII Corps* at least were not bright.

On the evening of the 22nd his orders, and those of General von Steuben, the commander of the *Eleventh Army*, who had joined him in Skoplje, were issued.[1] The *LXII Corps* was to retire to the line Debar–Kičevo–Brod, preparatory to continuing its march through Tetovo to Skoplje. The *302nd Division*, formerly in the *LXI Corps*, would come under its orders and cover its left on the Prilep–Brod road. Strong rear guards would block the passes on the flanks and in rear of the march. The *LXI Corps* would that same night begin its march through the Babuna Pass to Veles, *if necessary clearing a way for itself by fighting*. The newly-formed division under General Dieterich, which was divided into two groups covering Gradsko and Krivolak,[2] would retire step by step, the Gradsko Group on Veles, destroying the railway as it went, the Krivolak Group on Štip. The *First Army*, abandoning the line of the Vardar and the Bajimia, would dispute the advance of the enemy by way of Štip and Strumica and maintain touch with the *Second Army* in its old positions. Everywhere rear guards would hold back the pursuit as long as possible, especially on the

---

[1] " Weltkriegsende an der mazedonischen Front," p. 79.

[2] General Dieterich was the commander of the broken-up *6th Reserve Division* (see p. 132) who had been sent to take command of the *Landwehr* troops destined for the Struma valley. He had been summoned to Gradsko on the 20th and reached it next day amid a scene of frenzied panic—the town burning and under bombardment, and Bulgarian troops fleeing northwards in such numbers that they blocked his lorry for hours on the road. After some sort of order had been restored, his groups were made up as follows :—*Gradsko Group*—five German **Landsturm** companies, a battalion of the Bulgarian *66th Regiment*, two Bulgarian cavalry squadrons, a number of lines of communication or reinforcement companies of doubtful value, numerous machine guns, five batteries and an armoured train ; *Krivolak Group*—*66th Regiment* (less one battalion), the remnants of the *80th* and *87th Regiments* of the *3rd Division*, the Bulgarian *6th Cavalry Regiment*, machine guns, a German foot-artillery battalion, and soon afterwards two Bulgarian mountain batteries.

Monastir–Prilep front, where a further Allied advance would cut into the retreating columns.

1918.
23 Sept.

On the 23rd, as already stated, the Timok and Yugoslav Divisions of the Serbian Second Army forced the passage of the Vardar. The Yugoslav Division and the Cavalry Division met with really stiff opposition from the fresh *66th Regiment* of the *Krivolak Group*, fighting under the eye of the Commander-in-Chief, General Todorov, and it was not until late in the evening that it drove the enemy back on to the Čaške ridge, north of Kara Hojali. The First Army made more progress, and a column of the Drina Division, thrusting boldly towards the Babuna Pass, had some sharp fighting for the high ground west of Fariš against determined flank guards, mainly German, covering the pass. The Serbians were unable to overcome the opposition in time to prevent the passage of the Bulgarian *4th Division* and the *Reuter Division*.[1] On the right of the Armée Française d'Orient the French cavalry advancing from south of Monastir through Topolčani, and having covered upwards of 30 miles in 12 hours, entered Prilep, abandoned by the *302nd Division*. The cavalry was immediately followed by troops of the 11th Colonial Division, thrusting in from the south-east. The Army accomplished little north of Monastir, being checked at Kukurečani and Beranče by the Bulgarian *1st Division*. The enemy's *LXII Corps* was on this day not seriously interfered with, and its commander, General Fleck, was still coolly holding on on his right to let the long, slow, ox-drawn Bulgarian baggage columns withdraw in good order. His time was coming, and he may well have wished during the next few days that he had sacrificed a proportion of his trains to the profit of his troops.

That morning General Franchet d'Espérey issued fresh "Instructions for the Armies." In order to realize as quickly as possible the dispositions which he had laid down as marking the end of the first phase,[2] the following procedure would be adopted. As soon as the Serbian First Army reached the Prilep–Veles road, it would swing up its left and progress in a north-easterly instead of a north-westerly direction, its zone of advance being bounded by

---

[1] This formation was now broken up, the troops being divided among other divisions.

[2] See p. 130.

the Prilep–Veles and Prilep–Gradsko roads. On reaching the Vardar it would enlarge the bridgehead secured by the Second Army and push outposts towards Skoplje, Kliseli, and Štip. The Second Army would thrust simultaneously northwards towards Štip, and eastward to outflank the defences of the Gradec Planina and assure uninterrupted communication up the Vardar valley. The Armée Française d'Orient, continuing to carry out the mission assigned to it, would as soon as possible push forward a detachment of the 11th Colonial Division behind the left of the Serbian First Army to support it in the Veles area, and launch its cavalry in the direction of Skoplje in order to cut off the columns moving through the Kičevo–Tetovo corridor. The 1st Group of Divisions must at all costs establish a bridgehead on the Gradec Planina between Hudova and Demir Kapija. The British Army would continue to operate in the direction of Strumica and gain possession of the crest of the Belašica Planina between the Signal Allemand and Hudova. At the earliest possible moment it would push forward small detachments of infantry and cavalry on Strumica and then despatch cavalry patrols towards Petrić, Berovo, and Radovišta. The Greek I Corps on the Struma was to regroup its forces, so as to be prepared for the moment when it might be called upon to advance in the direction of the Rupel Pass.

**1918.
24 Sept.** On the 24th the progress towards the Vardar of the 1st Group of Divisions continued, and the heads of the columns reached the river at Smokvica and Davidovo. On the front of the Serbian Second Army the Timok Division was held up short of the crest of the Gradec Planina, but the Yugoslav reached the watershed between the Vardar and the Kriva Lakavica, thus opening the Štip road to the Cavalry Division, which marched on that town. It was, however, on the Army's left that the shrewdest blow was struck. At the confluence of Vardar and Crna the left wing of the Yugoslav Division had on the previous evening encountered very stout resistance from the *Gradsko Group* of General Dieterich's force, and had actually been counter-attacked with bayonet and bomb. The Voivode Stepanović had therefore called upon the 17th Colonial Division, which had been in support ever since the break-through. Two strong columns moved up to the support of the Serbians, but, faced by a barrage from the hostile batteries west of

Gradsko, General Pruneau decided to manœuvre the enemy by the west. By the morning of the 24th two battalions captured the Monastery of Čičevo, or Archangel, the scene of a long struggle in 1915. The enemy, thus outflanked— for he had no touch with the *4th Division* retreating up the Babuna Pass road to Veles—gave way to the pressure of the Serbians and fell back up the Veles road. Nineteen guns, some 40 locomotives, and great quantities of transport were captured at Gradsko Station. On the front of the First Army a column of the Drina Division entered the Babuna Pass on the heels of the retreating enemy, hustling his rear guard and taking prisoners from six different Bulgarian regiments. The 11th Colonial Division and the Greek 3rd Division, which was marching in rear of it, halted at Prilep in order to constitute two groups, one of which would advance on Veles, to the north-east, while the second and larger continued the movement to the north-west up the Prilep-Brod road. The Italian Division, which had been ordered to swing left on Kruševo, reached Urbjani. Of the 2nd Group of Divisions only the right made any progress, the 30th Division occupying Novoselani. The enemy had not yet retired from his old position from Monastir westward, though he had moved back baggage and some artillery, and perhaps thinned out his lines. The French 76th Division, launching an attack on Hill 1248, was repulsed by the Bulgarian *6th Division*. It was the enemy's last stand here. That night, in accordance with the orders of General von Scholtz, he slipped away and began his retreat.

1918.
24 Sept.

The situation was clearer now. The left was in fact becoming, as General Franchet d'Espérey had on the 31st August foreseen that it would become, the " marching " wing of the Allied array." All else was secondary now to the movement on Skoplje, important as were the other thrusts. If the British Army entered the Strumica valley it would have few natural obstacles in its path till it reached the Struma above the Rupel Pass and cut the main communication behind the enemy's left. The Serbian Second Army after the fall of Štip, now clearly imminent, would march on the Bulgarian frontier by the valley of the Bregalnica. Both these moves would have a very great effect upon the fortunes of the campaign, but they would not in themselves produce a definite decision. The kernel of the problem was whether the enemy's *LXI Corps*, retreating step by step astride the valley of the Vardar, could delay the Allied advance long enough to permit the *LXII Corps* to reach Skoplje before the pursuing Allies were in possession of that town. If not, the *LXII Corps* was doomed.

Map 1. A glance at a small-scale map will make this sufficiently clear. The Gostivar-Skoplje road, by which the whole corps was retreating, follows from Gostivar to Tetovo the valley of the upper Vardar. At Tetovo it turns sharply eastward to Skoplje. On the western side the road is overhung by the towering range of the Šar, with peaks over 7,000 feet in height. That barrier could not be crossed; it must be outflanked by the Kačanik defile; and for practical purposes the defile could only be reached through Skoplje.[1] If, therefore, the Allies could reach Skoplje first, in strength enough to hold it, the *LXII Corps*, with the four best divisions in the *Eleventh Army*—probably 60,000 men—was caught. Some troops might struggle over the pass to Prizren on the Albanian frontier; others might escape from Tetovo to Kačanik, if, indeed, that pass were not also blocked; but for the artillery, the baggage, and the bulk of the troops there would be no way out. Probably the corps as a body would lay down its arms.

Such was the race now beginning. The Allies, if they followed the Vardar valley, had to clear their course by fighting, but they had by far the shorter distance to cover. Who was to be first at Skoplje?

---

[1] There was, as will appear, a track direct from Tetovo to Kačanik, but it was impracticable for large bodies of troops or for guns.

CHAPTER XI.

THE FINAL OFFENSIVE: THE PURSUIT.

(Maps A, 8, 9; Sketches 7, 10.)

THE PURSUIT ON THE BRITISH FRONT, 25TH–30TH SEPTEMBER.

WE left the British Army and the foreign troops attached to it on the night of the 24th September pressing forward to the Bulgarian frontier, the advanced guard of the XII Corps on the Blaga Planina, the XVI Corps on the southern bank of the Bajimia Dere. According to the German account, the demoralization of the defeated *Eleventh Army* had spread to the troops of the *First*, whose defence had been brave and successful. It is probable that the bombing of British aircraft had done a good deal towards bringing this about. Certainly on the 25th September the British and Greeks between Lake Dojran and the Vardar were troubled more by the nature of the country than by the resistance of the enemy.

1918.
25 Sept.
Maps A, 8, 9.

General Milne had no fresh orders to issue, merely directing the corps commanders to continue the advance on the 25th " along the same lines and with the same object as today."

The orders of General Wilson, commanding the XII Corps, were also to a great extent a repetition of those issued on the evening of the 23rd, because the objectives then laid down had not yet been reached. The left regiment of the Crete Division was to establish itself on the Belašica Planina in touch with the 22nd Division, which was to capture the Signal Allemand. The 28th Division, now all assembled under the orders of the divisional commander, Major-General Croker, was to support the advance by pushing two brigades across the Kara Bail and on to the lower slopes of the Belašica about Bakče Obasi.

The 22nd Division had a task that was almost impossible, especially in view of its fatigue, so long as one stout-hearted Bulgarian remained behind a machine gun. Its 65th Brigade on the Blaga Planina could scarcely hope to reach the Signal Allemand, under conditions of mountain warfare, in one day unless either the resistance cracked or the Crete Division—which had a far stiffer climb from the plain—could turn the position by reaching the crest further east. Br.-General Majendie, thinking that it might be possible to seize this dominating point by a *coup de main* in the darkness, had, on learning that the Surrey Yeomanry had abandoned the task,[1] sent out a party of the 8/S. Wales Borderers, 50 strong, just before midnight on the 24th to make the attempt, but the little detachment was seen by the enemy and forced to return.

While the party was out, the brigadier received orders from his divisional commander, Major-General Duncan, to attack the Signal Allemand next day. Heavy artillery would bombard the position at dawn, and two 18-pdr. batteries of the C Brigade R.F.A. would be in close support. These batteries reached Asser Junction with some difficulty and in the course of the morning silenced a Bulgarian field battery in action in the open. Br.-General Majendie formed two columns, the right consisting of the 8/S. Wales Borderers and 9/King's Own under the command of Lieut.-Colonel R. C. Dobbs of the Borderers; the left, of the 9/East Lancashire with two sections of the 65th Machine-Gun Company The former was to follow the spur along which ran the Græco-Serbian frontier-line; the latter a parallel spur further west. The Surrey Yeomanry moved in support of the left column. Lest it may appear that this force was a formidable one, it must be added that the Borderers consisted of six platoons, the King's Own of one company, and the East Lancashire of three weak companies.

At 11.17 a.m. Br.-General Majendie received a report from the left column that it was reduced to 130 all ranks, having had a fair number of casualties and temporarily lost a still greater number of men who had gone astray in the scrub; it had no touch with the right column. Further reports which reached Major-General Duncan convinced him that the brigade was too exhausted to carry out its task, and at 1.35 p.m. he telephoned to the corps commander suggesting that the attack should be cancelled. General Wilson agreed, and it was finally decided to employ fresher troops, who could probably not be brought up in time to make an assault before the morning of the 27th.

---

[1] See p. 211.

Orderlies were therefore sent out to recall the columns, and the left one came in. The right column could not, however, be found. It was completely swallowed up in the thick scrub. No news of it was received until after nightfall, and no message from Lieut.-Colonel Dobbs until the following morning.

1918.
25 Sept.

The right column had been skilfully handled. Finding that the enemy's artillery had registered the track running towards the foot of the spur, Lieut.-Colonel Dobbs quitted it and made his way through the scrub beside it. Though the roughness and blindness of the country forced him to halt frequently in order to close up men and mules, he thus avoided casualties. The enemy's artillery had occasional glimpses of the column, but use of cover and of dead ground made the fire almost innocuous. On reaching the steep and thickly wooded spur itself the same method was adopted, the column keeping away from the crest and moving along the western slope. Progress was painful, but the column was hidden from the enemy. In the evening it emerged on the rocky heights above the level of the scrub, at a point which was for a moment thought to be the Signal Allemand itself, but which was soon found to be some hundreds of yards short of that peak. The Signal Allemand, moreover, was discovered to be fairly strongly held, and Lieut.-Colonel Dobbs, bitterly disappointed, decided that his force was too weak to carry it. With the aid of the left column he was convinced that he could have taken it, in his own words, "the opportunity of a lifetime." Before nightfall there was a short duel between the enemy's machine guns and the British Lewis guns. Then, about 8 p.m., a party of the enemy attacked the outposts with bombs. It was quickly driven off, and the British detachment remained in position throughout the following day.

The 83rd Brigade (Br.-General R. H. Hare) of the 28th Division, with the LIV Brigade R.F.A. attached, advanced over the Kara Bail by way of Hasanli and Pazarli, followed by the 85th. The steep and winding road proved almost beyond the powers of the artillery horses; in fact, although the guns were double-horsed, one battery and the brigade ammunition column were forced to give up the attempt for that day and to return to Černište. By evening the 83rd Brigade had reached Bakče Obasi, and the 85th was close behind, on the southern bank of the Kozli Dere.

General Briggs had ordered the advance of the XVI Corps on Kosturino to begin at daybreak, the Greek 14th Division using roads east of the main Dedeli–Kosturino road, the 26th Division that road and any tracks further west that it required. The Derbyshire Yeomanry in the van was to endeavour to penetrate the Kosturino Pass and reach Strumica.

Major-General Gay, commanding the 26th Division, considered that his best chance of capturing the pass was to push on during the night so as to occupy the high ground overlooking Kosturino by the early hours of the 25th, and issued orders to that effect. On the right the 79th Brigade (Br.-General A. J. Poole), moving up the main Dedeli-Kosturino road, found no difficulty in carrying out its task. At dawn an attack was launched on the enemy's position in front of Kosturino, with the aid of the left (36th) regiment of the Greek 14th Division, and the slight opposition was broken down. By 8.20 a.m. infantry patrols, preceded by a squadron of the Derbyshire Yeomanry, which had moved up through Kajali, were in Kosturino. On the right the Greek 9th Regiment reached the neighbourhood of Ormanli. On the left the 78th Brigade (Br.-General G. H. F. Wingate) marched through Valandova on Izliš. Br.-General Wingate had procured native guides, as the mule-track was barely discernible in the moonlight. This brigade met with stouter resistance, though only from a single company with machine guns, which held up the advance on the high ground south-west of Izliš from daybreak till 4 p.m. Then the enemy, after having inflicted 32 casualties on the brigade, abandoned the position. In rear of it three guns and five machine guns were found. British troops were thus the first to cross the frontier and set foot on Bulgarian soil.

On this day the Greek I Corps on the Struma was transferred from the command of General Milne to that of the Greek Commander-in-Chief, General Danglis.

We have seen that General Wilson considered that the Signal Allemand could be taken only by fresh troops. He therefore ordered the 22nd Division to stand fast on the 26th September, while Major-General Duncan moved the 2nd *bis* Zouaves up on to the Blaga Planina and made preparations for them to assault the position at daybreak next morning. The Crete Division was during the night of the 25th to continue its efforts to reach the crest of the

The Trail of the Retreat. On the track to Kosturino followed by the Greek 36th Regiment. (See Map 9.)

Belašica ; if it succeeded, the 28th Division was likewise to advance to the crest, at Point 1185, four miles west of the Signal Allemand. Early in the morning of the 26th there came news that the 9th Cretan Regiment had reached an important tactical point, not indeed on the crest, but only half a mile south of the Signal Allemand. General Wilson therefore ordered the 28th Division to advance to Point 1185 without delay.

1918.
26 Sept.

It was the hottest day of the pursuit so far, the maximum shade temperature being 95 degrees. This heat, the dust, and occasional grass fires proved very trying to the troops. The 85th Brigade (Lieut.-Colonel W. Y. Miller [1]), which had been ordered to pass through the 83rd, was also seriously delayed by having to get the guns up a ramp in the bed of the stream at Bakče Obasi, where the bridge had been destroyed by the enemy. The march was resumed at 2.15 p.m., but by nightfall only four 18-pdrs. had crossed the Kozli Dere, and when at 5 p.m. the advanced guard, the 2/East Surrey, came under machine-gun fire from Point 1185, only one gun was available to support it. The brigade therefore halted for the night with its head just short of the crest.

Meanwhile the 2nd *bis* Zouaves had reached Zeus Junction, where Major-General Duncan personally explained to Colonel Boré-Verrier what he desired. The regiment was to move up the boundary track, deploy 500 yards west of the summit, and passing through the detachment of Lieut.- Colonel Dobbs, assault the Signal Allemand at dawn. The Zouaves reached the position held by the British detachment, which had had a comparatively quiet day, at 1 a.m. on the 27th. There had been no shooting for some time now, and it seemed likely that the enemy had withdrawn. So, in fact, it proved. When the Zouaves advanced to the attack at 5 a.m. there was little or no resistance, and the Signal Allemand, which had caused so much trouble, fell very tamely. The endurance and courage of Lieut.-Colonel Dobbs's detachment, which had been completely isolated and exposed to an attack in superior numbers for the best part of 48 hours, furnishes one of the brightest episodes of

---

[1] The brigade commander, Br.-General K. M. Davie, had been ordered to exchange brigades with Br.-General R. E. Solly-Flood, commanding the 82nd Brigade of the 27th Division. Br.-General Solly-Flood did not reach 85th Brigade headquarters till next day.

the pursuit. It was the only unit or formation mentioned by General Milne in the body of that part of his despatch which dealt with the pursuit, and it well deserved the honour.

The next objective of the XVI Corps was Strumica. Before the advance of the 26th September began, while the Yeomanry were still watering horses, there was a dramatic incident. From the direction of Strumica there appeared a car, with a white flag on the bonnet. It contained two Bulgarian officers, the senior of whom was the bearer of a letter addressed to General Milne. This letter was signed by General Todorov and stated that the Bulgarian Government, with the consent of the Tsar, had authorized him to have recourse to General Milne's mediation with the Commander-in-Chief of the Allied Armies in order to obtain a 48 hours' cessation of hostilities, during which delegates would present themselves with proposals for an armistice. That General Franchet d'Espérey should suspend hostilities at such a moment was, as General Milne knew, out of the question. He sent on the *parlementaires* to Salonika without comment, and reported the contents of the letter to the War Office.

There was no serious opposition to the advance on Strumica, though the leading brigade of the 26th Division, the 79th, was shelled on entering the plain from the Kosturino defile. The first patrols reached Strumica at 11 a.m., and at 12.30 p.m. the Derbyshire Yeomanry rode through the town. The regiments of the Greek 14th Division, after a very fine march over mountain roads, reached Banjsko, Robovo, and Dabilja, on the three parallel roads which followed the valley of the Strumica river. The 79th Brigade of the 26th Division also passed through Strumica and covered the roads running north towards Berovo and Radovišta. The 78th halted at Popčevo. The 80th, the leading brigade of the 27th Division, moved up to Rabrovo, south-west of Kosturino, in case its aid should be required in the Strumica valley, and the other two brigades concentrated at Bogdanci. The division had been transferred to Army reserve, but was still administered by the XVI Corps.

This date was marked by a break-down in the supply arrangements of the XVI Corps. It was reported that this was due to two causes: the very bad state of the road between Stojakovo and Bogdanci, beyond which it was quite good; and the fact that the corps headquarters had taken over in the midst of the pursuit and had been unable to concentrate transport in its own hands. Another factor was the increasing distance between the troops and the rearward services under the control of G.H.Q. Br.-General E. D. Young, D.A. and Q.M.G. of the corps, informed Major-General Rycroft that the 26th and the 14th Greek Divisions were now on half-rations, and that unless G.H.Q. could supply them through the XII Corps zone by the road from Dojran which joined the Bogdanci-Kosturino road west of Gökčeli Bala, he would be unable to feed the troops in the Strumica valley. It was decided that this should be done and that the Bogdanci section should cease to be an artery of supply. Other arrangements were to remake the road between Dojran Station and town, cut to pieces by the traffic; to repair the culverts on the main road further north; to close down all railheads but Yanesh (XVI Corps) and Dojran (XII Corps) and use the personnel thus set free to augment the staffs at these two points; to insist on time-tables being followed and rigidly enforce traffic control; to use the lorries of the heavy artillery (which was now for the most part parked near Kalinova) for the salving of ammunition in the battery positions and its reissue after it had been examined; and to bring back in the returning supply lorries the surplus equipment of battalions which had already been reduced or were in the course of being reduced to two companies. A senior mechanical transport officer with a clerical staff was established at Advanced G.H.Q. at Yanesh to control the lorry transport to the XVI Corps.

1918.
26 Sept.

These measures had a useful effect, but they by no means completely restored the situation. The lorries allotted to various tasks could not always be collected in time, because their long runs had made them late or because they had broken down; light lorries, such as those used by the Italians and to a lesser extent by the French, would have been a godsend. As it was, the pace of the 26th Division might well have slackened but for the captured supply depots, which included meat on the hoof and *slivovitja*, the Bulgarian white plum-brandy, found to be a remarkable tonic to exhausted men.

On the morning of the 27th the Crete Division relieved the Zouaves on the Signal Allemand. The mission of the Cretans was now to sweep the crest of the Belašica Planina

27 Sept.

from west to east, in order to rid the troops in the Strumica valley of the galling fire of Bulgarian mountain batteries on the heights. The 85th Brigade of the 28th Division occupied Point 1185 at 5 a.m. without further opposition, and four hours later the 83rd Brigade passed through. Br.-General Hare decided on his own initiative to descend from the mountains into the Strumica valley. Actually, General Wilson, who had learnt of the difficulties of supply down there, had already at 8 a.m. issued orders to the 28th Division to stand fast. They did not reach the 83rd Brigade in time to stop it, and it marched down a mule-track, leaving all wheeled vehicles, including, of course, the guns of the LIV Brigade R.F.A., on the crest. It appeared from the very indifferent map that the path led to Banjsko, but it was actually two miles west of that point, at Svidovica, that the brigade emerged into the plain.

On the XVI Corps front the 26th Division, which was without food, was ordered to stand fast, with detachments covering the northern approaches to Strumica, and the only move made by Major-General Gay was to push forward the 78th Brigade from Popčevo to west of Strumica. Another car came through from the enemy's lines, with Mr. Walker of the United States Legation in Sofia and a Bulgarian officer, who were sent through British G.H.Q. to General Franchet d'Espérey at Salonika.[1] Later in the day the Bulgarian *parlementaires* who had come through the previous morning re-entered the enemy's lines. The Greek 14th Division could move without waiting for rations and was ordered by General Briggs to advance along the Petrić road, with the Derbyshire Yeomanry in the van, but not to go beyond Yeniköi. " A " Battery CXV Brigade R.F.A. was attached to the Yeomanry and " B " Battery, as well as the newly-arrived IV Highland Mountain Brigade,[2]

---

[1] The United States were not at war with Bulgaria, and an American representative had remained at Sofia.

[2] This formation had covered a great deal of country in the past week. Engaged in the attack on the Blaga Planina on the 19th, it had then, during the night of the 23rd, begun a march across the front to the northern shore of Lake Arjan. Thence on the 24th it moved north to near Bogdanci. On the 25th it was repeatedly in action in support of the 79th Brigade. It reached Kosturino that night and picked up its Bute Battery (previously with the 27th Division) which had had a long march from beyond the Vardar. Next day it went through into the plain. At a rough estimate it had covered 80 miles, in great part over mountain roads, in less than six days and nights. It was now to be on the move and in action until the Armistice came into force on the 30th.

The Pass into the Valley of the Strumica, near Strumica Town.

to the Greek Division. Progress was not nearly so good as on the previous day owing to artillery fire from the mountains on either side of the valley. The Derbyshire Yeomanry reached Sekernik, and the Greeks halted on a line from Gabrovo, on the southern road, to Radovo, on the main road to Petrić.

1918.
27 Sept.

There was now a prospect that the XVI Corps would shortly be able to sever the communications of the Bulgarian left wing in the Struma valley. Before that could be attained, however, there were two obstacles—apart from what resistance the enemy might make in the Strumica valley—which must be overcome. First, the Belašica Planina must be cleared, an extraordinarily difficult task for the now weary Crete Division. The second and more serious obstacle, at least to the British troops, was the failure of supply. That evening General Milne, in two successive messages to the corps, pointed out that the pursuit was now a problem of transport and supply, governed by the state of the Dojran-Strumica road, the reconstruction of which must be hastened by all possible means; he had authorized Major-General Livingstone, the Engineer-in-Chief, to issue orders direct to the two Chief Engineers for this purpose: all Army Troops companies, field companies, and Pioneer battalions available were to be turned on to the road. Next day, in fact, work was begun intensively on the whole length of the road, and new quarries were opened; but, as was to be expected, the full benefit of the new effort did not appear until about the 30th, when hostilities with Bulgaria ceased. Later in the night General Milne directed the XII Corps to withdraw all mounted units and horsed transport that could be spared, and also the LXXXII Brigade R.G.A. to south of Dojran in order to reduce traffic. The following morning he directed General Wilson to concentrate the 28th Division about Bakče Obasi, less the 83rd Brigade in the Strumica valley, which would come under the orders of the XVI Corps. Except for this brigade, the 28th Division therefore took no further part in the pursuit, any more than did the 27th Division. The 2nd *bis* Zouaves, relieved on the 27th by the Crete Division, was also ordered on the 28th to withdraw, in this case to Hasanli. The regiment halted for the night at Zeus Junction.

On the 28th, therefore, there was no forward movement by the XII Corps, except that the eastward sweep along the

28 Sept.

Belašica Planina by the Crete Division, whose 29th Regiment and mountain artillery had now rejoined,[1] was continued. On the crest the Cretans, hindered by grass fires, progressed only about a mile eastward from the Signal Allemand, though that in itself was no small feat. The 29th Regiment, climbing the mountains from north of Palmis, approached the crest. On the front of the 228th Brigade further east there were for the first time signs—explosions and the rearward movement of pack columns—that the enemy was about to abandon his position here.

The XVI Corps continued its progress down the Strumica. Early in the morning General Briggs met General d'Anselme, who informed him that the Archipelago Division of the 1st Group had reached the upper Strumica on the 27th, and that it would today be advancing along the Plaškovica Planina. The Derbyshire Yeomanry and the Greek 14th Division moved due eastward in the direction of Petrić, the advanced guard being a force of all arms under the orders of Lieut.-Colonel W. Neilson, consisting of the cavalry, "A" Battery CXV Brigade R.F.A., and a company of the Greek 9th Regiment. On the outskirts of Yeniköi it was held up by a comparatively strong force with machine guns and three batteries. The advanced guard was unable to make any headway, and was at night withdrawn behind the Greek line, the right of which was now on Mokrine.

The two brigades of the 26th Division did not march till afternoon. They were then moved north-east towards Berovo, with the object of covering the Greek left flank, which was being shelled from the Ogražden Planina, the 79th by the Hamzali road and the 78th by that through Yeni Mahale. The 79th made good Hamzali by nightfall and discovered a strong body of the enemy holding the pass above. The advanced guard of the 78th, the 7/Oxford and Bucks L.I. and one battery of the LVII Brigade R.F.A., reached Yeni Mahale, to find that the road, reported to be a good one, tailed off into a mountain track so steep as to be impracticable even for pack-mules. It therefore bivouacked there for the night.

In the course of the morning two more cars came through, the rear one a saloon with the blinds drawn. No one got out of it or showed himself till the cars reached

---

[1] See p. 207. These troops reached Dojran Station about 9 p.m. on the 26th.

BOMBING OF THE KRYESNA PASS   233

British Advanced G.H.Q. at Yanesh at 1 p.m. The party
consisted of M. Ljapchev, the Minister of Finance, General
Lukov, the commander of the *Second Army*, M. Radev,
Minister Plenipotentiary, the field officer who had previously
come through as *parlementaire*, and another Bulgarian
officer. General Milne sent them on to Salonika. He had a
short conversation with M. Ljapchev, which he reported to
the War Office. The Minister of Finance informed him that
the Prime Minister, M. Malinov, on assuming office three
months earlier, had inherited formal engagements to
Germany which he felt himself unable to break, though he
had made known his pro-Entente views before Bulgaria
entered the war. The defeat of the Bulgarian Armies had
restored his liberty of action. He now hoped that an
immediate armistice would be granted and that territorial
questions would be deferred until the peace conference. If
an armistice were granted the Government would oblige
their former allies to leave the country, resume full liberty
of action, reconstitute their forces, which were not yet
seriously damaged, and be in a position to follow the advice
of Great Britain.

1918.
28 Sept.

Though the plenipotentiaries were aware that the
conclusion of peace would be a difficult matter, it was
evident that they hoped to establish their position as
neutrals, if not, within a very short space, as allies. General
Milne knew that when they reached Salonika that evening
they would be disillusioned and that Bulgaria would have
to lie on the bed she had made for herself.

For the moment, however, his task was to cut off the
Bulgarian *Second Army* on the lower Struma. Every mile
that he advanced towards the upper Struma, which he
hoped to reach between the Rupel and Kryesna defiles,
would be a trump card in the hands of General Franchet
d'Espérey when he gathered the plenipotentiaries round a
table. That day had been marked by another exploit of
the Royal Air Force, which had twice heavily bombed the
steep-sided Kryesna defile, doing great damage to long
columns of transport retreating northward. General Milne
ordered the commander of the XVI Corps to continue on
the morrow the movement on Petrić, with the Greek 14th
Division, backed up if necessary by the 83rd Brigade. The
secondary movement by the 26th Division on Berovo was
also to be resumed. As there would possibly be a battle

this side of Petrić, he had returned the 27th Division to General Briggs's command, but now warned him to be sure how his supply situation stood before he brought it over the Kosturino Pass.[1] The division, which had concentrated about Čestovo and Dedeli, made ready to move, and in order to provide the most effective fighting force with the minimum of impedimenta, formed each of its infantry brigades into a single battalion of three companies, with 36 Lewis guns per battalion. As it proved, its intervention was not actually required.

1918.
29 Sept.
On the 29th the XII Corps took no part in the pursuit after 3 p.m., at which hour the only troops under its orders actively engaged, the Crete Division, passed to the command of General E. Zymbrakakis, commanding the Corps of National Defence.[2] The Crete Division continued to progress eastward on the Belašica, though slowly, and during the afternoon an officer made his way down the northern slopes and reached the lines of the 14th Division near Yeniköi. He stated that there was still some opposition from the enemy, hard to overcome on this difficult ground.

Meanwhile the 14th Division in the Strumica plain was being galled by artillery fire from the mountains on both flanks, but particularly from the Belašica, and was engaged in the only really hard fighting that took place in the whole course of the pursuit. At Yeniköi, in a strong position where the road entered a defile, Bulgarian infantry with numerous machine guns was making a determined stand. General Briggs, whose liking for the Greek troops was fully returned and whose relations with them were of the happiest, was up all day with them at Sekernik, and was able to observe with his own eyes how difficult was the task of the 14th Division. He saw a turning movement against the Bulgarian right flank break down with considerable loss, almost entirely owing to the fire from the Belašica. He had now got the 130th Siege Battery into action on the main Petrić road, and had had a promise from General

---

[1] See Appendix 19.
[2] General E. Zymbrakakis is not to be confused with his namesake, the commander of the Seres Division. The former's corps had been, as we have seen, broken up, the Archipelago Division being in the 1st Group, the Crete Division in the British XVI and later XII Corps, and the Seres Division having been sent to the Struma valley after its attacks when forming part of the XII Corps. General Franchet d'Espérey now put the Crete Division under General E. Zymbrakakis as a first step to the reconstitution of his corps.

Wilson that a 6-inch gun of the 43rd Siege Battery would bombard Yeniköi from the plain north of Lake Dojran on the morrow. Eager as he was to reach the Struma, he realized that it was not going to be an easy task if the flanking fire continued. He requested General Milne to urge upon General Zymbrakakis how essential it was that the Crete Division should quicken its sweep eastward.

1918.
29 Sept.

The advanced guard of the 79th Brigade, the 8/D.C.L.I. with " D " Battery CXVI Brigade R.F.A., advanced four miles up the pass from Hamzali on the Berovo road, and then, about a mile short of the crest, was brought to a halt by the accurate fire of mountain artillery and machine guns.

On the morning of the 30th both attacks were to have been renewed. The 83rd Brigade, which had moved forward to Trnovo, was to make a turning movement round the enemy's flank in conjunction with a frontal attack by the Greeks. On the Berovo road Br.-General Poole had ordered the 12/Hampshire to scale the mountains to the east so as to outflank the position on which the enemy had held up the 79th Brigade the previous day. But at 1.45 a.m. General Briggs, at his latest advanced headquarters, the village of Dabilja, received from G.H.Q. the following telegram :—

30 Sept.

" By reason of the Convention which has just been
" signed, hostilities with the Bulgarian Army will cease on
" Monday the 30th September at midday. All troops on
" both sides will remain where they are. Warn the Bul-
" garian troops by *parlementaires*. No further attack will
" be initiated by us after the receipt of this message."

General Briggs therefore cancelled the orders issued. The Greek 36th Regiment, however—whether before or after the receipt of this cancellation is not clear—went on and occupied Yeniköi before noon, pushing forward outposts to Barbarevo. The action at Yeniköi had cost the 14th Division 382 casualties ; but the British field and mountain artillery had come off lightly, considering the violence of the shelling, its losses being only three killed and six wounded.

In the whole course of the offensive the Anglo-Greek forces had captured 1,300 prisoners and 70 guns.

The total casualties of the Greek 14th Division were by far the heaviest incurred in the actual pursuit on the British front, being two officers and 96 other ranks killed,

18 officers and 434 other ranks wounded ; a total of 550.[1] The 26th Division had had 80 casualties since the 21st September. The only other British formation seriously engaged during the pursuit had been the 65th Brigade of the 22nd Division and the artillery which co-operated with it. The division had 90 casualties, or 112 if those of the attached Surrey Yeomanry and XVI Corps Cyclists be added. The Derbyshire Yeomanry, though it did very fine work and was in the van almost all through the pursuit, had only eight casualties. Neither the 27th nor the 28th Division had any at all.[2]

What the Medical Services describe as " non-battle " casualties " had been very numerous. The total number of British wounded admitted to hospital during the month —including therefore, the casualties in the Roche Noire Salient—was 3,137. The total number of sick admitted was more than three times as great, *viz* 9,855. To these must be added 1,953 Greeks.[3] During the pursuit itself, the proportion of sick to battle casualties was, of course, enormously higher. The two divisions which had suffered most from malaria, the 27th and 28th, evacuated some 5,000 sick between them, having had practically no fighting. Influenza and malaria accounted for all except a few hundreds of these non-battle casualties, the effects of the two diseases being in many cases combined. It was, in fine, the skeleton of an army that received the news of the Armistice and of the overwhelming victory to which it had at so much sacrifice contributed.

---

[1] Bujac, p. 164, *fn*.

[2] These figures, taken from the war diaries, do not accord with those given by the official medical history. For example, seven casualties are here attributed to the 27th Division and 14 to the 28th Division between the 22nd and the 30th September, while no less than 194 wounded are stated to have been admitted to casualty clearing stations from the 22nd Division in the same period. The divergence is easily explained by the fact that in the advance to the Grand Couronné men wounded in the attacks of the 18th and 19th, already shown in the returns for those attacks, were picked up, and that, as stated, a considerable number of British wounded were found in Bulgarian hospitals. There were also a number of cases of men accidentally wounded by the explosion of grenades when their unit was far from the front. Finally, there are sure to have been some men wounded on the 18th or 19th not admitted—perhaps because at the moment their wounds seemed of small account—until some days later. Nevertheless, the medical statistics are, it need hardly be said, the only completely reliable ones ; and the only figures which one can take as absolutely correct are those of wounded and sick for the whole month of September.

[3] " Medical Services : General History," Vol. IV, p. 147.

CAPTURE OF ŠTIP

THE GENERAL PURSUIT ON THE FRANCO-SERBIAN FRONT, 25TH–28TH SEPTEMBER.

The Serbian Armies and the Armée Française d'Orient were on the morning of the 25th September entering upon the decisive stage of the pursuit. The Serbian Second Army was directed upon the Bulgarian frontier at Carevoselo, the First on Veles and subsequently on Kumanovo, north of which there was no east-and-west road leading into Bulgaria for fifty miles. The Armée Française d'Orient had the double goal of Skoplje and Kičevo. During the night of the 24th September the enemy had abandoned Štip, and the Serbian Cavalry Division had entered the town on his heels.

1918. 25 Sept. Map 8. Sketches 7, 10.

On the 25th the 1st Group of Divisions established a bridgehead over the Vardar at Strumica Station, but the day was spent in closing the columns up to the river. On the front of the Serbian Second Army the Timok Division completely cleared the crest of the Gradec Planina. The main body of the Yugoslav Division crossed the Kriva Lakavica at Baltali, and the advanced guard reached Lipovdol, south-east of Štip. Wheeling slightly on its right, the First Army pushed on astride the Vardar, Morava Division on the east bank, Drina on the west, and Danube now in reserve. The two divisions drove the enemy back from village to village and from spur to spur, till by evening the Bulgarian *Dieterich Division* was back on the last heights from which Veles could be defended.

It will be recalled that on the 24th the right wing of the Armée Française d'Orient, consisting of the 11th Colonial and the Greek 3rd Division, had halted at Prilep, to constitute two groups, the smaller to march swiftly on Skoplje by way of Veles in support of the Cavalry Brigade, while the larger continued the pursuit in the direction of Brod. The Skoplje detachment, commanded by General Tranié, and consisting of the 22nd Colonial Brigade with field and mountain artillery, set out up the Babuna Pass road. As we shall see, Veles fell on the 26th, and the detachment had an uneventful progress until it reached the town on the morning of the 27th. The remainder of the two divisions, under General Farret, moved north-west up the Brod road, till checked by enemy rearguards on the Treska.[1] On its left the Italian 35th Division reached the outskirts of Kruševo, its right being at Godivle. The enemy having abandoned Hill 1248, the 2nd Group of Divisions reached the Semnica river north-west of Monastir. On the shore of Lake Prespa, between Lakes Prespa and Ohrid, and west of the latter the enemy's rear guards hung on until nightfall.

That evening General Franchet d'Espérey issued another " Instruction for the Armies,"[2] which chiefly concerned the Armée Française d'Orient. Five divisions, he observed to General Henrys, were now taking part in the pursuit towards Kičevo and Resan. This was contrary to his wishes; for Skoplje was now the more important of the two objectives of the Army. He therefore directed that the Tranié Detachment should be brought up to the strength of a division and that a second division should be ordered to march on Skoplje as soon as possible.

The enemy's *LXI Corps* had certainly on this date fulfilled its rôle, that of delaying the Allied advance up the Vardar while the *LXII Corps* made its way round to Skoplje. For the moment the race for Skoplje was going as well as the enemy's command could expect. A more immediate anxiety was the state of the *First Army* which, as we have seen, had made no serious resistance on the 25th to the British XVI Corps. Worse still, crowds of mutinous deserters from the *2nd* and *3rd Divisions* poured into Kyustendil and forced Bulgarian G.H.Q. to provide them with trains to take them home. G.H.Q. ceased to function that day, and on the 27th was withdrawn to Sofia, where General Todorov hoped it would be freed from interference of this sort.

The other news received by General von Scholtz, who had moved his headquarters back to Leskovac, south of Niš, was good. Two German divisions, the *Alpine Corps* from the Western Front and the *217th Division* from the Crimea, and several Austro-Hungarian divisions were on their way to his aid. All was not yet lost. His intention was to await their arrival at Kumanovo and then to launch a strong counter-attack down the Kumanovo–Kliseli–Štip

---

[1] This stream, a tributary of the Blato, is not to be confused with the considerable river of the same name which is a tributary of the Vardar.
[2] See Appendix 20.

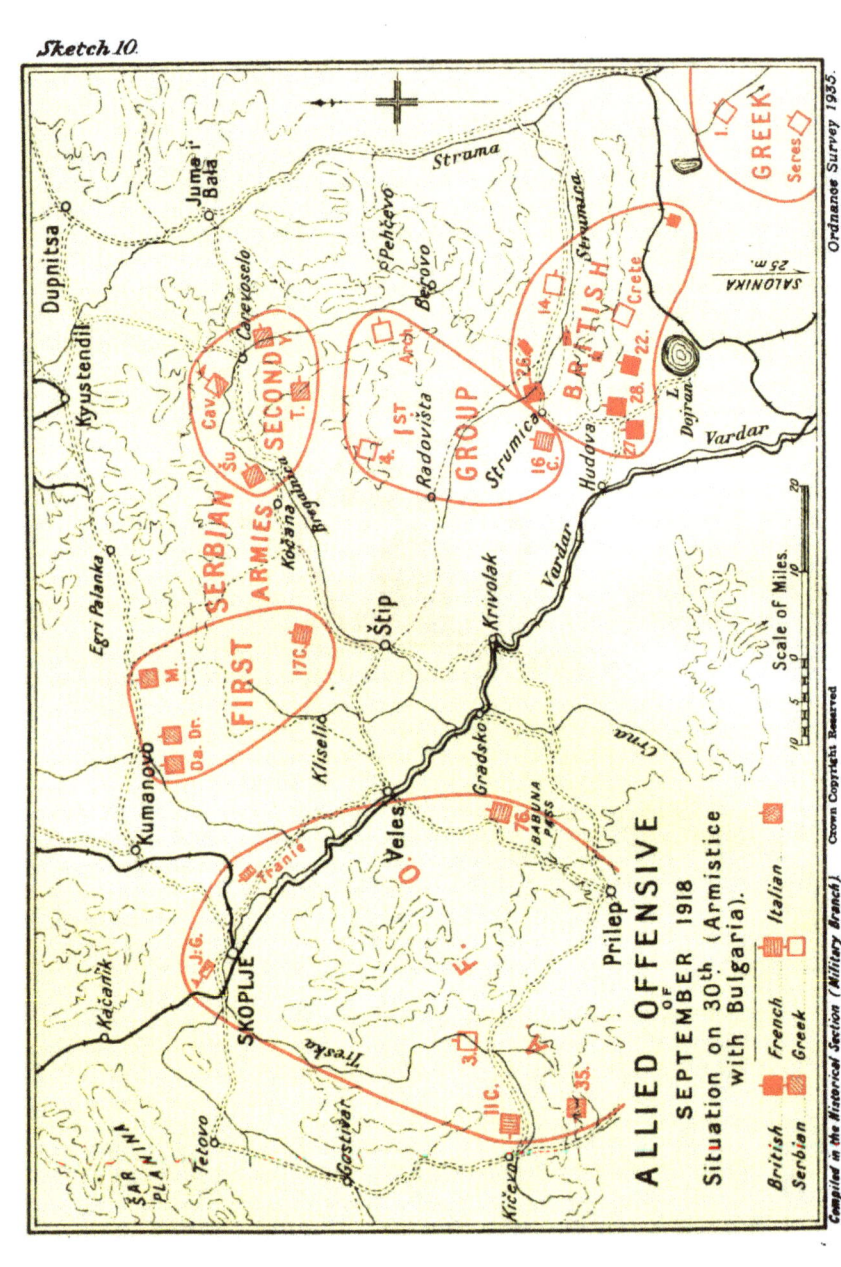

road. If successful, this would bring to a halt the Serbian advance eastward towards the Bulgarian frontier at Carevoselo. 1918. 25 Sept.

Bulgarian G.H.Q. would not, however, wait. On the morning of the 25th, evidently just before the mutineers broke in upon it, it ordered an immediate counter-attack to recover Štip. This was to be carried out from the northwest by the *2nd Division* and from the east by a detachment of the *First Army*, consisting of 12 battalions and 12 batteries, which had been concentrated at Radovišta. A detachment of all arms under General Windel, then at Kumanova, was to reach Kliseli by the morning of the 26th and to support the advance of the *2nd Division*.[1]

It was all in vain. On the morning of the 26th the Morava Division of the Serbian First Army anticipated the attack by driving the *2nd Division* out of Kišino. The Radovišta detachment made no progress against the Serbian Second Army, and General Windel's troops trickled forward only in time to be placed in reserve to the *2nd Division* as it withdrew to the Veles-Štip road. 26 Sept.

Meanwhile on the right the Serbian Second Army was exploiting its success, the indefatigable Yugoslav Division passing through Karbinci, five miles north of Štip, and the Cavalry Division occupying Kočana. South of Veles there was hot fighting, the left flank of the Morava Division on the east bank of the Vardar and the Drina on the west bank being held up by the Bulgarian and German troops of the *Dieterich Division*, which fought with real determination. Soon after nightfall, however, the enemy's rear guards abandoned the west bank and blew up the bridge. For some hours longer they maintained themselves in the eastern and northern portion of the town beyond the Vardar, but before daylight had withdrawn to the high ground at Novočani. There was not a man now on the west bank of

---

[1] General Windel, commanding a brigade of the *217th Division*, mentioned above, reached Kumanova on the 25th with the first echelon of the division—one battalion, two batteries, etc. The Bulgarian *55th Regiment*, withdrawn from the quiet front above Lake Tahinos on the Struma, and, according to the German account, the Bulgarian *3rd* and *7th Cavalry Regiments* were placed under his orders. The *7th Cavalry Regiment* came from the *Fourth Army* on the Ægean coast, but, as will be seen from the Bulgarian Order of Battle, there is no mention of the *3rd* in this theatre. It may be an error for *8th*, which regiment was with the *8th Division* on the lower Struma; on the other hand, a *3rd Regiment* doubtless existed, and it may have by now arrived from Bulgaria.

the Vardar. The gap between the troops of the *LXI Corps* north of Veles and the *302nd Division* of the *LXII Corps* in the Barbarec Pass on the Brod road was 30 miles wide. That gap consisted, it is true, of mountainous, wooded, and almost roadless country, but, as we shall see, the attacker was able to make use of it.

The Franco-Greek detachment under General Farret reached the entrance to the Barbarec Pass. The Italian Division entered Kruševo and crossed the Dragišec heights. The 156th and 76th Divisions reached Džvan on the main Kičevo road, and a regiment of the 30th reached Resan. Between the lakes the right of the 3rd Group of Divisions began to advance on the ancient city of Ohrid.

The rout of the enemy was almost accomplished now. It was not merely that the total of prisoners had doubled, having reached 10,000 with some 200 guns; not merely that the moral state of the Bulgarian forces appeared from the avowals of each succeeding batch of prisoners to be lower and lower; not even that the Serbian advance directly threatened Sofia and the rear of the Bulgarian *First* and *Second Armies*. The essential factor was that the separation of the *LXII Corps* on the Tetovo road from the rest of the Bulgarian forces was all but accomplished.

**1918.
27 Sept.** The 27th September marked another decisive stage. On the British front, as we have seen, the Greek 14th Division advanced eastward down the Strumica valley as far as Gabrovo. The 1st Group of Divisions crossed the Gradec Planina, already cleared by the Serbians, and its advanced guards on either side of the watershed entered the valleys of the Vodovča, a tributary of the Strumica, and of the upper Kriva Lakavica. The Serbian Second Army advanced north-eastward astride the Bregalnica, the Timok Division mounting the Plaškovica Planina, while the Yugoslav pushed eastward from Kočana. Its right, being now on the good Kočana road, approached the block-house at Kalimanci, 13 miles west of the Bulgarian frontier. Between the Bregalnica and the Vardar, the Morava Division of the First Army drove back the Bulgarian *2nd Division* and crossed the Veles–Štip road. On its left the Drina Division forded the Vardar. At Veles the Tranié Detachment also crossed, to reach the Veles–Skoplje road. On the Prilep–Kičevo road the French troops of General Farret forced the *302nd Division* step by step back through

ENEMY'S STAND ON GOLEK RIDGE

the Barbarec Pass. The Italian Division reached Mount Česma and the village of Cer. 1918. 28 Sept.

Next day, the 28th, the Greek Archipelago and 4th Divisions of the 1st Group crossed the watershed between the Kriva Lakavica and the Stara. The Serbian Second Army continued its movement on the frontier. At Bigla, three miles west of Carevoselo, the Cavalry Division and the advanced guard of the Yugoslav found the enemy in a strong position covering a defile on the main road. General von Scholtz had assembled at this vital point and on the Golek ridge to the south all the troops he could lay hands on, including four German battalions.[1] He had also withdrawn all the German troops from the *First Army*, and 5,000 of these—for the most part signallers and transport men, but with 22 guns—under General von Posseldt, were marching up the Struma from Petrić towards the same point. For that day the enemy held his ground.

The objective of the Serbian First Army was the Skoplje–Kumanova road, now packed with transport which was being unceasingly bombed by French and Greek aircraft. It forced the Bulgarian *2nd Division* back north of Kliseli, while the Tranié Detachment reached Vetersko on the Veles–Skoplje road. Progress was, however, slow. The enemy was still desperately striving to check the advance on Skoplje, and to a certain extent succeeding. On the Kičevo road General Farret's detachment of the 11th Colonial Division captured Brod and continued its advance on Kičevo, while the Greek 3rd Division, the way cleared for it by the French, turned down the valley of the Treska in the direction of Skoplje. On this flank the most serious threat to the enemy, whose *6th Division* only reached Kičevo on this day, while the *Ohrid* or *Composite Division* was struggling up the Black Drin north of Lake Ohrid, came from the Italian 35th Division. The centre of this division attacked the enemy, entrenched at Sop, though without success, while the right began a turning movement across the Kruška. The column of the 30th Division from Resan reached the crest of the Plakenoka Planina, and the

---

[1] Three of these were from the "Radovišta Group," whose activities have been described. They were our old acquaintance the *13th Saxon Reserve Jäger Battalion* and two battalions of the *12th Landwehr Infantry Regiment*. The fourth was the *1/256th* Battalion, a "propaganda battalion" from the Struma valley.

57th occupied Ohrid. The 76th Division was withdrawn from the line with orders to march rapidly through Prilep and Veles on Skoplje, in accordance with the Instruction issued by General Franchet d'Espérey on the 25th [1] and subsequent messages to the same effect.

It is interesting to observe how stubbornly General Henrys, commanding the Armée Française d'Orient, clung to his own conception of swinging westward on Kičevo, despite the urging of his Commander-in-Chief to put more weight into the thrust towards Skoplje. The point of view of the former is readily to be understood. The pressure of his westward thrusts was delaying the enemy on the Prilep–Kičevo road and on the Monastir–Kičevo road. There are even reports that units which had made good progress in their retreat towards Tetovo were brought back to face the threat of the Italians.[2] Nevertheless, there was a very real danger that at least the head of the enemy's *LXII Corps* would now reach Skoplje before the Allies and reunite with the *LXI*.

General Franchet d'Espérey now adopted a stronger tone. In the words of the official report he insisted " that " the bulk of the French divisions should be pushed as " quickly as possible on Skoplje . . . and that only small " detachments of all arms should be left in front of the " enemy's rear guards towards Kičevo." With his own hand he added to an instruction, addressed to General Henrys alone, two brief sentences which have something of Napoleonic abruptness and pith :—" La direction est au " nord et à l'est. Face à l'ouest, il n'y a que du nettoyage " et de la couverture." [3]

However, an abrupt change of direction by several divisions in semi-mountainous country takes time to operate. No new forces which General Henrys detached and swung north-eastward were now likely to be at Skoplje in time. It did not matter. Skoplje was none the less about to fall as the result of one of the most brilliant strokes of the whole battle.

---

[1] See p. 238.   [2] Villari, p. 239.   [3] Revol, p. 82.

THE CAPTURE OF SKOPLJE.

It has already been recorded that the first troops to reach Prilep were the French cavalry, which entered the town early in the afternoon of the 23rd September.[1] The brigade, which had no official title except that of the "Groupement de Cavalerie" and was better known as the "Brigade Jouinot-Gambetta" from the name of its commander, consisted of the 1st and 4th Chasseurs d'Afrique, a six-squadron regiment of Moroccan Spahis, and a section of armoured cars. It was a well-trained and a particularly well mounted force, whose Barb stallions were to prove themselves in the days to come more sure-footed and enduring than the pack mules. Its original mission had accorded with the conception of General Henrys, as outlined above. After gaining possession of Prilep it was to "wheel towards Kičevo in order to disorganize the retreating "columns, capture or destroy enemy artillery and convoys, "and push out reconnaissances to find out if the Stroška "Planina (north of the Prilep–Kičevo road) were held by "the enemy."[2] But, as the brigade rode northward in the bend of the Crna, General Franchet d'Espérey in his car caught it up, and personally directed General Jouinot-Gambetta to march straight on Skoplje after passing through Prilep.

1918.
23 Sept.
Map 8.
Sketch 10.

At Prilep General Jouinot-Gambetta received an order from General Henrys that he was to advance on Skoplje across the *massif* "north of the Prilep–Brod road." But, as will be clear from what has been written of the advance of the 11th Colonial Division, this route was barred, and a reconnaissance in force sent out in its direction on the 24th became engaged with the enemy in considerable strength. On the other hand, the Veles road was open as far as the Babuna Pass. General Jouinot-Gambetta therefore disregarded the order and marched on the Babuna Pass at 7 p.m. The advanced guard reached Izvor at 9 a.m. on

24 Sept.

---

[1] See p. 219.
[2] "Du rôle de la cavalerie dans l'Offensive en Orient," by General Guespereau (then commanding the Spahis) in "L'Armée d'Orient vue à "15 ans de distance" (Paris: *Revue des Balkans*). The following account is based partly on this article, partly on "Uskub, ou du Rôle de la Cavalerie d'Afrique dans la Victoire," by General Jouinot-Gambetta. The present writer has given a slightly fuller account in *The Fighting Forces*, June 1934.

1918. the 25th. Here the Spahis made touch with the Serbian
25 Sept. First Army and found it heavily engaged with the enemy's *4th Division*, which was defending Veles. The Spahis also came into action about Banjica. The road was closed, as were the tracks just west of it.

After considering all the reports, General Jouinot-Gambetta that evening made a vital decision. He would neither wait till the Serbians had opened a passage for him, nor take part in the infantry battle in order to assist them to do so. He would quit the Veles road at Štarigrad, and, leaving the Spahis to follow as soon as they could be disengaged, plunge into the mountains of the Golešnica Planina, and make his way across them, by the track through Drenovo, to Skoplje. No wheeled transport could accompany his march, though he might hope that his armoured cars would catch him up by the Veles–Skoplje road as soon as it was opened. It was doubtful, even, if the mounted men and pack animals would get through without heavy losses.

26 Sept. After a very trying march, during which for the most part the men had to lead their horses, Drenovo was reached at 8 p.m. on the 26th. After a halt of four hours and a night march, the leading regiments bivouacked, nearly 5,000 feet up, in or above the wild, rocky, and wooded gorge of the Kaidina river near Aldince. A few miles further
28 Sept. north there was a long halt on the morning of the 28th to allow the Spahis to rejoin, before descending to the Vardar valley. In the afternoon the brigade rode down and again halted at Dračevo, close to the railway, which patrols had found here unguarded. As night fell light after light appeared to the north, till a large area was covered with them. That could only be Skoplje, the goal.

General Jouinot-Gambetta had little notion as to what opposition he would have to meet and was not going to lose the advantage of surprise by carrying out reconnaissances in daylight. His reconnaissances would move out under cover of darkness; they would be closely followed by the leading squadrons of each regiment, and the attack would be launched as soon as there was light enough to see. To the Spahis he assigned the heights south of the town—the eastern end of the Karšjak ridge—which must be held at all costs after capture, since they commanded the town and the Tetovo road. The two regiments of Chasseurs d'Afrique were to advance up the valley of the Vardar and capture Skoplje, afterwards trying to find touch with the Tranié Detachment on the Veles road. He did not know that the infantry was still at Vetersko, 19 miles south-east of Skoplje in a direct line and nearer 30 owing to the windings of the road between Vetersko and Kaplan, or that its way was blocked by the remains of two divisions, *Dieterich's* and the *4th*.

1918. 28 Sept.

Nor did General Jouinot-Gambetta know that Skoplje had a garrison amply sufficient in numbers, if poor in quality, to hold up three cavalry regiments unsupported by any artillery but their little 37-mm. pack guns. This garrison, under the command of the German Colonel von Carlowitz, consisted, in fact, of six and a half battalions, four batteries, and an armoured train.[1] It was somewhat curiously disposed, a group on the right holding the Karšjak ridge, one on the left astride the Veles-Skoplje road north of Lake Kaplan, and a reserve at the station. The two groups, something like 13 miles apart, were linked only by patrols, and at that bad patrols; for they had allowed the French cavalry to approach the railway at Dračevo, half-way between the two groups, without giving the alarm. There had, indeed, been news during the night that French cavalry were approaching from the mountains, but its only effect had been to cause some hundreds of the Bulgarian recruits to stampede.

All went well for the cavalry. Following their patrols, the Spahis rode across the Markova river at 4.30 a.m. on the 29th, screened by driving mist. The Bulgarians on the heights beyond were driven off at the first onset. The 4th Chasseurs in the centre had a stiffer task, coming under the fire of the armoured train, which for a moment threw the regiment into confusion. The 1st Chasseurs, crossing to the left bank, were held up for a considerable time, during which three trains escaped. Both regiments, however, pushed on, and when the Spahis, leaving a squadron on the heights, crossed the bridge, entered the northern part of the

29 Sept.

---

[1] Two Bulgarian battalions and the German *217th Mountain Machine-Gun Detachment* under a Bulgarian regimental staff, four Bulgarian reinforcement battalions under a second regimental staff, the German *3rd Mountain Machine-Gun Detachment*, two companies German *Landsturm*, four Bulgarian batteries, and the armoured train which has been mentioned as engaged at Gradsko and which had subsequently been in action at Veles.

town, and secured the northern exits, the fight was virtually over. The Spahi squadrons subsequently attacked columns moving into Skoplje from Tetovo or fleeing north-westward towards the Kačanik defile. One column, consisting of two German heavy batteries, was overwhelmed by machine-gun fire, and five guns, ammunition wagons, supply wagons, and a number of prisoners were captured. The total number of prisoners here and in Skoplje amounted to 359, including 139 Germans. Between 300 and 400 oxen and sheep and stores of all sorts were also taken. Colonel von Carlowitz and a proportion of his force escaped up the valley of the Lepenac river to Eles-Han Station on the Mitrovica line. The armoured train, whose personnel had blown up the railway bridge at an early stage of the action, finally ran out under machine-gun fire to Hadžalar Station on the main Niš line. The detachment on the shore of Lake Kaplan formed front facing Skoplje from Hadžalar to Ibrahimovce on the Veles road.

It was indeed a remarkable operation, and would have been a still more brilliant success had General Jouinot-Gambetta been given the mountain artillery for which he had begged; for then it is possible that he would have caught the armoured train, which, in rear-guard actions always followed by demolition of the line, gave endless trouble during the weeks to come. If the attack had had luck on its side, it was the sort of luck which often attends the man who does the right thing. The fact that negotiations for an armistice were in progress may detract slightly from its merit, but does not really diminish its importance. For a French aeroplane came over the town, and then hastened back to Salonika with the news. That evening General Franchet d'Espérey was able to tell the Bulgarian delegates that the largest town of the new territories of Serbia, the second town after Belgrade in all Serbia, was in his hands, and that their *LXII Corps* was blocked on the Tetovo road.

The Armistice with Bulgaria.

We may now resume the main events of the 29th on the rest of the front. The 1st Group of Divisions reached the highest point on the Plaškovica Planina. The Serbian Second Army, after a fight lasting all day, forced the enemy

off the Golek and beyond the Bregalnica. In the evening 1918.
the Bulgarians abandoned Carevoselo and fell back to the 29 Sept.
frontier. The First Army made rapid progress northward,
the Drina Division reaching Malino; but neither its troops
nor those of the Tranié Detachment on the Veles–Skoplje
road were by nightfall in any position to reach out a hand to
General Jouinot-Gambetta in Skoplje. Still more remote
was the Greek 3rd Division in the valley of Treska; for, not
being equipped with transport for its difficult march, it had
to wait all day for a French pack column with two days'
food and some artillery ammunition to reach it. On its left
General Farret was held up in the valley of the Velika, and
the Italians made no progress against Sop. Here, in fact,
General Mombelli decided that a "full-dress" attack was
necessary, and occupied the day in preparing it. North of
the lakes the left of the Armée Française d'Orient continued
to advance, but this part of the front had now little effect
upon the main battle.

It is amusing to note the attitude of the two German
corps commanders when they heard that Skoplje was in the
hands of the enemy. General Surén, commanding the
LXI Corps, at once decided that his duty was to cover the
Kumanovo road. He appears to have made no effort to
help his colleague, and drew off northward. Leaving a rear
guard on the high ground north of Lake Kaplan, he made a
long march during the afternoon and night of the 29th,
halting again with his right on the road about Orlanci and
his left at Kešani. That retreat took as much out of his
troops as any two days of their recent rear-guard actions;
for, after ten days of great heat, the 29th was marked by
stormy weather and torrents of rain which turned the roads
into glue.[1]

To General Fleck, who heard of the capture of Skoplje
immediately on his arrival at his new headquarters in
Tetovo, the news appeared in a very different light. His
situation was indeed desperate. He was cut off from the

---

[1] The further advance of the Allied divisions, many of which did not
learn that the Armistice had been signed till after daylight on the 30th,
is not described here, as it was unopposed, but their final positions are
roughly indicated in Sketch 10. It should, however, be noted that in
this sketch, designed merely to give a general indication of the strategical
situation, divisions are shown in positions actually only reached by their
advanced troops, in some cases only by comparatively small advanced
guards.

rest of the Army and even from communication with his superiors; for his wireless was not working and he could not send a message by aeroplane owing to the density of the clouds and the heaviness of the rain.[1] He had three alternatives: to surrender; to attempt to scramble over the Šar either to the Kačanik defile or to Prizren on the Albanian frontier; to attempt to fight his way through. The first course was unthinkable. As for the second, a proportion of his infantry might have escaped, but, as has been explained, escape was an impossibility for the bulk of his force and for all his artillery and wheeled transport; even if it had been possible, such a movement would have defeated all the plans of General von Scholtz for a counter-offensive in conjunction with the reinforcing divisions. Without hesitation the corps commander decided to fight. At the commencement of the attack he would not be able to engage nearly all his force, his rear guard being about Šop and Kičevo, and the *Composite Division* three or four days' march away, only a few miles north of Debar. Still, he had a number of heavy batteries marching with the head of his column, and hour by hour he would be able to throw more troops into the battle, by making use of the light railway from Kičevo, through Gostivar and Tetovo, to Skoplje. He hastened the movement of his rearward formations and ordered the leading one, the Bulgarian *1st Division*, supported by a German machine-gun company and German and Bulgarian heavy artillery, to attack Skoplje next morning.

It was a pretty situation. One has observed that when a wasp is caught in a spider's web the captor is often as eager to set the victim free as the victim is to escape. But if one could assume the spider to be aware that other and more formidable members of his kind were hastening to his assistance one might suppose that he would not decline the combat. Such was the position of General Jouinot-Gambetta on the night of the 29th September and next morning. Perhaps, indeed, it was more serious; for he had not to do with the *LXII Corps* on the Tetovo road only. He had to keep an eye also to the northward, where there was still in being a remnant of the defeated right wing of

---

[1] "Weltkriegsende an der mazedonischen Front," p. 126. Yet, as we have seen, the French sent an aeroplane over Skoplje and discovered its capture by their cavalry.

BLOCKING OF BULGAR LXII CORPS 249

the Skoplje garrison ; and also to the east, where the left wing was in a position to threaten Skoplje and might at any moment receive aid from the *LXI Corps*. To hold out was of vital importance, if the fruits of his dash into Skoplje were not to be lost and his brilliant exploit made to appear a foolhardy escapade.

1918. 30 Sept.

By an early hour on the 30th the leading Bulgarian troops had crossed the Vardar bridge on the main road six miles west of Skoplje. Soon they were across the Mitrovica railway, and battalions were seen detraining on the Tetovo light railway only $3\frac{1}{2}$ miles from the town. Further south they were prevented by the fire of the French cavalry from climbing the Karšjak heights. But they had now brought up their artillery and begun to prepare their attack by fire. On the north side, too, there was movement, perhaps from the troops of Colonel von Carlowitz. How long could this last ?

All this time neither side knew of the Armistice. Apparently General Fleck was the first to hear of it, from his rear guard, which had been approached by French and Italian officers under white flags, bearing the news. General Jouinot-Gambetta received at 11.30 a.m. a message by aeroplane that the Armistice had been signed the previous night and would come into force at noon. About that hour, a staff officer sent out by General Fleck in an aeroplane returned with a message from General von Steuben that the Armistice had in fact been signed, and that the German forces would not recognize it. For some time after that the Bulgarian troops attacking Skoplje refused to believe the news, and the cavalry passed an anxious afternoon and night. At 8 a.m. on the 1st October the head of the Tranié Detachment was seen, and by noon it had relieved the cavalry in the positions of defence round Skoplje. It is idle to speculate what would have happened there but for the Armistice, though we may be sure that the 30th would have been a critical day for the cavalry.

According to German evidence the real responsibility for the Bulgarian surrender lies upon General Lukov, the commander of the *Second Army*.[1] Shortly after the launch of the Allied offensive, in which no part of his front was attacked, he telegraphed to Tsar Ferdinand begging him to

---

[1] " Weltkriegsende an der mazedonischen Front," p. 139.

open negotiations with the Allies.[1] The Tsar, whose attitude, again on German evidence, was firm throughout and who visited his troops to encourage them during the battle, repulsed the suggestion vigorously, but it spread abroad and encouraged the Malinov Government to make an effort on their own account. In the early hours of the 26th, as already recorded, Bulgarian *parlementaires* entered the British lines and were taken on to General Franchet d'Espérey. The latter sent them back on the 27th with the following message :—

"I have the honour to acknowledge receipt of the "letter of the 25th September 1918 which Your Excellency "has sent me through the General Officer Commanding-in- "Chief the British Army of the East. My answer, which I "am handing to the Bulgarian field officer, the bearer of the "letter in question, must, in view of the military situation, "be the following :—

"I can accord neither armistice nor suspension of arms "leading to the interruption of the operations in progress. "On the other hand, I will receive with fitting courtesy the "duly qualified delegates of the Royal Bulgarian Govern- "ment to whom Your Excellency refers in his letter. These "gentlemen should present themselves before the British "lines accompanied by an officer *parlementaire*."

The visit of Mr. Walker, sent by the United States Chargé d'Affaires, Mr. Murphy, was largely due to the fact that the Austrian wireless station refused to transmit an appeal which M. Malinov had requested the latter to make to President Wilson. General Franchet d'Espérey was instructed by M. Clemenceau to have no dealings with Mr. Murphy. On the 28th General Lukov, with the Minister of Finance, M. Ljapchev, and the former Minister at Bucharest, M. Radev, left *Second Army* headquarters at Sveti Vrach for Salonika. The news of the negotiations could not be kept secret, and its effect, coming upon the top of the heavy defeat, almost destroyed the last shreds of spirit in the Bulgarian nation. In Radomir, a little town twenty miles south-west of Sofia, a republic was proclaimed, and from 6,000 to 8,000 men marched on the capital. The military governor had only a handful of loyal troops—

---

[1] General Ludendorff in "My War Memories" (p. 712), says "on the "16th, or at latest the 17th."

chiefly the cadets of the military academy and a detachment of the Tsar's mounted Life Guard—but he was reinforced by the leading units of the German *217th Division*, arriving from the Crimea. He scattered the Republicans and drove them back. Nevertheless, it was only the presence of the German troops which permitted Bulgarian G.H.Q. to continue to work in Sofia and kept the city quiet. The Prime Minister sent the delegates at Salonika an urgent message to make what terms they could.

1918.
30 Sept.

General Franchet d'Espérey scouted the Bulgarian suggestion, which M. Ljapchev had outlined to General Milne, that Bulgaria should be treated more or less as a neutral, in return for which the delegates were authorized to guarantee that she would shortly employ her forces in the service of the Allies. The terms which he did grant were, however, not severe, though, of course, they were merely designed to render the country helpless, any question of punishment being left over for the peace conference to settle. The severest clause was due to the capture of Skoplje, which, as already stated, was reported to General Franchet d'Espérey before he put his signature to the document. By the terms of this clause all troops of the *Eleventh Army* west of the meridian of the town were to lay down their arms and to be treated as prisoners of war. The other principal points were the immediate evacuation by the Bulgarians of Greek and Serbian territory; the immediate demobilization of the Army except for three divisions and two cavalry regiments; the surrender of the arms, munitions, and transport of the demobilized elements; the ejection from Bulgaria within four weeks of German and Austro-Hungarian forces and of their diplomatic and consular representatives; the utilization by the Allies of the Bulgarian railways, roads, and ports; the occupation by the Allies of strategic positions in Bulgaria.

The number of prisoners actually captured prior to the Armistice was about 15,000. With the surrender of the formations of the *LXII Corps*, in some cases not until three or four days later, the figure was raised to 77,000, including three generals and 1,500 officers. Four hundred guns, 10,000 horses, 20,000 oxen and sheep formed part of the immense booty. In addition an army well nigh half a million strong was eliminated from the ranks of the enemy. The victory was complete.

The Tsar was sacrificed to the popular reaction. He was forced to abdicate on the 3rd October, and took refuge in Germany. Thanks, however, in the first instance to the German troops in Sofia, and subsequently to the popularity which the conduct of the Crown Prince had won for him with the returned soldiers and the nation at large, an anti-dynastic revolution was avoided, and Prince Boris ascended the throne in his father's stead. Thus of all the nations, Russia, Austria-Hungary, Germany, Turkey, and Bulgaria, which suffered final defeat in the Great War, Bulgaria was the only one in which the monarchy was preserved.

NOTE.

THE TERMS OF THE ARMISTICE WITH BULGARIA, SIGNED 29TH SEPTEMBER 1918.

Military Convention regulating the conditions for the suspension of hostilities between the Allied Powers and Bulgaria.

1. Immediate evacuation, in accordance with an arrangement to be concluded, of the territories still occupied in Greece and in Serbia. No cattle, grain, or food stuffs of any sort shall be removed from these territories. No damage shall be done on leaving them. The Bulgarian administration shall continue to operate in the districts of Bulgaria at present occupied by the Allies.

2. Immediate demobilization of the whole Bulgarian Army, except for the maintenance on a war footing of a group of all arms of three divisions (of 16 battalions each) and four cavalry regiments, which shall be employed, two divisions for the defence of the eastern frontier of Bulgaria and the Dobruja, and one division to guard the railways.

3. The arms, munitions, and military vehicles belonging to the demobilized elements shall be deposited at points to be fixed by the High Command of the Armies of the East; they will be stored by the Bulgarian authorities under Allied control. The horses will also be handed over to the Allies.

4. Return to Greece of the material of the Greek IV Army Corps taken from the Greek Army at the time of the occupation of Eastern Macedonia, so far as it has not been sent to Germany.

5. Bulgarian troops at present west of the meridian of Üsküb (Skoplje) and forming part of the *German Eleventh Army* shall lay down their arms and shall be considered until further notice prisoners of war. The officers will retain their arms.

6. Employment until the signature of peace of the Bulgarian prisoners in the East by the Allied Armies, without reciprocity as regards Allied prisoners of war. The latter will be handed over without delay to the Allied authorities, and civilians who have been deported will have complete liberty to return to their homes.

7. Germany and Austro-Hungary will be given a time limit of four weeks within which to withdraw their troops and military organization from Bulgaria. Within the same period the diplomatic and consular representatives of the Central Powers, as well as their nationals, must quit the territory of the Kingdom.

Orders for the cessation of hostilities will be given on the signature of the present convention.

SECRET ARTICLES.

1. The future passage of Allied military forces through Bulgarian territory and the use of railways, roads, rivers, and ports will be the subject of a special convention between the Bulgarian Government and the High Command of the Army of the East. Discussions to this effect will be begun within a period of a week at most. They will take into consideration also the control of the telephone, the telegraph, and the wireless stations.

2. A certain number of strategical points will be occupied in the interior of Bulgarian territory by the Great Powers of the Allies. This occupation will be provisional and purely as a guarantee. It will not occasion any coercion or arbitrary system of requisitioning. The Commander-in-Chief of the Armies gives the assurance that, except in extraordinary circumstances, Sofia will not be occupied.

3. The Commander-in-Chief reserves to himself the right to demand the complete cessation of intercourse between Bulgaria and her former Allies in case of need.

4. Opening of the Bulgarian ports to Allied and neutral ships.

FRANCHET D'ESPÉREY.
ANDRÉ LIAPCHEFF.
GENERAL LUKOFF.

CHAPTER XII.

THE LAST ACT.
(Maps 1, 8, 10.)

THE DANUBE OR CONSTANTINOPLE ?

1918.
Oct.
Maps 1, 8, 10.

THE war was not over, although Bulgaria was out of it. Germany and Austria-Hungary had given no recognition to the Armistice, and the former was now hastily extricating her troops from the Bulgarian wreckage. Turkey was still in the field. And yet, as it turned out, no British soldier was to fire another shot in the Balkans; and the harmless dropping of a few bombs by a German or Turkish aeroplane near Stavros was the enemy's last act of aggression against the British Salonika Army.

This ending to the World War was, however, hidden in the womb of the future when, on the 1st October, the day after the signature of the convention with Bulgaria, arrangements were made for the surrender of war material in accordance with Clause 3. It appeared that there might still be arduous tasks ahead, as, indeed, for the troops who had to advance to the Danube there actually were. Yet it was apparent that the Allies were now well on the road to final victory, and it was unlikely that that would be long delayed.

On the main battle-front in the west the British had broken the Hindenburg Line in the course of September and had at the end of the month begun with the Belgian Army an offensive in Flanders, which swept with dramatic speed over the ground that had been so fiercely disputed for the last four years. Further south the Franco-American assault known as the Battle of Champagne and Argonne was going forward successfully. In Palestine the Turks had been completely overthrown by the forces under General Allenby, and, on the very day in question, Damascus was captured. Signs of failing in the two chief belligerents of the Central Powers had appeared when, on the 15th September, the German Government made a definite offer of peace to Belgium and the Austro-Hungarian Government addressed to the United States of America a Note suggesting an " unofficial " peace conference.

The rout of Bulgaria and the elimination of her Army had taken the German Supreme Command completely by surprise. There had been warnings that all was not well with the Bulgarian forces, and failures, perhaps even serious loss of territory, had been anticipated from the coming Allied offensive; but nothing like this complete collapse. As has been stated, O.H.L. had answered the first cry of " Come over into Macedonia and help us ! " with the promise of a meagre reinforcement, a single German composite brigade and one Austro-Hungarian division.[1] But, as General Ludendorff at Spa marked the progress of the Allied offensive, he realized that, within a matter of days, the whole south-eastern front might dissolve at the moment when Germany was in a most desperate plight in the west.[2] The Allies would march into northern Serbia and thence attack Hungary, which would mean the *coup de grâce* to the Dual Monarchy. That was not all. Turkey would be almost completely stripped of defence. She had in her extremity been forced to depend for protection from the west on Bulgaria, little as she loved her ally. Her frontier here was covered by the Bulgarian *Second Army* on the Struma and the *Fourth Army* between the Struma and the Mesta. She had very few troops in Europe; her forces in Syria had been destroyed; the ragged remnant in Mesopotamia was inadequate for its task there and in any case could not be moved in time; from the Caucasus individual battalions might indeed be transported, but the shipping in the Black Sea was inadequate to carry more. Nothing, it seemed, could save Constantinople. Its fall would, in turn, open the Black Sea to the Allies. And from the Black Sea would come a fresh threat to Hungary by way of Rumania, who would doubtless rearm.

1918.
Oct.

In these circumstances Germany and Austria discovered that they could in fact send the aid which they had declared impossible. O.H.L. would provide a division from the Crimea, three divisions from the main Russian front—now, of course, inactive—and the *Alpine Corps*, a division equipped for mountain warfare, from France. The Austrian *Armeeoberkommando* promised a division from the Ukraine and two from Italy. As the three German divisions from

---

[1] See p. 194.
[2] Where not otherwise stated, this and the two succeeding paragraphs are based on Ludendorff, II, pp. 715–30.

the main Russian front had been about to start for France, the two Austrian divisions from Italy were also earmarked to go there, and the *Alpine Corps* came from there, this would have meant a loss to the Western Front of six divisions.[1] A large proportion of these troops were actually close at hand by the 30th September, the date of the Armistice. The German *217th Division* had, as has been mentioned, reached Sofia, and the Austrian *30th Division* was only just behind it on the Plevna–Sofia railway. The Austrian *9th Division* was even nearer the front at Vranje, the *Alpine Corps* was at Niš, and the *219th Division* moving to Niš from Paraćin.

The political action taken by General Ludendorff was even more significant. " I felt compelled," he writes, " to " take on myself the great responsibility of hastening the " end of the war, and for this purpose to move the Govern- " ment to decisive action." On the 26th September he summoned Secretary of State von Hintze, the Foreign Minister, to Spa. The outcome of the conference which took place on the 29th between Field-Marshal von Hindenburg, General Ludendorff, and Admiral von Hintze, and of a subsequent discussion with the Emperor the same day, was the proclamation of a representative parliamentary system in Germany, the supersession of the Imperial Chancellor Graf Hertling by Prince Max of Baden—and, on the 4th October, the German and Austro-Hungarian Notes to President Wilson proposing an armistice.

Before turning to consider Allied military policy in the Balkans after the defeat of Bulgaria, a word must be said of the situation of Rumania, which had considerable influence upon the trend of that policy. It has already been mentioned that on the 9th December 1917 Rumania had concluded an armistice known as the Truce of Focsani with the Central Powers.[2] Negotiations for peace had been slow for many reasons, among which were the existence in the country of a party which desired to fight to the end and the bitter rivalry between Germany, Austria-Hungary, Bulgaria,

---

[1] Actually only three German divisions, the *217th*, *219th*, and *Alpine Corps*, arrived. The *224th* got as far as the Banat and there, on the 2nd October, was ordered to France. The Austrians sent their *30th Division* from the Ukraine, the *9th* and *59th* from Italy; also the *4th Cavalry Division*. ("Weltkriegsende an der Mazedonischen Front," Sketch 2.)

[2] See p. 39.

AIMS OF GENERAL D'ESPÉREY

and Turkey when it came to the division of the spoils of victory. Eventually, on the 5th March 1918, a preliminary treaty was signed at Buftea, the general terms of which were embodied in the Treaty of Bucharest on the 7th May. Rumania pledged herself to demobilize and greatly reduce her Army and to surrender to the Central Powers a large proportion of her military equipment. In all the huge area occupied by the enemy's troops she had to submit to his economic demands; that is, she had to hand over complete control of her railways, her oil-fields,[1] and her corn-lands. The southern Dobruja was handed over to Bulgaria, while the northern part became the common property of the four victorious States. On the other hand, to the disgust of the German military authorities, the dynasty was spared, and Rumania was left in possession of Moldavia, where her Government maintained sovereign rights. She was even allowed to obtain a footing in Bessarabia, but that, of course, was at the expense of the Russian Bolshevists. The Court and Government remained at Jassy, where, as General Ludendorff remarks, the negotiators of the treaty had left the Entente a citadel.

1918. Oct.

Such were the general circumstances in which General Franchet d'Espérey issued his next instructions to the Armies. On the 30th, the day of the Armistice, he had not had time to mature plans, and merely directed that the Serbian First Army should continue the advance in the direction of Niš as soon as possible, while the Second established itself on the two main roads leading eastward into Bulgaria, that from Štip to Jum'a-i-Bala and that from Kumanovo to Kyustendil. Meanwhile all the Armies would disarm Bulgarian troops with whom they were actually in contact. The others could wait. On the 4th October General Milne visited the Allied Commander-in-Chief and was given his future plans in some detail.

The gaze of General Franchet d'Espérey was now fixed on the Danube. His first aim was to seize Niš; then he would debouch on a wide front in northern Serbia, forming a group of three Armies in line. On the right would be the British Army, with three British divisions, under General Milne; in the centre the Armée Française d'Orient with

---
[1] Very great damage had been done to the plants by a British Mission before they were occupied by the enemy, but they were by now giving something like their former yield.

four French, three Greek, and one Italian division, under General Henrys; on the left the Serbian Armies, with the six Serbian divisions, under Voivode Mišić. To operate against Turkey there would be a corps under General d'Anselme consisting of one French and one British division, to which Greek troops would be added later. For operations in Albania the French 57th Division, with small Serbian and Greek columns, would be employed. The strategic reserve would consist of two French divisions in Bulgaria and the two Greek corps in Eastern Macedonia.

The following moves would therefore take place. There was no change in the instructions issued to the Serbian First Army, which had been directed to gain possession of Niš. The Second Army was now to move north-westward and extend the front to the west to the Sanjak of Novi Pazar. As soon as communications could be re-established the first group of three French divisions, under the orders of General Patey, would begin to move up on the new Serbian right. The British Army would, for its part, begin to move northward on the 6th October, its zone of advance being bounded on the east by the Struma in the first instance and then by the road from Sofia to Lom Palanka on the Danube, and on the west by the route Strumica–Kyustendil–Pirot.

It was a vast undertaking for modern troops, who cannot march and fight in large formations unless backed up by the railway or at least by enormous quantities of mechanical transport on suitable roads. Broadly speaking, it was the intention of the Commander-in-Chief to allot to the Serbian Armies the Vardar–Morava corridor as the zone of advance. Here they would be without a railway; for the main Salonika-Niš line was already cut in dozens of places, would undoubtedly be cut all the way up to Belgrade, and could scarcely be put in running order even up to Skoplje for a couple of months. The right and central Armies, on the other hand, would make a detour and be brought up into line with the Serbians by the Bulgarian railways, which the Bulgarian Government would keep intact. These railways would afterwards be used for supply. It was the only possible solution of the problem. The Serbians were not "modern" in the sense indicated above. Hard, rustic, temperate, with few of the needs engendered by more fully developed civilizations, their troops constituted one of those "armées maigres" spoken

of by Duruy, and were ideal for such a task. They would
be freeing their own fatherland, and, if it came to living
upon it, they might be expected to fare better at the hands
of their own countrymen than would foreign troops. The
French and British must be kept regularly supplied with at
least the meat and bread or biscuit ration. Winter was at
hand, too, and blankets and horse-rugs would soon be
necessary. Billets would not always be available, and,
where they were not, bivouac sheets and perhaps tents
would be required. The multitude of miscellaneous stores
used by Armies might in some cases be dispensed with
temporarily, but not indefinitely.

1918.
Oct.

Even with the use of the Bulgarian railways it was,
however, likely to be extremely difficult to transport and to
supply such large bodies as General Franchet d'Espérey
contemplated moving up towards the Danube. In the first
place, the demolitions carried out by the enemy had disconnected the Bulgarian railways from those in the hands
of the Allies. The Constantinople line between Dojran
Station and the Struma could not be repaired under a month.
Up the Struma ran a narrow-gauge railway, which joined
the normal-gauge system at Radomir, south-west of Sofia ;
but the rolling stock on it was limited to 20 serviceable
engines and about 100 trucks, and the line ended at Rupel, so
that there was a gap of four miles between it and the normal-
gauge line at Vetrina Station. To fill that gap was also a
long process, as it involved practically rebuilding the road
bridge over the Struma at Rupel, where the light railway
must cross the river. When all the work was done, and
even supposing that further rolling stock were provided for
the Vetrina–Radomir light railway, that line would still be
a weak link with the Bulgarian normal gauge. And,
beyond that weak link, the normal-gauge system itself had
many deficiencies, such as poor bridges and sleepers laid
too wide apart—which meant very low speed—shortage
and bad repair of rolling stock. Worst of all, there was for
the moment hardly any coal, because the Pernik lignite
mines, worked until the Armistice by Serbian prisoners of
war, were disorganized and almost idle.

Another aspect of the problem engaged General Milne's
attention. Like Ludendorff, when he realized that Bulgaria
was about to collapse he at once anticipated that the Allies
would advance simultaneously to the Danube and to

Constantinople. Now, it was evident that General Franchet d'Espérey regarded an advance to Constantinople as an entirely subsidiary matter.

General Milne ordered the three divisions to begin their movement to the Struma on the 6th October, in accordance with the instructions of General Franchet d'Espérey, but he telegraphed both formally to the War Office and more freely to the C.I.G.S. himself his objections to the scheme. In the first place, he thought it regrettable that the troops of three different nationalities should be employed on the Danube. There had always been, in his view, too much mingling of nationalities. In some degree it had been inevitable hitherto, but now that the Armies were to be despatched in divergent directions there was an opportunity to sort them out. Nor was he so optimistic as General Franchet d'Espérey regarding the Danube venture, which he believed would be seriously crippled and delayed by bad communications. In any case, he had long been of opinion that, after the defeat of Bulgaria, Turkey should be the next British objective. It seemed to him that the opening up of the Black Sea, which would afford quick access to Rumania and permit supplies and stores to be transferred straight from ship to rail on the Bulgarian normal-gauge system, was likely to give earlier returns than the advance to the Danube. He therefore recommended that the troops of one nationality should be employed against Turkey, that that nationality should be British, that a British admiral should command in the naval operations and co-operate with the British Army, and that British troops should not be sent northward.

It is to be noted that neither in official nor in private messages did General Milne make use of the word "prestige." His attitude was based, as it had always been, on his conception of the military situation and on that alone. He preferred an "amphibious" operation against a belligerent who could be reached by such means to a distant expedition into the heart of the Continent. It was traditional British policy, well expressed in the rough principle : "Never, if "you have an alternative, go where the Navy cannot hold "out a hand to you."[1] General Milne's messages were in

---

[1] These words were used by Lieut.-General Sir George Cory, who was in 1918 chief General Staff officer to General Milne, in discussing verbally the episode in question with the compiler.

A CHANGE OF PLAN

full accord with sentiment in Whitehall, but there the question of prestige did arise, to reinforce his argument. When the Admiralty was instructed to prepare the terms of an armistice with Turkey, the First Sea Lord, Vice-Admiral Sir Rosslyn Wemyss, remarked that the first condition should be that the Allied fleet should enter the Black Sea, and that it should be placed under a British admiral, as "a proper recognition of Great Britain's share in the "Dardanelles campaign and the final Turkish downfall."[1] With regard to the Army the British Prime Minister took a similar tone. In Mr. Lloyd George's view the right wing of the Allied Armies had become the post of honour; the British Army had held it for three years, suffering severely in the process; now the French command suggested putting another Army in its place.

The upshot was that Mr. Lloyd George refused to accept the French plan. But, after a conference in Paris on the 7th, he was unable to persuade the French Ministers to adopt General Milne's, at least in entirety. There was a compromise, and a fresh directive was telegraphed to Salonika by M. Clemenceau that same day. The goals of the Entente were now the complete liberation of Serbia, the renewal of contact with Rumania and then with anti-Bolshevist southern Russia, and the isolation of Turkey. In a separate telegram it was laid down that the wing of the Allied Armies destined to march on Constantinople should be placed directly under the command of a British general, who would himself be under the orders of G.H.Q. of the Allied Armies of the East; that this wing should be mainly British but should include French, Italian, Serbian, and Greek detachments; and that British troops should also be represented in the operations to the northward.[2]

General Berthelot, the former chief of the French Military Mission to Rumania, was again sent out and, on the 7th October, placed at the disposal of General Franchet d'Espérey to direct, under his orders, Allied action in that country. The intention was to form under the command of General Berthelot an "Army of the Danube" of four divisions, and it was now decided that a British division should be one of them. With the aid of the new Army Rumania would rearm and attack Austria-Hungary. But

1918.
Oct.

---

[1] "Naval Operations," Vol. V, p. 351.   [2] Larcher, pp. 287-9.

all this could obviously not be effected in a moment. Apart from the difficulties of communication, there were at least two German divisions and a number of Austro-Hungarian regiments in occupied Rumania, and German reinforcements would certainly be sent in considerable numbers from Russia. Rumania herself was helpless, and could not move unless a hand were held out to her. If she could be reached she might be a strong reinforcement to the Allies; for it was known that she was prepared to mobilize and re-enter the war directly she was in a position to do so.

The British Move against Turkey.

Map 10. Before the plan was changed British troops had begun the move which was to have taken them to the Danube between Lom Palanka and Vidin. The 26th Division, in the Strumica valley, was ordered to march on the 6th October on Radomir. It was to advance in five groups, preceded by the Derbyshire Yeomanry and the XVI Corps Cyclists, down the Strumica to the Struma, and thence up the latter river. Only the first day's march had been carried out when it became necessary to halt the columns because Bulgarian transport was blocking the roads in front. The march was then continued, and by the 10th, the day on which General Milne was officially informed of the change of plan, the leading brigade had reached Livunovo in the Struma valley. As under the new scheme General Milne was still to find one division for the Army of the Danube, he decided to let the 26th Division go forward to Radomir, but withdrew the mounted troops which had been marching in the same direction. On the 13th he received from General Franchet d'Espérey the latter's detailed plan for the first stage of the operations against Turkey, and then changed his intention regarding the employment of the 26th Division.

The task of the Army under General Milne's command (consisting eventually of three British, one French, and three Greek Divisions, with Italian and Serbian detachments) was " to secure the passage of the Dardanelles to " a high seas fleet, which would undertake direct and " vigorous action against Constantinople with the object of " bringing the Turkish Government to terms." The first phase of this operation would be the seizure of the crossing-places of the Maritsa. This was to be effected by surprise, by an advanced guard consisting of the French 122nd Division and such British troops as were judged necessary; and surprise would be the easier because there were two Bulgarian regiments at Demotika, 21 miles south of Adrianople. An arrangement made between Turkey and Bulgaria, when the latter entered the Great War in 1915, now, in fact, played into the hands of the Allies. The frontier of 1913, which had been fixed at the conclusion of the Second Balkan War, ran 25 miles west of Adrianople. Turkey had, however, withdrawn the frontier to the Tunja down to Adrianople and thence behind the Maritsa to Sufli, handing over to Bulgaria the railway on the west bank to that point, but not the town of Adrianople itself. She had thus provided a gateway into her territory which the Bulgarians handed over without question to the Allies. The Bulgarian Government also placed the railway between Seres and Dedeagach, on which there were 15 engines and 150 trucks, at the disposal of General Milne's force.

1918. Oct.

If the Bulgarians were so accommodating, it struck General Milne that he might as well make use of their Sofia–Adrianople line also, to transport the 26th Division to Jisr Mustapha Pasha, and from there seize Adrianople by a *coup de main*. He at once sent Generals Briggs and Forestier-Walker to Sofia to find out if this could be done. The French 122nd Division he proposed should establish a bridgehead at Demotika, pushing on some units at least by rail, though all the transport would have to march. The other British division to be employed in the first instance would be the 22nd, which the Navy was prepared to transport from Stavros to Dedeagach, just west of the mouth of the Maritsa. General Franchet d'Espérey agreed with this plan, stipulating only that the 26th Division should be replaced as soon as possible by another division in the Army of the Danube. General Milne therefore ordered the 27th Division to begin moving to the Struma at Livunovo on the 16th.

The transport of the 22nd Division had to march the whole way to Dedeagach, *via* Drama, Kavalla, and Xanthi, as the Navy was unable to carry any animals or vehicles. A trying march it was, the roads being in a very bad state and the weather wet and cold. The cavalry, now grouped into a brigade under the orders of Lieut.-Colonel Neilson, also marched, leaving Neohori on the 22nd and reaching Dedeagach on the 30th. In the case of the 26th Division the transport had only to march to Kostanets, half-way between Sofia and Plovdiv, where it was entrained. Despite administrative confusion and lack of coal on the railway, which caused considerable delay, the transport by rail proved very much more expeditious than that by sea, and even the first column of the 26th Division's transport reached Mustapha Pasha on the same day as the personnel of the 22nd Division was landed at Dedeagach. The 77th Brigade entrained at Radomir on the 20th and arrived at Mustapha Pasha on the 21st; the other two brigades arrived by the 23rd. It so chanced that the garrison consisted of the Bulgarian *39th Regiment* which had held the Machukovo salient opposite the 78th Brigade. When that brigade reached Mustapha Pasha Station, the officers of the *39th Regiment* were on the platform to meet it, the regimental band was waiting to play it up to its camp, and transport was in readiness to carry the baggage. The cynic may declare that the Bulgarians were good judges of how the wind was now blowing, but the British brigade appreciated their welcome.

The personnel of the 22nd Division, on the other hand, did not land at Dedeagach for another week. According to the original design of Rear-Admiral M. Culme-Seymour, commanding the British Ægean Squadron, the force was to have been embarked at Stavros in 17 destroyers on the 23rd and landed at Dedeagach next day. Actually there were two postponements due to bad weather. Then the fleet sailed in the early hours of the 26th, but, being unable to disembark the troops in the open roadstead of Dedeagach owing to high wind and a choppy sea, was forced to return to Stavros. The landing finally took place on the morning of the 28th.

General Briggs had accompanied the 77th Brigade to Mustapha Pasha. On the 22nd—travelling with the local Bulgarian commander in his private coach—he made a reconnaissance by rail of the Maritsa all the way down to Ferejik, near the mouth, a distance of some 120 miles. He learnt that there were no Turkish troops to speak of on the frontier, the garrison of Adrianople being only one battalion with a couple of guns. His scheme was to rail the 77th Brigade after dusk on the 24th to Adrianople Station—on the right or west bank of the Maritsa. The brigade would then cross by ferries and seize the road bridges, after which the 79th Brigade would pass through it and enlarge the bridgehead by gaining possession of the forts on the high ground east and north-west of the town. On the 24th, however, having learnt that the French 122nd Division was unlikely to be in position at Demotika for another four days and that the landing of the 22nd Division at Dedeagach had been delayed, he telegraphed to General Milne that he had changed his views. He now considered it inadvisable to seize Adrianople until the 122nd Division had arrived, as such an action would probably cause the Turks to blow up the railway bridge across the Maritsa at Kuleh Burgas. General Milne authorized him to wait.

1918. Oct.

The British Commander-in-Chief was by this time aware that Turkey was on the brink of capitulation. The blow which she had been dealt in Palestine and Syria, where her Armies had been destroyed and where the British cavalry was now approaching Aleppo,[1] might well have forced her to throw in her hand within a very short time, but it was actually the Bulgarian collapse which caused her to sue for terms. She knew, better even than General Ludendorff, that she could not hope, with four skeleton divisions for the defence of both the Dardenelles and Constantinople, to hold up the eastward advance of the Allies. She therefore resigned herself to her fate.

As soon as the decision had been reached that the operations against Constantinople were to be carried out by a British general and a British admiral, the Admiralty directed Vice-Admiral the Hon. Sir S. A. Gough-Calthorpe, the British Commander-in-Chief in the Mediterranean, to go to Mudros harbour, where he arrived on the 11th October. The admiral had not long to wait before Turkey made a sign. On the 20th Major-General C. V. F. Townshend, the defender of Kut, who had been a prisoner in Turkish hands for two and a half years, arrived at Mudros. The new Grand Vizier, Marshal Izzet Pasha, who had been appointed by the Sultan to the post a week earlier, had sent him as his emissary to inform Admiral Calthorpe that Turkey was prepared to conclude a separate peace.

The admiral having been empowered to grant an

---

[1] The troops of the 5th Cavalry Division entered Aleppo on the 26th October. See " Egypt and Palestine," Vol. II, pp. 613–6.

armistice and having received instructions from the British Admiralty, Turkish envoys were invited to Mudros, where they arrived on the 26th. The French naval commander was excluded from the discussion, on the double ground that the Turkish envoys were accredited to Great Britain alone and that there would be serious delays if all points on which agreement had been reached had to be referred to the French Government. It was considered, too, that the Salonika negotiations with Bulgaria, in which the British had taken no part, might be taken as a precedent for the conduct of this affair. The fact that Great Britain had borne the brunt of the war against Turkey was also, as has been stated, a factor in the case. The French point of view was, however, that at Salonika the negotiations had been conducted by the Commander-in-Chief who had always been on the spot and had been responsible for the operations. Here, it appeared to French critics, Admiral Calthorpe had been sent to Mudros solely because he was senior to their own naval commander, Vice-Admiral Amet, and in order to remove the conduct of negotiations from the latter's hands.

The discussion with the Turkish envoys was considerably more protracted than that between General Franchet d'Espérey and the Bulgarian, and it was not till late in the evening of the 30th that the Armistice with Turkey was signed. By its main clauses the Dardanelles and Bosporus were to be opened and their forts occupied by the troops of the Allies; the Turkish Army was to be demobilized, except for certain troops required for the surveillance of frontiers and the maintenance of internal order; all war vessels in Turkish waters were to be surrendered; the Allies were given the right to occupy any strategic points the possession of which appeared necessary to their security; all Turkish ports were to be thrown open to Allied shipping; the outlying Turkish garrisons in the Hejaz, Assir, the Yemen, Syria, and Mesopotamia were to surrender to the nearest Allied commander; German and Austrian subjects, naval, military, and civilian, were to be evacuated from Turkey within a month; and Turkey was to terminate all relations with the Central Powers. Hostilities were to cease from noon, local time, on Thursday the 31st October.

At that hour the three Allied divisions were on or just behind the line of the Maritsa. On the right was the 22nd Division at Dedeagach, with a battalion covering the

THE TURKISH ARMISTICE

road bridge at Ipsala. The cavalry brigade was just north of Dedeagach. In the centre was the French 122nd Division at Gümüljina, with advanced troops on the right bank of the Maritsa at Demotika. These troops were under the command of General Wilson, with headquarters at Dedeagach. On the left was the 26th Division, under the orders of General Briggs, at Mustapha Pasha. A proportion of the artillery and transport of the three divisions had rejoined them, but the greater part was still strung out in rear. The Greek I Corps was echeloned between Kavalla and Drama.

Two battalions of the 228th Brigade, the 2/5th Durham Light Infantry and the 1st Garrison Battalion Seaforth Highlanders, under the command of Br.-General W. C. Ross, had been sent by direct order of General Franchet d'Espérey to occupy the Bulgarian Black Sea ports of Varna and Burgas. They had travelled *via* Radomir and Sofia, but had been delayed by lack of railway transport. The Seaforths were now at Burgas, but Varna was not occupied until the 5th November. On the 13th the Seaforth was re-embarked and despatched to Constantsa, in the Dobruja.

The arrival of the belated Indian reinforcements had begun, the first five battalions, 2/6th Gurkhas, 24th Punjabis, 2/Rajputs, 31st Punjabis, and 2/39th Garwhals, having reached Salonika on the 25th October. They were formally posted to the 65th, 66th, 67th, 83rd, and 84th Brigades respectively, but owing to the move of the 22nd Division the three allotted to it did not join for the time being.

The Opening of the Dardanelles.

Immediately the convention with Turkey had been signed, Admiral Calthorpe requested General Milne to send troops to carry out its provisions, that is, to occupy the defences of the Dardanelles and the Bosporus. Though Turkey had agreed to all his demands, the admiral was not prepared to enter the narrows with the fleet until the shores were lined with British troops, and the forts, batteries, and torpedo-tube stations were in their hands. General Milne proposed to send the infantry of one division for the purpose. On informing General Franchet d'Espérey, the latter replied that he would send a French regiment at the same time. In telegraphing this information to the War Office on the 1st November, General Milne urged that a British general, responsible only to his own Government, should be immediately appointed to supervise the carrying out of the convention and to regularize the demands of the Allies.

The War Office had just sent out a British Mission to the headquarters of the Allied Armies of the East, under Lieut.-General G. T. M. Bridges. General Bridges, who had reached Salonika on the 29th October, was now the official channel of communication between Generals Milne and Franchet d'Espérey, neither of whom, in fact, desired an intermediary, and was also to keep the War Office informed of all operations and intelligence affecting the Balkan theatre of war as a whole. He interviewed General Franchet d'Espérey, who replied that he considered the occupation of Constantinople a secondary matter, except that he must have a base there and must for the present use the main Constantinople–Sofia railway to supply his troops on the Danube. He fully agreed with General Milne that the appointment of a military chief to command the Allied forces of occupation was desirable. Next day, on instructions from Paris, he ordered one regiment of the 122nd Division, less transport and animals, to concentrate at Dedeagach for shipment through the Dardanelles; the remainder of the division was to be transported by rail to Stambul.

Once more General Milne was compelled to alter his dispositions. In the first place, Dedeagach proved so unsatisfactory a port owing to its exposure to the weather that it was necessary to send a division to the Dardanelles direct from Salonika, and to withdraw the division now at Dedeagach by road and rail into Macedonia. In the second place, the 27th Division, on its way north to the Danube, was held up by heavy falls of snow about Dupnitsa. General Milne therefore decided that the 26th Division, which was on the railway at Mustapha Pasha, should take its place in the Army of the Danube, that the 28th Division should embark for the Dardanelles, and that the 22nd and 27th Divisions should both return to British camps in Macedonia. The commander of the XII Corps, Lieut.-General Sir H. F. M. Wilson, was appointed " G.O.C. Allied Forces

Gallipoli and Bosporus." Admiral Calthorpe was appointed High Commissioner at Constantinople, his mission being confined to questions affecting the execution of the Armistice terms and to the protection of British interests; General Allenby in Syria, General Wingate in the Hejaz, and General Marshall in Mesopotamia were to continue to deal with matters in their own spheres. General Wilson was to remain under the general orders of General Milne, but the latter delegated to him authority to act in close co-operation with the admiral, who was the official channel of British policy in Constantinople.

1918. Nov.

Major-General Croker embarked at Salonika on the 7th November with the 83rd and 84th Brigades (including one Indian battalion apiece) and their machine-gun companies, the 449th Field Company R.E., two field ambulances, and a detachment of the Indian Mule Corps, to take over the Dardanelles defences. The 85th Brigade followed on the 12th. No artillery or wheeled transport accompanied the 28th Division and only 250 animals per brigade.

The end of the great drama of the Straits, one of the most vital of the war, was a comparatively quiet one. The troops of the 83rd and 84th Brigades disembarked without incident on both shores during the 10th and 11th. On the 10th Major-General G. N. Cory, M.G.G.S. of the British Salonika Army, landed at Constantinople from a British destroyer, to make preliminary arrangements and to take the earliest possible steps on behalf of British prisoners of war. On the 12th the Allied fleets steamed through. The delay caused by difficulties in sweeping up the mines had robbed the occasion of some part of its significance; for the Armistice with Germany had been concluded meanwhile, on the 11th, and the chief of the confederates, the last to remain in arms, was out of the war by the time that the ships passed in to the Marmara.

It was, nevertheless, an impressive sight. In view of the possibility of a last sortie by the *Goeben* and that large portion of the Russian Black Sea Fleet which was now in German hands, the British Ægean Squadron had been joined by the two Dreadnought battleships, *Superb* and *Temeraire*. It was the first-named, in which Admiral Calthorpe had hoisted his flag as Commander-in-Chief, that led the line, preceded by two destroyers. When the flagship reached Helles, where the riddled *River Clyde* still lay, a ghastly but glorious memory, upon the shore, the second fleet, the French, was not yet in sight. Behind that again were the Italian warships, and in rear the Greek. In silence the huge armada sailed through, the troops on shore saluting the flagships as they passed.

It was triumphal, yet scarcely a triumph. The memory of the lost chances, of the vast sacrifices of 1915 brooded upon the scene, typified by the hulk of the *River Clyde* and the ruined fort at Sedd el Bahr. The Dardanelles had not been forced; they had survived the war, impregnable.

The original intention of the French Commander-in-Chief had been that British troops should occupy the Dardanelles and French the Bosporus. This was cancelled by a decision of the two Governments, and it was decided that the forces of both nations should participate in the occupation of both straits, the command in the Dardanelles being exercised by the British and that in the Bosporus by the French, but the commanders in each case being under the orders of General Wilson. When, therefore, the 85th Brigade arrived on the 14th, it dropped one battalion at Constantinople to provide guards in the city and took over the defences on both shores of the Bosporus. The French troops of the 122nd Division then arrived to assume their share of the work, and by the 26th the new organization had been completed. The British 83rd Brigade now held the Asiatic forts of the Dardanelles and the French 45th Regiment the European, while the British 84th Brigade was in reserve on the Gallipoli Peninsula, the whole force commanded by Major-General Croker, with headquarters at Chanak. On the Bosporus one battalion of the British 85th Brigade held the European forts and one battalion of the French 84th Regiment the Asiatic, under the command of the French regimental commander, Colonel de Langlade. The remaining troops of the two formations were distributed on both shores, with battalions in Péra, Stambul, and Haidar Pasha. The French 148th Regiment was about San Stefano, west of Stambul, in reserve.

General Wilson, who had sailed with the fleet, landed on the 13th, and was received by a guard of honour of 300 British prisoners of war, wearing rough civilian clothes of Turkish homespun provided by the Ambassador of the Netherlands to replace the rags in which they had previously been clad. More of them were coming through from Turkey in Asia. These unfortunates represented the survival of the fittest, great numbers having died in captivity. {1918. Nov.}

It was a curious experience for British commanders and troops. Turkish officers in patent-leather riding boots bowed from the waist, exquisitely polite and maddeningly obstructive in guttural French. Lists of armaments were missing, but it was always some one other than the speaker that was responsible for them. Troops who should have been removed had stayed where they were, but they were always under the command of some other officer. Supplies and water transport promised had not arrived, but always through accidents beyond the courteous representative's control. Constantinople itself might have been a Greek city liberated from Turkish rule, so completely did the Turkish element efface itself and so great was the enthusiasm of the other elements. And in the city were over 10,000 German troops who had been unable to get away, including General Liman von Sanders, the former Commander-in-Chief in Palestine and Syria, who had several interviews with Major-General Cory. The Germans and Austrians were moved as soon as possible to the Asiatic shore of the Bosporus, where they were to remain until it was possible to repatriate them.

The Advance to the Danube.

The advance to the Danube was in the main a Serbian enterprise, and a marvellous achievement on the part of the Serbian troops. On the 1st October the two Serbian Armies had already been continuously engaged for sixteen days, not one of which but had been marked by fighting for some of their six divisions. The Yugoslav Division of the Second Army, in particular, had been always in the van, always moving, never out of action. Now these Armies went forward to the Danube as though they had been fresh troops. {Oct. Maps 8, 10.}

They advanced at a rate often exceeding ten miles a day. Almost by their own unaided efforts they drove before them a force which, numbered by formations, was ultimately of exactly their own strength, that is, six infantry divisions and one cavalry division.[1] They advanced over roads damaged by the enemy's retreat and on which the main bridges had been cut; they lived for the most part precariously upon a country already swept by requisitions, because their convoys could rarely catch them up; they were generally in rags and often bare-footed, having marched the soles out of their boots; and, hardy as they were, they were crippled by the universal influenza. Their pursuit was a return to old methods of warfare, recalling the Napoleonic days when considerable Armies had to march and fight so long as they had bread or biscuit and bullets. The elaborate modern organization of lines of communication and the system of regular supply from main depot to regulating station, from regulating station to railheads, from railheads to rendezvous, from rendezvous to refilling points, had disappeared. Had the Serbians waited for them to be reconstituted, there would have been no advance.

They had, of course, certain advantages in addition to their own iron strength. The fact that they were advancing through their own country and liberating it not only filled them with zeal for their task but assured them of the best that that country could provide. As a battalion entered a town or village, the inhabitants would bring out from their houses fowls, eggs, vegetables, even pigs, if they had escaped the enemy's requisitioning officers. The pursuing Serbians also made use of captured Bulgarian supplies and transport, and in many cases civilians marched with them, carrying food and even ammunition. There have come from Serbian officers epic pictures of the exploits of women—vignettes such as that of a mountain battery on some rocky trail followed by a file of Amazons each carrying a shell under either arm.

The Serbian ranks, thinned by wounds and sickness, were filled up by Bulgarian deserters of Serb nationality, by Serbian prisoners of war, by soldiers who had fallen out on the great retreat of three years before, hidden rifle and uniform, and remained quietly on their farms ever since. The Morava Division, which passed through the heart of its

---

[1] German *Alpine Corps*, *217th* and *219th* Divisions; Austro-Hungarian *9th*, *30th*, and *59th Divisions*, and *4th Cavalry Division*. This does not include the German troops already at the front and extricated from the Bulgarian Armies, which were formed into a composite division under the orders of General Dieterich, with the staff of the *6th Reserve Division*.

THE ADVANCE TO THE DANUBE 273

own recruiting area, the valley of the river from which it took its title, is said to have had when it reached the Danube a rifle strength twice or thrice as high as when it set out. The old *comitaji* leaders turned out with their bands and aided the regular forces without joining their ranks, harrying the enemy and shooting his transport animals in defiles. The enemy, too, was discouraged and weary. The first formation to attempt to bar the way, the Austrian *9th Division*, had come straight from Italy, where it had been severely handled, and contained a large proportion of Czech troops, always a fatal element of weakness in the Armies of the Dual Monarchy.

1918. Oct.

The first object of General Franchet d'Espérey being to gain possession of the rail and road junction of Niš, in order to cover the future development of the operations, the leading rôle now fell to the Serbian First Army, the Second having, as will be recalled, swung eastward towards the Bulgarian frontier. As the Serbian Cavalry Division was attached to the Second Army, the brigade of General Jouinot-Gambetta was put at the disposal of Voivode Bojović, commanding the First. The German counter-plan was that the Austrian *9th Division*, joined by the German troops of the *LXI Corps*, should delay the advance as long as possible on the line Priština–Vranje and cover the detrainment and deployment in its rear of the other reinforcing divisions. The German remnants of the *LXII Corps*, if they could not break out through Skoplje, were to make their way over the mountains through Priština to Niš. The roads and railways to the north were all clear—General von Scholtz had seen to that. He had had all Bulgarian columns and stragglers reaching Kumanovo turned east in the direction of Kyustendil so that they should not choke the Southern Morava corridor and prevent the escape of his Germans.

The energy with which the First Army of Voivode Bojović threw itself upon the Austrian *9th Division*, and the indifferent resistance of the latter, upset the German plan and brought the Serbians in front of Niš before the detrainment and deployment had been completed. The Serbians made contact with the enemy on the 3rd October, and after a short fight drove him back headlong. The Austrian division and the German troops of the *LXI Corps* poured back through the Mestarica Pass. The Serbians, now joined by their Cavalry Division, pursued in haste; a rear guard which attempted to hold them up at Leskovac was hustled out of it on the 7th, the French and Serbian cavalry swinging in on both flanks. Back went the luckless Austrians, and having lost 3,000 prisoners, having retreated between 60 and 70 miles in six days, passed through the line of the German *219th Division*, astride the Southern Morava south of Niš. On the right of the *219th Division*, the *Alpine Corps*, hastily detraining, was taking up a position on the high ground south of Prokuplje and west of the river. The *217th Division* which, as we recall, had been at Sofia, was arriving by rail at Bela Palanka and Pirot to come into line on the left. The Austrian *30th Division* was expected to detrain at Kruševac and Knjaževac on the 12th, but their *59th* and *4th Cavalry Divisions* were still far in rear.

The Battle of Niš began on the 10th, and the resistance of the Germans was only a degree more effective than that of the Austrians. By midday the Serbians were in the town. General von Steuben had ordered a retirement to Kruševac and Knjaževac, which had begun the previous night. His *Eleventh Army* was no longer under German command. General von Scholtz had been sent to Rumania to take over the defence of the Danube between the Iron Gates and Silistra, and the Austrian commander in the offensive of 1915 against Serbia, perhaps the most distinguished of Austrian soldiers, Field-Marshal von Kövess, had on the 10th assumed supreme command in the Balkans. Under his orders were General von Steuben, commanding the *Eleventh Army*; General Freiherr von Pflanzer-Baltin, commanding the Austro-Hungarian forces in Albania; the Military Governor of Serbia and Montenegro; and the commander of the garrison of Bosnia and Hercegovina. Field-Marshal von Kövess at once decided to withdraw behind the Danube and the Sava.

By the 15th October the Serbian First Army was again in contact with the enemy's main body, now reinforced by the Austrian *30th Division*. The new Austro-German line lay at first with left on Knjaževac, on the Timok, and with right behind the Western Morava. East of Kruševac, however, the enemy at the first attack swung back his right as a first step in his retreat to the Danube on either side of Belgrade. For the next four days the Serbian First Army,

while keeping up a steady pressure, launched no general 1918.
assault. Even it was exhausted. It was, moreover, await- Oct.
ing the powerful support on either flank which had been
promised.

General Tranié, whom we left in Skoplje, had been
ordered by the Allied Commander-in-Chief to cover the
deployment of the Serbian Second Army on the left of the
First. General Franchet d'Espérey was thus, it will be
seen, bringing the Second Army from the right wing on the
Bulgarian frontier over to the left, at the same moment as
he swung a French contingent of the Armée Française
d'Orient over to the right to be moved up by rail to the
Danube about Lom Palanka. It was a *chassé-croisé* which
could only complicate the already sufficient difficulties of
supply. On paper, his obvious course would have been to
send the Serbian Second Army up to the Danube at Lom
Palanka and Vidin, and to move the French up on the left
of the First Army. His decision was, nevertheless, sound.
In the first place the French troops, as has been explained,
needed the backing of the railway more than the Serbians;
in the second, it was impossible, for reasons of discipline if
not of humanity, to send the Serbians through Bulgaria
owing to the animosity of the two nations.

General Tranié, with his brigade of the French 11th
Colonial Division and two regiments of the Greek 3rd
Division, marched out from Skoplje on Kačanik. Meanwhile the German troops caught on the Tetovo road had
extricated themselves from the rest of the *LXII Corps*,
doomed to surrender, and burning their heavy baggage,
had made their way over the mountain track from Tetovo
to Kačanik. The Tranié Detachment was quickly on their
heels and hurried them northward, capturing almost all the
remainder of their transport and artillery. At Kačanik
itself 30 guns were taken on the 4th October; at Lipljan,
40 miles N.N.W. of Skoplje, another 22 guns, on the 7th.
It appeared almost incredible that the Germans should
have dragged them even so far, on such a road. That was,
so far as we are concerned, the end of General Fleck's force,
the remnants of which then managed to rejoin the *Eleventh
Army*, except the rear guard, which was cut off from the
main body. These troops turned westward into Montenegro and after an extraordinary anabasis reached the
Adriatic at Teodo Bay on the 23rd, whence they were

shipped to Fiume. On the 20th the relief of the Tranié Detachment, which had halted at Priština, was begun by the Serbian Second Army.

In Albania the Austrians were in full retreat, followed by the Italian XVI Corps, which had taken no part in the September offensive, and which now occupied Elbasan without opposition.

The right flank was also being made safe. A small French force of all arms reached the Danube at Vidin and Lom Palanka on the 19th, the Army Group of Field-Marshal von Mackensen behind the river making no attempt to eject it. Two French divisions, the 76th and 17th Colonial, under the orders of General Patey, next moved to the Bulgarian frontier at Egri Palanka, crossing the Serbian Second Army at Skoplje. Their supply was made easier by the fact that, after immense exertions, the railway had been repaired up to Veles, where the first train arrived on the 15th. The infantry moved by rail through Bulgaria, and that of the 17th Colonial Division was on the Serbian right or right rear at Pirot, with advanced guard at Knjaževac, by the 22nd.

These troops arrived in the midst of the Battle of Paraćin, the renewed attack of the First Serbian Army, which began on the 20th. Though the fighting was at times hot and marked by several German counter-attacks, there is no need to describe it in detail. It was, in fact, on the enemy's part, a delaying action only ; for his sole object was to put the Danube between himself and the pursuit as soon as possible. Paraćin was captured on the 23rd, and from then onwards the Serbian First Army pushed the enemy rear guards steadily back towards the Danube. On its right the Patey Group of Divisions interrupted the navigation on the Danube and had several brisk artillery engagements with the Austrian monitors. On its left, but echeloned far in rear, the Serbian Second Army advanced north of Mitrovica on Kraljevo and Čačak, in the valley of the Western Morava.

The German organization held out to the last, and the crossing of the Danube and Sava was effected quietly and in good order, by military bridges and steamers, between Smederovo and Šabac. The passage began on the 25th and was completed, under cover of fire from monitors of the Austro-Hungarian Danube Fleet, by the 1st November. Almost before the last boats had reached the Hungarian shore opposite Belgrade, Voivode Bojović made a triumphal entry into the capital. On the same day patrols of the Second Army reached the Drina. Serbia was completely cleared of the enemy. 1918. Nov.

The Danube had been the only goal announced to the Armies. The Commander-in-Chief had, however, informed his senior subordinates personally that he had no intention of halting on the river an hour longer than he could help. His next objective was to be Buda-Pesth.[1] Eventually, as he informed General Bridges, he intended to advance on Dresden.

Here, once again, his ideas were in conflict with those of the Supreme War Council. At a meeting of Marshals Foch and Haig, Generals Pershing, Bliss, di Robilant, and Wilson, in Paris on the 2nd November, a paper was drawn up suggesting the deployment of a great Italian force of from 30 to 40 divisions, including the five British and French Divisions then in Italy, between the Inn and the Danube, to move against Bavaria. Field-Marshal Haig, in particular, urged that such an advance directed against southern Germany, would be more effective than an advance across the Danube by the Armies under General Franchet d'Espérey, and that the rôle of the latter should be, at least for the time being, merely to cover the Italian concentration. Next day a formal proposal to this effect was drawn up by Marshal Foch, General Sir Henry Wilson, and the American and Italian Military Representatives on the Supreme War Council, Generals Bliss and di Robilant. The Italian Armies were to be concentrated in two groups, the first, of six Italian divisions, on the Upper Inn about Innsbruck, the second, of 20 to 30 divisions including the British and French, in the neighbourhood of Salzburg and Linz. These troops would have to be transported by the Brenner and Villach, and the railways were, of course, cut, just as they were in Macedonia. The most optimistic estimate by the British Section for the completion of the concentration was nine weeks from the date on which notice was given that it was required. The plan was approved by the Supreme War Council next day, and Marshal Foch was entrusted with the supreme strategical direction of operations against Germany on all fronts. General Franchet d'Espérey was to co-operate;

---

[1] Larcher, p. 250.

but all that was said of the Allied Armies of the East in the plan was that their employment with a view to reinforcing the main concentration at a later date would be studied.

There is an American phrase, symbolizing the refusal of the people of Missouri to take anything for granted, "You have to show us!" It appeared that the Allied Armies of the East had to show the Supreme War Council still more before it believed in them. Even now, after all that had been accomplished, those responsible for Allied policy considered that the Italians could effect more, beyond the barrier of the Alps, than could the forces from Macedonia, who had reached the Central European plains.

General Franchet d'Espérey thought otherwise, and once again went on with the preparation of his plans without awaiting authorization to carry them into effect. True, he was still to a great extent, in his own words, " prisoner of " his communications." He had only nine divisions in northern Serbia,[1] and did not contemplate employing more for the time being. But he knew that Austria-Hungary was reeling, that the spirit of the German troops was cracking, and that no great resistance need be expected. Besides, he was preparing a grandiose scheme in Rumania. The Army of the Danube, three or four divisions under General d'Anselme, whom he had placed at the disposal of General Berthelot, was to assemble between Ruschuk and Nikopol on the Danube, here the boundary between Bulgaria and Rumania. It would cross the river and drive back the German garrison of Rumania ; Rumania would rise ; her reconstituted Armies would be turned against the Central Powers ; some 20 divisions in all would advance into Bohemia, where already preparations were being made to create Czecho-Slovak armed forces. Already he had placed at Ruschuk an infantry regiment with artillery, drawn from the 76th Division of the Patey Group, to cover the assembly of the Army of the Danube, which he did not expect to complete until the latter part of November. Before any troops other than the covering force had reached the Danube in Bulgaria, before the Serbians had crossed it higher up on their front, the Austrian Empire passed out of the war in dismemberment and ruin.

---

[1] The Greek 3rd Division, the third division of the Patey Group, had now reached Niš.

THE AUSTRIAN, GERMAN, AND HUNGARIAN ARMISTICES.

If the Bulgarian Army had been weakened by war-weariness, that of Austria-Hungary was far more advanced in decay, the disruption of the races which formed the Empire being in its case as potent a cause as fatigue, hunger, disillusionment, and losses in battle. On the 24th October the knock-out blow was delivered in Italy. The Italians and their Allies met with some opposition to their first attacks, but after the foremost defences had been overrun the Austrian front collapsed, so that there was no prolonged operation as in Macedonia. It was a headlong rout, with the Italians pursuing by forced marches. The Armistice convention was signed at the Villa Giusti, the headquarters of General Diaz, on the 3rd November, ten days after the launch of the attack; it might have been signed within a week of it and before that with Turkey, had not delay been caused by discussion at Versailles, where the conditions to be accorded to Germany and Austria-Hungary were being debated simultaneously. Hostilities both in Italy and Macedonia, so far as the Austrians were concerned, came to an end at 3 p.m. on the 4th.

1918.
Nov.
Map 10.

We say "the Austrians" advisedly; for Austria could now speak only for herself, though the Italians in their own interests disregarded the political upheaval which took place while the last battle was in progress. The Czecho-Slovaks of Bohemia had already declared their independence. In the midst of the fighting two other States broke away. On the 29th October the Yugoslav National Council at Agram declared the independence of the Yugoslavs, and took over the Austro-Hungarian Navy at Pola, which was manned to a great extent by their nationals. They claimed that the fleet was now the possession of the State which would come into being, with Serbia at its head, and containing the Yugoslav provinces of the old Austro-Hungarian Empire, that it was, in fact, an Allied fleet, and would be used in the service of the Allies. Having in their hands a draft of armistice conditions in which the naval forces of Austria-Hungary were treated as a hostile fleet, the Italians refused to recognize the Yugoslav naval authorities at Pola. They signed their Armistice convention and rigidly enforced its terms. This hardly concerned General Franchet d'Espérey, except that he had both Serbian and Italian forces under his command, and that the Serbians were already very suspicious of the Italians and their designs on the eastern coast of the Adriatic. The emergence from the ruins of another independent State, Hungary, which refused to recognize the Armistice of the Villa Giusti, affected him, on the contrary, very closely. A revolution broke out in Buda-Pesth on the 31st October, and on the following day an independent Government was formed, with Count Karolyi as prime minister.

Karolyi issued orders that on the 4th November the Hungarian troops were to hand in their arms and return to their homes. On the 5th, however, he changed his mind, issued a proclamation that Hungary was threatened by its Rumanian, Czech, and Slav neighbours, and ordered the troops to rejoin their regiments. In reality, Karolyi's power was a shadow; soldiers' councils on the Russian model were being constituted; and the country was on the eve of anarchy.

Germany was still a belligerent, and General Franchet d'Espérey was determined to strike at her through Hungary, forcing the Hungarian authorities to transport his troops by their railways and to hand over all the Danube shipping within their reach for the same purpose. He went up to Belgrade with the Crown Prince of Serbia, made his entry into the capital at his side on the 7th, and then met the Hungarian delegation, with Karolyi at its head. The negotiations were prolonged by the obduracy of the Hungarians, and the Commander-in-Chief threatened to continue hostilities and to march on Buda-Pesth. Before terms were concluded Rumania was ready to re-enter the war and did so officially on the 10th, the day on which Allied troops first crossed the Danube and set foot upon her soil. The Army of the Danube had by this time two regiments at Ruschuk, two battalions at Sistova, and two at Nikopol, all with artillery. In the early morning two French battalions crossed the Danube at Ruschuk by surprise and established a bridgehead; on the 11th crossings were also effected at Sistova and Nikopol. There was little or no resistance. The Serbian First Army also crossed the river on its front without opposition. But no further move on the part of the Allied Armies was needed; for, on that same day, the Armistice with Germany was concluded and the active hostilities of the Great War came to an end.

Hungary, however, had refused to resign herself to her lot while Germany continued the struggle, and, nominally at all events, she was actually the last belligerent on the side of the Central Powers to capitulate, on the 13th. General Franchet d'Espérey had by that time left Belgrade, and the convention was signed on his behalf by General Henrys and the Voivode Mišić.

1918. Nov.

The main conditions were the evacuation by Hungarian troops and the occupation by the Allies of a great area comprising roughly all the territory south of the Maros to its junction with the Tisza and south of the Drava to the frontier of Slavonia-Croatia; the demobilization of the Hungarian Armies with the exception of six infantry and two cavalry divisions; the right of the Allies to occupy such strategic positions as they considered necessary and to use the railways for their military requirements; the surrender to the Allies of six Danubian monitors and a number of passenger steamers, tugs, etc.; the surrender to the Allies of 25,000 horses; the surrender of war material at points to be fixed by the Allied Commander-in-Chief; the immediate liberation of Allied prisoners of war and interned civilians; the evacuation by rail of all German troops within fifteen days of the signature of the Austrian Armistice convention by General Diaz, that is, by the 19th; assistance by Hungary in the victualling of the Allied troops of occupation—requisitions to be permitted so long as they were not arbitrary, and to be paid for at current rates; obligation on the part of Hungary to discontinue relations with Germany and to forbid all transport of troops and munitions destined for the German forces in Rumania, without the special permission of the Allied Commander-in-Chief; undertaking by the Allies not to interfere in the internal administration of Hungary.

The Armies of Field-Marshal von Mackensen in Rumania, which had been reinforced by a number of divisions from Russia of doubtful quality and already tainted with Bolshevism, were by the 11th November a large force on paper, of about 10 divisions. They were already attempting to withdraw—their right through Arad and Buda-Pesth, their main body through Transylvania—but had made little progress; and, owing to the confusion on the Hungarian railways and the lack of coal, it was quite impossible to evacuate them by the 19th. On the other hand, it was undesirable that they should be interned and become a charge upon the resources of Rumania for an indefinite period. The time-limit was therefore extended, and the Germans were gradually sent home.

The 79th Brigade of the British 26th Division, destined as we recall to form part of the Army of the Danube, reached Ruschuk between the 8th and 12th November. On the 23rd the 12/Hampshire was sent by ship down the Danube to Cernavoda, to keep an eye on the Dobruja, where it seemed likely that Rumanians and Bulgarians would come to blows. On the 26th, by which date the rest of the division was closing up to the Danube, it was decided that a composite brigade, of one battalion from each infantry brigade, under the command of Br.-General Poole, should represent the British Army at Bucharest on the occasion of the re-entry of the King of Rumania into his capital. Lack of barges to cross the Danube made this impossible, so that eventually only one battalion of the 79th Brigade, the 10/Devonshire, was able to go. It was accompanied by the divisional commander, Major-General Gay, and the brigade commander, Br.-General Poole, with representatives of their staffs. Br.-General Ross, commanding the 228th Brigade, also attended the ceremony as a visitor.

1918. Dec. The detachment crossed the river on the 27th and marched to Bucharest, arriving two days later. The entry of the King took place on the 1st December.

The scene, with which the record of the trials and endurances of the Salonika Army may be concluded, was joyous and splendid, the whole population of Bucharest and its neighbourhood turning out to welcome back from their temporary capital of Jassy the King and Queen who had confronted an evil fate with so much dignity, courage, and loyalty. The 10/Devonshire took part in the lining of the route. After the King and Queen had passed a procession was formed, and the Allied troops marched past them, the British being welcomed by the huge crowd with particular warmth. A *Te Deum* was afterwards celebrated in the cathedral. That night there was a banquet at the Palace, attended by the three British generals and Major-General Gay's senior staff officers. Next day the British-born Queen of Rumania received all the British officers at the Palace, while the citizens entertained the troops. Set free after two years from the heavy yoke of the invader, Bucharest was almost crazed with delight.

But the Devonshire had to return to a cold and weary watch upon the Danube, with the rest of the division, which shortly afterwards occupied also the ports of the Dobruja. The Allied Armies of the East were to be scattered far and wide, from Batum to the Adriatic, and the British troops were to be scattered as widely as any. They were to be seen in the streets of almost all the cities of the Near East, quiet and well-behaved, untouched by the spirit of Bolshevism which affected some of their former comrades in Macedonia, mildly interested, but convinced of the superior interest of Bootle or Brixton. They were to be involved in the struggle of Red and White in Russia and in the new war between Greek and Turk which burst out from the still smouldering ashes of the old. Everywhere in the Near East the confusion of the Great War was to be succeeded by fresh confusion, sometimes worse than the former, because accompanied by starvation. But the main story ends with the great victory in Macedonia and with its first-fruits : the reconquest of Serbia, the opening of the Dardanelles, and the deliverance of Rumania.[1]

It was three years since the landing of the Allies at Salonika, nearly three years since Germany first made merry over the " Allied internment camp." Now it had all ended in victory. Greater events dwarfed that victory, as throughout those three years they had dwarfed and thrust into the background the whole campaign. Neither of them aroused much interest among the general public of the conquerors or of the vanquished. There were no bays for the Allied Armies of the East. It sounds incredible, but there are many witnesses to prove it, that when victory in the Great War had its apotheosis in Paris on the 14th July 1919, when in their triumphal march the troops passed the august winged figures, each symbolic of a victorious battle, in the Champs Elysées, the only Macedonian names upon the scrolls which met their eyes were " Pogradec " and " Skra di Legen." No Monastir, no Dobropolje, upon those tablets of glory ! Perhaps the first real tribute came from

---

[1] A " Summary of Events concerning the British Army of the Black Sea, December 1918 to May 1919 " will be found in Appendix 1. Both there and in the preface it is explained why the record of events is carried no further.

an enemy, the supreme commander of the late hostile coalition. It came from Field-Marshal von Hindenburg and appeared in the war memoirs of his right-hand man, General Ludendorff. It had the force of being contemporary with the event itself, being part of the statement made by the Field-Marshal to the Imperial Chancellor, on the 3rd October. The situation was too grave for anything but the truth, though it is just possible that, sub-consciously, the Field-Marshal was seeking to throw a larger share than was due of blame for the German defeat in the west upon the Bulgarian surrender in Macedonia.

"As a result of the collapse of the Macedonian front, and
"of the weakening of our reserves in the west, which this
"has necessitated, and in view of the impossibility of
"making good the very heavy losses of the last few days,
"there appears to be now no possibility, so far as human
"judgment goes, of winning peace from our enemies by
"force of arms. . . . In these circumstances the only right
"course is to bring the war to a close."

CHAPTER XIII.

CONCLUSION.

Some Open Questions.

A SHORT discussion of the conduct of the war in Macedonia may be prefaced by a few lines which the same writer set at the head of a similar discussion of the Palestine Campaign. He repeats them simply because he is unable to better their expression of his idea.

"The lessons to be learnt from the campaigns in Sinai, "Palestine, and Syria are many and valuable, but like "those of all historical events they are broad and general "in character. History does not repeat itself exactly on "the field of battle any more than in the council-chamber, "and it is seldom possible to draw from it precise deductions "such as the mathematician, the chemist, and even to some "extent the philosopher, present to us."

Dogmatism in deduction, above all in considering "the "might have been," is a danger always besetting the military historian and the military student, because in the case of military history present and future problems are constantly—and very properly—being considered in the light of the past. The dogmatist will build a great edifice on foundations which he is not able to test. It is wiser to choose only those that we know to be reasonably sound, and then not to build too high. That principle will not, however, prevent us from considering others of which we cannot be assured and from assessing their possible value. In times of emergency they too may serve their turn. In any case, such dogmatism is not more dangerous than the tendency of an opposite school of thought to ignore all lessons because, misled by the dissimilarity of the circumstances of successive wars, it fails to recognize that similar problems recur in slightly different forms. Another sort of criticism also, which does not seek to build, but only to destroy what is ill-constructed, is of value because it may help to prevent the repetition of past mistakes.

As we look back upon the part played by the Allies in Macedonia throughout the war there arise two problems:

the first and major one concerning what might have been accomplished; the second concerning what was actually accomplished. The former is a truly vast subject, which it is not possible or perhaps worth while—if we observe the caution suggested above—to treat in detail. It may be divided into four periods: that prior to the Gallipoli campaign; that at the end of 1915, when the Allies did actually intervene and landed at Salonika; that in the late summer of 1916, when Rumania entered the war; and that in the spring of 1917, when the Allied Armies in Macedonia took the offensive.

In the opening stage, that of the summer of 1914, there was in the Balkans no question of a war of coalitions. Germany, Austria-Hungary, France, and Russia, expecting a short war, were fighting for a decision in the most accessible theatres. Great Britain had ready only her small professional Army—at first, indeed, only part of it—and it had been pledged to the support of France and Belgium. Italy, Turkey, Rumania, Greece, and Bulgaria were none of them belligerents. The first round in the Balkans was between Austria and Serbia alone. But after a measure of stabilization had taken place, after the Austrian Armies opposing Russia had retreated to the San in September, after those which had attacked Serbia had been forced back over the Drina in August, after the Battle of the Aisne had been fought in France, some observers began to realize that the war might not after all be a short one. A few of them turned their eyes to the Balkans and to that Vardar-Morava corridor which led into Central Europe.

One of these was Colonel de Lardemelle, who was to appear for a moment as a divisional commander in Macedonia and to be broken by General Sarrail.[1] He was then Chief of the Staff of the Fifth Army, commanded by the man who was to achieve final victory in Macedonia, General Franchet d'Espérey. The general, who had himself visited the Balkans more than once and made some study of their military conditions, directed his staff officer to draw up a project, suggested some modifications, signed it, and had it placed in the hands of the French Government in November 1914. It proposed the concentration on the Danube, by way of Salonika and any other lines of communication

---

[1] See Vol. I, p. 79, *fn.*

AN EARLY FRENCH PROJECT 287

available, of a French Army of some 10 divisions, to join the Serbian and Rumanian Armies, followed if possible by the Bulgarian and Greek. The Serbians would take the offensive in Bosnia; the French would either cross the Danube and advance on Buda-Pesth or cross the Sava and advance on Vienna. The project depended upon the naval co-operation of Great Britain and the military assistance of Russia. Though only a sketch, it took account of the deficiencies of the communications in Macedonia.[1]

The crux of the problem was Bulgaria, lying all along the flank of the Vardar-Morava corridor, almost touching it at Strumica Station and again at Vranje. Unless her help or her neutrality—and what oath would have guaranteed her neutrality?—were assured, the venture would have been too risky. It may be that the landing of the French troops would have been a decisive argument with her, but this is not certain; and once the troops were landed, the promoters of the enterprise would have been fully committed to it. We have seen that the political arguments and promises of the Entente failed to win over Bulgaria, and that neither Rumania nor Greece would move for fear of her. Almost equally important was the opposition of the French Commander-in-Chief, General Joffre, who realized that the scheme would place him in a position of considerable inferiority to the Germans on the Western Front, and that, on the other hand, they could when they chose reach the Danube more quickly than the French. So, though M. Briand induced the French Cabinet to view the plan with favour, it never went beyond the stage of discussion. The same is true of Mr. Lloyd George's similar project in January 1915, though he had new arguments, namely, that by then the Austrians had suffered a really disastrous defeat at the hands of the Serbians,[2] and that there was a continuous line of trenches from end to end of the Western Front.

One can say only of these plans that *if* the agreement of General Joffre and the British War Office could have been won for them, *if* the Bulgarian question could have been satisfactorily settled, there was promise in them. Probably they could never have been put into force in the absence of a supreme direction of the conduct of the war. If they had

---

[1] Larcher, pp. 41-4.   [2] See Vol. I, pp. 25-9.

been, they would not have produced a strategical surprise. Germany could concentrate troops on the Danube as readily as in France ; if France sought a new front, she could only expect to find Germany in her path once more.

Then came the turn of the Gallipoli venture, in its conception purely a British scheme, which had, or might have had the advantage of both strategical and tactical surprise, which struck, with the aid of sea power, at a point where no serious German interference was to be expected for a long time to come, and which offered quicker returns. There is little reason now to doubt that the attempt to force the Dardanelles might have succeeded had it been otherwise handled. It was, however, a substitute for a campaign on the Danube, and until the late summer, when the resources of the Entente had somewhat increased and the Gallipoli campaign was heading for failure, an attempt to conduct both diversions simultaneously was not seriously contemplated.

While the Gallipoli campaign was in progress the great Austro-German offensive of the summer of 1915, beginning with the Break-through of Gorlice in May, dealt Russia the hardest blow she received in the course of the war, chilled the heart of Rumania, and perhaps finally tipped the balance, where Bulgaria was concerned, on the side of the Central Powers. The enemy was now working upon a co-ordinated programme. Theoretically, there was no unified command on his side—that was not to come until the 6th September 1916—any more than on the side of the Entente. Practically, the strong character and technical knowledge of Falkenhayn and the dependence of Austria-Hungary upon German aid, owing to Germany's greater resources and superior organization, had given the German Chief of the General Staff so great an ascendancy over the more brilliant but erratic Austrian Conrad that the former was enabled in major matters to impose his will upon the latter. To a very large extent, then, the Central Powers had a supreme direction of the war in 1915, while the Entente had none. The handling of the Gorlice offensive and the later Austro-German-Bulgarian offensive against Serbia, on the one hand, that of the Gallipoli campaign and the landing of troops of the Entente at Salonika to aid Serbia, on the other, were to be the pointings of the moral.

The tragic record of delays and divided counsels in the

autumn of 1915 has been given very fully in the previous volume,[1] and is to be found in still more detail and from a rather different point of view in "Military Operations: "Gallipoli," Volume II. It may appear to the student, in an armchair and with all the facts at his disposal, to be one of singular ineptitude, but at the time the complications of the problem were bewildering. The British desired to try one more throw at Gallipoli or to land in the Gulf of Iskanderun; the French desired to land at Salonika, but their higher command desired to carry out the Champagne–Loos offensive; the Greek Prime Minister invited the Allies to land on Greek soil, while the Greek King forbade them to do so; individual members of the French and British Governments were sharply divided in their views, and it was the Macedonian question which, rather than any other cause, brought about the fall of the French Ministry on the 29th October 1915; General Joffre had agreed to a landing at Salonika, but the British General Staff was strongly opposed to it. When the landing did take place it was too late fully to accomplish its purpose of saving the Serbian Armies, though, as has been shown, it did help to prevent their being encircled and completely destroyed.[2] Nothing can now be added to the conclusion reached in the previous volume that " early co-ordinated and determined action by " the Allies might, at the least, have frightened Bulgaria out " of her engagements (to the Central Powers), brought " Greece into the field, and further limited the extent of the " Serbian disaster," except that such action could have been achieved only by a single controlling authority.

The Entente had accomplished something, but not much, and was now tied down to Macedonia. Its forces escaped a certain risk—how great, one cannot estimate—of being driven into the sea when Falkenhayn halted the victorious Bulgarians on the Greek frontier. After many hesitations it was decided to remain in Macedonia, at first in fortifications covering the port of Salonika, then on the frontier, in touch at certain points with the enemy. This had at least the negative advantages of denying the possible submarine base of Salonika to the enemy, providing a rallying-ground for the Serbians who had reached the Adriatic ports, and keeping open the threat of an advance into Central Europe by the Vardar–Morava corridor. The

[1] See Vol. I, Chapters II and III.   [2] See Vol. I, p. vii.

Armies at Salonika were strongly reinforced, by the Serbians, by Italian and Russian contingents, and by further French troops. In the first half of 1916 there was a continuous struggle between the British and French General Staffs, the latter advocating an offensive, the former refusing to take part in one. It was the prospect of Rumanian intervention which finally decided Britain to fall in with the French views, but subject to important qualifications and without having as yet done anything to speak of to equip her forces for a campaign of movement in this country.

There followed the minor offensive on the shore of Lake Dojran and the advance beyond the Struma during August and September 1916, the Bulgarian invasion of Greek territory and advance against the Allied flanks, and the long series of engagements known as the Battle of Monastir. Throughout this period the British effort was restricted to small actions and raids and to the relief of French and Italian troops required to take part in the main battle. Whatever the shortcomings of its conduct, the Battle of Monastir resulted in an Allied victory which shook the spirit of the Bulgarians and brought German reinforcements post-haste in response to their despairing appeals. The exhaustion of the attackers and the lack of reserves, even more than the coming of a late winter, prevented the success from being exploited. Meanwhile Rumania had wasted time in bargaining, delayed her declaration of war on Austria-Hungary till after the Russian June offensive had been brought to a halt, conducted her operations when she did move on a faulty plan, and in little over three months been utterly routed. Here we can positively say that an opportunity was lost. The chance of conducting operations against Bulgaria by Rumania from the north with powerful aid from Russia in the Dobruja, coupled with an offensive from Salonika, was most promising. But operations on exterior lines, above all others, demand a well-thought-out general plan, unified control, co-ordination, timing, and resolution. (It will be remembered that in this campaign the Central Powers, for once, operated on exterior lines.) Unfortunately, France and Britain could not control Rumania's actions; nor were they responsible for the lack of training of her forces; nor, apparently, were they able to induce Russia to give her support of any value. Also, they had the Battle of the Somme on their hands. But the

LOST OPPORTUNITIES

Somme was a drag also on Germany's wheels, as were the Italian Trentino offensive on those of Austria, the campaigns in Mesopotamia, Sinai, and the Caucasus on those of Turkey, and the Battle of Monastir itself upon those of Bulgaria. Yet German, Austrian, and Bulgarian troops co-operated effectively in the overthrow of Rumania, whereas the unco-ordinated efforts of the Allies were by comparison fruitless.

So, we reach the spring offensive of 1917. By this time the British Army had at last been equipped with transport suited to the country and had been reinforced by an infantry division and some badly needed heavy artillery. This offensive is an appalling chapter of accidents. Undeserved ill fortune played a part in it, and the threat of a Greek attack in the rear had a crippling effect; but bad judgment, faulty organization, discouragement, and mistrust were all too prominent. With better backing from home, better leadership, better organization, and a spirit of mutual confidence throughout the Armies, it seems once again certain that far more could have been accomplished.

The British Government, unfavourably impressed by the conduct of this offensive and influenced by the shortage of shipping, then washed their hands of the affair and turned to Palestine, leaving the French to settle the Greek question. They withdrew two infantry divisions, the bulk of the cavalry, and a large proportion of the heavy artillery. They cut down the pack-transport establishment which had only just been reached. They set their minds resolutely against the idea of any further active operations in Macedonia, and it was over a year before they again entertained it. It was this attitude, the discredit into which this theatre of war had fallen, the miasma of futility which overhung it, as much as lack of means, which put an offensive in the following autumn out of the question.

As for the spring of 1918, that was overshadowed by the German offensive in France. The initiative had passed to the enemy, and energies in Macedonia were diverted to defence. After the successes gained at the Skra di Legen and in Albania, the French again began to consider a major offensive; the steps by which the assent of the Allies was gained for it have been described in detail.

We may conclude without hesitation that an opportunity was lost at every one of the four stages, with the possible exception of the first. The scope of the opportunity is another matter. In other words, we have not answered the question: Could the decisive victory in Macedonia have been won earlier?

We have seen that two years before the end, on the 30th October 1916, General Milne had sounded a note of optimism in this respect, in striking contrast to the general British pessimism regarding Macedonia. He had given it as his opinion that even large-scale local operations, such as those of the Battle of Monastir then in progress, might " at " any moment cause a break-up in the Bulgarian Army," which did not relish a long and trying campaign. Bulgaria had not, like Serbia, entered the war by compulsion, to fight for her life. She had been led into it by her Tsar; and, so far as there was any national motive for her intervention, it was merely haste to back what appeared to be the winning side and to avenge the humiliations of the Second Balkan War. The fortitude and endurance of Serbia were not to be expected from her. With 20 divisions General Milne would have been prepared to carry out a general attack with limited objectives. With 29 divisions he would have been prepared to embark upon a major offensive.[1] It is very interesting to note that when General Franchet d'Espérey launched his offensive in September 1918, he had at his disposal—if we include one half-trained Greek division which he did not employ—precisely this number.[2]

General Milne's appreciation was, of course, written when Russia and Rumania were still in the war, but, on the other hand, when there was one Turkish division and the equivalent of one German division in Macedonia. He added the important qualification that the enemy should not be further reinforced by German or Turkish divisions. Soon afterwards Turkey almost ceased to count in this theatre, but Germany did not. Throughout 1917 she had always about two divisions in Macedonia, and it seems certain that, prior to the year 1918, there was no period of

---

[1] See Vol. I, pp. 203–5.
[2] One may add the infantry of practically another division by taking into account the British 228th Brigade, the 2nd *bis* Zouaves, the 58th Battalion of Chasseurs-à-pied, Albanian and Indo-Chinese battalions, etc. With the exception of the Zouaves and Chasseurs-à-pied, these troops were only suitable either for holding the line or for operations on very thinly-held fronts, but they were useful in both respects.

the war, even those of her greatest stress, when she would not have been able to provide some further reinforcements if Bulgaria were in serious trouble. She had for this purpose invaluable troops in her *Jäger* battalions, which were of the highest quality and accustomed to acting independently or in improvised formations. She could generally spare regiments from her Eastern Front, where as time went on she increasingly dominated the Russians. If in 1917 an Allied offensive had taken the form of a lightning stroke and had broken the front completely, despite the presence of two German divisions, these reinforcements might have suffered the fate of those of September and October 1918, that is, have arrived in time only to be involved in the Bulgarian disaster and retreat to the Danube afterwards. If, however, it had been a slow and deliberate operation, they would have had an opportunity to close the breaches made in the Bulgarian ranks, and in country lending itself so excellently to defence they would have done so if the Allied strength had not been overwhelming.

The conditions of a decisive victory in Macedonia were, therefore, either that the original rupture of the Bulgarian front should be achieved by one sudden, tremendous blow, or that Germany should be harder pressed for troops than she ever was prior to 1918. In 1918 it is true that she had large reserves on her Russian front, where the war was over, and that she used some of them in Macedonia; but they were not for the most part of good quality. In greater or less degree they had been contaminated by Bolshevism, and the achievements of many of them when they arrived were indifferent. Another condition was that the Allied Armies of the East should have been at least as strong as they were in September 1918, whereas prior to 1918 only three or four of the Greek divisions were available, and the Serbian Armies were skeleton formations until they received their Yugoslav reinforcements.[1] It is not easy to see where substitutes for these additional troops could have been found.

There is one factor which has not yet been mentioned in this review, though it has cropped up constantly in the record of the campaign. That is the medical factor. It may be represented by the one word, "malaria," because, though malaria was responsible for only a third of the total

---

[1] See p. 68.

admissions of British troops to hospital,[1] it was by far the biggest agent, and because it ravaged the whole Army and affected practically all the troops, not only those in hospital. Where the British Salonika Army was concerned there is some ground for treating malaria as the predominant factor in all operations. Such is the view of at least one senior officer of the British medical services,[2] who writes :—

"In any attack or even in a strategical move, the great
"question for the particular G.O.C. in charge of the opera-
"tion always was, 'How many fit men can I raise for the
"'prosecution of the operation; and, during the time of
"'the operation, how many men are likely to fall out with
"'disease, chiefly malaria?'... Many of our failures
"would have had a very different end had they been
"entrusted to fit troops.... To have brought the cam-
"paign to a speedy end, a huge army would have been
"needed.... The bigger the army, the quicker it went
"down with malaria, and we couldn't have had hospitals
"enough to house half a million men." This argument applies to British troops to a very much greater extent than to Serbian or Greek, but it has to be reckoned with in some degree for all the contingents. Anti-malarial measures might, as has been indicated in these volumes, have been more thorough, especially in the earlier period, if the means had been supplied. That would have decreased the gravity of the problem, but would not have solved it. In short, in building up a striking force, an enormous wastage from malaria, a certain proportion of which was permanent wastage, had to be taken into account.

Another point to be considered is the effect of the German submarine campaign upon sea-borne supply. This campaign was at its height in 1917, caused a grave shortage of shipping, and tended to incline British opinion to the prosecution of operations in Palestine, where the forces engaged were not so largely dependent on shipping in the Mediterranean and therefore not so much at the mercy of the submarine. It aggravated the difficulties and risks of any renewed effort in Macedonia after the close of the Battle of Monastir.

Finally, there are the deficiencies of internal communications, both those within the zone of the Allied

---

[1] See Appendix 21 for battle and non-battle casualties.
[2] Major-General W. H. S. Nickerson, who was in turn A.D.M.S. of the 28th Division and D.D.M.S. of the XII Corps.

Armies of the East and those which they could not reach until they had broken the enemy's front, but which they would require for an advance to the Danube or into Bulgaria. The former could be, and were, vastly improved, and more could have been effected with greater resources. Yet, even if there had been still more road-making, and more mechanical transport had been supplied, it is doubtful if a very much larger force could have been maintained without a considerable increase of standard-gauge railway track—without, say, the substitution of standard-gauge for narrow on the Sarakli-Stavros line, or, for operations west of the Vardar, the doubling of the Monastir railway as far as Vertekop. The deficiencies of the latter no foresight could wholly remedy. The Niš railway was certain to be destroyed, and its reconstruction was certain to be a slow business. The roads would have to be used much as the enemy left them. It will be suggested that in these circumstances a serious pursuit was scarcely possible except for troops of a special type.

Such appear to be the main points for and against the possibility of decisive victory in Macedonia earlier than it was actually achieved. One is very loth to deny that there was such a possibility. Perhaps, too, an operation short of the "sudden tremendous blow," which has been postulated as essential to decisive victory, an operation on the lines of that projected by General Milne in his appreciation of the 30th October 1916, might have been equally effective at that time, before the complete overthrow of Rumania. For either, the Entente would have had to concentrate greater strength and above all to provide more material than it ever did, but, it is submitted, not beyond its resources, in view of the great returns promised by success. It would have had to create a unified control of the conduct of the war, such as not even the Supreme War Council provided, and a local unified control, working smoothly and efficiently, such as was not provided until the arrival of General Guillaumat. The former was very difficult, but it ought not to have been impossible ; the latter should have been easy. There would never have been any certainty of success, but the chances of it would have been, at the lowest, as good as those of most of the major offensives on the Western Front ; and the cost in human life of either success or failure would have been considerably less.

It is not suggested that any victory in the Balkans would have brought Germany to sue for peace unless combined with a considerable measure of success in France; the idea that a purely defensive policy in the West, coupled with a main effort in the Balkans, would have accomplished this appears to be illusory. Yet it is an exaggeration to say that Britain and France were compelled to stand on the defensive in the Balkans unless they stood purely on the defensive in the West.

So, it seems, the argument cannot be prevented from moving in a circle. Given the mistakes of the Allies in the early stages and the wastage which they involved, given the delay in going to the aid of Serbia, given the decision of Britain to devote enormous resources to offensive campaigns in Palestine and Mesopotamia—though it is not here suggested that this decision was necessarily mistaken—given the errors of Rumania, it may well be that it was beyond the power of the Allies to mount a major offensive in Macedonia until the Greek Army was at full strength in the autumn of 1918. Even in these circumstances earlier operations here might have played a larger and more useful part in the general effort. But, could we conceive the cleaning of the slate, then we could go much further. The importance of the Balkans in a war involving nearly all Europe, the strategic significance of the Vardar–Morava corridor as a gateway to Central Europe would then have been clearly recognized.

The second question, as to what was actually achieved, as to the contribution of the victory in Macedonia to the final victory in the whole war, can be answered more quickly, though it has given rise to a great deal of discussion. Germany was on the brink of defeat by military operations on the Western Front coupled with the pressure of the naval blockade. Austria-Hungary was already worn out and ready to collapse at any moment. The elimination of Bulgaria was, nevertheless, a disastrous blow, both morally and strategically. It opened the road to the Danube and compelled the Central Powers, if they would avoid invasion, to create a new front, a task which they found beyond their resources, or to sue for peace immediately. It caused Turkey to throw in her hand at a moment when, despite her disaster in Palestine, she might conceivably have held out for some little time longer. The German evidence shows, when fair allowance is made for national vanity and desire to shift the blame to other shoulders, that, following upon the Allied victories in France, it hastened and made certain the end. More than that cannot be said, but that in itself is important. Marshal Franchet d'Espérey, an ardent believer in the possibility of earlier victory, makes no higher claim for the victory that was gained when he writes :—

" C'est grâce à cette poursuite sans merci que la chute
" des Empires Centraux fut précipitée irrémédiablement et
" sans pertes." [1]

SOME DEDUCTIONS.

The campaign in Macedonia has in one respect a unique interest for military students. In other theatres of war, notably in the Italian, there were operations at far greater altitudes ; but the Battle of the Dobropolje may be taken as the only major operation of the Great War in a European theatre, leading to a decision, which was carried out at heights of from 5,000 to 7,000 feet.[2] The battle of rupture, the enlargement of the breach, and the pursuit may, in fact, be studied together as essentially an operation of mountain warfare on a very large scale. The pursuit itself, and especially the second stage, the Serbian pursuit of the Germans and Austrians to the Danube after the Bulgarian Armistice, has another special interest. As it progressed, it became more and more an operation without lines of communication. In the end, it recalled to a large extent conditions prior to the introduction of the railway and the internal-combustion engine on the road, conditions in which fast-moving troops could not expect heavy transport to keep up with them and had to rely as a matter of course on rations far inferior in quantity and quality to the modern emergency ration, or even to live on the country altogether.

---

[1] Larcher, p. 9.
[2] The peaks of the Transylvanian Alps, in which Falkenhayn carried out his offensive against Rumania, are considerably higher than those of the Moglena Mountains, but the chain is cut by many gaps and the passes are comparatively low. The mean height of the Asiago Plateau in northern Italy is roughly the same as the crest of the Moglena ridge at the point attacked, but this is not broken country. Moreover, the Austrian attacks were from higher ground, and the Italians were on the defensive. In any case, no decision was obtained here.

CONCLUSION

It is to be hoped that some of the lessons of this twentieth-century mountain warfare, as revealed by the offensive of September 1918, will appear from the chapters in which it is described. A brief consideration of the strategy and tactics of the offensive, with a few notes on equipment and supply may, however, be of value.

It is perhaps in the nature of a commonplace that the main difference between warfare in mountainous country and warfare in the plain is the greater influence on the former of terrain and communications. In any country the choice of the section of front to be attacked will be to a certain extent governed by the direction of the roads leading up to it and through it, and of those on its flanks. In relatively flat country, however, this consideration is a secondary one, especially in highly developed country where more or less suitable roads can usually be found leading in any required direction; it is also one the importance of which is every day decreasing with the development of cross-country transport. In mountainous country it still remains the essential consideration, because transport and artillery on wheels, however propelled and even if the wheels turn an endless cogged chain, must in general follow the valleys. In country of this sort the most suitable objective is likely to be a junction of routes. There will also be opportunities of bringing about the surrender or destruction of hostile forces by the mere blocking of routes—opportunities likely to be very rare in the plain. It is also a logical conclusion that if the front of attack be selected for these reasons, the first objective will not be chosen primarily because it is the easiest. It may, in fact, be the most difficult.

All these points are brought out by the offensive of September 1918 on the Franco-Serbian front. The breakthrough was made in the only sector where the Bulgarian front exactly coincided with the frontier-crest. The attack was directed against the only section of the crest itself where the defensive organization was highly developed, but it avoided the long advance over rising ground, all very suitable for defence and fortified in depth, which would have been necessary at any point between the Vetrenik and the Vardar. Again, the Allied Commander-in-Chief insisted with all the weight of his authority that the capture of the key to the second position of defence, the Kozyak spur,

FEATURES OF MOUNTAIN WARFARE 299

should be achieved, not by a second operation, but by a continuation of the original operation, without pause. That objective taken, the ground dropped gradually to the valley of the Vardar, and the general lie of the valleys—and therefore of the routes, such as they were—was favourable to an advance on the river between Demir Kapija and Gradsko. We have seen the importance of the northwestern half of this front, between Krivolak and Gradsko, where so many rail and road communications joined, crossed, or approached one another.[1] The capture of Skoplje and the blocking of at least a quarter of the enemy's forces in the Tetovo corridor is a striking illustration of the other feature of mountain warfare which has been mentioned.

There is yet another feature illustrated by the earlier stages of the attack. In mountainous country, if the communications in the direction of the advance are relatively good, it is almost certain that the lateral communications will be inferior to them, because the former will follow the valleys, or in rare cases the spurs, while the latter will cross them. The result of these conditions will normally be that the time factor is against the defender, that it is more difficult for him to concentrate troops at suitable points for counterattacks on a large scale than it would be in the plain. The attacker will therefore run less risk of being caught and crushed in a pocket of his own making and need have less fear for his flanks when pushing on deeper into such a pocket. The advantages of the defender, so obvious at first sight, are greatly weakened by this consideration.

On the other hand, the difficulty of lateral communication will affect the attacker also. If he desires to change the direction of his advance or of any section of it, as General Franchet d'Espérey desired to change that of the Armée Française d'Orient from Kičevo to Skoplje, he can only do so slowly, either by a movement of troops laterally, " against the grain " of the ground, or by the employment of troops not yet fully committed and probably far in rear.[2] In short, no modification of his original scheme will be easy. This certainly appears to qualify the maxim of Bourcet evolved in the Maritime Alps in the War of the Austrian

---

[1] See p. 125.
[2] See p. 242.

Succession, that every plan "should have a second com-"partment." [1]

There are certain other aspects which are so obvious that they need only be mentioned in a work intended mainly for professional readers or students already acquainted with the tendencies of modern warfare. The first of these is the immense importance of aircraft in the mountains, to observe what is taking place in the valleys; and this applies not only to the enemy's situation and movements, but to those of friendly troops, who may not be able to communicate quickly with the rear. Again, it is patent that, the fewer the roads and the more the enemy's troops are confined to such as there are, the more deadly and demoralizing will be bombing attacks upon them from the air, especially where they pass through defiles. The discontinuity of the front, what the French call its *compartimentage*, and its corollary that fewer troops to the mile are likely to be employed in the mountains than in the plain, are equally commonplaces. So is the fact that in the mountains the advance will be supported by less artillery than in the plains. It is, however, worth while noting what actually happened in this respect in Macedonia.

As already recorded, a very powerful concentration of artillery was effected to prepare and support the rupture of the front. After that only a very small fraction of either field or heavy artillery was able to follow the infantry. Generally speaking, the mountain artillery did well, and, after being constantly employed with the most valuable results in the pursuit, got through to the Danube. The field artillery almost disappeared on the road; in no case did a division reach the Danube with more than one-third of its field guns. The field artillery of the 17th Colonial Division began the pursuit on the 17th September with one section per battery, that is, 18 guns in all instead of 36; a single battery came into action in front of Gradsko on the 23rd; and the artillery, on arrival on the Danube, consisted of two batteries of two pieces each with 100 rounds a piece. A few horse-drawn and tractor-drawn French and Serbian heavy batteries also went right through, but they hardly ever came into action.[2] In rather less difficult circum-

---
[1] See Spenser Wilkinson's "The Defence of Piedmont" and Liddell Hart's "The Ghost of Napoleon."
[2] "Etude sur la Guerre de Montagne," p. 79.

stances and a shorter pursuit, on the British front, the amount of field artillery following the infantry was very limited and that of the heavy artillery still more so.

Here certainly is an aspect of General Franchet d'Espérey's problem in which commanders of 1934 would have an advantage over him. Yet it must be realized that even a force equipped with the most modern type of mechanical traction for artillery would have required petrol-carrying vehicles of great strength and high horse-power, themselves heavy consumers of fuel in proportion to their capacity. It would also seem that the danger of blocking circulation in defiles would have been as great with artillery which was drawn and supplied with ammunition by mechanically propelled vehicles as was actually the case. In mountain warfare energetic and well-led troops have constantly made their way with the backing of less artillery than that in hands of the defence, and, so far as can be seen, they will always have to do so. In the pursuit of a beaten army it will always pay to press on regardless of this consideration, and in the mountains above all.

The value of cavalry led by a commander determined to reach his goal at any hazard, even in country on the face of it most unfavourable, is strikingly illustrated by the march of the brigade of General Jouinot-Gambetta on Skoplje. Had it been possible to treat in greater detail the main Franco-Serbian offensive, it would have been made clear that both the French and the Serbian cavalry rendered most useful service on other occasions also. On the British front, the enemy did not make a serious stand until just at the end, in front of Yeniköi, but the Derbyshire Yeomanry was opposed all the way, and its work was extremely valuable throughout the pursuit. "Their only fault," General Milne wrote of his Yeomanry, "was their "lack of numbers."

It is of interest to note that the offensive fulfilled the anticipations of the Commander-in-Chief very closely in most respects, but that as regards the lines of supply his calculations were upset. In his preliminary orders and instructions he refers constantly to the importance of opening up the Vardar valley, which he regarded as vital to the services of supply. He also hoped that the Monastir–Prilep road, the best road west of the Vardar on the enemy's side of the line, would be quickly available for use on that flank, the railhead for which would then be Monastir. What actually happened was that the Serbian Armies had to be maintained, especially as regards ammunition, wholly for some time and mainly until the Armistice with Bulgaria, across the Moglena mountains, and that the right wing of the Armée Française d'Orient was dependent for much longer than was anticipated on the roads in the bend of the Crna.

The reason was, in part, the failure of the British attacks at Dojran, as regards the Vardar valley, and, as regards the Monastir plain, the unexpected persistence of the enemy in clinging to his positions in that quarter. But even after the 1st Group of Divisions had reached the Vardar, the destruction of the railway by the retreating enemy proved so thorough that by the 29th September railhead had only reached Kilometre 75, just south of Gevgeli Station.[1] Such conditions may often recur. They demand that particular attention shall be paid beforehand to the roads leading up to the sector of attack; that these, should they be deficient in number or damaged by fire, shall be increased or thoroughly repaired, and pushed forward as close as possible to the front line; and that every possible provision shall be made to link them speedily with the enemy's road system. In the case of this attack the linking had to take place at the most difficult points, on the summit of the ridge. A second serious handicap was that the enemy, who relied to a great extent on light railways, telpherage, and ropeways, had, by comparison with the Allies, neglected his roads.

Mountain warfare must always impose upon the troops taking part in it, especially the dismounted arms, considerable physical effort. The suitability of the Serbians for this type of warfare has been brought out in these pages, but there is also valuable information from the French regarding the superiority of men bred in mountains and hilly country even in highly civilized lands. The French 57th Division, which arrived at Salonika in October 1915, was largely made up of peasants and farmers from the mountainous regions of the Doubs, the Jura, and the Vosges. From the 3rd November to the 15th December the 371st Infantry Regiment was continually engaged in

---

[1] Revol, p. 115.

SPECIAL TROOPS REQUIRED

marching and fighting. In the retreat from Serbia it covered an average of over 20 miles a day. After the actions of Furka on the 11th December,[1] the 242nd Regiment marched for 36 hours through hill country, without leaving a straggler behind. On the other hand, a regiment composed of young classes, not from a mountainous region, operating in Albania in the final offensive, was completely worn out in eleven days and had to be withdrawn to the rear. At the best, French troops required substantial rations, and, if their morale was to be fully maintained, a regular supply of wine, the latter being particularly difficult to transport through the mountains. North African troops, excellently suited to mountain warfare, were unfortunately not represented in the Colonial divisions in Macedonia. None of these had regiments of Arab or Berber Tirailleurs as in France; instead, each Colonial regiment had one Senegalese in addition to two white battalions. But the Moroccan Spahis showed, in more than one long-distance cavalry raid in Albania, carrying six days' flour and rice on their horses, how hard such men can live. The French critics sum up the evidence on this point with the statement :—

"En montagne, des troupes d'élite devraient être "uniquement composées de montagnards rustiques, se "contentant d'un faible ravitaillement." [2]

They point out, however, that special training is a fair substitute for what may be called the "birth qualification" in the making of mountain warriors.

Whether we consider the Macedonian Campaign purely in the light of history or as a source from which useful suggestions as to policy, strategy, tactics, and training may be drawn, it seems that there is material for thought in all this where we as a nation are concerned. We have become predominantly an urban population. Our Regular divisions and brigades have no territorial basis, and even old county regiments are to-day often recruited in great part from the cities, sometimes from cities outside their counties. Still more anomalous is it that our Highland regiments, instead of being composed entirely of mountaineers, are also largely recruited from cities and big towns, in their case because they are too numerous for the Highlands to support. So it comes about that, though we have in Scotland and Wales

---

[1] See Vol. I, p. 75.
[2] "Étude sur la Guerre de Montagne," pp. 20–1.

populations naturally suited to mountain warfare, we are unable to reserve any of the troops drawn from them for such employment. To extend the picture to the Empire as a whole, we have a very wide selection of troops suited to the most varied conditions, without being able to specialize except in small local wars. The Great War saw curious misfits: Regular divisions (the 27th and 28th) seasoned to heat in the East suffering wastage from the cold of the first winter in Flanders; South Africans filling the hospitals, and Indians wholly unaccustomed to bush fighting, in East Africa; Gurkhas from the mountains of Nepal and Jats from the fringes of the hot Sind desert in the waterlogged trenches about Neuve Chapelle, while New Army battalions were climbing Sari Bair and Welsh Territorials were being smitten by sunstroke at Aden. Such misfits were often inevitable, though some of them were gradually re-sorted. Our organization makes it impossible wholly to avoid them, and this is especially true as regards the British Army itself.

Our troops may be expected to be quicker-witted and mentally more adaptable than those of countries largely agricultural; our Territorial Army would certainly have a far higher standard of civil education. On the other hand, the townsman, though he can support fatigue as well as another, cannot do so for long on short commons. His spirit may carry him through terrible exposure, but in the long run that exposure will exact from him a heavier toll in sickness than from the countryman. He will probably have less defence against diseases such as malaria.

It is, however, above all in the advance and pursuit through mountains that townsmen are likely to be at a disadvantage by comparison with countrymen, and especially with mountaineers or hillmen. It will be impossible to create from the former one of those " armées " maigres " which the conditions of the pursuit in Macedonia demanded and which may be needed in similar country in the future. That problem should be frankly faced. The transport of bivouac-shelters, great-coats, and even packs in mechanically driven vehicles may be extremely useful, but in really primitive country it represents a gamble. In such country it might well actually worsen the situation. Vital avenues of supply might be blocked, vital stores of fuel might be used up, and the soldier who would otherwise only have had to buckle his belt tighter might be starved from lack of food or from cold. Yet the alternative of expecting British troops to " march light " in the old sense of the phrase is hardly possible now.

These considerations in some measure justify British objections to the Macedonian Campaign. It seemed that the excellent troops sent out from France to Salonika were not being employed to the best advantage, that they would have been more valuable and have pulled their weight more fully in some more suitable theatre of war. They suggest caution in becoming committed to such a campaign in the future, unless we are able to employ, from our large resources, the type of troops best fitted for its conditions. On the technical side warfare is changing fast, but there are certain principles which do not change readily with the progress of technical science, and among them are the broad principles of mountain warfare.

If ever it should come about that a British Government finds itself hesitating between two theatres of war, the balance ought to be heavily weighted against that which, for climatic, physical, or medical reasons, is the less suited to the qualities and aptitudes of its troops.

APPENDIX 1.

SUMMARY OF EVENTS
CONCERNING THE
BRITISH ARMY OF THE BLACK SEA,[1]
DECEMBER 1918 TO MAY 1919.

ON the 14th December 1918 British G.H.Q. left Salonika for Constantinople by sea; on the 17th it was established at the Military School in Péra. On the 11th January 1919 General Milne was instructed to assume executive control of the Constantinople police. This was carried out by Lieut.-General Sir H. F. M. Wilson, who formed an Inter-Allied Commission of Control, on which France and Italy were represented as well as Great Britain. Small Allied police posts were established throughout the city, chiefly at points where Christian and Moslem were likely to come to blows; but the method relied upon in general was to limit outside interference to the minimum and to work through the Turkish police, whose reliability and authority every effort was made to improve. In very difficult conditions complete tranquillity was maintained, and serious crime became less prevalent in Constantinople than in other large European cities. The sanitary control was taken over simultaneously by another commission, and resulted in a marked improvement of the health of the population.

Prior to the arrival of G.H.Q., on the 5th December, the War Office informed General Milne of the decision that all forces in the Balkans, including European Turkey, would remain under the general control of General Franchet d'Espérey. Troops which it had been decided to send to the eastern shore of the Black Sea would not be placed under his command. Despite this division of responsibility, it actually fell in practice to the British to carry out the disarmament and reduction of the Turkish forces in Thrace, as well as of the great bulk of the Armies, which were in Asia Minor, under the terms of the Armistice.

There were at least 400,000 Turkish troops under arms. It was soon discovered that for the purpose of watching the frontier, but still more for that of maintaining internal order, Turkey would require to keep a considerable force. After much discussion it was agreed that this was to be limited to twenty miniature divisions, each with an establishment of 1,500 infantry and a small proportion of artillery and machine gunners. Except in the vicinity of Constantinople no two divisions were to be stationed in the same town.

As regards the rest of the Army, the personnel was to be rapidly demobilized after the return of units to their territorial centres, and all munitions of war were subsequently to be collected. The process of demobilization was slow and was interrupted by deliberate obstruction on the part of local Turkish commanders; but generally speaking it was eventually achieved. The least satisfactory area was that about Erzerum, where the Turkish *XV Corps* was never brought down to the authorized limit. It was not unnatural that there should have been trouble here,

---

[1] In retrospect, this title is generally used from the date of the arrival of G.H.Q. at Constantinople, but it does not appear to have been officially assumed until the 13th May 1919.

APPENDIX I

since these troops had been victorious up to the last and in the mass knew very little of the defeats suffered by Turkey elsewhere.

The task of disarmament was, however, far more difficult. Winter conditions in the inaccessible interior of Anatolia made impossible the movement of arms and munitions on a large scale, even with Turkish good will; and it was therefore decided to issue no instructions for their surrender until the spring. Depots were scattered all over the country, and to have stationed Allied guards at each of them would have entailed splitting up the rapidly decreasing force at General Milne's disposal into small, dangerously dispersed, and isolated detachments. General Milne therefore decided to entrust the collection to the Turkish Ministry of War. So far as could be judged, the Peace Treaty would probably permit Turkey to retain her armament or a great part of it, so that it was to the interest of the Ministry to collect as much as possible rather than have it dispersed or destroyed. To simplify the problem, it was decided to demand only breech-blocks of guns and bolts of rifles. Machine guns, however, were to be brought complete to Constantinople, where the locks and side-plates were to be taken over. Depots were provided where the arms would be in the keeping of Allied military guards, but under Turkish care and maintenance.

The plan worked well enough, even the Nationalist leaders, Mustapha Kemal Pasha and Jemal Pasha, sending in large consignments from their areas, though again about Erzerum there was failure to comply with the regulations. Huge quantities of arms had been delivered when the events of May 1919 at Smyrna brought the process suddenly and completely to an end.

Mention has been made of the decision to send a force to Batum, on the Black Sea, to enforce the conditions of the Armistice with Turkey and to safeguard railway communications with Baku, on the western shore of the Caspian. In 1918, following the Russian collapse, the Turks had invaded the Caucasus. A British detachment known as "Dunsterforce" had occupied Baku from the 4th August to the 14th September, when it had been compelled to evacuate the place under heavy pressure from the Turks. The latter were eager to complete their conquest of the Caucasus before withdrawal was forced upon them, and fighting with White Russian and Armenian forces continued after the Armistice. In order to check this ambition, the 39th Brigade, which formed part of the Mesopotamian Expeditionary Force, reoccupied Baku on the 17th November. On the eastern shore of the Caspian, Krasnovodsk was already in the hands of a small British detachment from North Persia and of a large body of Russians, the latter being, however, completely unreliable. On the arrival at Baku of Major-General W. M. Thomson, commanding the 39th Brigade, the Krasnovodsk detachment came under his orders. The force which it had been decided to despatch to Batum was to form a link between Constantinople and the 39th Brigade on the Caspian and to reopen the oil pipe-line between Baku and Batum.

The 27th Division was selected for the task. Major-General Forestier-Walker arrived at Batum with a composite brigade of his division on the 22nd December. The first news which greeted him was that there had been an outbreak of hostilities south of Tiflis, on the Batum–Baku railway, between the forces of the new Republics of Armenia and Georgia. A staff officer with a small escort at once set out for Tiflis, and persuaded the two parties to cease fighting. Negotiations were opened at Tiflis under the presidency of Major-General W. H. Rycroft, who happened to be making a tour of inspection in the Caucasus, and an armistice was arranged. Finally, on the 17th January 1919, peace was signed between Armenia and Georgia. This was only the first of several local conflicts, between Georgians and the Volunteer Russian Army, between Armenians and Tatars, in which British troops had to intervene.

By the 9th January the greater part of the 27th Division had reached Batum ; a brigade had been established at Tiflis ; and contact had been made with the 39th Brigade at Baku. On the 15th the latter force, including the detachment at Krasnovodsk, came under the orders of General Milne, and on the same date a composite force of all arms under Major-General W. Malleson which was stationed on and within the frontier of Trans-Caspia, at Askabad, Meshed, and Merv, also passed to his command. On the 16th the Commander-in-Chief left Constantinople for a tour in the Caucasus and Trans-Caspia. He reported to the War Office that in his view the British forces in the latter area, exclusive of the little garrison at Krasnovodsk, should be gradually withdrawn. On the 13th February he was informed that the War Office fully agreed with his suggestion. Major-General Malleson's force would be withdrawn across the Persian frontier, which it would continue to protect from the risk of Bolshevist invasion, and would be placed under the orders of the Commander-in-Chief in India. The last British troops left Askabad on the 1st April, and on the 15th of that month the force ceased to be under General Milne's command. The Trans-Caspian front was taken over by a Russian commander appointed by General Denikin.

Meanwhile the British Army of the Black Sea had been considerably reduced. At the beginning of February the headquarters of the XVI Corps was abolished, Lieut.-General Sir C. J. Briggs being appointed Chief of the British Military Mission to General Denikin in South Russia. On the 16th of that month General Briggs reached Ekaterinodar. In March the 22nd Division was disbanded. The 26th Division handed over the Southern Dobruja to the Italian Army on the 20th April. One brigade was moved to Egypt, and the rest of the division was broken up, five battalions being transferred to the 27th Division in relief of Regular battalions, which were reduced to cadre and sent home to be reformed.

Questions such as those of the control of the railways, the administration of the oil industry, the assistance given to the American Missions which were carrying out relief work, and the political relationships of Armenia, Georgia, and the Tatar Republic of Azerbaijan, are outside the scope of this very brief summary ; still more so is that of the British Military Mission in South Russia, which did not come under General Milne's orders until he was called upon to take measures for its safety. The most suitable point at which to make an end appears to be the landing of the Greek Army at Smyrna, which took place, by decision of the Supreme War Council, on the 15th May 1919. This marks the beginning of what developed into a new war ; were we to continue the record of events, we should find no halting place short of the evacuation of Turkey, which was not complete until October 1923. All this later period properly belongs to the post-war volume, if, as suggested in the preface, one is eventually compiled.[1]

Here it remains only to be said that the landing at Smyrna was accompanied by regrettable excesses, bad enough in themselves but exaggerated by rumour, which aroused among the Turks bitter resentment against the Allies. For the time being, at any rate, the British, whose naval forces had ensured a safe landing to the Greeks, were chiefly reproached. The Turkish Government, hitherto strong enough to carry out the terms of the Armistice, suffered serious loss of power and prestige

---

[1] See p. viii. A summary of the main events, movements, and reorganizations in the Army of the Black Sea will be found in the sections devoted to the 27th and 28th Divisions, the latter especially, in the official volume, " History of the Great War : Order of Battle of Divisions, Part I—The Regular British Divisions," compiled by Major A. F. Becke (H.M. Stationery Office).

to the profit of the Nationalist movement in Asia Minor. From that moment the surrender of arms ceased and a completely new phase began.

At the end of May the dispositions of the Army of the Black Sea were as follows :—

27th Division :—Headquarters at Tiflis.
    39th Brigade at Baku with a battalion in each of the Caspian ports of Krasnovodsk and Petrovsk.
    80th Brigade at Batum, with a battalion at Gagri, on the Black Sea, 140 miles north-west of Batum.
    81st Brigade at Tiflis, with a battalion at Nakhichevan, on the Arazes.
    82nd Brigade at Erivan and Tiflis.

28th Division :—Headquarters at Moda, south of Haidar Pasha.
    83rd Brigade on eastern shore of Dardanelles.
    84th Brigade in the Haidar Pasha area.
    85th Brigade in Péra, with two battalions on the western shore of the Bosporus.

Army Troops :—A battalion each at Péra, Haidar Pasha, and Salonika ; Garrison battalions at Ismid, Batum, Eskisshehr, and Salonika.

APPENDIX 2.

ORDER OF BATTLE
OF THE
ALLIED ARMIES OF THE EAST,
14TH SEPTEMBER 1918

COMMANDEMENT DES ARMÉES ALLIÉES EN ORIENT.

Commander-in-Chief .. .. .. General Franchet d'Espérey.
Chief of the Staff .. .. .. General Charpy.
Sub-Chief of the Staff .. .. Colonel Trousson.

ARMÉE FRANÇAISE D'ORIENT.

G.O.C. .. .. General Henrys.
Chief of the Staff .. .. .. Colonel Expert-Besançon.

2ND GROUP OF DIVISIONS.

G.O.C. .. .. General Patey.
    30th, 76th, and 11th Colonial Divisions, 156th Division (less one Regt.), one Regt. Greek 3rd Division.

3RD GROUP OF DIVISIONS.

G.O.C. .. .. General de Lobit.
  57th Division, one Regt. 156th Division; 2 Serbian Bns., one Albanian, one Algerian, one Indo-Chinese Bn., and the *Tabor* of Essad Pasha.
Italian 35th Division.
Greek 3rd Division (less one Regt.).
Army Troops: Groupement de Cavalerie (1st and 4th Chasseurs d'Afrique, Regt. de Marche des Spahis Maroccains).
(The above formations formed the A.F.O.; those which follow were directly under the C.A.A.).

1ST GROUP OF DIVISIONS.

G.O.C. .. .. General d'Anselme.
  16th Colonial Division, Greek Archipelago and 4th Divisions.

SERBIAN ARMIES.

Commander-in-Chief .. .. .. The Prince Regent Alexander.
Chief of the Staff .. .. .. Voivode Mišić.

FIRST ARMY.

G.O.C. .. .. Voivode Bojović.
  Morava, Drina, and Danube Divisions.

SECOND ARMY.

G.O.C. .. .. Voivode Stepanović.
  Šumadija, Timok, and Yugoslav Divisions, French 126th and 17th Colonial Divisions.

Army Group Troops: Cavalry Division.

BRITISH SALONIKA ARMY.[1]

Commander-in-Chief .. .. .. General G. F. Milne.

XII CORPS.

G.O.C. .. .. Lieut.-General Sir H. F. M. Wilson.
  22nd, 26th, and 27th Divisions, 83rd Brigade (less 2 Bns.), Greek Seres Division, 2nd bis Regt. de Zouaves.

XVI CORPS.

G.O.C. .. .. Lieut.-General Sir C. J. Briggs.
  28th Division (less 83rd Brigade H.Q. and one Bn.), Greek Crete Division.

GREEK I CORPS.

G.O.C. .. .. General Paraskevopoulos.
  Greek 1st, 2nd, and 13th Divisions.

---

[1] A detailed Order of Battle is given in Appendix 3.

APPENDICES 2 AND 3   311

FRENCH G.H.Q. TROOPS.
Greek 9th and 14th Divisions.

Greek Army.
Commander-in-Chief .. .. .. *General Danglis.*

Greek Corps of National Defence.
G.O.C. .. .. *General E. Zymbrakakis.*
Archipelago Division (attached 1st Group of Divisions), Seres Division (attached British XII Corps), Crete Division (attached British XVI Corps).

Greek I Corps (attached British Salonika Army).
G.O.C. .. .. *General Paraskevopoulos.*
1st, 2nd, and 13th Divisions.

Greek II Corps.
G.O.C. .. .. *General Miliotis.*
3rd Division (attached Armée Française d'Orient), 4th Division (attached 1st Group of Divisions), 14th Division (French G.H.Q Troops).
9th Division (French G.H.Q. Troops).

APPENDIX 3.

ORDER OF BATTLE
OF THE
BRITISH SALONIKA ARMY,
14TH SEPTEMBER 1918

GENERAL HEADQUARTERS.

Commander-in-Chief	General G. F. Milne, K.C.B., D.S.O.
Major-General, General Staff ..	Major-General G. N. Cory, C.B., D.S.O.
Deputy Adjutant-General ..	Major-General H. J. Everett, C.B., C.M.G.
Deputy Quartermaster-General	Major-General W. H. Rycroft, K.C.M.G., D.S.O.
Attached—	
Major-General, Royal Artillery ..	Major-General W. H. Onslow, C.B., C.M.G.
Engineer in Chief	Major-General H. A. A. Livingstone, C.B., C.M.G.

XII Corps.

G.O.C.	Lieut.-General Sir H. F. M. Wilson, K.C.B., K.C.M.G.
Br.-General, General Staff	Br.-General F. G. Fuller, C.M.G.
Deputy Adjutant and Quartermaster-General	Br.-General E. J. F. Vaughan, D.S.O.
G.O.C. Royal Artillery	Br.-General H. D. White-Thomson, C.B., C.M.G., D.S.O.
Chief Engineer	Br.-General C. G. W. Hunter, C.M.G., D.S.O.

22nd Division.

G.O.C. .. Major-General J. Duncan, C.M.G., D.S.O.

65th Brigade .. Br.-General B. J. Majendie, D.S.O.
    9/King's Own.
    9/East Lancashire.
    8/S. Wales Borderers.

66th Brigade .. Br.-General F. S. Montague Bates, C.M.G., D.S.O.
    12/Cheshire.
    9/South Lancashire.
    8/Shropshire L.I.

67th Brigade .. Br.-General A. D. Macpherson, C.M.G., D.S.O.
    11/R. Welch Fusiliers.
    7/S. Wales Borderers.
    11/Welch.

Artillery .. XCVIII, XCIX, C, and CI Brigades, R.F.A.
Engineers .. 99th, 100th, and 127th Field Companies R.E.
Pioneers .. 9/Border Regiment.

26th Division.

G.O.C. .. Major-General A. W. Gay, C.B., C.M.G., D.S.O.

77th Brigade .. Br.-General W. A. Blake, C.M.G., D.S.O.
    8/R. Scots Fus.
    11/Cameronians (Scot. Rif.).
    12/Arg. and Suth. Highrs.

78th Brigade .. Br.-General G. F. H. Wingate, D.S.O.
    11/Worcestershire.
    7/Ox. and Bucks L.I.
    7/R. Berkshire.

79th Brigade .. Br.-General A. J. Poole, C.M.G.
    10/Devons.
    8/D.C.L.I.
    12/Hampshire.

Artillery .. LVII, CXIV, CXV, and CXVI Brigades, R.F.A.
Engineers .. 107th, 108th, and 131st Field Companies R.E.
Pioneers .. 8/Ox. and Bucks L.I.

APPENDIX 3

27th Division.

G.O.C. ..	Major-General G. T. Forestier-Walker, C.B.
80th Brigade ..	Br. General W. J. N. Cooke-Collis, D.S.O.

    2/Shropshire L.I.
    3/K.R.R.C.
    4/Rifle Brigade.

81st Brigade ..	Br.-General B. F. Widdrington, C.M.G., D.S.O.

    1/Royal Scots.
    2/Cameron Highrs.
    1/Arg. and Suth. Highrs.

82nd Brigade ..	Br.-General R. E. Solly-Flood, C.M.G., D.S.O.

    2/Gloucestershire.
    2/D.C.L.I.
    10/Hampshire.

Artillery ..	I, XIX, XX, and CXXIX Brigades, R.F.A.
Engineers ..	17th, 500th, and 501st Field Companies R.E.
Pioneers ..	26/Middlesex.

Attached to XII Corps—

Greek Seres Division.

G.O.C. ..	General Zymbrakakis.

1st, 2nd, and 3rd Regiments of Corps of Nat. Defence.
2nd bis Regiment de Zouaves .. Colonel Boré-Verrier.
83rd Brigade (less two battalions). See under XVI Corps.

Corps Troops.

1/1st Lothians and Border Horse (less one squadron).
12th Cyclist Battalion.

XVI CORPS.

G.O.C. ..	Lieut.-General Sir C. J. Briggs, K.C.B., K.C.M.G.
Br.-General, General Staff ..	Br.-General H. L. Knight, D.S.O.
Deputy Adjutant and Quartermaster-General ..	Br.-General E. D. Young, C.M.G.
G.O.C. Royal Artillery ..	Br.-General H. E. T. Kelly, C.M.G.
Chief Engineer ..	Br.-General H. L. Pritchard, C.M.G., D.S.O.

28th Division.

G.O.C. ..	Major-General H. L. Croker, C.B., C.M.G.
83rd Brigade [1] ..	Br.-General R. H. Hare, C.M.G., M.V.O., D.S.O.

    2/King's Own.
    2/East Yorkshire.
    1/York and Lancs.

---

[1] Headquarters, 2/King's Own, 83rd Machine-Gun Company and Trench-Mortar Battery were attached to the XII Corps.

APPENDIX 3

84th Brigade .. .. Br.-General F. C. Nisbet, D.S.O.
   1/Suffolk.
   2/Cheshire.
   1/Welch.
85th Brigade .. .. Br.-General K. M. Davie, D.S.O.
   2/The Buffs.
   2/East Surrey.
   3/Middlesex.
Artillery .. .. III, LIV, XXXI, and CXXX Brigades, R.F.A.
Engineers .. .. 38th, 449th, and 506th Field Companies R.E.
Pioneers .. .. 23/Welch.

Attached to 28th Division—
228th Brigade .. .. Br.-General W. C. Ross, C.B., C.M.G.
   2/5 Durham L.I.
   2nd Garr. Bn. The King's.
   22nd Garr. Bn. the Rifle Brigade.
   1st Garr. Bn. Seaforth Highrs.

Attached to XVI Corps—
              Greek Crete Division.
G.O.C. .. .. General Spiliades.
   8th, 9th, and 29th Regiments of Corps of Nat. Defence.
Greek 3rd Cavalry Regiment.

              Corps Troops.
1/1st Surrey Yeomanry (less one squadron).
16th Cyclist Battalion.

            GENERAL HEADQUARTERS TROOPS.
Air Force Contingent—
            16th Wing, Royal Air Force.
Commander .. .. Lieut.-Colonel G. E. Todd.
                         Nos. 17, 47, and 150 Squadrons R.A.F., No. 22 Balloon Company (two sections), and Salonika Aircraft Park.
Mounted Troops .. .. .. 1/1st Derbyshire Yeomanry.

Artillery—
G.O.C. Heavy Artillery [1] .. .. Br.-General P. L. Holbrooke, D.S.O.
                         XX Brigade R.G.A. (four 60-pdr. batteries), XXXVII Brigade R.G.A. (five 6-inch howitzer batteries), LXI Brigade R.G.A. (three 6-inch howitzer batteries and one 8-inch howitzer battery), LXXV Brigade R.G.A. (four 60-pdr. batteries, of which the 190th was attached to the XVI

---

[1] Headquarters Heavy Artillery was attached to the XII Corps. All the heavy artillery, except as otherwise specified, was also attached to that corps.

APPENDIX 3 315

	Corps), LXXXII Brigade R.G.A. (three 60-pdr. batteries and one 5-gun 6-inch gun battery, of the last of which one gun was attached to the XVI Corps and one gun to the Greek I Corps), 84th Siege Battery R.G.A. (two 4·7-inch guns attached Serbian Armies, two 6-inch Naval guns in Entrenched Camp Defences).
	III Mountain Artillery Brigade R.G.A. (three 2·75-inch batteries, attached XVI Corps).
	IV Highland Mountain Artillery Brigade R.G.A. (attached XVI Corps, less Bute Battery attached to XII Corps).
	Nos. 24, 32, 73, 74, 90, 91, 94, 95, 97, 98, 99, 141 Anti-Aircraft Sections R.G.A.
Engineers	420th Field Company, and 37th, 137th, 139th, 140th, 143rd, 286th, and 287th Army Troops Companies, No. 8 Survey Company R.E.

NOTES.—There were two Garrison battalions on the Lines of Communication.

The transport included under G.H.Q. Troops consisted of 32 Mechanical Transport Companies A.S.C., which included those attached to the siege batteries and motor ambulance convoys. Ten further companies—two heavy and eight light—were attached to the Serbian Armies. The horse transport consisted of eight Auxiliary Horse Transport Companies, four Auxiliary Pack Companies, and one Reserve Park; and four Indian Mule Cart Corps units.

In addition to the troops given above, each division had a Signal Company R.E., a Divisional Train (partly wheeled and partly pack), three Field Ambulances, a Sanitary Section, and a Mobile Veterinary Section.

The divisional artillery in every case consisted of three brigades each of two 6-gun 18-pdr. batteries and one 4-gun 4·5-inch howitzer battery, and of one brigade of three 4-gun 18-pdr. batteries—thus each division was armed with 48 18-pdrs. and 12 4·5-inch howitzers.

Each brigade had a Machine-Gun Company, a Light Trench-Mortar Battery (eight 3-inch Stokes guns). The establishment of Lewis guns had just been increased from 20 to 32 per battalion, but it does not appear that all battalions had yet received their extra guns. The Derbyshire Yeomanry had a Machine-gun Section of two guns and also 12 Hotchkiss guns; the weak Corps Cavalry Regiments had no machine guns and only eight Hotchkiss.

There were three 2-inch Medium Trench-Mortar Batteries (not officially numbered by the War Office) and 12 6-inch Medium Newton Trench Mortars, all attached to the XII Corps.

The garrisons of the Ægean islands (see Vol. I, p. 370) had been taken over by the Navy.

APPENDIX 4.

ORDER OF BATTLE
OF THE
BULGARIAN AND GERMAN FORCES IN MACEDONIA, 14TH SEPTEMBER 1918

BULGARIAN GENERAL HEADQUARTERS.

Commander-in-Chief	Prince Boris.
Deputy Commander-in-Chief ..	General Todorov.
Chief of the Staff	Major-General Burmov.

MACEDONIAN ARMY GROUP.

G.O.C.	General v. Scholtz.
Chief of the Staff	Colonel Graf v. Schwerin.

GERMAN ELEVENTH ARMY.

G.O.C. .. .. General v. Steuben.

LXI CORPS.

G.O.C. .. .. Lieut.-General Surén.
 2nd Division [1] :—(10th and 30th Regts.), (28th and 44th Regts.), (21st and 43rd Regts.). Attached :—16th, 53rd, 81st, and 9th (L. of C.) Regts., 12th Saxon Jäger Bn.
 4th Division :—(7th and 31st Regts.), (47th and 48th Regts.).
 302nd Division :—(8th, 9th, 27th, and 69th Regts.), 12th Saxon Res. Jäger Bn.

LXII CORPS.

G.O.C. .. .. Lieut.-General Fleck.
 1st Division :—(1st and 6th Regts.), (25th Regt.), (41st and 42nd Regts.).
 6th Division :—(3rd and 15th Regts.), (51st and 52nd Regts.).
 Composite (Ohrid) Division :—(19th and 82nd Regts.), (36th, 71st, and 72nd Regts.), 2nd Storm Bn., Austro-Hungarian 6th Grenadier-Jäger Bn.
 Detachment of the Lakes [2] :—(35th, 70th, and one Bn. 36th Regts.).
  (Directly under the Eleventh Army.)
 3rd Division :—(11th and 24th Regts.), (29th and 32nd Regts.), (45th and 46th Regts.). Attached :—14th, 49th, 80th, and 87th Regts., one Bn. 18th Regt., 2 Bns. German 12th Landwehr Regt.

BULGARIAN FIRST ARMY.

G.O.C. .. .. Lieut.-General Nerezov.
 5th Division :—(2nd and 5th Regts.), (18th and 20th Regts.), (50th and 83rd Regts.). Attached :—54th and 65th Regts.
 9th Division :—(17th Regt.), (33rd and 34th Regts.), (57th and 58th Regts.).
 Mountain Division :—(67th and 68th Regts.), 39th Regt. and one Bn. 4th Regt.

---

[1] To save space, brigades are not given, but where regiments were placed under a brigade headquarters they are enclosed in brackets.
[2] That is, between Lakes Prespa and Ohrid.

APPENDIX 4 317

1st Macedonian Brigade (from 11th Division) :—60th and 61st Regts.
First Army Troops :—4th and 66th Regts.
Army Group Troops :—75th Regt., German 13th Saxon Res. Jäger, 2/256th, and 2/375th Bns.
(The two Armies above formed part of the Macedonian Army Group ; the two below were directly under Bulgarian G.H.Q.)

BULGARIAN SECOND ARMY.

G.O.C. .. .. Major-General Lukov.
  7th Division :—(13th and 84th Regts.), (22nd and 26th Regts.), Disciplinary Regt.
  8th Division :—(12th and 23rd Regts.), (56th Regt.). Attached :—85th Regt., 8th and 10th Cavalry Regts.
  11th Division :—(59th and 62nd Regts.), (63rd and 64th Regts.). Attached :—4th Cavalry Regt.

BULGARIAN FOURTH ARMY.

G.O.C. .. .. Lieut.-General Toshev.
  10th Division :—(37th and 38th Regts.), (86th Regt.). Attached :—88th Regt., one Bn. Bulgarian 11th Landwehr Regt.
  Ægean Defence Force :—(1st and 10th Bulgarian Landwehr Regts.).
  1st Cavalry Division :—(1st Cavalry Regt.), (5th Cavalry Regt.), (7th Cavalry Regt.).
  2nd Cavalry Division :—(Bulgarian 8th Landwehr Regt., one Bn. Bulgarian 11th Landwehr Regt.), (Guard and 11th Cavalry Regts.).
Fourth Army Troops :—40th Regt., 12th Frontier Bn.

NOTE.—In the above Order of Battle, artillery, pioneers, machine-gun units, and detached cavalry squadrons are omitted, but the totals are given on p. 145. Nor are the composite battalians included. There are also unaccounted for one battalion of the German 12th Landwehr Regiment (perhaps in the train at this date) and one battalion 8th Landwehr Regt. In addition, there were three German Landsturm battalions on the L. of C., which were engaged at Skoplje, and a German battalion formed from depots and L. of C. formations. The German units on the front fill four pages of the German official monograph. They were largely composed of signal units, transport, etc., but included approximately 200 guns, 16 mountain-machine-gun detachments, and four squadrons. There were also five Austro-Hungarian batteries.

The headquarters of the Macedonian Army Group, Eleventh Army, LXI and LXII Corps, and 302nd Division were German formations. It may be added that these two corps headquarters have been shown by means of Roman numerals throughout, for the sake of clarity, but that according to the German custom they have no right to them. They were not strictly speaking " corps headquarters " but " Generalkommandos," that is, temporary formations more nearly corresponding to the French headquarters of " Groupements de Divisions," and are as such shown by means of Arabic numerals by the Germans.

APPENDIX 5.

INSTRUCTIONS FOR THE GENERAL COMMANDING-IN-CHIEF THE ALLIED ARMIES OF THE EAST.

(TRANSLATION.)

Paris,
16th December 1917.

Secret.
État-Major de l'Armée.
Groupe de l'Avant.
3° Bureau A.
No. 12838 BS/3.

I.

Maps 1, 3.   The Allied Armies of the East, placed under the command of General Guillaumat, will be based not only upon Salonika but upon the whole of Greece.

II.

The mission of the Allied Armies is, first, to prevent the enemy from conquering Greece. With this object, they have in the first place to maintain the integrity of the conquered territory from the sea to the Albanian Lakes, while as far as possible remaining in contact with the Italian troops in the region of Valona.

Secondly, should the Allied forces be compelled to yield ground, it will be their duty to continue to deny to the enemy any access to Greece, particularly to the region east of the Pindus, maintaining possession as long as possible of the Entrenched Camp of Salonika and combining their action with that of the Italian forces at Valona.

III.

As soon as our defensive organization has been carried out, or is on its way to completion, the Commander-in-Chief will consider the possibilities of an offensive against the enemy's Armies, according to the conditions of the moment and in the manner which will best serve the interests of the Coalition.

IV.

In making preliminary arrangements for the entry into the field of the Greek Army, the Commander-in-Chief will :—

Decide upon the role to be assigned to this Army, at first in defence and later in the offensive ;

Define its zone of action ;

Make arrangements for it to take over this zone.

In order to obtain the greatest value from it, its independent status must be respected.

V.

It will also be his duty, by precautionary measures taken in agreement with General Ferrero or with the Greek Government, to ensure the protection of the naval base of Corfu, the maintenance of which assures our communications across the Adriatic.

FOCH,
    General,
    Chief of the General Staff.

CLEMENCEAU,
    President of the Council,
    Minister of War.

APPENDIX 5

POINTS TO WHICH THE ATTENTION OF THE GENERAL COMMANDING-IN-CHIEF THE ALLIED ARMIES OF THE EAST IS DIRECTED.

(TRANSLATION.)

Paris,
9th December 1917.

Secret.
État-Major de l'Armée.
Groupe de l'Avant.
3° Bureau A.
No. 12838 bis BS/3.

1. PRESENT SITUATION.

   1. *Allied defensive Organization:* 1st and successive positions. — Outline of defences, strength of obstacles (wire), dugouts, means of communication (telephone, wireless, visual), maps (artillery maps).

   2. *Communications:* Roads. — Outline of track, Possibilities of development, Lorries.

      Railways: Normal gauge and light — Wagons, Locomotives, State of efficiency.

   3. *Proposals for the improvement of the above defensive organization and communications.*

   4. *Condition of the Allied Troops.*

      A. *Higher Formations:*

      Distribution — Troops in line, Troops in reserve.
      Defence Scheme.
      Plans for the reinforcement of positions (battery positions).
      Scheme for the relief and resting of troops,
      Condition of the Serbian and Russian troops.

      B. *Artillery:*

      Distribution — Field Arty. Heavy. Tr. Mortars, etc. — Including artillery in each sector and mobile artillery capable of employment as a reserve.

2. POINTS CONCERNING THE ALLIED ARMIES OF THE EAST.

   It is the duty of the Allied Armies of the East:

   A. *To base themselves not only upon Salonika but upon the whole of Greece.*

   This entails:—
   The preparation of new sea bases (Itea, Piræus, Volos),
   The development of railway communication with Greece,
   The improvement of the road system between Greece and Macedonia,
   The provision of successive supply bases.

B. *To prevent the enemy from conquering Greece*, and with this object, *to maintain the integrity of the conquered territory from the sea to the Albanian Lakes, keeping contact as far as possible with the Italian troops at Valona.*

The execution of this essential duty involves the drawing up of a defence scheme providing for :—

The strengthening of the defensive system (successive positions),

The organization of the front (communications, telephone system),

The reduction to a minimum of the effectives in first line and the formation of reserves as strong as possible and well disposed.

C. *To prepare for the eventual assumption of the offensive.*

Such preparations demand :—

The fixing of the objectives,

An estimate of the means required to attain them (infantry divisions, artillery),

Allotment of tasks to the various Allied forces.

With regard to the employment of the Greek Army, the principles we should adopt would seem to be as follows :—

Its independent status must be respected,

Its zone of operations, which must at first be defensive, should be allotted in accordance with the part to be assigned to this Army in the offensive,

It will no doubt be possible to allow it to operate, when the time comes, in the region where it has interest in doing so ; for this will ensure its good will. Its political interest will probably direct it to the conquest of **Eastern** Macedonia, that is, to Kavalla. To make such action possible, the Roman road in the direction of Vrasta must be repaired ; the Greek Government would do this now if they were requested.

For similar reasons it would no doubt be advisable to concentrate the Greek Army in the region of the Struma, in contact with the British Army.

3. POINTS OF IMPORTANCE REGARDING THE INTERNAL ORGANIZATION OF THE FRENCH FORCES.

Establishment of the French Army of the East as an independent formation by providing it with an Army organization and the necessary services :—

Decentralization of the Salonika Base,

Provision of successive supply depots,

Review of commands throughout the force,

Review of staffs.

4. POINTS REGARDING THE ITALIAN TROOPS.

The Commander-in-Chief will, in conjunction with the commander of the Italian 35th Division, examine the conditions in which that formation can be placed on the extreme left of the line of the Allied Armies of the East, in accordance with the demand put forward by the Comando Supremo.

It must be understood that in its new position the Italian 35th Division will remain under the orders of the Commander-in-Chief.

5. POINTS REGARDING THE RUSSIAN CONTINGENT.
      It will be for the Commander-in-Chief to decide at what moment the Russian division shall be withdrawn from the Macedonian front, if circumstances demand. The method of disposing of these troops will, in case of need, be communicated to him by the Government.

16/12/17.[1]
                                              FOCH.

APPENDIX 6.

THE PRESIDENT OF THE COUNCIL, MINISTER OF WAR, TO THE GENERAL COMMANDING-IN-CHIEF THE ALLIED ARMIES OF THE EAST.

(TRANSLATION.)

État-Major de l'Armée.   Paris,
3⁹ Bureau A.   23rd June 1918.
No. 9565 BS/5.

      The enemy is now striving with all the means at his disposal to obtain a decision on the Franco-British front. It therefore behoves the Allied Armies in the outer theatres and especially on the Eastern Front to assume a definitely aggressive attitude.

THE PRESENT SITUATION IN MACEDONIA IS PARTICULARLY FAVOURABLE TO OFFENSIVE ACTIVITY.

      The military power of the Allied Armies is now reaching its maximum.
      Germany, who has concentrated all her resources in France, can hardly support the Bulgarian Army, which, left to itself as a result of the withdrawal of the German troops, is suffering from a moral crisis which obviously diminishes its capacity for resistance. The internal situation of Bulgaria is, into the bargain, such that an Allied military success may bring about serious political repercussions.
      In the present situation, the Allied Armies of Macedonia have, therefore, for the moment liberty of action which permits them to impose their will upon the enemy.

IT IS NECESSARY TO EXPLOIT WITHOUT DELAY THIS FAVOURABLE SITUATION.

      If Germany does not obtain before the autumn a decision on the Western Front, she will have breathing space to transfer a portion of her effort to Macedonia, in order to settle affairs in the East. The best means of assuring ourselves against the possibility of such an attack are to forestall it by attacking ourselves.

---

[1] The date at the foot is doubtless that of the signature, which would not be appended till the general instructions had been signed by M. Clemenceau.

APPENDIX 6

THE OBJECT TO BE AIMED AT IN THE OFFENSIVE ACTION OF THE ALLIED ARMIES OF THE EAST must be to break through the Bulgarian system of defence, in order to force the enemy to make an important withdrawal, such as will open to the Serbian and Greek Armies access to their lost territories.

This result cannot be attained except by a general and combined action by all the forces constituting the Allied Armies of the East.

Nevertheless, such a general action cannot be contemplated immediately: the comparatively slender resources in artillery and aviation at the disposal of the Allied Armies of the East limit correspondingly the extent of the fronts on which attacks with the object of breaking through can be conducted simultaneously.

Moreover, the choice of possible zones of action is for the moment restricted by reason of the climate, which during the hot season is unfavourable to the development of major operations in the marshy regions of the low plains and of the valleys.

These two factors make it necessary for the general offensive to be preceded by a series of local offensives

spread out over a period of time;
conducted with growing intensity in accordance with a comprehensive plan, with objectives destined to prepare and to facilitate the final decisive action, which will set the crown upon them.

These local actions might well be carried out in the sector of the Serbian Army and in that which will be entrusted to the Greek Army, in order to respond to their aspirations as well as to exalt their morale and perfect their fighting value.

To SUM UP, the Allied Armies of the East must, despite the severity of the hot weather, continue the series of operations begun happily at the Skra di Legen and in eastern Albania, and by successive efforts of increasing scope bring about progressively the dislocation of the enemy's front. They will thus render possible the launch of a general offensive, which must be carried out before the autumn and from which we are entitled to hope for considerable results.

It was with these ideas that General Guillaumat, before returning to France, broadening the scheme of his earlier projects in accordance with the new possibilities, set on foot the preparation of offensive operations by the Allied Armies of the East.

You will not fail to see that the need for avoiding any loss of time demands that we should push forward the realization of this general plan without delay.

I ask you in consequence, and in the higher interests of the Coalition, to be good enough to apply all your energies to the fulfilment of the programme outlined above, and to let me know as soon as possible what decisions you have reached as to bringing it into effect.

CLEMENCEAU.

APPENDIX 7.

GENERAL FRANCHET D'ESPÉREY, G.C.M.G., G.C.V.O., COMMANDER-IN-CHIEF, ALLIED ARMIES,

TO

GENERAL MILNE, K.C.B., D.S.O., COMMANDER-IN-CHIEF, BRITISH ARMY.

(TRANSLATION.)

Secret.
Commandement en Chef
 des Armées Alliées.
État-Major Général.
3ᵉ Bureau.
No. 4602/3.

Q.G.A.A.,
24th July 1918.

I have the honour to address to you my instructions concerning **Maps A, 4, 5.** the participation of the British Army in the general offensive to be carried out by the Allied Armies on the Eastern Front before the autumn.

This general offensive is to be undertaken in the broader interests of the Coalition and also in the interests of the Army of the East.

Its execution will be facilitated by the obvious moral crisis existing in the Bulgarian Army and people, whom the Germans, deeply engaged on the Western Front, can no longer support with swift and effective aid.

This favourable situation must be exploited without delay; for if Germany does not obtain a decision before the autumn on the Western Front she will be free to transfer a proportion of her effort to Macedonia in order to settle affairs in the East. The best means of assuring ourselves against the possibility of such an attack are to forestall it by attacking ourselves.

The object to be aimed at in our offensive action must be to break through the Bulgarian system of defence.

This result cannot be attained except by *a general and combined action* by all the forces constituting the Allied Armies of the East.

In this general action, the broad lines of which I have had the honour to explain to you verbally, the rôle of the British Army will be the following:

Deprive the Bulgarian First Army of all freedom of manœuvre by attacking it, pin it down by fighting, and take advantage of the perturbation caused by the operations against other parts of the enemy's front so as to change into a rout any inclination to retire, and drive back his beaten troops beyond the Belašica Planina so as to assure for our use in future operations the Vardar valley communications (rail and roads), the importance of which is capital.

The methods employed will be the following:

1. *During the period of preparation* for the attacks (that is to say, from the 15th August):

On the whole front west of Lake Dojran maintain lively artillery activity, so as to disquiet the enemy and retain on this part of the front the large quantity of Bulgarian artillery which is there at present. These demonstrations are to have the effect of keeping the enemy's attention on this point, in order to enhance the effects of surprise on other parts of the front.

On the whole front held by the British Army take measures to harass the enemy from the moment at which the offensive actions begin, and prevent him from carrying out an undisturbed retirement; be prepared to carry out a rapid pursuit if need be. For this purpose it is necessary that the extension and restoration of communications beyond the front line should be studied and that the necessary material should be held in readiness.

2. *After the launch of the attacks on other parts of the Eastern Front*, and when these have made a certain progress:

Attack with determination the enemy's positions east of the Vardar, so as to drive back the Bulgarian forces and cut their communication with Strumica, taking all measures to ensure that the phase of exploitation shall follow immediately the rupture of the enemy's front.

In order to attain this result, the first objective should be the " P " Ridge and the neighbouring heights west of Lake Dojran, the possession of which is of the highest importance to the enemy in this region.

It appears that the best means of capturing the " P " Ridge will be a heavy frontal attack, *with artillery preparation*, west of the lake, by two divisions (one British and one Greek), combined with a *surprise* flank attack,[1] *without artillery preparation*, by one Greek division, on that part of the enemy's front extending from the Belašica Planina to Lake Dojran (north of the lake).

The *means* at the disposal of the British Army, in addition to its own resources, will be:

Two Greek Divisions;
One group of three Greek 6-inch batteries;
The armoured train of 19-cm. (two guns).

These troops will be placed at your disposal in good time.

This general offensive must be brought to an end before the coming of the cold weather, owing to the difficulties of communication in winter.

I have therefore the honour to request you to be so good as to undertake vigorously from now onward, despite the severity of the hot weather, the study and preparation of the operation entrusted to the British Army, so that it can be launched at the beginning of the last fortnight of September.

I should be obliged if you would furnish me with the plans drawn up with this object.

We must—and here I am sure that you will agree with me—convince those who have to carry out our orders that, if the present situation on the Eastern Front justifies hopes which it would have been vain to conceive a year ago, the success of the offensive is none the less dependent upon speed in preparation and vigour in execution.

On your left the 1st Group of Divisions will be prepared to combine its action with yours in order to prevent the enemy from giving us the slip. Instructions, which I will forward to you, to this effect will be given to it.

FRANCHET D'ESPÉREY.

---

[1] *Attaque à revers* in the original.

APPENDIX 8.

TELEGRAM FROM GENERAL MILNE TO WAR OFFICE

Troopers, London.
G.C. 306 cipher.
25th July 1918.

Reference your 61932 cipher D.M.O. July 10th. I have today received instructions from the Allied Commander-in-Chief to make preparations for a serious offensive operation with my force during the 2nd half of September. This offensive action on my front will entail the use of at least 3 British divisions and I am to be given 2 Greek divisions to assist. It is, however, to follow and to be conditional on attacks in other parts of this theatre and also will depend to some extent on the state of the Bulgar Army and on events elsewhere. This action on the part of my force will be likely to be successful only if you are prepared to bring us up to fighting pitch by sending the necessary reinforcements and ammunition by the date mentioned. I should be glad to know how I stand as regards this operation having regard to the last sentence in the wire from Proemial No. 27875 cipher dated 13th January 1917,[1] and also to what extent the deficiencies of this force in personnel and munitions are likely to be made good in the time. Taking all things into consideration it seems to be sound and right that we in this theatre should be prepared to take advantage of the situation which might present itself this autumn, as I pointed out in my G.C.291 cipher dated July 22nd.[2] Chief, Britforce.

APPENDIX 9.

TELEGRAM FROM WAR OFFICE TO GENERAL MILNE

G.O.C.-in-C., G.H.Q., Salonika.
63181 cipher D.M.O.
11 p.m. 27-7-18.

Your G.C. 306 dated 25th July. It is my opinion that unless an offensive on your front is likely to produce military results of a far-reaching kind it would not achieve any useful political purpose, whilst a failure, or only partial success, would encourage the Bulgars and relieve the Germans of a considerable source of anxiety. It is essential, to produce the required results, that the offensive should take place at a time when Germany cannot with safety detach troops from the Western Front,

---

[1] The sentence referred to enjoined General Milne to refer the question to the War Office if he thought it desirable to take part in operations other than those at that time agreed to by the Allied Governments.

[2] See p. 108.

otherwise the enemy's interior lines will enable him to reinforce more rapidly and neutralize our efforts. In September this essential condition will not exist and conditions will not be favourable for an offensive in the Balkans before the spring of 1919. It is in the spring too that our troops are at their fittest and have recovered from the effects of malaria, which during the autumn incapacitates a large proportion. The above objections, of course, do not apply to the exploitation of any change which may occur before that time in the political situation in the Balkans.

I cannot hold out any hope under the existing circumstances that reinforcements and ammunition in excess of the usual allotment will be available this autumn.

APPENDIX 10.

GENERAL FRANCHET D'ESPÉREY, G.C.M.G., G.C.V.O., COMMANDER-IN-CHIEF, ALLIED ARMIES,

TO

GENERAL MILNE, K.C.B., D.S.O., COMMANDER-IN-CHIEF, BRITISH ARMY.

(Translation.)

Rigoureusement secret.
Commandement en Chef des Armées Alliées.
État-Major Général.
3ᵉ Bureau.
No. 4725/3.

Q.G.A.A.
4th August 1918.

Maps A, 4   I have the honour to communicate to you, for your information, an extract from the instructions which have been given to the 1st Group of Divisions for its participation in the operations envisaged in my letter No. 4602/3 of the 25th July (actually dated 24th):

" The rôle of the 1st Group in the general offensive will be the
" following :—
   " 1. *During the period of preparation for the attacks.*—On the whole
" front east of Lunzi maintain such activity as will disquiet the enemy
" and retain on this part of the front, which is always a tender spot in
" the estimation of the Bulgarians (particularly in front of the Skra
" sector) the considerable infantry and artillery effectives which are
" there at present. These demonstrations are to be carried out in order
" to enhance the effects of surprise on other parts of the front.
   " 2. *At the moment of the launch of the attacks.*—On the whole front
" harass the enemy to prevent him from moving his reserves and keep
" him under the threat of an attack ;
   " Be prepared to carry out a rapid pursuit should the enemy attempt
" to slip away ; prepare in advance with this end in view the extension
" and restoration of communications beyond the front.
   " 3. *When the progress of the attacks threatening the enemy's com-*
" *munications begins to shake him.*—Deliver a sudden attack in the general
" direction of Huma, Kojnska, Miletkovo, Davidovo ; if the enemy
" gives way, begin exploitation at once and drive him, *l'épee dans les*

" *reins*, to the Vardar, so as to prevent him from crossing it; establish
" touch with the English and Serbian forces.
" This attack will be launched on the order of the General Com-
" manding-in-Chief. It will be carried out with all the means at the
" disposal of the 1st Group."

Further, in continuation of the letter cited, I have the honour to inform you that the Greek divisions at your disposal for the operations will be:
1. The Crete Division (3 Regiments), which is to be available on the 20th August in the rearward zone of the 1st Group.
2. The Seres Division (3 Regiments), which is to be available about the 1st September in the same rearward zone.

As regards the Crete Division, I request you to be good enough to get into direct communication with the General commanding the 1st Group in order to arrange its move into the British zone from the 20th August.

As to the Seres Division, details will be sent to you later.

In both cases I consider it absolutely necessary not to inform these Greek divisions of their destination until the latest possible moment.

By Order, the Chief of the Staff,

CH. CHARPY.

APPENDIX 11.

GENERAL INSTRUCTIONS

FOR

THE EXPLOITATION

(TRANSLATION.)

Rigoureusement secret.
Commandement en Chef des Armées Alliées.
État-Major Général.
3º Bureau.
No. 4949/3.
Map, 1/200,000.

Q.G.A.A.
31st August 1918.

The general offensive which is to be carried out shortly by the Allied **Maps 4, 6.** Armies of the East is unlikely to bear all its fruit unless, after the period of the rupture of the enemy's front, exploitation of the success is undertaken without delay.

In this instruction the general directives for this exploitation are given; its object is to co-ordinate the efforts of the Armies. All executants, down to Divisional Commanders, should be made acquainted with the General Plan in so far as it concerns them. But complete copies of this instruction must not go below Armies.

A. THE MANŒUVRE TO BE CARRIED OUT.

The general offensive has for goal the rupture of the enemy's front and the break-up of the Bulgarian Armies with a view to obtaining a decisive success.

(a) A main central attack conducted by the Franco-Serbian forces. These Franco-Serbians will drive back the Bulgarian *2nd* and *3rd Divisions*, and march as soon as possible on the region Negotino–Kavadarci, so as to cut the Bulgarian Armies in two.

(b) When this central attack has made progress and when it constitutes a threat to the line of communication of the Vardar, Anglo-Franco-Greek forces will attack the Bulgarian *First Army* east of the Vardar in order to prevent it from re-establishing itself and to free the line of communication of the Vardar, which is of the highest importance.

This attack of the right flank and the central attack will be connected by the 1st Group of Divisions.

(c) The advance of the central attack will then make possible a combined attack conducted by part of its troops and by the A.F.O. in the direction of Prilep, and the development of our success to westward and northward as far as the region of Üsküb (Skoplje).

The operations outlined shortly in paras. (a), (b), and (c) above will then be completed on the right by an operation carried out in co-operation by part of the British forces and formations of the Greek Army, with the object of bringing about the fall of the defences on the Belašica Planina and putting the Rupel Pass into our hands. In addition, as circumstances dictate, an operation may be carried out by the Greek Army on the middle and lower Struma with the object of disorganizing the Bulgarian forces on this part of the front and of covering the right of the general array of the Allied Armies.

This series of operations will constitute the *First Phase* of our offensive.

In this First Phase, the development of which will be discussed below in greater detail, we are aiming above all at the destruction of the organized forces of the enemy; we are covering ourselves against an eventual reaction on the part of the enemy (more especially by way of the Vardar valley); and we are seeking to provide ourselves with a base, served by good communications with the rear, with a view to the execution of the *Second Phase* of our operations.

At the end of the First Phase the dispositions should be as follows:—

1. *A.F.O.*
   Main Body:—Üsküb (Skoplje) area.
   Advanced Guard:—Kumanova area, watching the approaches to Niš and Kyustendil.
   Flank Detachment—Kačanik and Kalkandelen (Tetovo).

2. *Serbian Armies.*
   Main Body:—Veles-Štip area.
   Advanced Guards on the roads towards Sofia: the Kočana road and the track leading *via* Kliseli to the road from Egri Palanka and Kyustendil.

3. *British Army.*
   Main Body:—Strumica valley.
   Advanced Guard on the road to Berovo.

4. *Greek Army.*
   Main Body:—Demir Hisar, Rupel, Petrić area.
   Advanced Guards on the Livunovo–Jum'aja and Nevrokop roads.

5. *1st Group of Divisions.*
   Main Body:—In the Hudova–Demir Kapija region, holding the crest of the Blaguša and Gradec Planina (in touch with the Serbians and British).
   Advanced Guard pushed forward in the upper valley of the Strumica on Radovišta.

NOTE.—As soon as circumstances permit, the 1st Group of Divisions will be gradually withdrawn from the front by the extension of the British and Serbian fronts, and will constitute the *General Reserve of the C.-in.-C.* This general reserve will comprise three French divisions—the 16th and 17th Colonial and the 122nd. It will be disposed in depth in the area Gradsko–Negotino–Demir Kapija–Hudova.

A map, 1/200,000, is enclosed indicating the general dispositions which should be assumed at the end of the First Phase (prior to the disposal in general reserve of the 1st Group of Divisions) and the zones of action laid down for the Armies.

The use by certain Armies of means of communication within the zone of another Army will be regulated at the proper time.

In the *Second Phase*, we are unlikely to find ourselves faced by considerable organized forces on large fronts; the resistance of an enemy whose morale will have been gravely weakened will probably be met with only in patches, and supported by weak artillery.

It is therefore likely, even if the Germans intervene, that we shall be able to impose our will on the enemy more easily than in the First Phase, on condition that our operations are co-ordinated and that our system of communication with the rear functions normally.

We have therefore the right to set ourselves at this moment distant and audacious objectives, which will be the enemy's vital points.

The development of the First Phase will be discussed below; as regards the Second Phase, further instructions will lay down in good time its objectives and the conditions under which it will be carried out.

IMPORTANT NOTE.—Between these two phases, which are separated here merely for convenience, there should in reality be no check in continuity. In no Army, in fact, should these instructions be taken as limiting endeavour, should a favourable opportunity present itself; the efforts of all should be in the direction of developing the success, always, however, in co-operation with their neighbours.

B. FIRST PHASE.

I. *Missions of the Groups.*

1. *Central Franco-Serbian Group under the command of the Voivode Mišić.*

Serbian Second Army.—After the period of the break-through, the two pursuit divisions, the Yugoslav and Timok, preceded by light detachments, will be pushed forward as early as possible, the former in the direction of Kavadarci and Negotino, the latter in that of Demir Kapija, to cut the Vardar line of communication.

Two main routes, practicable for motor traffic, will provide their communications, that is :—

Yugoslav : Rožden, Mrežećko, Dubnista, Kavadarci.
Timok : Topolec Pass, Konopista, Bunarce, Demir Kapija.
These two divisions will be followed and supported by :—
Yugoslav, by the 17th Colonial Division.
Timok, by the Šumadija.

The 122nd Division will not be required for the time being and will pass into general reserve, at the disposal of the Commander-in-Chief of the Allied Armies.

During this phase of the battle, the pursuit divisions should press in boldly like a wedge into the heart of the enemy's position, covering their flanks by detachments to be relieved automatically by the supporting divisions. All the executants should be imbued with the idea that on the speed of the advance depends the success of the offensive of the Allied Armies and that this speed is the best insurance against surprise; for it will spread disorganization in the enemy's ranks and so allow us to dare all. The advance must therefore be pressed without respite, *to the extreme limit of endurance* of men and horses and making use of every means to break down such resistance as may be encountered.

On arrival at the confluence of the Crna and the Vardar, the bridges are to be seized so as to prepare for a subsequent resumption of movement and to free the railway. The breach should be enlarged by lateral thrusts, in order to allow the neighbouring Groups to make progress.

Serbian First Army.—This Army, which will support the left of the advance of the Second Army, must as soon as possible seize the bridges over the Crna (Rasim Bey, Vrbečko, and further north), and form bridgeheads beyond the river.

Later, it will combine its efforts with those of the A.F.O. to enlarge the breach made in the enemy's position.

For this purpose, it will attack in the direction of Prilep–Bela Vodica (widening its front in the direction of Trojaci and Drenovon) in touch with the A.F.O.

The Commander-in-Chief will, at the proper time, assure the synchronization of the attacks destined to clear the Prilep area.

2. *Right Anglo-Franco-Greek Group under the orders of General Milne.*

Its attacks will be launched on the order of the Commander-in-Chief when the advance of the central attack has shaken the Bulgarian *First Army*.

As soon as the breach is made it must be enlarged by lateral thrusts to right and left. Forces held in reserve for the pursuit must be pushed rapidly forward, but the right flank must be carefully watched towards the Belašica Planina.

A vigorous pursuit will allow us to obtain here considerable tactical results against the troops of the Bulgarian *9th* and *5th Divisions*, whose natural line of communication (the Vardar valley) will be threatened by the Serbian advance and whose retreat can be conducted only by the Strumica defile ; all efforts should therefore have the object of cutting their retreat in this direction and then of driving back beyond the chain of the Belašica Planina such elements as have escaped, so as to free the Vardar Railway, which is of the highest importance.

The British 27th Division will simultaneously grapple with the enemy in the direction of Gevgeli and Pardovica, maintaining touch on its left with the 1st Group of Divisions. As soon as the forward movement of the formations of this group has approached the Vardar, the 27th Division will rejoin the main body of the British forces on the left bank of the river, the 1st Group alone operating on the right bank.

3. *1st Group of Divisions.*

The sector of this Group stretches across the tumbled *massif* of Gandash-Dzena, one detachment (of the strength of a division) west of the watershed, in the plain of the Moglenitsa, two divisions to the east of it. This situation determines the rôle of the elements of the 1st Group.

(i) Left Division (between the Bistritsa and the Suchitsa : see 1/50,000 Map).

Mission : To support the right of the Šumadija Division during the period of the break-through and the Timok Division during the first part of the period of exploitation.[1]

With this object :

(a) When the Šumadija Division begins its descent to the ravine of the Poröi, it will act in the direction of Zborsko and the Preslap in such a way as to pin down the enemy's forces on this side and deny to them the free use of the only route which crosses the line of the crests between the upper basins of the Poröi and of the Belitsa.

---

[1] With this end in view there will be close liaison between the headquarters of the detachment and the Šumadija and Timok Divisions.

(b) Proceed to clear the upper valleys of these rivers.

(c) Establish touch with the Serbian pursuit division towards the Studenavoda and the Col of Golubac.

(d) Later, cover the right flank of the Serbian advance by means of small detachments operating on the high *massif* Kojuh-Dzena.

(ii) Right Divisions.

Their attack in the direction of Miletkovo, Davidovo, will be launched, either on the initiative of the General Officer Commanding the 1st Group, if signs of a withdrawal are noticed, or on the order of the Commander-in-Chief, after the attacks east of the Vardar.

The pursuit will be directed on Davidovo-Hudova, in touch with the British Group, in such a way as to gain possession of the crest of the Blaguša and Gradec Planina, which are indispensable to us if we are to make use of the Vardar Railway.

At Demir Kapija touch will be gained with the Serbian Group.

The repair of the roads in the Vardar valley will be carried out as early as possible by the 1st Group of Divisions; the repair of the railway will be the task of the *Direction de l'Arrière*.[1]

4. *Armée Française d'Orient*.

Its attacks will be launched :

Either on the order of the General Officer Commanding the A.F.O., if a withdrawal on the part of the enemy is anticipated,

or on the order of the Commander-in-Chief, in conjunction with a movement towards the north-west by the Serbian First Army (see below).

They will set the seal upon the success and will afford us subsequent opportunities for manœuvre.

With this object :

The A.F.O. will in the first instance operate in the general direction of Prilep, in touch with the Serbian First Army, so as to break the enemy array west of the Crna, or at least force him to retreat.

At this stage, developing its action, the A.F.O. will take as its objective the important road junction of Kičevo, so as to manœuvre out of position the Bulgarian forces still in the region of the lakes.

Then, becoming the marching wing of the Allied array, the A.F.O. will continue its movement, its left thrown forward, so as to attain at the end of the First Phase the line Veles–Üskūb (Skoplje).

The outflanking movement on Üskūb *via* Kalkandelen (Tetovo) should press forward rapidly. At the same time a strong detachment, in co-operation with the 3rd Group of Divisions, will clear the region of the lakes and form on our left flank a solid obstacle against any possible reactions by the enemy from Albania.

The success of this manœuvre on the part of the A.F.O. is of extreme importance, because it will permit us to cover our flank to northward at dangerous points and provide us with a solid and sufficiently developed base for the Second Phase of the operations.

The provisional detachment of the A.F.O. (a division in strength) which is in line on the right bank of the Crna will have a special mission in the early stages. Conforming to the movement of the Serbian First Army and operating in echelon in rear of its left, it will move in the general direction of Razim Bey, so as to complete the clearance of the right bank of the Crna and cover the left of the attack.

Close liaison must for this purpose be established between the headquarters of this detachment and the Serbian First Army.

5. *Cavalry*.

The French and Serbian Divisions will be assembled at the moment when the attacks are launched, the former south of Monastir, the latter

---

[1] A rough British equivalent would be " Headquarters, Lines of Communication." (Compiler's note.)

in the region of Voshtaran. Their subsequent employment will be determined by the lie of the ground.

(a) In the First Phase they will, as a rule, be united under one command [1] and attached to the A.F.O., for employment in pursuit in the plain of Prilep after the period of the break-through.

(b) Action by large formations of cavalry being impossible among the *massifs* of the mountainous area between Lake Prespa and Kalkandelen (Tetovo), the best policy will then be to despatch the bulk of the cavalry to the Stip area (very suitable for cavalry) to cover the general array of the Armies and establish contact with the enemy forces either towards the north or towards the east.

6. *Greek Army.*

The operations of the Greek Army will be dealt with in special instructions. The various formations of this Army will be employed in the following manner:

(a) The 3rd Division will be attached to the A.F.O.

(b) After the 1st Group of Divisions has come into general reserve, the Archipelago Division will rejoin the Corps of National Defence and the 4th Division the main body of the Greek Army.

(c) The Corps of National Defence will be attached to the British Army. In the early stages its Corps Troops and the Archipelago Division will be at the disposal of the 1st Group of Divisions. After this Group has come into general reserve, the Corps Troops and the Archipelago Division will rejoin their Corps.

(d) The main body of the Greek Army will comprise the I Corps and the II Corps (less the 3rd Division), to which the 4th Division will subsequently be added (see para. (b)).

C. DISPOSITIONS OF THE ARMIES.

1. Experience on all fronts proves that early tactical successes are always developed too late, because the reserves are too distant.[2]

The dispositions assumed by the Armies before becoming committed to the attack should therefore be such as to ensure that the advance "takes off" without delay; while certain reserves will make thrusts to right and left to enlarge the breaches and increase the booty, others must press forward resolutely.

It must never be forgotten that, owing to the mountainous nature of the country and the shortage in horses in the Bulgarian Army, the Bulgarian batteries cannot be withdrawn and will fall into our hands if we threaten the communications; and that, on the other hand, such threats to the communications will seriously weaken the morale of troops fighting on a front divided into compartments.

2. With a view to future operations, reserves must be reconstituted at each stage whenever possible. This is the sole means by which commanders can influence the course of the battle.

3. Keep subordinates well informed of your intentions and of the situation, and urge them always to display initiative and the spirit of co-operation. In a general action such as we are about to undertake against an enemy whose morale is already shaken in certain formations, there can never be too much boldness from the moment when the front has been broken.

---

[1] The Serbian Army will, however, if necessary have a call upon one regiment of the Serbian Cavalry Division for employment on its front from the beginning of the pursuit.

[2] Here, owing to the comparative weakness of the enemy in artillery, reserves can be closed up without risk.

In mountain warfare, above all, small detachments boldly and skilfully handled may obtain great results.

March in several columns so as to outflank the enemy directly one column meets with resistance. Each column should be covered by an advanced guard and should keep touch with the neighbouring columns. Watch your flanks and your rear.

4. All possible measures must be taken before the attacks to facilitate supply: advanced dumps, improvement of communications, assembly of personnel and material for road-making, etc.

The *Direction de l'Arrière* is responsible for putting into working order the permanent way to Üsküb (Skoplje) on account of its particular importance.

The British Army is responsible for putting into working order the line from Salonika to Demir Hisar.

GENERAL FRANCHET D'ESPÉREY.

The Chief of the General Staff,
CH. CHARPY.

APPENDIX 12.

XII CORPS INSTRUCTIONS

FOR THE

PREPARATIONS FOR ATTACK.

Secret.
G/8/497.
Reference 1/20,000, Dojran 3A.

Yanesh,
7th September 1918.

These instructions supersede those contained in XII Corps No. **Map 5.** G/8/425, dated 16th August (as amended by XII Corps No. G/8/451, **Sketch 8.** dated 19th August) and XII Corps No. G/8/360, dated 3rd August, which are accordingly cancelled.

I. *Intention.*

The attack will depend upon, and form part of, larger offensive operations in this theatre, the immediate military object of which is to break through the Bulgar defences.

II. *Situation.*

Owing to the present very favourable situation of the Allies on the Western front, to the disturbed political situation within Bulgaria, and the low morale of the Bulgar Army, the greatest confidence is justified in the thorough success of the Allied operations on the Macedonian front in general and of the attack by the XII Corps in particular.

III. *General Principles.*

(1) All ranks, especially officers, must be infected with this spirit of complete confidence by every means possible. It should inspire the whole operation and the training for it.

(2) Surprise—rapidity of movement—determination not to be checked—these will form the basis of the attack.

(3) Having in view the situation given above, the greatest boldness will be admissible in driving home and exploiting initial successes, though the necessary consolidation of the main objectives must not be thereby interfered with.

(4) Preparations for the warfare of movement, which will result from a thorough "break through" of the enemy's defences, will now be commenced throughout the Corps, care being taken that these do not reveal our intentions.

IV. *Secrecy.*

The greatest care and ingenuity will be exercised by all ranks, not only to preserve secrecy (which is vital to the success of the attack), as to the real objectives and the troops to be employed, but also to deceive those who need not know the truth.

V. *Ruses.*

Both the 22nd Division and a Greek Division attached to the XII Corps for this attack will be situated in training camps within one day's march of the forward area until a very short period prior to the attack.

As surprise is so important, and as (even with the minor operations which are being carried out on the XII Corps front, with the object of misleading the enemy) it is almost impossible to prevent him knowing that a major operation is projected at some point on this front, the arrangement of visual ruses to deceive as to the true front of attack will be undertaken by all three British Divisions on the following lines.

To prevent the enemy knowing when or to what portion of our front the two divisions in training move, the extra camps which will be necessary for the Greek Division in the forward area will be pitched as early as possible, and these, and the camps vacated by the 22nd Division, when they go to their training camps, will be left standing. The 26th and 27th Divisions will similarly pitch dummy camps to more than counter-balance the above. (They will be informed by the 22nd Division as to the amount of extra canvas which is being pitched for the Greek Division.)

When the time comes for the Divisions in training to move to the camps already prepared for them in the forward area they will do so in one night, leaving their training camps standing until after the attack.

Divisional Commanders will, in consultation, arrange for any other ruses which may suggest themselves, to the same end.

VI. *Main Attack.*

(1) *Objective.*—The object of the main attack is to gain possession of the "P" Ridge and neighbouring high ground, and to exploit this success by all available means.

(2) *Enemy's organization for defence.*—The defensive organization of the enemy on the front of attack consists of three continuous systems of defence.

(i) *An advanced line* extending from the Lake about 600 yards south of Dojran Town through the Petit Couronné–O.6–Sugar Loaf–P. 4¼.

(ii) *An intermediate line* from the Lake to a point about a kilometre north of Dojran Town through the Orb–the Hilt–the Tongue–P. 4.

(iii) *A main line* from the Lake shore at a point east of Piton Chauve –East Bastion–Black Hill–Grand Couronné–P. 3–Dolina.

In rear of this main line there are certain fortified localities, notably Piton Chauve, Koh-i-Noor and P. 2.

NOTE.—For the purposes of identification the enemy trenches have been lettered and numbered as shown on a map, 1/10,000, which will be issued shortly, and the above lines of defence will accordingly be referred to as follows:—

    (i) The Advanced line .. .. The X Z line.
    (ii) The Intermediate line .. .. .. The W D line.
    (iii) The Main line .. .. The T line.

In addition to the above, certain localities have been fortified by the enemy between the Advanced and Intermediate lines, notably Hill 340 and Dojran Hill.

(3) *Enemy dispositions.*—The dispositions of the enemy between Lake Dojran and the river Vardar, as far as known, are described in an accompanying memorandum.

(4) *Troops available.*—The troops available for the attack are:—

    The 22nd Division.
    The Greek (Seres) Division.
    The 83rd Infantry Brigade (less two Battalions).
    The 2me bis (French) Regiment of Zouaves.
    The XII Corps Cavalry Regiment.

The artillery available to support the attack is as follows:—

Mountain guns—2·75-inch		4	
,, ,, (Greek) 65-mm.		4	
,, ,, (Greek) 75-mm.		12	= 20
18-pdrs. from 22nd Div.		48	
,, ,, 26th Div.		22	
,, ,, 27th Div.		24	= 94
4·5-inch Howitzers		36	= 36
6-inch ,, 26 cwt.		32	
6 ,, ,, 30 ,,		4	= 36
8-inch Howitzers		4	= 4
60-pdrs.		36	= 36
6-inch Mk. VII		1	
6 ,, Mk. XI		2	
19-cm. Railway mountings		2	= 5
Total			231
Medium Trench Mortars			24

(5) *Plan of Attack.*—The general plan of attack is as follows:—

The 22nd Division with one regiment of the Seres Division attached will advance, generally speaking, from the area Hill 380, P. 4¼, Horseshoe, Berks Hill, and attack the enemy's position " P " Ridge, Grand Couronné, inclusive. This will be termed the Left Attack.

Simultaneously with this attack the Seres Division, less one regiment, supported by the 83rd Infantry Brigade (less two battalions) will advance from B Sector front line trenches and Rocky Knob, and attack in a north-westerly direction, their objective being the line Dojran Hill—Hill 340, which will be consolidated. From here an advance will be made against the enemy's works on The Orb, and an attack delivered against the Grand Couronné in conjunction with the Left Attack. This will be termed the Right Attack.

At the same time, between the Right and Left Attacks, a demonstration will be carried out from the trenches of C Sector, against the enemy's trenches from O.4 to O.5½, by the 83rd Infantry Brigade.

Meanwhile troops of the 26th Division which will be holding the portion of the Corps front from the Horseshoe exclusive, to the Vardar, in order to support the left flank of the Main Attack, will simultaneously make a subsidiary attack against the enemy's advanced works on the line Emerald Hill–Ruby Hill–Flat Iron Hill, which will be consolidated.

The 2me bis Regiment of Zouaves and the XII Corps Cavalry Regiment will be in Corps Reserve.

(6) *Artillery action.*—In order to obtain the advantage of surprise, artillery action previous to the attack will be limited to as short a period as possible. It will consist of two days devoted to wire-cutting and registration, and the following night, namely, that previous to the attack, devoted to bombardment of selected areas and neutralization of artillery by special shell. In addition harassing fire, by long range guns, will be directed during the night against the enemy's communications.

For two hours previous to the attack harassing fire will be directed upon the enemy's front trenches to drown any sound of our troops in positions of assembly.

At Z hours our barrage will be brought down upon the enemy's front-line trench system, and will advance in accordance with a plan which will be prepared by the G.O.C. R.A. XII Corps. Howitzers will bombard selected points of attack and will lift to more distant objectives, finally forming a protective barrage for consolidation.

Black Hill, on the right flank of the Right Attack, will be masked with smoke barrage.

The left flank of the Left Attack will be secured by artillery fire if threatened.

Meanwhile, as soon as light permits, the enemy's Divisional Headquarters at Furka will be bombarded.

The hostile artillery will be neutralized by counter-battery groups.

The organization and distribution of the artillery for the above tasks will be described in the XII Corps Artillery Plan which will be issued shortly.

(7) *Action by the Royal Air Force.*—In addition to artillery work the Royal Air Force will provide infantry contact patrols, and machines for bombing and harassing with machine guns any enemy on the move behind the front, also a flight for harassing more distant targets, and reconnaissance.

VII. *Boundaries.*

The boundary between the Seres Division and the 22nd Division will be: –Volovec Village inclusive to the Seres Division–the summit of the Grand Couronné–The Orb inclusive to the Seres Division, Mansion Ravine to where the Krastali–Dojran Road crosses it, inclusive to the Seres Division, Dagger Ravine inclusive to the 22nd Division, Jumeaux Ravine (between Dagger and Hand Ravines) inclusive to the Seres Division, Hand Ravine No. 2 till it cuts our trench system, inclusive to 22nd Division, our front line trench system inclusive to the Seres Division to Christmas Ravine. Christmas Ravine and Vladaya Ravine to where the Rates Road crosses it, Rates Road by Rates Village to the Fountain on the main road, all inclusive to the 22nd Division.

The boundary between 22nd Division and 26th Division will be –Oswald's Hill–Silver Willow–E. 13, all inclusive to the 26th Division –Point 303 (just west of Castle Hill) inclusive to 22nd Division–Bagatelle –Mektoub–Tertre Vert, all inclusive to 26th Division, thence the existing Divisional boundary.

VIII. *Distribution of the troops.*

The whole of the artillery of the XII Corps (less 26 18-pdr. guns under the orders of the 26th Division, and 24 18-pdr. guns under the orders of the 27th Division) will be under the orders of the G.O.C. R.A. XII Corps, except as stated below :—

(*a*) *Right Attack.*—The Right attack will be carried out by the Seres Division, less one regiment and one company of engineers allotted to the Left attack.

The attack will be supported by the 83rd Brigade (less two battalions) to which will be attached the 127th Field Company R.E., from the 22nd Division.

Three batteries 75-mm. Greek Mountain guns will be placed under the orders of the G.O.C. Seres Division when the line Dojran Hill–Hill 340 has been attained.

(*b*) *Left Attack.*—The Left attack will be carried out by the 22nd Division (less 127th Field Company R.E.), and the following attached troops :—

        One Regiment, Seres Division.
        One Company of Engineers, Seres Division.
        One British Mountain Battery.
        One Greek 65-mm. Mountain Battery.

Two batteries 18-pdrs. from the Left barrage will be placed under the orders of the G.O.C. 22nd Division as soon as the objectives Pusoubra [1] –Grand Couronné have been attained, or any way at dusk on Y day.

(*c*) *Demonstration.*—The troops of the 83rd Brigade occupying the trenches of C Sector (The Tortue) will demonstrate against the enemy's trenches O.4 to O.5¼ by fire effect and small patrols which, however, will not cross the enemy's wire. The object of the demonstration will be to draw the enemy's barrage.

(*d*) *Subsidiary Attack.*—The force to be employed in this attack is left to the discretion of the G.O.C. 26th Division.

IX. *Method of Attack.*

The Right Attack after overcoming the enemy's resistance in his advanced line defences O.1 to O.3 will advance at once to the line Dojran Hill–Teton Hill–Hill 340, while a force, specially detailed for the purpose, will deal with the garrisons of the Petit Couronné and O.5¼.

On reaching the line Dojran Hill–Hill 340, it will be consolidated by troops detailed for the purpose, while a portion of the force will continue its advance without pause, and will at once attack the Orb.

From here an attack will be launched against the Grand Couronné with the troops of the Left Attack, if the progress already made by that attack has not made such action unnecessary.

During this attack steps will be taken to ensure that a sufficient garrison is retained on the Orb to protect the right flank of the attack. Meanwhile the enemy's troops on Black Hill and the Casque will be masked as far as possible by the artillery.

In the event of success every effort will be made to exploit the situation and prevent the enemy removing their guns from the Volovec area, while at the same time the positions captured are secured.

The Left Attack will be directed successively and as rapidly as possible against the enemy's three lines of defence :—

    (*a*) O.6–Sugar Loaf–P. 4¼.
    (*b*) The Hilt–The Tongue–P. 4.
    (*c*) The Grand Couronné–Pusoubra–Dolina.

If the troops on any portion of their front are held up or delayed they will be best assisted by the neighbouring troops pushing forward vigorously to their next objective, and this will be clearly explained to all ranks.

---

[1] Pusoubra is the map name of the peak known to the British as P. 3.

The occupation of the " P " Ridge will be considered the primary objective of the Left Attack, and the G.O.C. 22nd Division will dispose his reserves with this in view.

The attack on the Grand Couronné by the right of the Left Attack will not be delayed to await the co-operation of the Right Attack, but in the event of unforseen circumstances delaying the attack such co-operation should be looked for.

On gaining the enemy's main line of defence steps will at once be taken to occupy the enemy's works on Koh-i-Noor and P. 2, which will be included in the line to be consolidated. Every effort will be made to further exploit the success and to prevent the enemy from withdrawing guns from the area dominated by the positions gained.

Subsidiary Attack.—This attack will be arranged to synchronize as much as possible with the main attack, and when the objectives have been reached the line Emerald Hill, Flat Iron Hill, Goldies Hill, will be consolidated.

X. *Defence of our Main Lines.*

The General Officers Commanding 22nd and 26th Divisions will be responsible for the security of our main line of defence during the attack within their areas.

For this purpose the 26th Division will place half a battalion of infantry at the disposal of the G.O.C. 22nd Division to hold the Horseshoe position.

The General Officer Commanding 83rd Infantry Brigade will be responsible for the security of our main line of defence during the attack within the area allotted to the Seres Division.

XI. *Date and Time of Attack.*

The attack will be delivered on Y day, which will be notified in due course, and at Z hours, which will be about dawn on Y day, and which will be the moment at which our barrage descends.

XII. *Divisional Plans.*

The General Officers Commanding the 22nd and 26th Divisions will make preparations accordingly and submit plans at as early a date as possible for the attacks of their respective divisions.

In the meantime, in anticipation of the arrival of the Commander of the Seres Division, Br.-General R. H. Hare, C.M.G., M.V.O., D.S.O., Commanding the 83rd Brigade, will act as his Deputy and will be responsible for making all the necessary preparations, and for submitting a plan for the Right Attack. He will also subsequently be responsible for conveying and interpreting the orders of the XII Corps Commander to the G.O.C. Seres Division, and to the troops under his command.

Liaison between the Corps, the 22nd Division, and Br.-General R. H. Hare will be undertaken by Lieut.-Colonel P. L. Hanbury, D.S.O., who will have his Headquarters with the XII Corps.

XIII. *Further Action by Divisions.*

The Divisions in the Corps will keep specially close contact with the enemy by means of energetic patrols along the whole front, and will be prepared to press forward in the event of the operations in this theatre causing a general retreat of the Bulgarian Forces. Further instructions will be issued on this subject.

F. G. FULLER.
Brigadier-General,
General Staff, XII Corps.

Issued at 2 p.m.

APPENDIX 13.

22ND DIVISION ORDER NO. 120.

15th September 1918.

Secret.
Reference Maps 1/10,000 " Couronné " and latest 1/20,000 Sheets.

I. *General Intention.*

(1) On Y day the XII Corps will attack and seize the " P " Ridge **Map 5.** and the neighbouring high ground. This attack will commence at Z **Sketch 8.** hour (the hour at which the first artillery barrage comes down). The date of Y day and the time of Z hour will be notified later.

(2) The main Corps attack will be divided into the " Right Attack " and the " Left Attack." The " Right Attack " will be carried out by the Greek Seres Division (less one regiment) and attached troops. The " Left Attack " will be carried out by the 22nd Division and attached troops.

(3) The 2me bis of Zouaves and XII Corps Cavalry Regiment will be in corps reserve.

(4) The 65th Infantry Brigade and 66th Machine-Gun Company will be in Army reserve.

II. *Objectives.*

(1) (*a*) The final objective of the " Left Attack " is the line Grand Couronné–Koh-i-noor–P. 2–Dolina, and this will be the " Line of Consolidation." It is absolutely essential that the attack on the " P " Ridge should succeed in order to enable the remainder of the attack to progress. The attack on the " P " Ridge must therefore be driven home at all costs and regardless of the progress of the other attacks. Brigade reserves will be close up to deal with any check on the " P " Ridge.

(*b*) As soon as the final objective has been gained, and our protective barrage permits, the success will be exploited by all means available, especially by pushing forward patrols to capture the enemy's guns in the vicinity.

(2) (*a*) The " Right Attack " will at the same time advance to the line Dojran Hill, Teton Hill, and Hill 340 and consolidate it, and from here advance against the enemy's works on the Orb.

(*b*) The above attack will include the capture of Petit Couronné.

(*c*) If found necessary, this attack will also co-operate with the " Left Attack " in the assault on Grand Couronné.

(3) A demonstration will be carried out opposite O.4–O.5 (both inclusive) by a battalion of the 83rd Infantry Brigade attached to the Seres Division at the same time as the " Right " and " Left Attacks."

(4) The 26th Division will at the same time demonstrate on the left of the " Left Attack " against the enemy's advanced line Emerald Hill–Ruby Hill—Flatiron Hill.

III. *Plan of Attack.*

(1) The " Left Attack " will be directed successively and as rapidly as possible against the various objectives in the enemy's lines of defence (as given in paras. II (1) and V) until reaching the line Squirrel Wood [1] –T. 177 (south-west of Plume)–Warren–Dolina.

---

[1] Squirrel Wood has not been identified. It was probably in the low ground south-west of the Sceptre.

(2) A pause will be made on this line to allow of reorganization on it before the final objectives are assaulted at Z plus 80 minutes.

(3) No pause will be made at either the first or second objectives, except in the case of O.6, which will be occupied and held until the "Right Attack" has established itself on Petit Couronné and Hill 340.

(4) The necessary mopping up will be carried out in all cases by small parties which will follow on when their work is finished, but the advance will on no account be checked for them.

IV. *Troops available for the "Left Attack."*

Commander—Major-General J. Duncan, C.B., C.M.G., D.S.O., commanding the 22nd Division, with Battle Headquarters at Hill 420.

 22nd Division (less 65th Infantry Brigade in Army reserve and the 127th Field Company R.E. attached to the Seres Division).
 77th Infantry Brigade.
 3rd Regiment Seres Division, with one company of Génie and 3 companies of Machine Guns (each 8 guns).
 65th Machine-Gun Company. 67th Machine-Gun Company.
 One section 77th Machine-Gun Company.
 The Bute Mountain Battery.
 One Greek 65-mm. Battery.

Two 18-pdr. batteries will come under the orders of the G.O.C. 22nd Division as soon as the objectives Grand Couronné–Pusobra have been attained, or, in any case, at dusk on Y day.

V. *Division of the "Left Attack."*

The "Left Attack" will be carried out on a front of 3 Brigades (Right, Centre, and Left). Tactical boundaries between divisions and separating brigades are as given in 22nd Division General Staff Instruction No. 2, paras. (vii), (viii), (6).

The following gives the allotment of troops, commanders, headquarters, and objectives:—

(a) *Right Brigade Attack*:
 Commander—Br.-General A. D. Macpherson, C.M.G., D.S.O., commanding the 67th Infantry Brigade.
  Headquarters—Christmas.
  Troops—67th Infantry Brigade, 3 Sections 67th Machine-Gun Company (Forward Guns), 67th Trench Mortar Battery (less 4 trench mortars).
  Objectives—
   1st.—O.6 (to be held till "Right Attack" gains Petit Couronné and Hill 340). Barrage lifts off it at Z plus 10 minutes.
   2nd.—Hilt–Knot–Tassel. Barrage lifts off it at Z plus 30 minutes.
   3rd.—There is no definite third objective for this attack; it will consist of an advance towards the northern edge of Squirrel Wood from which to be ready to assault the 4th objective.
   4th.—Grand Couronné. Barrage lifts off it at Z plus 80 minutes.

It is anticipated that the above assault on Grand Couronné will be delivered at about the same time as the assault by troops of the "Right Attack" on the Orb. On gaining possession of the Orb, the troops of the Seres Division will push forward patrols to get in touch with the troops of the 67th Infantry Brigade. If this touch is not gained it may be necessary thereafter to carry out the attack on Grand Couronné in co-operation with troops of the Seres Division.

This combined attack would be preceded by a regular artillery bombardment, under arrangements already made between the two divisions.

APPENDIX 13 341

As soon as Grand Couronné is completely in our hands, the 22nd Division will assume responsibility for its defence.

(b) *Centre Brigade Attack* :
Commander—Colonel Pagos.
Headquarters—Hills Camp.
Troops—3rd Regiment (Seres Division), 24 Machine Guns (Forward Guns), one section Greek Génie, 4 Trench Mortars of the 67th Trench-Mortar Battery.
Objectives—
1st.—Sugar Loaf–the Corne. Barrage lifts off it at Z plus 3 minutes.
2nd.—The Tongue–Maze. Barrage lifts off it at Z plus 11 minutes.
3rd.—The enemy's main trench west of its junction with the long C.T. (running from south to north) 70 yards east of T. 177—the support trench T. 185—the Warren, including its whole system of main and support trenches and C.Ts. Barrage lifts off the main trenches at Z plus 35 minutes, and off support trenches at Z plus 42 minutes.
4th.—The Grand Shoulder–Koh-i-Noor. Barrage lifts off it at Z plus 80 minutes.

(c) *Left Brigade Attack* :
Commander—Br.-General F. S. Montague Bates, C.M.G., D.S.O., commanding the 66th Infantry Brigade.
Headquarters—Pillar.
Troops—66th Infantry Brigade, 3 Sections 66th Machine-Gun [1] Company (Forward Guns), 66th Trench Mortar Battery.
Objectives—
1st.—P. 4¼. Barrage lifts off it at Z plus 3 minutes.
2nd.—Zebera (P. 4). Barrage lifts off it at Z plus 8 minutes.
3rd.—Pusobra (P. 3). Barrage lifts off the south end at Z plus 20 minutes.
Little Dolina. Barrage lifts off it at Z plus 37 minutes.
4th.—Dolina. Barrage lifts off the east end of Dolina at Z plus 37 minutes and off west end of Dolina at Z plus 51 minutes.
5th.—Triangle–P. 2. Barrage lifts off it at Z plus 80 minutes.
6th.—P. 1. Barrage lifts off it at Z plus 95 minutes.

(d) *Divisional Reserve* :
(i) 77th Infantry Brigade, 9th Border Regiment (Pioneers), 99th and 100th Field Companies R.E. and one Company Greek Génie (less one section).
(ii) This Reserve will be placed as follows :—
77th Infantry Brigade Headquarters at the Pillar.
One Battalion at " W " Camp.
One Battalion at Pillar.
One Battalion (less two companies holding the line) at Oxford.
Two companies of above Battalion holding the line D. 6 (inclusive) to E. 13 (exclusive) at S.P. 2 and S.P. 3.
9th Border Regiment (Pioneers) (less two companies) at Oxford.
Two companies 9th Border Regiment (Pioneers) at Pillar (under C.R.E. as long as tactical situation admits).
99th and 100th Field Companies R.E. at camp north of Table (under C.R.E. ready to move up).
Greek Company of Génie (less one section) at Oxford (under C.R.E.).

(e) *Troops holding the Line* :
(i) On the night Y minus 3/Y minus 2, Headquarters 66th Infantry Brigade will open at Pillar and its commander will assume responsibility for the defence of the line from D. 6 (inclusive) to E. 13 (exclusive).

---

[1] As will be seen from para. I (4) of this order, the 66th Machine-Gun Company was actually attached to the 65th Brigade in Army Reserve. This is a slip and should read "3 Sections 65th Machine-Gun Company."

Two companies of a battalion of the 77th Infantry Brigade will come under his orders for this purpose, while the Headquarters and remaining two companies of this battalion will again come under the commander 77th Infantry Brigade, and will be withdrawn to Kidney Camp.

(ii) On Y minus 2 day, the 83rd Infantry Brigade will take over the responsibility for the line as far west as C. 10 (inclusive) and at the same time the commander 67th Infantry Brigade will assume responsibility for the defence of the line from this point to D. 6 (exclusive).

VI. *Action of the Artillery.*

(1) The operations will be preceded by two days' wire-cutting and one night's special bombardment.

Harassing fire will be carried out on the nights Y minus 2/Y minus 1, and Y minus 1/Y, to keep the gaps in the enemy's wire open.

On this latter night there will also be a smoke bombardment combined with the other harassing fire to screen the assembly of the attacking troops from enemy observation, as well as to drown sound.

(2) On Y day the barrage will commence at Z hour.

Each attack will be preceded by a rolling barrage and howitzer blocks as given in the Artillery Plans.

The Koh-i-Noor Group (two 18-pdr. batteries, a Greek battery of 65-mm. mountain guns), and the independent Bute Mountain Battery will be ready, under the hand of the Divisional Commander, from the time the main objective is gained or from dusk on Y day, to move forward directly required in close support of the infantry, to pursue the enemy with fire and to assist in the barrage of the " Line of Consolidation."

VII. *Action of Machine Guns.*

(1) The Machine Guns are divided into " Forward " and " Rearward " guns. The Forward guns are under the Brigadiers concerned, but have a final definite objective detailed by the Division. The remaining guns are Rearward guns for barrage purposes under the D.M.G.O. Forward guns are allotted to Brigades as shown in para. V.

(2) On the two nights preceding the operation, machine guns will assist the field guns and howitzers with harassing fire to keep the gaps in the enemy's wire open, and on the latter of these two nights to drown the noise of the assembly.

(3) During the attack, machine-gun barrages will be put down by Rearward guns (and by Forward guns as directed by G.Os.C. Brigades) in front of the various objectives and finally will form a protective barrage in front of the " Line of Consolidation."

VIII. *Action of Pioneers and Engineers.*

(1) Pioneers and Engineers will be in Divisional Reserve at the disposal of the G.O.C., placed as given in para. V (*d*).

(2) The 99th and 100th Field Companies R.E., one Company of Greek Génie (less 1 section), and two Companies of Pioneers will, as far as the tactical situation permits, be available for immediate use under the C.R.E., chiefly on the following pre-allotted tasks: preparation of Doljeli–Volovec and Krastali–Dojran roads, and of a mule track between Doljeli and P. 4 ; the preparation of water supplies in the new area ; labelling the new positions, etc.

IX. *Action of the R.A.F.*

(1) Contact patrols will fly over our line as follows :—

(*a*) Over the " Line of Reorganization " (W.D. Line) at Z plus 45 minutes.

(*b*) Over the Final Objective, " Line of Consolidation," at Z plus 95 minutes.

APPENDIX 13

(2) At these times the infantry in the front line *only* will indicate their positions (when the patrol aeroplane calls with its Klaxon horn) with both ground flares and with their tin discs.

(3) Other Contact patrols will be sent out at times as found desirable by the G.O.C. Division, and in these cases warning to the infantry will not be possible. They must, however, be on the look-out and indicate their positions as mentioned above whenever a low-flying aeroplane calls with its horn.

(4) Battalions will remember that they can communicate with a low-flying machine at any time by means of their Popham Panel.

X. *Evacuation of Wounded.*

(1) Wounded and sick will be evacuated under regimental arrangements as far as Regimental Aid Posts.

(2) From here they will be brought back by Field Ambulances, through Advanced Dressing Stations at Christmas, Senelle, " W," Oxford, Pillar, Horseshoe, and Col de Rates, to Main Dressing Stations at 323, Asagi Mahalla, and Chugunsi.

(3) From these Main Dressing Stations they are evacuated under arrangements made by XII Corps to the 28th or 31st C.C.S. or to the Base.

XI. *The Move Up to Assembly Positions and Forming-up Places.*

(1) On Y minus 3/Y minus 2, and Y minus 2/Y minus 1 nights, the attacking troops will move up to Forward Camps under orders specially issued.

(2) The actual movement from these Forward Camps into the Forming-up Places will take place on Y minus 1/Y night.

XII. *Signals.*

The following Signals will be used :—

(1) To mean " I have reached this point," referring to most forward line only—Ground Flares lit at about 30 yards apart and tin discs revealed (see also para. IX).

(2) To mean " I am being attacked and require artillery support "—S.O.S. :—

(*a*) By Day—Either two 1½-inch Parachute White Lights fired in rapid succession or two Red Verey Lights fired in rapid succession.

(NOTE.—The reason 1½-inch Parachute Lights are used besides the coloured light signal is that the red Verey Lights are not as visible by day as the more distinctive Parachute Lights.)

(*b*) By Night—Two Red Verey Lights fired in rapid succession.

XIII. *Liaison.*

(1) Liaison between neighbouring units will be arranged by telephone and visual.

(2) Besides this, personal liaison with the Right Attack (Seres Division) is arranged for by British officers attached to and accompanying the Left Attacking Battalions of that Division.

(3) Personal Liaison between the 22nd Divisional Headquarters and the 3rd Greek Regiment is arranged for by the attachment of a number of British officers and N.C.Os. to the Regimental and Battalion Headquarters of the latter Regiment.

XIV. *Disposal of Prisoners.*

(1) Prisoners will be collected at Brigade Battle Headquarters in small batches and will be sent by brigades under escort to three Forward

Collecting Stations at Vladaya Ravine, Pearse, and Gokcelli. (Each of these is in telephone communication with the Main Divisional Collecting Station at Chugunsi, where there is a cage).

(2) From this Main Collecting Station the Corps will take over all prisoners.

XV. *Divisional Battle Headquarters.*

These will be opened at Hill 420 at 10 p.m. on Y minus 1 day, and will remain open there until further instructions on the subject are issued by the Division. Reports will be sent accordingly.

XVI. *Synchronization of Watches.*

This will be carried out at 9.30 a.m. and 9.30 p.m. daily under arrangements which will be made by this office. This will commence from a date to be notified later.

XVII. *Further Action.*

All Units and Headquarters will be ready to become mobile for an indefinite period. Heavy kits will therefore be packed and put away and Mobile Advanced Establishments prepared.

Acknowledge.

Issued at 10 p.m.

T. G. G. ANDERSON,
Lieut.-Colonel, G.S., 22nd Division.

Headquarters 22nd Division.

APPENDIX 14.

PLAN OF OPERATIONS OF THE CRETAN DIVISION.

XVI Corps General Staff.
G. 295/54.

Secret.   *7th September.*

Reference Maps 1/20,000 and 1/50,000.

1. *Intention :*

Map 7.
Sketch 9.

The attack, as outlined below, will depend upon larger offensive operations in this theatre, and will be carried out in conjunction with an attack made by the XII Corps (to which is attached the Seres Division) against the enemy's positions west of Lake Dojran.

The object is to break through the enemy defences and to exploit any success gained.

Preparations are to be made so that the attack can take place on the night 17th/18th instant.

2. *Objectives :*

1st Objective :—The enemy's main line between Battery Cross and Lake Dojran.

2nd Objective :—The enemy's second line on the crest of the Blaga Planina.

3. *General Considerations :*

The success of this attack depends upon surprise, which will be effected as follows :—

(a) By the absence of previous artillery bombardment.

APPENDIX 14

(b) By placing the units of the division in forward positions at the last moment, where they must remain unseen by the enemy.

(c) By good order and silence during the advance, from the moment the attacking troops leave the forward positions of assembly.

(d) By the dash of the attacking troops during the advance and the rapidity of their action.

4. *Plan of Attack :*

(a) The attack by the Cretan Division will be made by 2 regiments finding the front lines and supports ; the remaining regiment will be in reserve at the disposal of the G.O.C. Cretan Division, and will operate on the left flank of the division against the enemy's right.

The boundary between the two leading regiments will be the point where the track crosses the railway 250 metres N.E. of Broken Bridge–Bulamac–Karali–Gevshekli North–Kara Pazarli, thence track to Point 208, N. of Nikolic–Point 512–to crest of Blaga Planina.

The Right Boundary of the regiment on the right will be Chakli Station–Derveshli–Battery Cross–to crest of Blaga Planina.

The Left Boundary of the regiment on the left will be Mud Crossing and the northern edge of the marshy ground bordering Lake Dojran.

(b) The attack will be protected on the N.E. flank by a British brigade. One other British brigade will also move forward in Corps reserve.

(c) (i) The artillery of the Cretan Division will operate under the orders of the artillery commander of the division, who must be in close liaison with the two leading regiments. It will be necessary for the artillery of the division to move forward with the infantry as far as the line Ehatli–Gevshekli South, before they can expect to support the infantry successfully and assist in breaching the enemy's line.

(ii) As soon as the infantry have taken the outpost line, the field artillery of the 28th Division, under the orders of the C.R.A. 28th Division, will advance as follows :—

3 batteries of 4·5-inch howitzers to positions west of Bulamac ;
7 batteries of 18-pdrs. to the line of the Akinjali Dere.

As soon as light allows these batteries will bombard the enemy's main-line trenches from The Whale to Dojran Lake.

A British artillery liaison officer will be attached to the staff of each of the 2 attacking regiments.

(d) The engineers of the division will be disposed as follows :—
A half-company with each of the leading regiments ;
One company with the regiment in reserve.

5. *Instructions concerning the Attack :*

(i) The night before the attack, the units of the division will be assembled as follows :—

Right regiment with one artillery group and half-company R.E. (*sic*) at Rabovo.

Left regiment with one artillery group and half-company R.E. at Popovo.

Reserve regiment with one company R.E. in the ravines east of The Oval.

In these positions the troops will remain concealed during the day.

(ii) On the night of the attack the 2 leading regiments will be conducted by British guides to positions on the railway facing their objectives, with the right resting on Chakli Station and the left on Mud Crossing, with covering parties in front.

(iii) At an hour to be fixed by the G.O.C. XVI Corps the 2 leading regiments will advance on their objectives within the boundaries mentioned.

In each battalion careful arrangements must be made to ensure that connection is maintained between columns laterally and from front to rear.

(iv) The enemy's outpost line on the front, South edge of Gulemenli Wood–Kodzakoria–Akinjali Wood will be rushed in silence, without firing and without artillery support. Rockets (gold and silver rain) will be sent up when this line has fallen.

(v) The advance from the railway will be timed so that the leading battalions will have taken the outpost line by daybreak. As soon as this line has fallen, the advance on the enemy's main line will continue. The sooner the main line is reached, the less chance will there be of enemy reinforcements reaching it.

(vi) The regiment in reserve will be moved to the low ground S.E. of the railway in time to be on the railway about Mud Crossing by daylight; its further advance will be regulated by the G.O.C. Cretan Division. The IV Highland Mountain Brigade (2 batteries) will be attached to this regiment.

(vii) The obstacle formed by the enemy's wire in front of his main position must to a great extent be overcome by means of wire-cutting parties, since entire reliance cannot be placed upon the mountain artillery being able to do this.

(viii) When the crest of the Blaga Planina has been captured, the troops will consolidate to guard against counter-attack and to enable field artillery to be brought up if required for the continuance of the operations.

(ix) Coloured flags will be carried for the purpose of indicating to the artillery and aeroplanes the positions reached by the leading infantry.

Tin discs will also be carried to indicate the position of the leading infantry to the contact aeroplanes.

The contact aeroplane will fly over the attacking troops at various times during the advance, and, on it sounding the Klaxon horn, the *leading* infantry will show the discs and also wave the flags.

(x) Ammunition columns (S.M.A.) of Cretan Division Mountain Artillery will be established about the junction of the Karadzali Dere and Hoja Suju, where they will replenish the echelons de combat as required.

Ammunition to replenish S.M.A. will be sent in vehicles of XVI Corps Ammunition Column to this position from the Popovo Ammunition Depot.

A British mounted orderly with a Greek interpreter will be provided for the S.M.A. to enable them to demand ammunition as required from the depot.

6. *Approach March:*

On the night previous to that on which the Cretan Division moves to the areas referred to in para. 5 (i), the units will move forward from their present camps, assisted by British guides, to the following areas, where they will remain concealed during the day:—

Right Regiment.
1 Artillery Group.
½ Company R.E. (*sic*).
} Area Corapli–Jeni Mahale, S.E. of Baisili.

Left Regiment.
1 Artillery Group.
¼ Company R.E.
} Area Gulemenli–Indzekli, W. of Baisili.

Reserve Regiment.
1 Company R.E.
} Area Gulemenli–Indzekli, W. of Baisili.

The G.O.C. will make careful arrangements before the units move from their present camps to ensure that:—

(i) The ammunition supply is complete.

(ii) No unnecessary impedimenta accompanies the troops, but is left under charge of a guard in present camps.

7. *Troops taking part in the Operations*:

In addition to the Cretan Division, the following troops will take part in the operations :—

28th Division, including 3 F.A. Brigades and 2 Mountain Brigades (*i.e.* Artillery).
XVI Corps Cavalry.
3rd Greek Cavalry Regiment.
1 6-inch Gun.
1 Heavy Battery, 60-pdr. guns (4 guns). } For counter-battery work.

H. L. KNIGHT,
Br.-General, General Staff, XVI Corps.

APPENDIX 15.

XII CORPS ORDER NO. 33.

Secret.   *18th September 1918.*
Reference Maps Couronné 1/10,000 ; Dojran 1/20,000.

1. The attack will be renewed tomorrow morning, September 19th, **Map 5.** as follows :— **Sketch 8.**

(A) The Seres Division, supported by one battalion 83rd Brigade, will attack the Orb and the Hilt and subsequently the Grand Couronné, up to but exclusive of the Rockies.

(B) The 22nd Division, 77th Infantry Brigade, and 2nd Bis Regt. de Zouaves, under G.O.C. 22nd Division, will attack the " W " and " T " lines, the latter inclusive of the Rockies, and the west side of Grand Couronné, and also including the " P " Ridge, Little Dolina, and Dolina.

The boundary between the two attacks (A) and (B) will be as follows :—

Summit of the Grand Couronné (inclusive to Seres Division)–the Rockies (inclusive to 22nd Division)–the Hilt–Sword Ravine–Dagger Ravine (all inclusive to Seres Division)–Jumeaux Ravine–Dorset Ravine (inclusive to 22nd Division)–point where the track crosses the Vladaya Ravine, 1254/1821–thence as before.

22nd Division will be responsible for defence of the line from La Tortue inclusive to E. 13.

2. A preparatory bombardment will be arranged, and the barrages for the two attacks co-ordinated, by the G.O.C.R.A. XII Corps.

3. Z hours will be 5.15 a.m.

4. Acknowledge.

Issued at 5 p.m.

P. L. HANBURY, Lt.-Colonel, G.S.,
for
Brigadier-General, General Staff.

Appendix 16.

TELEGRAM FROM O.H.L. TO BULGARIAN G.H.Q.

(Translation.)

To General Todorov. Reference your No. 11515. As Your Excellency is aware Germany is now engaged in a most terrific struggle on the Western Front. All our forces will be required for that purpose. There doubtless the issue of the Great War will be decided. I am therefore compelled to refuse the request of the Scholtz Headquarters that a whole German division be sent to Macedonia. I can put at the disposal of the Army Group only some units of a reinforced infantry brigade which will have to be transported from Sevastopol. I will also try to free further troops, but for the present I cannot definitely say what units. Prior to the receipt of Your Excellency's telegram I had been in communication with the High Command Baden concerning the reinforcement of the Macedonian front by Austro-Hungarian troops but have not yet received a reply. I am extremely sorry that I am unable to do more to satisfy Your Excellency's request. In the present highly critical military situation the Bulgarian High Command must try to deal with the situation with the forces now at its disposal which are not less numerous than those of the enemy and must reconcile itself to a possible loss of territory. I think I must leave it thus to Your Excellency, suggesting that you for your part come to some arrangement with the High Command Baden concerning the despatch of help.

Signed, for the High Command,
GENERAL-FIELD-MARSHAL VON HINDENBURG.

NOTE.—The copy preserved in the British archives is not dated, but it is indicated that it was forwarded by the Bulgarian Ministry of War to General Todorov at G.H.Q. on the 19th September.

Appendix 17.

TELEGRAM FROM FRENCH G.H.Q.

(Translation.)

22nd September 1918.

5159/3.

Serbian Army, British Army, A.F.O., 1st Group.

The enemy is in retreat on the whole front between Monastir and Lake Dojran. We have now to rout him, to take prisoners from his ranks, and to capture his material by an unceasing and resolute pursuit. Outflank resistance and push forward light detachments, which should establish themselves on his line of retreat. The cavalry, whose hour is come, should in all cases preceed the infantry columns and open the way for them.—
FRANCHET D'ESPÉREY.

Appendix 18.

TELEGRAPHIC ORDER BY G.H.Q.

22/9/18.

XII Corps, XVI Corps.
G. 715.

Advance to be continued with greatest possible speed. XII Corps **Maps A, 9.** to clear Blaga Planina and occupy Kara Bail. XVI Corps to press on to line Pt. 408, Pt. 358, Miletkovo bridge, and across the Bajimia Dere. 1st Groupement ordered to Miletkovo–Davidovo. 26th Divn. to wire progress to 27th Divn. periodically. Boundary will be Cinarli–Dedeli road inclusive to XVI Corps. Corps to get into touch at Cerniśte at 9 a.m. or as may be mutually arranged.

Appendix 19.

TELEGRAPHIC ORDER BY G.H.Q.

28/9.

Adv. XVI Corps, XVI Corps, Adv. XII Corps, XII Corps.
G.A. 810.

You will continue the movement towards Petrić with the 14th Greek **Maps A, 9.** Division and also towards Berovo with the other troops at your disposal. 83rd Brigade will come under your orders during the day to back up the 14th Greek Division. Watch your supply situation closely and wire me during the day how you stand, because on that must depend the localities to which you bring the 27th Division. Is the Strumica–Berovo road fit for lorry traffic? Answer urgently required. Addressed Adv. XVI Corps, repeated XVI Corps, Adv. XII Corps, and XII Corps.

(NOTE.—A wire subsequently despatched laid down that the movement towards Petrić was the more important and that that should be the first objective. The movement towards Berovo was to be continued sufficiently to keep the left flank clear.)

Appendix 20.

INSTRUCTION FOR THE ARMIES.

(TRANSLATION.)

Q.G.A.A.
25th September 1918.

Secret.
Commandement en Chef
  des Armées Alliées.
État-Major Général.
3ᵉ Bureau.
No. 5200/3.

1. *Situation on the Front of the Armies.*—*In the centre*, the resistance **Map 8.** of the enemy on the heights north-east of the Vardar between the

Bregalnica and the Gradec heights was broken yesterday evening by the Serbian Second Army after a series of brilliant engagements ; it captured Štip and is now pushing advanced guards towards Kočana and towards Kliseli. On its part the Serbian First Army has increased its swing towards the north-east, and its advanced guards are at the gates of Veles.

On the right, the 1st Group of Divisions and the British Army, in touch about Valandovo, are attacking the Gradec–Belašica range ; the British Army has crossed the Bulgarian frontier by the Kosturino Pass.

On the left, the A.F.O. is pushing its cavalry and a composite detachment on Üsküb (Skoplje) by way of Veles. The enemy is in retreat north-east of Monastir, pursued by our columns on the routes leading to Kičevo and Resan.

2. This situation, which is developing in accordance with our anticipations, calls for but small modifications in the instructions previously given to the Armies.

3. *Serbian Army.*—No change.

4. *A.F.O.*—Five divisions are now taking part in the pursuit on Kičevo and Resan ; their directions are convergent. It is therefore of the highest importance to regroup the larger formations as speedily as possible so as not to employ in this difficult country and off the true line so large a proportion of our strength. On the contrary, our weight should be shifted more and more in the direction of Skoplje. This is at once the direction in which we shall achieve the greatest success and that in which the intervention of German reinforcements may threaten us most seriously.

(*a*) The detachment directed on Skoplje will be reinforced as quickly as possible in infantry and artillery (including 155-mm. guns) so that we have on this flank the strength of at least a complete division.

(*b*) A second division will be regrouped as quickly as possible in the area between Monastir and Prilep, to be directed upon the region of Skoplje.

Mobile heavy artillery units, which cannot be employed in the mountainous region through which the enemy is retreating, will also be regrouped and despatched to the Skoplje area.

(*c*) At the same time the Army will direct the 3rd Group of Divisions to exert strong pressure to the northward, in order to threaten first of all and subsequently to cut the Resan–Ohrid road.

5. *1st Group of Divisions.*—As soon as the Gradec–Belašica heights have been captured, advance without delay into the valley of the Strumica on Radovišta, in order to form a connecting link between the Serbian and the British Armies. Subsequently, gain possession of the *massif* of the Plaškovica Planina, which the Serbian and British Armies will turn from north and west in order to make touch about the important cross-roads of Carevoselo.

So far as possible maintain a Greek division in reserve in the region of Hudova.

The line of communication of the forces operating north of the Gradec *massif* will be the Kosturino–Strumica defile, common to the British Army. The British Army is responsible for the policing and upkeep of this route.

6. *British Army.*—With a proportion of its forces, push on in the direction of Strumica, later of Berovo, and finally of Carevoselo, as indicated above.

With the forces operating north of Lake Dojran subdue the resistance on the Belašica chain by means of a sweep eastward, in the plain towards Petrić and Livunovo, and on the crest towards Rupel.

Prepare for the rapid reconstruction of the railway to Demir Hisar.

7. *Hellenic Army.*—The eastern sweep of a portion of the forces of

the British Group will make possible a rapid advance of those of the Greek I Corps on Demir Hisar and Rupel, so as to gain possession of the defile in the shortest possible time.

From now onwards make all preparations for this action.

In addition, push out strong reconnaissances, each of the value of a battalion at least and with artillery, on the front Demir Hisar-Seres to harass the enemy and prevent him from slipping away. Be ready to profit by any sign of withdrawal to go forward on his heels and secure possession of the heights east of Demir Hisar. The Hellenic troops on the Struma will take it as an honour that they will no longer be held back from participation in the operations in which the Hellenic troops already engaged are playing so brilliant a part.

FRANCHET D'ESPÉREY.

APPENDIX 21.

A NOTE ON CASUALTIES.

The following figures, which give the casualties among British and Dominion (*i.e.*, Indian) troops during the campaign, are taken from " Medical Services : Casualties and Medical Statistics," Chapter XII.

BATTLE CASUALTIES.

	Officers	Other Ranks	Total
Killed and died of wounds ..	221	3,875	4,096
Missing..	74	1,510	1,584
Prisoners of war	7	1,187	1,194
Wounded	855	16,033	16,888
Total	1,157	22,605	23,762

NON-BATTLE CASUALTIES.

	Officers	Other Ranks	Total
Died of disease or injury ..	76	3,668	3,744
Sick or injured	13,767	463,751	477,518
Total	13,843	467,419	481,262

CASUALTIES FROM MALARIA ALONE.
Admissions to hospital 162,517
Deaths 787
Evacuated to U.K. under scheme of 1917-18 34,762

APPENDIX 21

AVERAGE RATION STRENGTHS.

Year	British Troops	Indian Troops	Local Labour	Total
1915	60,889	—	—	60,889
1916	123,394	2,616	—	126,010
1917	182,583	2,108	17,574	202,265
1918	128,747	3,764	27,408	159,947

GENERAL INDEX.[1]

Aftonides, Commandant, 164
" Agents, 28th Divisional," 27
Air raids. *See* Royal Flying Corps and Royal Air Force.
Albania, French and Italian operations in, 16, 31, 91, 118, 276
Alexander, Crown Prince of Serbia, 11, 34, 48, 103, 131, 280
Allenby, Gen. Sir E. H. H., 41, 111, 124, 125, 254, 269
Allied Armies of the East, reductions in, 31; dispositions of, Dec. 1917, 48; mission of, Dec. 1917, 49; Defence Scheme of, spring of 1918, 70–6; discussion of offensive by, spring 1918, 77; their operations in Albania, May–June 1918, 91, 118; their strength, Sept. 1918, 131, 133; morale of, 133; offensive of, 147 and *passim*; their advance to Danube, 271–80; belittlement of their achievements, 283
Allied Railway Commission, 53, 59
Amet, Vice-Admiral, 266
Anderson, Lieut.-Col. T. G. G., 166 (*f.n.*)
Anselme, Gen. d', 48, 131, 196, 199, 202, 204, 210, 214, 232, 258, 278
Armée d'Orient, 32, 129
Armée Française d'Orient, its operations in Albania, 16, 31, 91, 117; 48, 50, 54; its rôle in Defence Scheme, 71; its rôle in final offensive, 130; in exploitation of success, 196–202, 220–2, 237–47; its cavalry in capture of Skoplje, 243; its rôle in advance to Danube, 257, 275; 302
Armistices—
with Bulgaria, negotiations for, 228–33, 246–50; convention signed, 235, 251; terms of, 251–3
with Turkey, 266
with Austria, 279
with Germany, 280
with Hungary, 281
Army of the Danube, 261, 262, 268, 278, 280, 282

Army Reserve, 6, 13, 14, 36
Artillery, heavy artillery sent to Palestine, 4, 13; on Dojran front, 16, 86, 88, 90; an 8-in. how. battery received, 58; siege batteries from Palestine, 62; in capture of Skra di Legen, 90; shortage of ammunition stocks, 113; situation on Dojran front as regards offensive, 114; reinforcements refused, 114; demands for gas shell, 115; its activity on Dojran front, Aug. 1918, 119; supply and expenditure of ammunition in Battle of Dojran, 122; in capture of Roche Noire Salient, 142; in Battle of Dojran, 163, 165, 169, 172, 175, 191; field artillery dissolves in pursuit, 300
Asser, Br.-Gen. V., 216
Austria-Hungary, refuses to recognize Bulgarian Armistice, 254; sends reinforcements to Macedonia, 255, 272; signs armistice with Italy, 279

Baillie, Lieut.-Col. D. G., 28, 29
Barrère, M., French Ambassador in Rome, 32
Base Training Camp (Infantry Reinforcements), 57
Bates, Br.-Gen. F. S. Montague, 45, 168, 183
Bayley, Br.-Gen. G. E., 87
Beckett, Lieut.-Col. J. D. M., 28
Belin, Gen., 107
Berry, Br.-Gen. P. P. E. de, 176
Berthelot, Gen., 36, 68, 261, 278
Bishop, Lieut.-Col. B. F., 171
Blackwood, Lieut.-Col. A. P., 44
Blake, Br.-Gen. W. A., 180, 181
Bliss, Gen. Tasker H., 107, 277
Bojović, Gen. (afterwards Voivode), 48, 71, 104, 128, 153, 273, 277
Bordeaux, Gen., 64, 68
Boré-Verrier, Lieut.-Col., 179, 183, 227
Boris, Crown Prince of Bulgaria, 198, 199, 252

---

[1] The Appendices are not indexed either here or in the Index to Arms, Formations, and Units.

354 GENERAL INDEX

Bourcet, French General in War of Austrian Succession, maxims of, 195, 299
Bourchier, Lieut.-Col. R. W., 169 (*f.n.*), 191
Braquet, Gen., 64
Breslau (German-Turkish light cruiser), 56
Brest-Litovsk, Armistice and Treaty of, 39
Briand, M. Aristide, 287
Bridges, Lieut.-Gen. Sir G. T. M., 268, 277
Briggs, Lieut.-Gen. Sir C. J., 25, 62; his instructions for local operations, April 1918, 80; brings operations to an end, 84; enquires into failure, 85; 93; his views on Bulgarian morale, 96; Greek I Corps under his orders, 97, 138; favours offensive at mouth of Struma, 108; his orders for Battle of Dojran, 172; Greek I Corps withdrawn from, 173; relieves Crete Divn., 177, 204; 190, 206; takes command of British left wing, 207; his orders during pursuit, 211, 226, 230, 234; receives news of Armistice, 235; 263; his plan for seizure of Adrianople, 264; advises delay, 265; 267
British Ægean Squadron, 264, 269
British Army of the Black Sea, 283
British Mission to G.H.Q., Allied Armies, 268
British Salonika Army, its gloomy prospect in spring of 1917, 1; troops withdrawn from to Palestine, 2, 4, 12, 14; and to France, 76, 93, 94; training and instruction in, 6, 57; relaxations of, 8; discipline and morale of, 10, 100; aids refugees from Salonika Fire, 21; hands over left bank of Vardar to French, Nov. 1917, 35; effects of German March offensive on, 58, 76; relieves French on left bank of Vardar, March 1918, 61; dispositions of, April 1918, 63; rôle of in Defence Scheme, 71; takes over right bank of Vardar, 94; dispositions of, 15th July 1918, 97; lack of leave in, 100; luckless rôle of, 112; proposal to transfer officers to Egypt, 122; plans for final offensive, 130; Greek troops attached to, Sept.

British Salonika Army (*continued*)—
1918, 130, 131; its preparations for offensive, 135–41; in Battle of Dojran, Sept. 1918, 159–92; outbreak of influenza in, 166; in pursuit, 202, 223; depleted state of, 203; its orders from Gen. d'Espérey, 23rd Sept., 220; Bulgarian delegates enter its lines, 232; its first rôle after Bulgarian Armistice, 257; its revised rôle, 261; its move against Turkey, 262; occupies Dardanelles, 269; scattered over Near East, 283
Brooke, Major W. H., 9
Bruchmüller, Col., 38
Brusilov, Russian Gen., 10
Bucharest, Treaty of, 257
Buftea, Treaty of, 257
Bulgarian Army, does not interfere with British sports, 9; rumours that it was contemplating an offensive, 17; its dispositions in Dec. 1917, 46; its increased activity in Feb. 1918, 54; desertions from, 95; artillery activity of at Dojran, June 1918, 99; its dispositions in Sept. 1918, 131; its strength then, 133, 145; morale of, 133; story of " contract" with Germany for its employment, 134; its front broken in Battle of the Dobropolje, 147–58; its dispositions at Dojran, Sept. 1918, 160; its high morale there, 161; in Battle of Dojran, 163–90; retreats on British front, 204–16; deterioration of its morale, 217; mutiny in, 238, 250; its right blocked at Skoplje, 246
Bunoust, Gen., 129
Burges, Lieut.-Col. D., V.C., 170

Cadorna, Gen., 74
Cairnes, Lieut.-Col. J. E., 191
Cambon, M. Paul, 111 (*f.n.*)
Cambrai, Battle of, 41
Cameron, Lieut.-Col. O. S., 142 (*f.n.*)
Campbell, Lieut.-Col. J. A., 185
Captures—
by Allies in Sept. 1918, 251
by British, at Homondos, 27; at Salmah, 30; at Butkovo Jum'a, 45; in Roche Noire Salient, 144; by XII Corps in Battle of Dojran, 18th Sept., 171, 185

GENERAL INDEX 355

Captures (*continued*)—
  by British and Greeks in offensive, Sept., 235
  by French, in Albania, 16, 118; in Battle of the Dobropolje, 152
  by Greeks, at Skra di Legen, 90
  by Italians, in Albania, 118
Carey, Br.-Gen. H. E., 169 (*f.n.*), 188, 191
Carlowitz, Col. v., 245, 246, 249
Carter, Br.-Gen. B. C. M., 28 (*f.n.*)
Castelnau, Gen. de, 53
Casualties—
  British, at Homondos, 27; at Salmah, 30; in raid on Boyau Hill, 30; in Struma operations, April 1918, 85; in Dojran raids, April 1918, 87; and in May, 88; in Roche Noire Salient, 144; in Battle of Dojran, 171, 177, 185; in pursuit, 235
  Bulgarian, in Battle of Dojran, 186
  French, in Battle of the Dobropolje, 152
  Greek, at Skra di Legen, 90; in Battle of Dojran, 171, 177; in pursuit on British front, 235
Cecil, Lord Robert, 106, 111 (*f.n.*)
Charpy, Col. (later Gen.), 48
Clarke, Major-Gen. T. E., 12
Clegg-Hill, Lieut.-Col. Hon. A. R., 170
Clemenceau, M. Georges, becomes President of the Council and War Minister, 46; his instructions to Gen. Guillaumat, 49, 73; considers offensive in Macedonia, 77; his instructions to Gen. d'Espérey, June 1918, 104; orders preparations for offensive, 106, 109; authorizes offensive, 112; supports Gen. Milne's demands for ammunition, 115; his instructions to Gen. d'Espérey, 7th Oct. 1918, 261
Cobbe, Lieut.-Col. I. S., 191
Colbeck, Lieut.-Col. B. B., 191
Conferences of Allies, Paris (25th July 1917), 12; London (7th Aug. 1917), 12; Rapallo (6th Nov. 1917), 41; Calais (26th Feb. 1917), 42; London (4th Sept. 1918), 111; Paris (7th Oct. 1918), 261
Conrad v. Hoetzendorff, Gen., 288
Constantine, King of Greece, 2, 31, 66, 132, 289

Contaratos, Gen., 94
Cooke-Collis, Lieut.-Col. (later Br.-Gen.) W. J. N., 12 (*f.n.*), 63, 82, 214
Corfu, convalescent depot at, 7
Corkran, Br.-Gen. C. E., 34, 113 (*f.n.*)
Corps Mounted Troops (XVI Corps), 24, 28
Cory, Br.-Gen. (later Lieut.-Gen.) Sir G. N., 12, 75, 260 (*f.n.*), 269, 271
Cottrell, Lieut.-Col. R. F., 191
Croker, Major-Gen. H. L., 6, 223, 269, 270
Culme-Seymour, Rear-Adm. M., 264

Danglis, Gen., 66, 131, 226
Davie, Lieut.-Col. (later Br.-Gen.) K. M., 28 (*f.n.*), 174, 175, 227 (*f.n.*)
Delaunay, Lieut.-Col., 53
Delmé-Radcliffe, Br.-Gen. C., 70
Derby, Earl of, 106
Descoins, Col., 32
Diaz, Gen., 111, 279, 281
Dieterich, German Gen., 218, 220, 272 (*f.n.*)
Dietrichs, Russian Gen., 10
Dobbs, Lieut.-Col. R. C., 224, 225, 227
Dobropolje, Battle of the, 147-58
Dojran, The Battle of, the positions attacked, 159; attack of XII Corps, 18th Sept. 1918, 163-72; attack of XVI Corps, 18th Sept., 172-7; attack of XII Corps, 19th Sept., 178-85; casualties of, 185; comments on, 186-90; artillery dispositions in, 191; Bulgarian dispositions in, 192; 302
Dojran front, minor operations on, 15, 30, 45, 86, 119
Dukhonin, Gen., 39
Duncan, Major-Gen. J., 138, 168, 171, 178, 179, 180, 182, 184, 185, 224, 226, 227

Enaux, Commandant, 104
Endymion (British Cruiser), 43
Engineers, Royal, mosquito-proof huts made by, 7; theatres built by, 9; Survey work by, 17-21; work on light railways, 34; work on defences, 55; sound-ranging, 59, 114; work on roads, 73; Signals, 101, 141; flash-

356 GENERAL INDEX

Engineers, Royal (*continued*)—
spotting, 114; Indian Sappers and Miners unsuitable to replace, 121 (*f.n.*); preparations for offensive, 140; water-supply, 140; road-making for attack of XVI Corps, 173; bridging in pursuit, 211, 214; road-making in pursuit, 231; railway work, Oct. 1918, 259

Entrenched Camp of Salonika, 3, 18, 49; rôle of in Defence Scheme, 52, 74

Erskine, Lieut.-Col. J. D. B., 171

Essad Pasha, 17, 32, 33

Everett, Br.-Gen.(later Major-Gen.) H. J., 12

Expeditionary Force Canteen, 9

Eydoux, Gen., 64

Falconar Stewart, Lieut.-Col. R., 181

Falkenhayn, Gen. v., 36, 124, 288, 289, 297 (*f.n.*)

Farret, Gen., 237, 240, 241, 247

Ferdinand, King of Rumania, 282

Ferdinand, Tsar of Bulgaria, 195; sues for an Armistice, 26th Sept. 1918, 228; 249; abdicates, 252; his responsibility for Bulgaria's entry into the war, 292

Ferrero, Gen., 49, 91, 118

Fleck, Gen., 219, 247, 249, 275

Fleuriau, M. de, 111 (*f.n.*)

Foch, Gen., his instructions to Gen. Guillaumat, 49, 76, 87; receives report from Gen. Guillaumat, 77; 101; his instructions to Gen. Franchet d'Espérey, 104; desires offensive in Macedonia, 111; given strategical direction of all operations against Germany, 277

Focsani, Truce of, 40, 256

Forbes, Lieut.-Col. R. R., 15

Forestier-Walker, Major-Gen. G. T., 8, 25, 81, 143, 213, 216, 263

Fox hunting in Macedonia, 8

Franchet d'Espérey, Gen., 79, 97 (*f.n.*); arrival of, 102; receives instructions from home, 104; ordered to prepare for offensive, 106, 109; instructs Gen. Milne to begin preparations, 109, 119; gets permission to attack, 112; supports Gen. Milne's demands for ammunition, 115; his plan for offensive, 124; his insistence on speed, 128; his optimism, 130; his instructions to Gen.

Franchet d'Espérey (*continued*)—
Milne for final offensive, 135; defines rôle of French 1st Group of Divisions, 136; 137; his remarkable " Instructions for Exploitation," 138; leaves date of attack to Voivode Mišić, 147; 152; informs Gen. Milne that efforts must be made to profit by Serbian break-through, 172; 190, 196; his orders of 21st Sept., 200; his instructions to British on 19th Sept., 202; real originator of Allied military policy in Balkans, 203; hands over Greek 14th Divn. to Gen. Milne, 204 (*f.n.*); urges relentless pursuit, 207; 217; his orders of 23rd Sept., 219; sees his anticipations fulfilled, 221; receives Bulgarian *parlementaires*, 228, 250; and Bulgarian delegates, 233, 250; withdraws Crete Divn. from British command, 234 (*f.n.*); his orders of 25th Sept., 238, and of 28th, 242; orders French cavalry to march on Skoplje, 243; informs Bulgarian delegates of capture of Skoplje, 246; declines to suspend hostilities, 27th Sept., 250; grants an armistice to Bulgaria, 251; his plan after Bulgarian. Armistice, 257; considers advance on Constantinople a secondary matter, 260; 268; 263, 270; eager to gain possession of Niš, 273; his dispositions, 275; determined to invade Germany through Hungary, 277; meets Hungarian delegation at Belgrade, 280; an advocate of offensive in Macedonia in Nov. 1914, 286; his view of results of campaign, 297; his conduct of the operations, 298, 299; his calculations upset regarding lines of supply, 301

French Army, question of leave in, 11; takes over defence of left bank of Vardar, 35; hands back left bank of Vardar to British, 61; 10,000 troops to be sent to France, 77; divisions handed over to Serbians for offensive, 128; part played by them in Battle of the Dobropolje, 149–52; 2nd *bis* Zouaves attached British Army, 178; formation of Armée du Danube, 261

GENERAL INDEX 357

French Army (*continued*)—
See *also* Armée Française d'Orient.
French Foreign Legion, 10
French Military Missions—
to Greece, 52, 64, 67
to Rumania, 36, 38, 67, 261
Fuller, Br.-Gen. F. G., 166 (*f.n.*)

Gallipoli Campaign, 288
Gargalides, Lieut.-Col., 197
Gay, Major-Gen. A. W., 226, 230, 282
Génin, Gen., 52
German Supreme Command, employment of a " Central Reserve," 38, 40 ; attitude of to Macedonia, 42 ; refuses reinforcements to Bulgaria, 194 ; sends reinforcements, 238, 255 ; refuses to recognize Bulgarian Armistice, 254.
German Troops in Macedonia, 46 ; withdrawals from, 78 ; in Battle of the Dobropolje, 154 ; extricated from Bulgarian Armies after Armistice, 254 ; reinforcements to Macedonia, Sept.-Oct. 1918, 255, 272
Germany, refuses to recognize Bulgarian Armistice ; makes offer of peace to Belgium, 15th Sept. 1918, 254 ; Armistice with, 280
Gérôme, Gen., 35, 48
Geshov, Gen., 160
Gillman, Major-Gen. W., 11
Goeben (German-Turkish battleship), 56, 269
Gordon, Lieut.-Col. G. H., 191
Gough-Calthorpe, Vice-Admiral the Hon. Sir S. A., 265, 267, 269
Gradsko-Krivolak, the " sensitive point " on Bulgarian front, 125, 132
Gramat, Gen., 68
Grant, Br.-Gen. C. J. C., 78
Granville, Earl, 59, 93
Gray, Lieut.-Col. W. K., 191
Great Britain, attitude of to campaign, 2, 12, 41, 287, 291 ; efforts of to reconcile Italy and Greece, 33 ; recognizes Provisional Government in Russia, 37 ; sends aid to Italy, 40 ; decides to make Palestine the only offensive theatre, 41 ; shares in loan to Greece, 64 ; supplies food to Greek Army, 65 ; agrees to offensive in Macedonia, 112 ; lessons of campaign for, 303

Greek Army, 17 ; mobilization of, 31, 59, 64, 91 ; 35 ; troops put at disposal of British, 61, 92, 94, 130 ; qualities of, 64, 68, 98, 189 ; its local operations on Struma, April 1918, 81 ; captures Skra di Legen, 89 ; takes over defence of Struma, 95 ; its shortage of equipment, 98 ; split up for final offensive, 131 ; its indifference to German propaganda, 133 ; Seres Divn. in Battle of Dojran, 163-71, 178-190 ; Crete Divn. in Battle of Dojran, 172-7 ; 14th Divn. in pursuit, 202-12, 222-35 ; I Corps withdrawn from British command, 226
Grossetti, Gen., 11, 48
Guillaumat, Gen., arrives, 46 ; personality of, 48 ; his instructions from home, 49 ; his views regarding Italian Contingent, 51 ; his impressions of British Army, 52 ; general confidence in, 54 ; 56, 61, 65, 69 ; his Defence Scheme, 70 ; it is criticized at Versailles, 73 ; but approved of by Gen. Milne, 76 ; refuses to consider evacuation of Salonika, 75 ; agrees to withdrawal of 12 British battns., 76 ; discusses possibility of offensive, 77 ; recall of, 79, 101 ; local operations ordered by, 80, 87 ; decides to capture Skra di Legen, 89 ; his profit from success, 90 ; his operations in Albania, May-June 1918, 91 ; 92, 94, 97 (*f.n.*) ; departure of, 101 ; part played by in support of Gen. d'Espérey, 104, 106, 107, 111, 112 ; makes unified control in Macedonia work smoothly, 295

Haig, Field-Marshal Sir D., 277
Hammond, Col. F. D., 53
Hanbury, Lieut.-Col. P. L., 166 (*f.n.*)
Hare, Br.-Gen. R. H., 54, 84, 138, 164, 209, 225, 230
Heneage, Lieut.-Col. A. P., 191
Henrys, Gen., appointed to command A.F.O., 48 ; 71, 102, 130, 131 ; his views on Battle of Dojran, 190 ; his advance on Kičevo, 201, 238 ; his interpretation of Gen. d'Espérey's orders, 242, 243 ; his rôle in advance to

Henrys, Gen. (*continued*)—
Danube, 258; signs Hungarian Armistice, 281
Hertling, Graf (German Chancellor), 256
Heywood, Lieut.-Col. T. G. G., 194 (*f.n.*)
Hindenburg, Field-Marshal v., 194 (*f.n.*), 256; acknowledges importance of Allied victory in Macedonia, 284
Hintze, Admiral v. (German Foreign Minister), 256
Hoffmann, Major-Gen. Max, 36, 38, 39
Holbrooke, Br.-Gen. P. L., 116, 123, 191
Homondos, first raid on, 15; second raid on, 25
Hungary, will not recognize Austrian Armistice, 280; signs her own, 281

Indian Troops for Macedonia, 121, 203; arrival of, 267
Influenza, 166, 205, 236, 272
Intelligence Service, British, 23, 145, 160 (*f.n.*)
Isonzo, Twelfth Battle of the, 40
Italian Comando Supremo, 40, 51, 70, 118, 119
Italy, her attitude and operations in Albania, 32, 47, 91, 118, 276; Austro-German offensive against, Oct. 1917, 40; friction with Greece, 51; refuses to send Yugoslav volunteers to Macedonia, 69; agrees to offensive in Macedonia, 112; her proposed invasion of Germany, 277
Izzet Pasha, Marshal, 265

Jackson, Lieut.-Col. B. A., 182
Jacquemot, Gen., 16
Jekov, Gen., 132
Joannou, Gen., 90
Joffre, Gen., 287, 289
Jouinot-Gambetta, Gen., 243, 246, 248, 273, 301

Karolyi, Count, 280
Kashing, S.S., 123
Keogh, Surg.-Gen. Sir A., 58
Kerenski, Alexander, 37, 39
Knight, Br.-Gen. H. L., 12 (*f.n.*)
Koritza, " Republic " of, 32
Kornilov, Gen., 39
Kourospoulos, Col., 197
Kouvaković, Col., 68, 69

Kövess, Field-Marshal v., C.-in-C. in Balkans, 274
Krilenko, Ensign (Bolshevist Commander-in-Chief), 39
Krivolak, importance of. *See* Gradsko-Krivolak

Labour, Mediterranean, 55, 56, 101 (*f.n.*), 140
Langlade, Col. de, 270
Lardemelle, Col. (later Gen.) de, 286
Lawson, Lieut.-Gen. H., 10
Leave, lack of, 34, 100
Leopold, of Bavaria, Field-Marshal Prince, 38
Lewis Guns, increased establishment of, 122, 138 (*f.n.*)
Liman von Sanders, Gen., 271
Livingstone, Major-Gen. H. A. A., 52, 55, 56, 73, 231
Ljapchev, M. (Bulgarian Finance Minister), 233, 250, 253
Lloyd George, Rt. Hon. D., asks for recall of Gen. Sarrail, 2; asks for information regarding campaign, Nov. 1917, 41; 105 (*f.n.*); agrees to offensive in Macedonia, 111, 112; disagrees with Gen. d'Espérey's plan, 7th Oct. 1918, 261; 287
Lobit, Gen. de, 48
Ludendorff, Gen., 36, 38, 39, 40, 255; decides to sue for peace, 256; his dislike of Treaty of Bucharest, 257; 259, 265, 284
Lukov, Gen., 132, 233, 249, 250, 253
Lyautey, Gen., 48

Macedonia, an isolated theatre of war owing to defeat of Russia and Rumania, 1, 36–42; climatic conditions of, 140; campaign in helps to bring down Central Powers, 284, 296; problems of campaign in discussed, 285 *et seq.*; as an example of modern mountain warfare, 297 *et seq.*
Machine Guns, Tactics of, 86; in Battle of Dojran, 165
Mackay, Captain D., 120
Mackensen, Field-Marshal v., 36, 69, 124, 276, 281
Macpherson, Br.-Gen. A. D., 168
Mahon, Lieut.-Gen. Sir B., 53
Majendie, Br.-Gen. B. L., 87 (*f.n.*), 182, 184, 210, 224
Malaria, 1, 5; methods to combat, 7, 94; casualties from, 7, 31, 58, 94, 100; decision to send home

GENERAL INDEX 359

Malaria (*continued*)—
chronic cases, 58, 100; rise in sick rate after exertion, 63; results in no divisions being withdrawn, March 1918, 76; effect of on battalions sent to France, 94; effect of in pursuit, combined with influenza, 236; an immensely important factor in campaign, 293
Malinov, M. (Prime Minister of Bulgaria), 134, 233, 250
Man-power, economies in, 10, 57
Marasesci, Battle of, 38
Marie, Queen of Rumania, 282
Marshall, Gen. Sir W. R., 269
Maude, Lieut.-Gen. Sir F. S., 124
Max, Prince, of Baden, 256
Maynard, Br.-Gen. C. C. M., 25, 30, 44
Mayne, Lieut.-Col. H. B., 191
Mesopotamian Campaign, 41, 42, 296
Miller, Lieut.-Col. W. Y., 227
Milne, Gen. G. F., his optimistic views in May 1917, 3; despatches troops to Palestine, 4, 13; his method of holding line in summer of 1917, 6, 13; his remarks on subject of malaria, 7, 94; 8; his visit to Serbian Armies, 11; sends senior officers to more active fronts, 11; 15; decides to reoccupy Struma Valley in Oct. 1917, 24; 33; welcomes arrival of Gen. Guillaumat, 48, 51; is informed of instructions given to Gen. Guillaumat, 49; 52, 55, 56, 61; receives outline of Gen. Guillaumat's Defence Scheme, 70; draws up scheme for British Army, 73; his views on an offensive in Macedonia, April 1918, 78; and in July, 107; his plans for local activity, April 1918, 80; 92, 96; instructed to prepare for offensive in Sept. 1918, 109; his heavy responsibilities, 112; his demands for extra artillery refused, 113; his demands for gas shell cut down, 115; asks for extra trench mortars, 117; directed to maintain artillery activity during preparations for offensive, 119; unable to form machine-gun battalions, 122; 129, 131, 135; his instructions for offensive from Gen. d'Espérey, 135; submits

Milne, Gen. G. F. (*continued*)—
plans to Gen. d'Espérey, 137; receives "Instructions for Exploitation," 138; lends Stokes mortars to French, 151 (*f.n.*); his instructions in event of success at Dojran, 166; informed by Gen. d'Espérey that pressure must be maintained, 172; orders cessation of attacks, 19th Sept., 185; 190; asks for reinforcements, 202; 204; his dispositions for pursuit, 207; his orders for 23rd Sept., 208; anxious to hasten pursuit, 210, 231; 223; Greek I Corps withdrawn from his command, 226; receives Bulgarian *parlementaires*, 228; and Bulgarian delegates, 232; orders advance on Petrić, 233; informed of Gen. d'Espérey's plan, 4th Oct., 257; his objection to it, 259; his revised rôle, 10th Oct. 1918, 261; his plan for advance against Turkey, 263; postpones attack on Adrianople, 265; sends a divisions to Dardanelles, 267; on value of cavalry in pursuit, 301; his views in Oct. 1916, 292, 295
Milner, Viscount, 111 (*f.n.*)
Minis, Col., 176
Mišić, Voivode, Serbian Chief of the Staff, 104; outstanding ability of, 128; 131; in command in Battle of the Dobropolje, 147 *et seq.*; 196 *et seq.*; his rôle in advance to Danube, 258; signs Hungarian Armistice, 281
Molesworth, Lieut.-Col. H. E., 191
Mombelli, Gen., 247
Monastir, Battle of (1916), 11, 126, 290
Mondésir, Gen. de, 68
Mountain warfare, final offensive as an example of, 297 *et seq.*
Murphy, Mr. (U.S. Minister at Sofia), 250
Murray, Gen. Sir A. J., 4

Naper, Lieut.-Col. L. A. D., 191
Navy, 21; in Gulf of Orfano, 43, 78; assists Italians in Albania, 118; lands British troops at Dedeagach, 263; passes through Dardanelles, 269
Negropontis, Gen., 93
Neilson, Lieut.-Col. (later Br.-Gen.) W., 24, 232, 263

GENERAL INDEX

Nerezov, Gen., 132, 160, 192
Nicholas II, Tsar of Russia, 36
Nickerson, Major-Gen. W. H. S., 294
Nider, Gen., 64
Niklov, Major-Gen., 158
Niš, Battle of, 274
Nisbet, Br.-Gen. F. C., 83, 174, 175
Nivelle, Gen., 2

Offensive of 1917, 36, 291
Offensive of 1918, plan of, 124; Allied superiority on front of assault, 128; launch of, 147; exploitation of success in, 193–249
Onslow, Major-Gen. W. H., 52, 216
Orphanidis, Col., 205, 206
Otranto Barrage, the, 119

" P " Ridge. *See* Dojran, Battle of
Pagos, Col., 168
Painlevé, M. Paul, 46
Palestine Campaign, 4, 12, 41, 111, 134, 254, 296
Palk, Lieut. R., 83
Paraćin, Battle of, 276
Paraskevopoulos, Gen., 65, 97, 138
Parnourias, Lieut.-Col., 191
Parsons, Lieut.-Col. W. F., 191
Patey, Gen., 49, 258, 276, 278
Pérès, Lieut.-Col., 197
Pershing, Gen., 277
Pétain, Gen., 101
Pflanzer-Baltin, Gen. Freiherr v., 274
Piave, Battle of (15th June 1918), 96
Pitt, Major R. B., 215
Pleydell-Railston, Lieut.-Col. H. G., 8, 26
Plumer, Gen. Sir H., 40
Plunkett, Br.-Gen. E. A., 113, 150
Pogradec, capture of, 16
Polites, M. Nicolas, 93
Poole, Br.-Gen. A. J., 172, 226, 235, 282
Posseldt, Gen. v., 241
Pritchard, Br.-Gen. H. L., 173
Pruneau, Gen., 149, 221

Radev, M. (Bulgarian delegate), 233, 250
Raids, 15, 16, 17, 25, 28, 30, 44, 54, 78, 80, 86, 88, 90, 213. *See also* Dojran front, Homondos, Struma Valley, etc.

Railways, light railway construction, 34, 100; Allied Railway Commission, 53, 59; control of Greek, 59; situation of on Moglena front, 127; strain of offensive on, 141; state of in Bulgaria, 259; delays in repairing lines damaged by enemy, 302; limited capacity of Macedonian, 295
Reade, Major-Gen. R. N. R., 64
Red Cross Society, British, 9
Regnault, Gen., 10, 48, 49
Reuter, Gen. v., 153, 155, 157, 158
Rhodes, Col. G. D., 141
Ribot, M. Alexandre, 2
River Clyde, 269
Roberts, Br.-Gen. A. C., 12 (*f.n.*)
Roberts, Private D., 169
Robertson, Gen. Sir W. R., his views on campaign, 3; 34; superseded as C.I.G.S., 62
Robilant, Gen. di, 277
Roche Noire Salient, Capture of, 141
Rondet, Col., 156, 197, 216
Ross, Sir Ronald, 58, 95
Ross, Br.-Gen. W. C., 208 (*f.n.*), 267, 282
Royal Air Force, formation of, 59; exploits of, 88, 99; liaison with artillery, 114; rôle of in Battle of Dojran, 166; bombs retreating enemy, 204, 206, 222, 233
Royal Flying Corps, raids by, 14, 79; bombs *Goeben*, 56; reinforcements received by, 59. *See also* Royal Air Force.
Royal Naval Air Service, 14
Rumania, situation of in 1917, 2, 36, 256; left in possession of Moldavia, 257; is ready to rearm, 261, 278; liberated, 282; campaign of in 1916, 290
Rushev, Major-Gen., 157, 158
Russia, situation of in early 1917, 2, 3; revolution in, 36; summer offensive of 1917 in, 37, 69
Russian Black Sea Fleet, 269
Russian Contingent in Macedonia, 10, 31, 51
Rycroft, Major-Gen. W. H., 12, 114, 229

Sackville-West, Major-Gen. C. J., 74, 105, 106, 110
Salmah, raid on, 28
Salmond, Major-Gen. W. G. H., 207
Salonika Fire, the, 21

GENERAL INDEX

Sarrail, Gen., his recall demanded, 2; refuses to relieve British troops, 4, 13; 8, 11, 14, 31, 33, 34; relieves British troops, 35; 42; recalled, 46; his achievement, 47; his views regarding French Contingent, 50; 61, 103, 286

Savin, Lieut.-Col., 197

Scholtz, Gen. v., 132, 153, 157, 193; his measures during Allied Offensive, 194, 198; orders a withdrawal, 217; receives reinforcements, 238; tries to cover Bulgarian frontier, 241; 248, 273; superseded, 274

Schools—
Army Training (Infantry), 57; Army Artillery, 57; Army Signal, 57; Army Anti-Gas, 57; Army Lewis Gun, 57

Schwerin, Col. Graf v., 194

Serbia, Crown Prince or Prince Regent of. *See* Alexander.

Serbian Armies, unrest in, 11; fatigue of, 31; British representative attached to, 33; Yugoslav reinforcements received by, 68, 293; rôle of in offensive, 127; qualities of, 127, 258, 271; in Battle of Dobropolje, 147–58; exploitation of success by, 193–202, 216–22, 237–47; capture of Veles by, 239; reach Bulgarian frontier, 247; rôle of in advance to Danube, 258, 271–80; their victory at Niš, 274; and Paraćin, 276; re-enter Belgrade, 277

Serbian Government, protests at withdrawal of British troops, 12

Shipping. *See* Transport by Sea.

Skoplje, Capture of, 243, 299

Skra di Legen, Combat of the, 89, 291

Smuts, Lieut.-Gen. J. C., 66

Solly-Flood, Lieut.-Col. (later Br.-Gen.) R. E., 44, 141, 227 (*f.n.*)

Sonnino, Baron, 33

Spencer, Lieut.-Col. A. A. W., 173

Spiliades, Gen., 174, 175, 176, 208 (*f.n.*)

Staveley, Capt. C. M. (R.N.), 43

Stepanović, Voivode, 128, 152, 197, 198, 220

Steuben, Gen. v., 131, 153, 157, 158, 193, 218, 249, 274

Struma Valley, withdrawal from for summer of 1917, 4; malaria in, 7; fox hunting in, 8; re-

Struma Valley (*continued*)—
occupation of in Oct. 1917, 24; operations in, Oct. 1917, 25–30; and April 1918, 80–6; partial withdrawal from for summer of 1918, 93; minor Greek operation in, Sept. 1918, 173

Submarine campaign in Mediterranean, 2, 294

Summerhill Camp, 7, 56

Summer Line, 4, 93, 173

Superb, British battleship, 269

Supply and Transport, problems of in pursuit, 228, 231, 295, 301

Supreme War Council, 41; Military Representatives criticize Gen. Guillaumat, 73; part played by in final offensive, 102–11; surprised by its success, 203; its plans in early Nov., 277; 295

Surén, Gen., 157, 158, 247

Survey, British, in Macedonia, 17

Tanks, unsuitability of on British front, 120

Taranto route to England, 34, 69, 94, 100, 114; delays on, 116, 123

Temeraire, British battleship, 269

Thiry, Col., 136

Todd, Lieut.-Col. G. E., 206

Todorov, Gen. (Bulgarian C.-in-C.), 132, 194, 219; sues for an Armistice, 26th Sept. 1918, 228; 238

Topart, Gen., 96, 150, 151

Toshev, Gen., 132

Townshend, Major-Gen. C. V. F., 265

Training, 6, 57, 137, 141

Tranié, Gen., 237, 240, 247, 249, 274

Transport by Sea, difficulties and risks of, 2, 10, 65, 294; shortage of shipping, 34, 100, 294

Turkey, defenceless state of, Oct. 1918, 255, 265; British move against, 262–71; Armistice with, 266

Turkish Army, troops leave Macedonia for Palestine, 17

United States of America, 42

Vazov, Gen., 161, 192

Venizelos, M. Eleutherios, 31, 59; asks for French Mission, 64; his prestige advanced by Combat of Skra di Legen, 91; objects to withdrawal of British troops, 93; 98, 289

Wake, Br.-Gen. Sir Hereward, 105
Walker, Mr. (of U.S. Legation in Sofia), 230, 250
War Cabinet, meeting of, 2 ; Gen. Robertson's appreciation addressed to, 3 ; discusses defence in Macedonia, 75 ; decides not to withdraw divisions from Macedonia, March 1918, 76
Wemyss, Vice-Admiral Sir R. E., 261
Weygand, Gen., 74
Whitehead, Capt. C. M., 182, 184
White Thomson, Br.-Gen. H. D., 191
Widdrington, Br.-Gen. B. F., 25, 82, 214
Wilson, Lieut.-Gen. Sir Henry (C.I.G.S.), 40, 62 ; Military Representative on S.W.C., 74 ; criticizes Gen. Guillaumat's Defence Scheme, 75 ; hopes to reduce British Contingent in Macedonia, 76 ; dislikes prospect of offensive, April 1918, 78 ; still dislikes it, July 1918, 109 ; at conference authorizing it, 4th Sept. 1918, 111 ; 112 ; appealed to by Gen. Milne for reinforcements, 202 ; informed of Gen. Milne's objection to French plans, 6th Oct. 1918, 260
Wilson, Lieut.-Gen. Sir H. F. M., his orders for Battle of Dojran, 163 ; is against a renewed attack on 18th Sept., 172 ; his orders for attack on 19th, 178 ;

Wilson, Lieut.-Gen. Sir H. F. M. (*continued*)—
again considers a renewed attack unjustified, 185 ; 204 ; orders preparations for pursuit, 205, 206 ; troops under his command in pursuit, 207 ; his orders, 24th Sept., 223 ; postpones attack on Signal Allemand, 224 ; orders 28th Divn. to advance to Belašica Planina, 26th Sept., 227 ; 230, 231, 234, 267 ; appointed G.O.C. Allied Forces, Gallipoli and Bosporus, 268, 270
Wilson, President, 250, 256
Windel, Gen., 239
Wingate, Br.-Gen. G. H. F., 209, 226
Wingate, Gen. Sir R., 269
Winter Line, 24, 174
Wood, Major H., 18, 19
Woollcombe, Lieut.-Gen. Sir C. L., 75, 76

Young, Lieut.-Col. (later Br.-Gen.) E. D., 12 (*f.n.*), 229
Young Men's Christian Association, 10
Yugoslav National Council, 279
Yugoslav Reinforcements to Serbian Armies. *See* Serbian Armies

Zymbrakakis, Gen. (cmndg. Seres Divn.), 164, 167, 178
Zymbrakakis, Gen. E. (cmndg. Corps of Nat. Defence), 65, 234

INDEX TO
ARMS, FORMATIONS, AND UNITS.

Artillery—
 Batteries, Field—
  11th—15, 25 (f.n.); 18th—176; 22nd—44, 173, 174; 39th—25 (f.n.); 62nd—176; 95th—28; 96th—25 (f.n.); 118th—173, 174; 133rd—28; D/1—25 (f.n.), 142 (f.n.); A/CXIV—99; A/CXV—230, 232; B/CXV—230; D/CXVI—235; D/CXXIX—25 (f.n.), 28, 142 (f.n.); D/CXXX—44, 174
 Batteries, Garrison, Heavy—
  20th—90, 208; 143rd—96, 142 (f.n.); 153rd—15, 142 (f.n.); 180th—96, 142 (f.n.); 181st—13; 188th—208; 190th—90, 172, 208 (f.n.); 192nd—208; 196th—208
 Batteries, Garrison, Mountain—
  Argyll—24; Bute—142, 172, 191, 204, 215, 230 (f.n.)
 Batteries, Garrison, Siege—
  43rd—13, 163, 172, 208 (f.n.), 235; 84th—13 (f.n.), 129 (f.n.); 127th—96, 142 (f.n.); 130th—208, 234; 132nd—208; 134th—13; 205th—13; 209th—4; 292nd—4; 320th—62, 208; 322nd—62; 395th—62; 396th—142 (f.n.); 424th—58, 90, 142 (f.n.), 183; 445th—62
 Brigades, Field—
  I—25, 142 (f.n.); III—174, 176; XIX—142 (f.n.), 215; XX—142 (f.n.); XXXI—174, 176; LIV—174, 176, 225, 230; LVII—232; C—210, 224; CXIV—99; CXV—230; CXXIX—142 (f.n.), 215; CXXX—174, 175
 Brigades, Garrison, Mountain—
  III—174; IV Highland—44, 172, 174, 230
 Brigades, or Groups, Heavy Artillery—
  XX—191, 204, 208, 216; XXXVII—204, 208, 216; LXI—62; LXVI—216; LXXV—208; LXXXII—208, 231

Cavalry—
 Brigades (Yeomanry)—
  7th Mounted, 4; 8th Mounted, 4; Cavalry Brigade (temporarily formed Oct. 1918), 263, 267
 Regiments (Yeomanry)—
  1/1st Derbyshire, 4, 5, 24, 97, 205, 207, 209, 211, 226, 228, 230, 232, 236, 262, 301
  1/1st Lothians and Border Horse, 163, 205
  1/1st Surrey, 5, 15, 24, 172, 210, 224, 236
Corps—
 XII, 4, 5, 6, 9, 14, 16, 20, 30, 51; dispositions of, April 1918, 63; local activity of, April 1918, 80, 86; dispositions of, 15th July 1918, 97; artillery bombardments, Aug. 1918, 119; expenditure of ammunition by in Battle of Dojran, 123; its rôle in final offensive, 137, 159; its attack, 18th Sept. 1918, 163–72; and 19th Sept., 178–91; in pursuit, 207–16, 223–34; in move against Turkey, 263
 XVI, 4, 6, 12 (f.n.), 13, 14; operations in Struma Valley, Oct. 1917, 25–30; 44, 51, 55; Greek troops attached to, 62, 93; dispositions of, April 1918, 63; operations April 1918, 80–6; relieved on Struma by Greeks, 94; dispositions of, 15th July 1918, 97; its rôle in final offensive, 137, 162; its attack, 18th Sept., 172–7; in pursuit, 207–12, 223–35; in move against Turkey, 263
Cyclists—
 XII Corps Bn., 209
 XVI Corps, 6, 24, 28, 97, 236, 262
Divisions—
 10th (Irish), 6, 7, 13, 14, 15, 17, 95 (f.n.)
 22nd, 6, 16, 35, 63, 86, 88, 90, 94, 97; its rôle in Battle of Dojran, 137, 163; its attack, 18th Sept., 168–72; and 19th

Divisions (*continued*)—
  22nd (*continued*)—
    Sept., 178–90; 202, 204; in pursuit, 207–12, 223–8; its move to Dedeagach, 263; withdraws to Macedonia, 268
  26th, 6, 35, 63, 90, 94, 97; artillery activity on front of, Aug. 1918, 120, 137; 164; its minor operation during Battle of Dojran, 165, 172; 77th Bde. attached to 22nd Divn. for attack, 166, 178–85; 202; in pursuit, Sept. 1918, 205–12, 226–35; its advance into Bulgaria, 262; and to the Maritsa, 263, 267; joins Army of Danube, 268, 282
  27th, 6, 7, 8; operations in Struma Valley, Oct. 1917, 24–30; and April 1918, 81; moves west of Vardar, 94, 96; artillery activity on front of, 120; 137, 140; in capture of Roche Noire Salient, 141, 163, 167; under orders of Gen. d'Anselme, 202, 204; crosses Vardar, 211, 214; its move into Bulgaria, 263; withdraws to Macedonia, 268
  28th, 6, 7, 9, 24, 27, 28, 63, 81; operations in Struma Valley, April 1918, 83; 96, 98, 123; 137; in battle of Dojran, 172–7; transferred to XII Corps, 207, 211; in pursuit, 223–35; goes to Dardanelles, 268
  60th (London), 4, 13, 95 (*f.n.*)
Engineers—
  Field Companies—
    100th—210; 143rd—211; 449th (Northumbrian)—54, 269; 501st (1/2nd Wessex)—215; 506th (Hampshire)—44
  Other Units—
    8th Field Survey Co., 19
    Flash-spotting Section, 20
    Sound-ranging Sections, 20
    38th Air Line Section, 141
    286th Army Troops Co., 173
    Base Park, 56
Flying Corps (R.F.C.) later Royal Air Force—
  Balloon Sections, 26th—166; 27th—166
  Squadrons, No. 17—59, 166; No. 47—59, 166; No. 150—59, 166; Wing, Sixteenth—206

Infantry—
  Brigades—
    65th—15, 45, 86, 87, 166, 171, 178, 182, 184, 185, 205, 210, 223, 236, 267
    66th—45, 168, 170, 171, 178, 180, 182, 183, 185, 267
    67th—90, 168, 171, 178, 185, 267
    77th—30, 138, 166, 178, 179, 184, 185, 264
    78th—5, 35, 205, 209, 211, 226, 228, 230, 232, 264
    79th—17, 63, 172, 186, 205, 211, 226, 228, 230 (*f.n.*), 232, 235, 265, 282
    80th—5, 12, 43, 63, 81, 96 (*f.n.*), 211, 214, 215, 228
    81st—15, 25, 27, 63, 81, 96 (*f.n.*), 144, 213, 214, 215
    82nd—25, 27, 28, 43, 44, 63, 79, 96 (*f.n.*), 141, 144, 213, 214, 227
    83rd—27, 54, 63, 84, 138, 163, 165, 172, 173, 185, 204, 206, 207, 208, 209, 210, 225, 227, 230, 231, 233, 235, 267, 269, 270
    84th—7, 27, 44, 63, 83, 174, 175, 177, 211, 267, 269, 270
    85th—27, 28, 51, 63, 174, 175, 177, 211, 225, 227, 230, 269, 270
    228th—6, 14, 27, 62, 63, 95, 97, 172, 173, 174, 205, 207, 208 (*f.n.*), 232, 267, 292 (*f.n.*)
    Composite Brigade, in Battle of Dojran, 173, 174
  Regiments—
    Infantry of the Line and Territorial—
      Argyll and Sutherland Highlanders, 1st Bn., 25
      ——, 12th Bn., 30, 179, 180, 181, 182
      Black Watch (Royal Highlanders), 10th Bn., 94
      ——, 13th (Scottish Horse) Bn., 8, 15, 25, 94
      Border, 9th Bn. (Pioneers), 178, 185
      Buffs (East Kent), 2nd Bn., 51, 175
      Cameron Highlanders, 2nd Bn., 25, 213, 214
      ——, 10th Bn. (Lovat's Scouts), 28, 94
      Cheshire, 2nd Bn., 44, 83, 85, 175, 176

INDEX TO ARMS, FORMATIONS, AND UNITS 365

Infantry (*continued*)—
  Regiments (*continued*)—
    Infantry of the Line and Territorial (*continued*)—
    Cheshire, 12th Bn., 16, 45, 168, 170, 171, 182
    Devonshire, 10th Bn., 282
    Duke of Cornwall's L.I., 2nd Bn., 29
    ——, 8th Bn., 17, 172, 235
    Durham L.I., 2/5th Bn., 267
    East Lancashire, 9th Bn., 184, 224
    East Surrey, 2nd Bn., 52, 175, 227
    East Yorkshire, 2nd Bn., 173
    Gloucestershire, 2nd Bn., 27, 28, 79, 141
    ——, 9th Bn., 94
    Hampshire, 10th Bn., 27, 28, 29, 141
    ——, 12th Bn., 172, 235, 282
    King's (Liverpool), 14th Bn., 94
    King's Own (Royal Lancaster), 2nd Bn., 55, 138, 179
    ——, 9th Bn., 45, 87, 182, 224
    King's Royal Rifle Corps, 3rd Bn., 214
    ——, 4th Bn., 82, 94
    Lancashire Fusiliers, 12th Bn., 15, 16, 87, 94
    Manchester, 13th Bn., 94
    Northumberland Fusiliers, 2nd Bn., 94
    Oxford and Bucks L.I., 7th Bn., 232
    Rifle Brigade, 4th Bn., 82, 85
    ——, 22nd (Garrison) Bn., 62
    Royal Fusiliers, 3rd Bn., 94
    Royal Scots, 1st Bn., 15, 26, 144, 214

Infantry (*continued*)—
  Regiments (*continued*)—
    Infantry of the Line and Territorial (*continued*)—
    Scots Fusiliers, Royal, 8th Bn., 181, 182
    Scottish Rifles, 11th Bn., 180, 182
    Seaforth Highlanders, 1st Garrison Bn., 267
    Shropshire L.I., King's, 8th Bn., 168, 171
    South Lancashire, 9th Bn., 16, 168, 170, 171
    South Wales Borderers, 7th Bn., 90, 168, 170, 171, 182
    ——, 8th Bn., 224
    Welch, 1st Bn., 44, 177
    ——, 11th Bn., 168, 171
    ——, 23rd Bn. (Pioneers), 174
    Welch Fusiliers, Royal, 11th Bn., 88, 168, 171
    Wiltshire, 7th Bn., 94
    York and Lancaster, 1st Bn., 55, 84, 173
    Yorkshire L.I., King's Own, 1st Bn., 9, 84, 94
  Regiments (Indian)—
    Garwhals, 2/39th Bn., 267
    Gurkhas, 2/6th Bn., 267
    Punjabis, 24th Bn., 267
    ——, 31st Bn., 267
    Rajputs, 2nd Bn., 267
  Labour Companies—
    95th, 173 ; 96th, 211
  Machine-Gun Battery—
    6th Armoured M.B.—4
  Machine-Gun Companies—
    65th—88, 224 ; 67th—88 ; 82nd—28 ; 84th—44
  Trench Mortars—
    Battery—
      81st Light—15

OFFICIAL HISTORY OF THE GREAT WAR
FRANCE & BELGIUM

Official History of the Great War — France & Belgium was the grandest official history ever produced in Britain. Its purpose was to provide "within reasonable compass an authoritative account, suitable for general readers and for students at military schools."

Due to the number of full-colour maps bound in each volume many previous attempts to reprint this valuable reference ether floundered, or were produced with the maps in monochrome.

We have reissued our derivative editions NOW in both regular softback and hardback bindings, with smart new jacket artwork, and a refreshing of the internal pages with semi-silk paper for better reproduction of the important colour cartography.

Order directly from
www.naval-military-press.com

The Complete France & Belgium Series, text volumes with colour bound-in maps volumes included are:

1914 Volume I
Mons, the retreat to the Seine, the Marne and the Aisne

1914 Volume II
Antwerp, La Bassée, Arnetieres, Messines and Ypres

1915 Volume I
Winter 1914-15: Battle of Neuve Chapelle: Battles of Ypres

1915 Volume II
Battles of Aubers Ridge, Festubert, and Loos

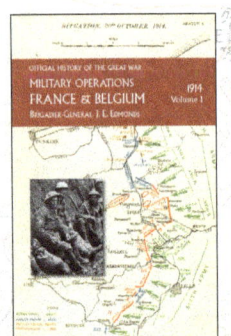
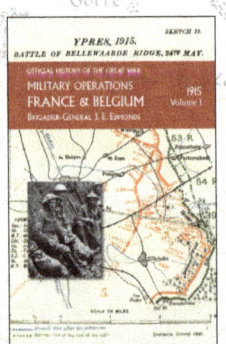
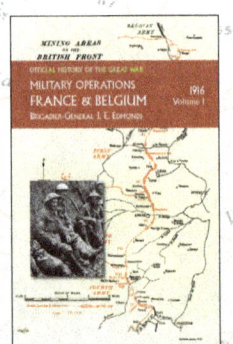
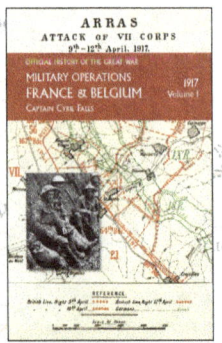

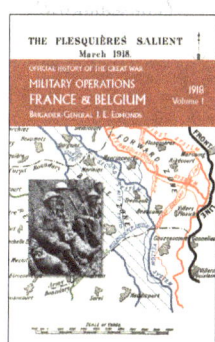 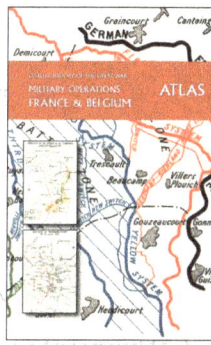 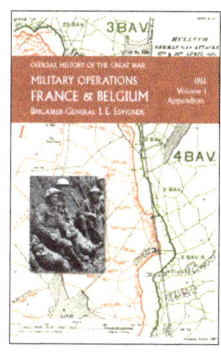 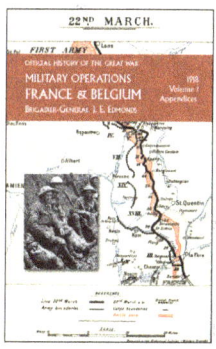

1916 Volume I
Sir Douglas Haig's Command to the 1st July: Battle of the Somme

1916 Volume II
2nd July 1916 to the end of the Battles of the Somme

1917 Volume I
German Retreat to the Hindenburg Line and the Battle of Arras

1917 Volume II
Messines and Third Ypres (Passchendaele)

1917 Volume III
The Battle of Cambrai

1918 Volume I
The German March Offensive and its Preliminaries

1918 Volume II
March-April: Continuation of the German Offensives

1918 Volume III
May-July: The German Diversion Offensives and First Allied Counter-Attack

1918 Volume IV
The Franco-British Offensive

1918 Volume V
26th September – 11th November. The Advance to Victory

1916. Volume I. Appendices

1916. Volume II. Appendices

1917. Volume I. Appendices

1918. Volume I. Appendices

Transportation on the Western Front

The Occupation of the Rhineland 1918-29

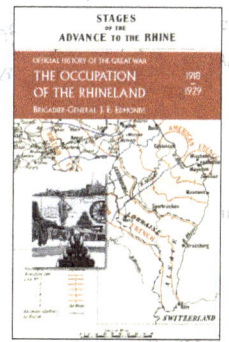 

www.ingramcontent.com/pod-product-compliance
Lightning Source LLC
Chambersburg PA
CBHW070804300426
44111CB00014B/2425